D1013567

SECOND EDITION

Questioning Sociology

CANADIAN PERSPECTIVES

Edited by **MYRA J. HIRD** and **GEORGE PAVLICH**

OXFORD
UNIVERSITY PRESS

OXFORD
UNIVERSITY PRESS

Oxford University Press is a department of the University of Oxford.

It furthers the University's objective of excellence in research, scholarship, and education by publishing worldwide. Oxford is a registered trade mark of Oxford University Press in the UK and in certain other countries.

Published in Canada by
Oxford University Press
8 Sampson Mews, Suite 204,
Don Mills, Ontario M3C 0H5 Canada

www.oupcanada.com

Copyright © Oxford University Press Canada 2012

The moral rights of the author have been asserted

Database right Oxford University Press (maker)

First Edition published in 2006

All rights reserved. No part of this publication may be reproduced, stored in a retrieval system, or transmitted, in any form or by any means, without the prior permission in writing of Oxford University Press, or as expressly permitted by law, by licence, or under terms agreed with the appropriate reprographics rights organization. Enquiries concerning reproduction outside the scope of the above should be sent to the Permissions Department at the address above or through the following url: www.oupcanada.com/permission/permission_request.php

Every effort has been made to determine and contact copyright holders. In the case of any omissions, the publisher will be pleased to make suitable acknowledgement in future editions.

Library and Archives Canada Cataloguing in Publication

Questioning sociology : Canadian perspectives / edited by Myra J.
Hird and George Pavlich. -- 2nd ed.

Includes bibliographical references and index.
ISBN 978-0-19-544031-7

1. Canada--Social conditions--Textbooks. 2. Sociology--Textbooks.
I. Hird, Myra J II. Pavlich, George Clifford

HN103.5.Q84 2012   301.0971   C2012-900064-7

Cover image: Lilly3/iStockphoto

This book is printed on permanent (acid-free) paper ∞.

Printed and bound in the United States of America.

2 3 4 — 15 14 13

Contents

Acknowledgments

The editors wish to thank all the contributors for their insight and collegiality—the product is fitting testament to their enormous creativity and talent. We would like to acknowledge the thoughtfulness, support, encouragement, and assistance of Caroline Starr, Mark Thompson, and Tanuja Weerasooriya at Oxford University Press.

George Pavlich acknowledges Myra Hird for her insight and a friendship of many years. I dedicate my efforts to Carla Spinola, Seth Pavlich, and Tally Pavlich.

Myra Hird thanks George Pavlich for his enduring friendship and dedicates this book to Eshe, Inis, and Anth.

Contributors

Barry D. Adam
Professor, Department of Sociology and Anthropology, University of Windsor, Windsor, ON.

Rob Beamish
Associate Professor, Department of Sociology, Queen's University, Kingston, ON.

Annette Burfoot
Associate Professor, Department of Sociology, Queen's University, Kingston, ON.

Curtis Clarke
Director, Alberta Solicitor General Staff College, Edmonton, AB.

Lisa Cockburn
Ph.D. candidate, Department of Sociology, Queen's University, ON.

Philippe Couton
Associate Professor, Department of Sociology, University of Ottawa, Ottawa, ON.

Dawn H. Currie
Professor, Department of Sociology, University of British Columbia, Vancouver, BC.

Erin Dej
Ph.D. candidate, Department of Criminology, University of Ottawa, Ottawa, ON.

Nob Doran
Professor, Department of Social Sciences, University of New Brunswick Saint John, Saint John, NB.

Daniel Downes
Associate Professor, Department of Information and Communications Studies, University of New Brunswick Saint John, Saint John, NB.

Kelly Hannah-Moffat
Professor, Department of Sociology, University of Toronto at Mississauga, Mississauga, ON.

Lois Harder
Professor, Department of Political
Science, University of Alberta,
Edmonton, AB.

Myra J. Hird
Professor, Department of Sociology,
Queen's University, Kingston, ON.

Bryan Hogeveen
Associate Professor, Department
of Sociology, University of Alberta,
Edmonton, AB.

Jennifer Jarman
Associate Professor, Department
of Sociology, Dalhousie University,
Halifax, NS.

Stephen Katz
Professor, Department of Sociology,
Trent University, Peterborough, ON.

Deirdre M. Kelly
Professor, Department of Educational
Studies, University of British
Columbia, Vancouver, BC.

Catherine Krull
Associate Professor, Department
of Sociology (cross appointed with
Women's Studies), Queen's University,
Kingston, ON.

Patrick Lalonde
M.A. candidate in the Department
of Sociology, Anthropology, and
Criminology, University of Windsor,
Windsor, ON.

Randy Lippert
Professor (Sociology), Department
of Sociology and Anthropology,
University of Windsor, Windsor, ON.

Patricia Monture
Professor, Department of Sociology,
University of Saskatchewan,
Saskatoon, SK.

Dawn Moore
Associate Professor of Legal Studies,
Department of Law, Carleton
University, Ottawa, ON.

George Pavlich
Professor of Law and Sociology,
University of Alberta, Edmonton, AB.

R.A. Sydie
Professor and Emeritus, Department
of Sociology, University of Alberta,
Edmonton, AB.

Lorne Tepperman
Professor, Department of Sociology,
University of Toronto, Toronto, ON.

Mark Vardy
Ph.D. candidate, Department of
Sociology, Queen's University,
Kingston, ON.

Introduction: Sociological Questions

George Pavlich and Myra J. Hird

What Is Sociology?

As with other disciplines, this question attracts almost as many responses as the number of texts in which it is raised. Not wishing to add a static response to that dubious record, we will avoid describing sociology as a field definable by a fixed object of study, a core set of theoretical texts, a required theoretical approach, or even as a discipline held together by the use of one (scientific?) method.[1] Instead, this book identifies sociology more as an ever-evolving craft, as a process of systematically understanding and reflecting upon our historically specific interactions with others and the wider consequences of these interactions. Framed thus, sociology emerges as a changing but systematic attempt to create, assemble, or reassemble concepts to examine the assumptions that shape our social being at given moments in history.

Such a view echoes the work of an influential sociologist, C. Wright Mills (1916–62), who saw sociology as providing the space to create a uniquely sociological imagination. For Mills (1959), the sociological imagination may be described as a 'quality of mind' that seeks to 'achieve lucid summations of what is going on in the world' (5). As the basis of sociology, this frame of mind promises 'an understanding of the intimate realities of ourselves in connection with larger social realities' (15). Sociology, for Mills, develops this quality of mind by making imaginative leaps to connect the most intimate of personal 'troubles' (experienced by particular individuals) to a history of the most general structures that shape a given society. Such leaps enable us to develop broader understandings of ourselves by connecting our current self-identities and wider socio-historical formations. The understandings help us to address the social patterns 'of which we are at once creatures and creators' (164).

The sociological imagination forms one part of the history of sociology—a history that reaches back beyond Mills' writings to the work of nineteenth- and early-twentieth-century theorists such as Karl Marx, Max Weber, Émile Durkheim, August Comte, and Herbert Spencer. These theorists' influential thinking permeates the ideas and research found in this book. For instance, in the late nineteenth century, Karl Marx (1818–83) developed a comprehensive critique of capitalist society based upon the unequal relations individuals have to modes of production, labour, and property, which continues to inspire radical sociological analyses of societies and their political economies today. Also writing in the late nineteenth and early twentieth centuries, Max Weber (1864–1920) provided a theory of how one kind of rational (means-ends) way of thinking had radically transformed most areas of society, creating distinctively modern political, economic, legal, cultural, and social institutions. A good example of this rationalization process occurred in the administration of modern societies, which increasingly relied on formal bureaucracies that operate with great efficiency but come at the cost of ridding the world of magical enchantment and reducing life to a cold 'iron cage' of rationality. Weber's analysis of bureaucracy still inspires critical sociological analyses of organizations, rationalization, and authority today. Auguste Comte (1798–1857), who coined the term 'sociology' in the early nineteenth century, developed positivist sociology to derive absolute knowledge about how societies progress. Writing in the nineteenth and early twentieth centuries, Émile Durkheim (1858–1917) focused his attention on understanding both how individuals are shaped by independent 'social facts' and how the structures of given societies are shaped by basic underlying factors, such as the changing divisions of labour within a group. Nineteenth-century theorist Herbert Spencer (1820–1903) was keenly interested in applying Darwinian evolutionary theory to society, and coined the phrase 'survival of the fittest' to describe how individuals interact with each other in society. Although quite different in their various ideas and theories, what each of these founding sociological theorists shared was a commitment to situating individual beliefs, values, and actions within a wider group and societal context. Put another way, each of these founding theorists argued both that individuals cannot be understood outside of their societal milieu and that sociology offers a unique way of analyzing this social context.

In keeping with this fundamental starting point, and working within Mills' sociological imagination as a helpful and accessible way of thinking about the relationships between individuals and society, this introduction explores different facets of the sociological imagination in four related sections. The first section uses hypothetical examples to describe key characteristics of the sociological imagination, while the second situates sociological thinking against other disciplines. The third section outlines three influential theoretical approaches in sociology often used to help create sociological imaginations. In the fourth section, we discuss the basic role that questions play in formulating a sociological imagination. Reflecting a central theme of this book, this section shows how fundamental questions can arrest everyday views of the world and open us up to a sociological imagination.

Sociologists and the Sociological Imagination

What sort of thinking is distinctive, though not necessarily exclusive, to sociology? In responding to this question, and to elaborate upon Mills' previously noted 'frame of mind', it is important to differentiate between two of many possible ways of thinking about the world; namely, the *everyday* approach and the *sociological* approach.[2] Typically, we rely on everyday, taken-for-granted assumptions to help us negotiate our lives. I may, for instance, know that I am in a hurry because I am late for an appointment. This perception encourages me to drive faster, or speed up my walking pace. In such circumstances, we seldom stop to consider the underlying assumptions of time, or the actions that follow from our common impressions of time. We do not ordinarily question underlying assumptions made when claiming to 'be in a hurry' or trying to 'keep an appointment'. For instance, we seldom examine how the idea of 'hurry' relates to socially established conventions of time, or how these ideas are ingrained in the sorts of individuals that we are. The common-sense meaning maps we use to guide us through life, once learned through socialization, become taken-for-granted frameworks. They condition our everyday thinking and actions.

To take a related example, I might ask someone, 'Excuse me, what is the time please?' Ordinarily, I do not expect that person to engage me in a philosophical discussion of time, or a history of how global time standards came to be established, and so on. In our everyday thinking, when we ask someone what the time is, we expect an answer like, 'Oh! It is a quarter past five.' In turn, I am likely to thank the person, and through the interaction both questioner and respondent embrace a shared common-sense view of time.

However, suppose the respondent happened to be a sociology major conducting fieldwork and responds thus: 'What do you mean "Do I have the time?" What is time? In what sense can one have it? Do you mean to imply that I, as a human being, can own the time?' This response is likely to strike one as facetious, if not downright rude. But it would also disturb the everyday commonsense meanings that we commonly ascribe to the term 'time'. Through this different interaction, the sociology major may prompt you to consider alternative possibilities. You may, for instance, think differently when understanding and responding to your world. Were this to happen, the questions would have encouraged you to examine assumptions grounding your common-sense ways of acting around time. In the process, you might begin to experience a quality of mind that is akin to Mills' sociological imagination.

The point could also be made through an even simpler example. Say I wish to hang a picture on the wall, and so reach for my hammer. In this situation, I typically do not raise questions about the nature of the hammer's existence (Is it real? What is the true nature of a hammer? Who defines what a hammer is?). I simply want to use it to drive a nail into the wall. However, there are situations that propel me to reflect on the being of the hammer. Let us suppose that after repeated and accurate swings of the hammer, the nail simply does not budge. I might hold the hammer up to scrutiny, asking, 'What is this confounded thing, and what is wrong with it?' These sorts of questions explicitly focus our thoughts on the hammer's existence, and prompt us to adopt an attitude beyond ordinary ways of existing. Again, events interrupt everyday patterns of thought to provoke fundamental questions, paving the way for reflective frames of mind to surface.

These examples suggest that we harbour several distinct qualities of mind. First, there are our ordinary, everyday, commonsensical patterns of thought (for example, seeking the correct time to make a meeting, or thinking about how to place the nail in the wall to hang the picture). This is the usual, familiar attitude through which we approach our worlds. When we think in this way, we simply rely on typical, everyday concepts of time, the hammer, etc. Second, and by contrast, there are moments that arrest our everyday, common-sense thought and action. Here we question the activities, tools, and concepts with which we are engaged. The challenging response of the sociology major, or the hammer's failure, provokes me into thinking about my assumptions of time, or the hammer's existence.

As noted, the second mode of thinking encapsulates the quality of mind akin to a sociological imagination. This sort of thinking requires a leap in which we, as participants in given social contexts, suspend our comfortable, everyday understandings of things. We do so in order to think differently about the ways in which we interact with others. This reflective jump is the foundation of sociological ways of thinking, speaking, and writing. It appeals to theoretical languages that may be related to, but yet are quite different from, the everyday languages that make up our 'common sense'.

In this sense, it is not too much of a push to suggest that becoming a sociologist is somewhat akin to learning a new (analytic) language, and this requires a particular sort of preparation. To think sociologically, we remain participants of ordinary life. We do our shopping, play sports, visit with friends, go to work, etc. But, in addition, we must learn to pore over particular aspects of that life from a different vantage (e.g., collective, socio-historical, critical), using the concepts derived from a dynamic, systematic, theoretical, and empirically informed language. This involves a process of learning how to think about collective life differently from the ways provided by everyday social meanings.

A basic tool for negotiating the passage from everyday to reflexive sociological thinking is none other than the difficult, the arresting, the provocative, even if always elusive, *question*.

In this sense, as discussed later in this introduction, sociological thinking most often starts at moments of astute questioning. Such questioning challenges the limits of ordinary, common-sense frames of meaning. It may lead us beyond the vocabulary and grammar of everyday thinking to sociology's conceptual languages. But how does sociological thinking relate to other academic disciplines?

The Sociological Imagination and Other Disciplines

Suppose you are drinking coffee on the deck of your friend's small urban back garden. Dew glistens on the green leaves of a maple tree, reflecting the bright morning sunlight. This tree is undoubtedly the outstanding feature of an otherwise bleak garden. Your friend's mood is glum as she reflects on her inability to pay mounting bills and debts. As a single parent, she supports a child and, when not trying to make ends meet, spends time trying to find a job that will accommodate her child care responsibilities.

She tells of her inability to buy the basics, such as groceries, water, and electricity. Your friend has come upon hard times of late, and she talks now of knowing what the term 'poverty' means. She even confesses to thinking about pilfering some 'good food', and has entertained ways of committing benefit fraud. Each time, however, she has thought better of it and let her life take its increasingly strained course. She has become frazzled by her predicament and blames the changing times; more specifically, she points to increasing calls for the erosion of social welfare and the increased cost of heating, water, and electricity. Unable to find a job that will allow her to tend the children, she has become dependent upon social services, and is perturbed by the identity this has foisted upon her. She stares meaningfully into her cup, and sighs deeply. You place your hand, reassuringly, on her shoulder.

There are many ways to analyze this snippet of life. In academic life, different approaches are often used to distinguish specific disciplines (e.g., engineering, anthropology, medicine, history, chemistry). However, the boundaries between disciplines are never clearly defined; their borders are usually contested, they change over time, new disciplines are created, others are merged, and there are often explicit calls for interdisciplinary work. But universities still distinguish between disciplines, although in different ways. They usually isolate social sciences and humanities from the natural sciences, medicine, etc., viewing the former as focusing on the human dimensions of a situation.

Referring to the above example of your friend's situation, a so-called natural science such as plant biology might refer to the species of maple tree in question, enlightening us how energy from the sun helps to sustain, through photosynthesis, the life of the tree with its bright colours. A physicist could examine the properties of sun's refracted light through the prism-like bubbles of liquid. Chemists may seek to establish whether the liquid in view is water, or some other translucent substance secreted by the tree. The physiologist might collaborate with medical colleagues, and indeed our noted chemist, to study the potential effects of coffee on the human body.

Within the social sciences, the economist might describe redistributions of money flow in free market contexts, explaining your friend's current plight as a result of basic adjustments to markets. Psychologists, by contrast, might discuss the elements of mind that explain your friend's depressed mood, and prescribe possible treatments for her 'frazzled' state. Those of a more psychoanalytic bent may interpret what lies buried in her expressive sigh or your comforting gesture. Feminist psychologists may locate the effects of patriarchal power relations that disproportionately disadvantage women. Political scientists would likely point to underlying changes to previous welfare state formations, to the ways in which the state is nowadays pressured by neo-liberal calls to surrender (sell off) many public services to private enterprise (e.g., water facilities, electricity). Classical criminologists might point to the supposed cost-benefit, rational, calculations that your friend makes before thinking about stealing. They would undoubtedly note her free choice to obey the law rather than face the punishments dealt to those who fall foul of it.

Sociologists are likely to approach the setting in the back garden through a rather different set of perspectives. The use of the plural form of the term 'perspective' is deliberate, for there is little consensus on the exact ways in which sociology ought to proceed. However, there are distinguishing approaches and practices of those who aim to develop specifically *sociological* (rather than, say, economic, political, etc.) approaches. Without suggesting there are absolute distinctions, one might say that sociology tends to be involved with naming, understanding, and critically evaluating collective patterns through which people live out their lives. These are often referred to as the *societal* aspects of contexts.

Yet, as noted, sociological imaginations are generated from many different theoretical approaches and license diverse practices, from surveys, laboratory experiments and statistical analyses to participant observation, interviews, interpretative analysis, theorizing, critique, and political engagement. The sociological imaginations of this book's chapters, however, tend to draw on three main traditions, asking questions involving sociological traditions that themselves highlight different aspects of society: subjective interaction, social structures, and social transformation. It is important to stress that most of the chapters draw simultaneously—in some measure at least—on aspects of all these traditions and in various ways. Several also draw on other theoretical orientations, but to address all of these would take the present discussion too far away from its introductory aims.

Three Sociological Approaches

Subjective Troubles

First, some sociologists develop a sociological imagination from theoretical traditions centred on how we interact with other subjects. These interactions create meanings that shape our views of the world and so affect how we act. The sociological traditions are concerned with interpreting and explaining social relationships—they deal with the meanings and actions that these relationships generate. A key figure in developing this approach, Max Weber, defines social relationships thus: 'The term "social relationship" will be used to designate the situation where two or more persons are engaged in conduct wherein each takes account of the behavior of the other in a meaningful way and is therefore oriented in these terms' (1980, 63). He distinguishes between behaviour (say, a random movement of your hand) and socially meaningful behaviour (say, a wave). He calls the latter 'social action'. For Weber, sociology is only concerned with *social* actions and relationships.

Weberian-inspired sociological imaginations therefore focus on social actions, shared meanings, and relationships between subjects. They focus on *inter-subjectively* created meanings that guide people's actions.[3] With reference to the example in the previous section, they might emphasize how you and your friend interact using meanings that both understand. They would examine how these meanings allow you to interact with each other and the object world. They may also ask how processes of socialization (that is, how you are taught to embrace the meanings of a given society) have helped to create you and your friend as particular kinds of individuals (subjects) capable of functioning in *this* society.

Within this approach, sociologists are likely to ask the following sorts of questions: Why do you behave and think in the ways you do? How do social interactions shape one's world view, and how does the latter affect the ways people subsequently behave? How do the meanings by which you make sense of the world lead you to act more or less predictably? What wider social history makes possible the thoughts and actions that colour your friend's and your social worlds? How do you come to interpret images, actions, gestures, and words in particular ways?

To be sure, over time, there are many different ways in which people can identify themselves and each other as subjects. For example, imagine a thirteenth-century serf is transmuted to a conversation you are having with a friend today. This serf, who hails from a radically different social context, would likely not understand the meanings you and your friend use to communicate effortlessly with one another. The serf may not even see him or herself as an individual subject, as someone with private thoughts, capable of free ownership, and so on. The identity of an unfree peasant (serf) is the creature of a very different social world, belonging to a way of being that was shaped by an entirely different social context. Consequently, a peasant's view of the world (and understanding of his or her location within that) would be very different from current beliefs.

The serf example challenges the idea that individual subjects are essentially and universally the same. At the very least, it indicates that subjects assume very different forms, and their understandings of themselves and their worlds vary greatly—depending upon the social contexts from which they emerge. Thus, Weberian-inspired sociological approaches require us to shelve the everyday view that I am essentially (i.e., at my core) a constant, unchangeable, and absolute individual. These approaches draw on a theoretical tradition that views subjects as malleable creators (agents) and creatures (products, effects) of a given social history and context. They enable specific questions, such as those in the first part of this book, directed toward the possibility that various images of the self (as free agent with a particular sexual orientation and ethnicity) are produced out of social interactions within a socio-historical context.

This idea, that perceptions of the self are a product of social interactions within a socio-historical context is associated with what is known as structuralism and post-structuralism. These are complex ways of understanding the world, but briefly, structuralism refers to the idea that cultural products such as language and texts have an underlying structure. In other words, structuralism provides a way of understanding objects in any given society as having a fundamental structure. Noam Chomsky, for instance, argued that all languages share a 'universal grammar'; children learn the individual language of the society into which they are born, but every language is similarly structured by a set of rules. In sociology, structuralism takes various forms but clings to the idea that systematic enquiry can discover regular, recurring, and ordered patterns of social behaviour (e.g., from the micro rituals of crossing streets at traffic lights or the way students file into lecture halls, to the regular ways that the education system feeds into economic and political systems). Structuralists describe these patterns as *social structures,* which are thought to create individual human subjects. For structuralist thinkers, if individual subjects appear to have a stable nature—a core—then this is precisely because of the relative stability of primary social structures.

The essays in Part 1, and many other chapters of the book, also draw on what may be loosely termed 'post-structuralist' approaches.[4] This set of approaches expands upon and responds to the structuralist view. Post-structuralists agree that subjects (e.g., people, I, you, he, she) are created identities, but they challenge the view that social structures exist in any absolute way. For them, subjects are always products of unpredictable and changing (thus not regular) historical contexts. From this perspective, any attempt to discover regular social patterns is not possible—any such claims are always beliefs, artificial impositions. All things (including language, knowledge, images of truth, the sociologists, the subject, etc.) are located within ongoing and unnecessary flows of history. Two key French theorists often associated with post-structuralism, but who do not identify themselves as such, are Jacques Derrida and Michel Foucault. Derrida's work in part indicates that language is assembled and used in very different ways—in current practices in our contexts, language is used in such a way as to create particular images of the subject (see Derrida 1976). For example, the use of the first person as the subject of language often imparts the impression that individuals are absolute beings with a core essence (e.g., the statements 'I am rational', 'I am happy', etc., use language in such a way as to create images of a unified or fixed 'I').

Foucault also rejects the idea of a stable subject, but he emphasises power relations as the key to understanding how particular images of individuals and selves are created (Foucault 1980a). In addition, both theorists challenge the idea that there are universal truths to discover; for them, truths (say, about subjects and social structures) are always achievements of hard truth-producing 'work' in particular contexts. Some feminist writers modify this approach to accommodate distinctive ways to redress the plight of women in contemporary societies (Weedon 1997). The sociological imaginations of Part 1 tap post-structuralist traditions to question various everyday senses that people have of themselves as 'selves', free beings, sexual beings, citizens, and political agents.

Some might ponder how Mills' sociological imagination, which grows out of classical sociological thinking, could relate to a post-structural challenge to hierarchies of such classical thinking. Our response is simply this: diverse post-structuralist orientations do not eschew the classics but rather read them through different interpretative lenses to expose classical sociological thinking to marginalized 'others' (e.g., women, people of colour, indigenous people) who are excluded by particular theories of society. In so opening classical sociology to its others, post-structuralist thought renders the questioning posture championed by Mills' sociological imagination in new ways, and so enables a revitalized way of imagining how to be with others. To be sure, as we shall see later in this introduction, this approach suggests a rather different version of critical thinking. The approach to critique does not follow the usual attempt to secure absolute judgments of existing societies—judgments that claim to be able to show society how it might adopt progressive change. Instead, post-structuralist thinking is more concerned with relentlessly opening existing social contexts to what they might become (see Pavlich 2000; 2005). It does so, in large measure, through the art of continuous and never-ending questioning—the very heart of any sociological imagination.

Imagining the Social

Another tradition used to generate sociological imaginations views collective life as a distinct object in its own right. Imagine the idea this way: While walking home from university you happen to glimpse a fair-sized flock of Canada geese flying overhead. You are struck by the overall patterns created as the geese dart and fly in their various courses. Interestingly, one can focus attention on the antics of a particular goose, the interactions of a smaller grouping, or indeed on the changing shapes of the whole flock. The sociological tradition referenced in Part 2 of this book tends to focus on collective groupings, or the whole flock. These sociological approaches typically explain wide social structures by referring to other social structures, not to individual characteristics. In these approaches, the collective whole is explained through the component (social) groupings, and such groupings, in turn, serve to explain why individual geese act as they do.

As a forerunner of this approach, Émile Durkheim observed that society should be seen as an entity in and of itself, made up of social facts. For him, sociology ought to explain any society by focusing explicitly on its underlying 'social facts'.[5] Durkheim (1938) regarded sociology as a unique science that would take 'social facts' (not individuals) as its basic object of study. From this perspective, sociologists might explain why an individual acts in a particular way, by turning not to psychological or even economic factors, but specifically to *social* facts. These social facts may be actualized through individuals and even the interactions between individuals. But, for Durkheim, they exist independently of any one individual; that is, they are detached from, and then serve as a constraining force over, a particular individual's actions. A Durkheimian sociological approach might tend to use scientific methods to explain human behaviour by studying how social facts are related to one another. Thus, to explain why an individual committed a criminal act, a Durkheimian sociologist would not look to, say, the psychological (or genetic) makeup of the offender. Instead, he or she might look to explain the social facts of crime in relation to other social facts (for example, describe general crime rates and then relate them to corresponding poverty rates, or economic growth rates, to explain the emergence of particular, individual crimes).

Developing this sort of imagination, Durkheimian-inspired sociologists might ask this of our example above of your friend's situation: can the social fact of increasing impoverishment be explained by wider economic (e.g., free market) and political (e.g., the decline of the welfare state) changes? How can scientific methods be employed to study the social facts of this situation? For instance, in your friend's case, what social facts lie behind her particular reliance on social welfare? Is the fact of growing social inequality in Canadian society related to the facts of free market economic arrangements, or to class, gender, and ethnicity? What scientifically based policy recommendations and interventions might help to change society for the better?

The chapters of Part 2 develop various sociological imaginations around the theme of the 'social'. Though diverse, many of these essays also implicitly embrace the post-structural idea that the social does not exist absolutely; if it exists at all, this is so because of given 'systems of truth' located within a given history. These essays suggest an imagination directed toward showing how the social, as a concept, could generate fairer, public-spirited, compassionate, gender-equal, non-imperialist, and just ways of associating with others.

Critical sociology

Third, a well-established critical sociological tradition nurtures various critical imaginations. These imaginations seek to understand the injustices of given contexts, with an underlying objective of finding effective ways of bringing about incremental, or indeed revolutionary, social change. Many budding sociologists may have direct experience of what it means to be poor, to witness the destruction of beautiful environments for short-term pecuniary gain, to bear the brunt of coercive control, or to be on the receiving end of prejudicial discriminations based on ascribed gender, ethnicity, sexual identity, youth, old age, deviance, eccentricities, and so on. Glimpsing the harsh effects of unequal chances to live a preferred life, being touched by the glint in the eye of the downtrodden child, seeing the ruthless effects of social exclusion, bearing the brunt of cold discriminations, or experiencing the horrors of intolerance, some seize upon sociology to make sense of—in order to fight against—social injustice. Sociology, in such quarters, serves as a theoretical awakening, a means of discursively explaining experiences of injustice and directing political action in search of social change.

There are many different sociological imaginations of this ilk, but most tend to assume a macro (wide) focus, and might approach our example of your friend's situation through questions like this: What social patterns and structures have created the conditions in which your friend must now negotiate who she is and what to do in her day-to-day life? How is her individual situation a product of wider power formations that advantage some people (e.g., the wealthy) and disadvantage other groups (e.g., the lower class, women, the young, the elderly, ethnic minorities) within Canada? What collectively shaped ideas, decisions, and actions make it possible for some people to own property and permit others to rent from them (e.g., a capitalist society based on the private property ownership)? What socio-political decisions create conditions for, and frame, the type of life your friend now lives? How are these decisions made, by whom are they made, and what sort of effects do they have? How have the economic arrangements of the day favoured the wealthy or powerful at the expense of the poor or oppressed? In whose interest is it to continue the free market policies that entrench a particular brand of capitalism? What sorts of institutions are created to develop, enforce, and monitor wider decisions as policies? What can be done to change the present society to bring about a different (fairer, more just, equal) society (see Marx and Engels 1948, 1970)?

The chapters of Part 3 mobilize aspects of this tradition—but with the aim of developing a sociological imagination that deliberately examines the ways in which sociological knowledge can speak to power relations by naming and indicating the effects of particular 'truths' in everyday life. Again, post-structuralist themes are implicitly tapped in this part's chapters that consider power and knowledge to emerge as closely connected processes (that is, truth is created through power relations, just as knowledge helps to set up particular power relations—see Foucault 1977, 1980). What is taken to be true in any social context is a socio-political achievement, not an independent discovery. As such, critical sociological imaginations are particularly concerned to ensure that knowledge that challenges current social forms be given a legitimate voice. Without critical analyses, there is little to challenge current social forms with all their injustices, inequalities, and so on (Pavlich 2000). The dangers of tyranny are never far away when critique is disallowed, and this is precisely why the authors of the chapters in Part 3 call for new knowledge-producing environments—ones that encourage, rather than stifle and silence, critical imaginations.

No doubt, over the past four decades critical sociologists have confronted the validity of modes of critique embraced by their analyses (Pavlich, 2005). For example, many social critics have rejected the view that critique or critical thinking necessarily involves judgments of given societies based on absolute, universal, or certain criteria deemed capable of defining progressive social change. If nothing else, postmodern analyses of the 1980s and 1990s forcefully challenged the idea that universally agreed upon criteria may ever be achieved (is this idea not simply an illusion, a myth, of modern thinking?), far less that such criteria might assuredly guide universal social progress. Indeed, one might ponder whether modern versions of foundational criteria can be made to apply to all societies without replicating an imperial approach that most critical theorists question (recall that 'others' are always created by universal declarations). As well, writers such as Jean-François Lyotard (1984) noted how modern critical forms, based mostly on founded judgment, were facing an increasing crisis of legitimacy in social contexts where belief in absolute conceptions of knowledge had been seriously challenged by surrounding events (world wars, apartheid, the Holocaust, etc.). Such events were not prevented by, and in some cases actually derived support from, modernity's rationally inspired quest for universal criteria as the basis for judging how to 'advance' society. In the wake of these events, an uncertainty contoured many societies as more people questioned the view that absolute, universal criteria could serve as a basis for pointing to social progress. One response to this situation has been the quest not to abandon critical thinking, and commentators have sought new 'grammars of critique' appropriate to current socio-historical horizons (see Pavlich 2000, 2005). Such grammars are increasingly less attached to founded judgment as a way of practising critical thinking, and more concerned with attempts to permanently open social beings to imagine what they might become. Fundamental questioning and the resultant sociological imaginations, we argue, are central to grammars of critique that downplay the role of universally founded judgment.

Why the Questions?

To sum up, we have noted several approaches that inform the sociological imaginations of this text. In general, one might say that most sociologists are involved with naming, understanding, critically questioning, and/or seeking to change the collective patterns and groupings in which people live out their lives—these are often referred to as the *societal* aspects of life. Is there one sure way to develop this imagination? As Mills makes clear, there is no hard and fast blueprint, but we have already noted a basic tool for that task: an ability to raise fundamental questions about our collective being.

Even a cursory glance at the present text reveals its emphasis on questions. The title *Questioning Sociology* conveys the message from the outset. The introduction has itself tried to communicate a sense of sociological thinking by posing questions. In addition, every contributing chapter is developed out of a specific question. Despite the chapters' differences, all adopt a questioning, interrogative stance. In each case, various examples of the sociological imagination emerge as a result of responses to questions that require analysts to *reflect* on collective issues.

The practice of *asking questions* that lead beyond the limits of everyday commonsense is thus a basic methodological resource for sociological thinking. That is, to repeat the logic adopted, sociological thinking occurs at moments when we suspend our participation in everyday, common-sense ways of understanding and acting in the world. It starts by reflecting on those understandings and actions. Instead of using common-sense meanings to negotiate our way through life, sociologists look to other (sociological) meaning horizons. Developing a sociological imagination is very much like learning a different language, a new vocabulary, syntax, grammar, diction, style of expression, and so on. This language may be related to everyday life, but it involves a specifically reflective, *questioning*, orientation that leads us beyond the limits of familiar commonsense understandings.

Yet sociology explores ideas and actions in a language that is neither homogeneous nor complete—it is always evolving and changing. Since sociological thinking reflects on moments in history, and since these moments are constantly changing and never beyond question, sociology itself must remain open to new ways of exploring social life. In particular, sociological qualities of mind require us to go beyond the limits of given (everyday) ways of communicating. They require us to question the objects, concepts, and images that are simply assumed in ordinary life.

Learning to think sociologically, thus, is without end, because there is no final or finite language to learn. Sociology does not have one canon or doctrine that all sociologists must observe. Instead, the languages of sociology are multiple, dynamic, and forever developing through new ideas, texts, presentations, and so on.

However, sociology's methodological reliance on questions is even more basic. For example, underlying all versions of the sociological imagination is a question that many sociologists must face: What methods are appropriate to address the collective aspects of our lives? Can the scientific methods of the natural sciences (physics, chemistry, etc.) be transposed to a different context to explain social facts?[6] Or is the subject matter of sociology so different that it requires its own unique methods of analysis? If so, in what ways are the objects of sociology different from those of the natural sciences (say, sexuality versus gravity)? What methods can best address such objects? Is sociology a discipline that must remain committed to studying its objects using scientific methods (Durkheim 1938)? Should it interpret social meanings with the greatest possible conceptual precision in order to understand social being (Weber 1968)? Should sociology aim to describe a 'taken-for-granted' reality, or critically assess how that reality is created in context? Should it, by contrast, analyze a given society against a justified image of an ideal, advanced, equal, or rational society? Should sociology, for instance, not only name the social structures responsible for your friend's poverty, but also suggest ways in which those structures can be changed to bring about a better society (Marx 1970)? This last question implies that societies are able to change. It also supposes that sociological analysis can help point both to appropriate directions for change and the mechanisms for achieving such changes (e.g., through revolution—see Marx and Engels 1948, 1970).

At the same time, it is important to emphasize that such questioning applies not only to social challenges but also to the very discipline of sociology. If any systematic pattern of thinking (a discipline?) is to grow and remain nourished, it must permanently remain open to new ideas, new theories, and new approaches. As such, sociological questions may just as importantly and valuably question the historical practices and thinking of sociology. The very practice of questioning sociology should therefore be treated not as a threat but as the lifeblood to secure vibrant, open, and always responsive approaches to how we might become with others. Overall, the basic point is this: while sociologists use particular kinds of questions to arouse the sociological imagination, they also make abundant use of questions to reflect on their own practices. The reign of the question is therefore basic to developing a sociological imagination. Were sociology to have a motto, it would, no doubt, look something like this: 'Question, Question, and Question Again!'

Notes

1. Indeed, as Anthony Giddens (1987) puts it, 'Like all other social sciences . . . sociology is an inherently controversial endeavour. That is to say, it is characterised by continuing disputes about its very nature' (2–3).
2. Like the topics of earnest dinner conversations with good friends, where people argue over the world's plight and try to solve its most intractable problems, sociology does often examine pressing issues. However, unlike spontaneous meal-based musings, sociologists have—perhaps even before August Comte's *Cours de Philosophie Positive* (1838) put the term 'sociology' into wider circulation— historically positioned their discussions as systematic analysis. Indeed, Comte claimed sociology as the royal science—the queen of all sciences—because unlike others (physics, chemistry,

etc.) it dealt with the basis of collective being: human morality. This made it logically prior to all other sciences because without stable social moorings, without peaceful social arrangements, all else becomes impossible. Could sophisticated computers be invented, understood, developed, and deployed if a society were incapable of preventing its members from annihilating one other? First things first, according to Comte, and sociology's promise to explain peaceful, rational co-existence is among the first of sciences.

3. See Weber (1968) and Berger (1974).

4. For a more detailed discussion of post-structuralism, see Seidman (1998) and Calhoun (1995, 113–16).

5. For Durkheim (1938), *'A social fact is a way of acting, fixed or not, capable of exercising on the individual an external constraint; [or again] every way of acting which is general throughout a given society, while at the same time existing in its own right independent of individual interpretations'* (13, emphasis in the original).

6. Some say this question betrays a deep-seated insecurity about the relative status of *social*— as opposed to say *natural*—sciences. Disturbed by the charge that sociology is not a 'real' science, or that it is always a depraved cousin to its natural ('hard science') counterparts, many sociologists respond by clinging inveterately to 'science' like nobody else. They try to be more scientific than any other scientist. No doubt this unfertile obsession has its own sociological pedigree, and its legacy *has* yielded many taxonomies, classifications, and descriptions of the seemingly obvious. Visit the far reaches of an older library and locate yourself at the spot where sociology texts are filed. Look for the dusty tomes of yore that—if ever pried from the unsullied comfort of long-forgotten shelves—herald the functions of this or that social system, or more ambitiously posit the absolute nature of all social existence. This 'science' falls prey to the ravages of time, and its claims to final truth are exposed as rooted in a given time and place.

PART I

Subjective Troubles

The first part of this book explores questions regarding how we identify ourselves as particular individuals or small groupings of people. It tackles questions of the self, the 'I', our emotions, our families, which seem so immediate to us, and various outcomes of complex relations with others. In different ways, the chapters in Part 1 challenge the view that 'I' (the individual's sense of self) is a primitive, fixed, primary being that exists in advance of any social interactions. Each chapter points to different means through which this 'I', self, or small grouping, is created by broader social relations.

George Pavlich's chapter, 'Am I Free?', begins by challenging everyday views that selves are naturally free (that is, I am different from a stone or a flower because my nature as a human being is not fully determined—I am free to choose, within wide limits, how to act). Pavlich taps into this view by noting the extent to which Canadian society is based on images of individual freedom. Its founding liberal philosophy assumes that individuals are by nature free and that state power often curbs that freedom. Against this familiar view, Pavlich explores the possibility that neither the so-called individual (the 'I'), nor the supposed freedom often attached to such individuals, actually exists before interactions with others. Rather, both our conceptions of 'individuals' and 'freedom' are products of social interactions at given moments in history. If this is so, then, drawing on the work of Michel Foucault, one might argue that historical power relations and freedom are not necessarily opposite ideas, as is often thought. This leads Pavlich to imagine a rather counterintuitive idea: namely, that power is sometimes exercised precisely by enforcing 'free' individual identities. This is especially the case for liberal democracies in which governments claim the right to govern in part because they guarantee individual freedoms (freedom of speech, assembly, religion, and so on). However, if power is exercised by requiring each 'I' to be free in specified ways, then we are forced to reconsider what we mean when we say 'I am free.' In seeking to be free, individuals can end up endorsing a freedom that effectively allows them a narrow choice—namely, that of choosing their own chains.

Chapter 2 considers two of the most fundamental of human questions, 'Who am I?' and 'What can I become', by invoking a particular sociological imagination. Dawn Currie and Deirdre Kelly draw on empirical research conducted to expose girls' experiences of peer relations. This research provides a basis for exploring how an individual's sense of self is sustained by various complex interactions among the social, political, economic, and cultural structures that surround the individual. Responding to the question 'Who am I?', Currie and Kelly focus attention on how adolescent girls are actively involved in developing images of 'self' through social contexts, described as a search for selfhood. Here, they work out who they take themselves (the 'I') to be. Based on interviews with girls between the ages of 12 and 16, the research challenges two divergent strands of thinking: not only mainstream sociology and its failure to investigate identity projects of non-dominant groups (mistaking dominant identities for the norm) but also the view that girls are simply passive victims of 'adolescent femininity'. Currie and Kelly instead analyze the words of adolescent girls that describe the numerous pressures to 'fit in', to conform to conservative and traditional notions about how girls should dress, talk, act, and relate to others. Although these pressures are both intense and relentless, the researchers are clear that adolescent girls are active agents too. They make use of opportunities to resist wider relational structures and pressures. While girls who resist do not necessarily create entirely 'free' subjectivities, they are at least able to construct alternative, sometimes oppositional, understandings of themselves.

Myra Hird's chapter, 'Am I a Woman?', takes up the discussion of gender in Currie and Kelly's chapter in a different way. Hird argues that sociologists often champion the idea that gender profoundly shapes an individual's experience of the world. From this vantage point, whether an individual is identified as a woman or a man has significant consequences for the way other people relate to that individual, their occupation, family life, salary, health, intimacy, and so on. Many feminist sociologists share this view of gender. They often accuse sociology in general of ignoring or at least downplaying the significance of gender in determining an individual's life course. However, Hird invites us to consider questions of gender in another way. She notes that sociologists tend to separate the term 'gender' from 'sex': gender refers to socially constructed elements of personhood (femininity and masculinity), while sex refers to biological characteristics (what makes us either female or male). Her chapter challenges this distinction by arguing that our assumptions about sex as something natural limits the ways by which we are able to analyze gender. Sex, she contends, is also a socially generated category. Indeed, Hird maintains that the so-called opposite sexes are actually more similar than they are different. On that basis, she invites readers to consider what social interactions might look like without prevalent concepts of either sex or gender.

Chapter 4, by Barry D. Adam, explores another dimension of the 'I' and the self by responding to the question 'Why be queer?' In his formulation of a sociological imagination, Adam details the complex mechanisms through which social relations within Western society define, manage, and regulate sexuality. He begins by outlining a complex history of social processes that led to the 'invention of homosexuality as a juridical and medical category'. The processes also generated a negative bias—a homophobia—against those who identify as lesbian, gay, bisexual, and transgendered people. Dominant institutional structures within society, such as the law, medicine (especially psychiatry and psychology), and educational and public policy arenas, encourage us to identify as selves who align with prevailing gendering practices. Despite the considerable costs of defining oneself as queer, Adam convincingly challenges 'the ugly taskmaster of homophobia'. He argues against its tyrannical social censures that fail to comprehend the benefits to be gained from diversity in all its forms. He concludes by noting that if all selves were to reject homophobia, those selves' personal horizons would be greatly expanded and enhanced. This in turn could potentially help many more people to be 'at peace with themselves'.

In Chapter 5, Stephen Katz questions a conventional view that our emotions are unique to each of us, and moves to consider how a sociological imagination might approach the matter of our emotions. He does so by engaging a field of inquiry referred to as the sociology of emotions, which examines how certain emotions are 'tethered to particular social contexts'. Drawing on various social analysts, he examines emotions as products of particular historical, cultural, social and political contexts. Without denying the power of personal emotional experiences, Katz argues that emotions provide 'signposts' to the ways in which our social contexts help to create our 'interior lives'. Echoing a theme of this part of the book, the sociology of emotions allows us to glimpse how subtly the self and its internal emotions may be socially produced. Similarly, research on identity and aging tells us that different visions of self are considered normal during specific stages of life. Such norms reflect prevailing images of normality and abnormality, deviance, and difference. And that is crucial to self-definitions in contexts where selves are encouraged to define themselves in relation to others.

Erin Dej continues this theme in Chapter 6 by asking readers to rethink and explore the social bases of mental phenomena referred to as 'mental illness'. She notes that 'when we hear the words "mental illness" we think of someone who is very sick, who behaves strangely, who makes us uncomfortable, who maybe even scares us, and who does not fit in with everyday society.' Her chapter questions such perceptions by examining how the history of various scientifically orientated psychiatric institutions, diagnostic practices, and officially sanctioned treatments embraced by a dominant medical model have shaped our beliefs about mental illness. Dej then examines how this model was challenged in the 1960s by a growing deinstitutionalization movement that called for the abolition of mental hospitals and for appropriately humane community-based services. Even if that movement failed to live up to its ideals, it did spawn a social approach to mental phenomena that took root in antipsychiatry and the mad movement. Whatever their shortfalls, these approaches have broadened the approach to mental issues and potentially provide a different paradigm for approaching mental illness in ways that maximize rights, freedoms, and privileges of all people.

In the concluding chapter of Part 1, Catherine Krull questions another frequently taken-for-granted idea that many assume exists quite unproblematically: the family. She notes that despite the massively growing diversity of what we consider to be family in Canada, an image of a 'traditional' nuclear family (with a male breadwinner/female care-giver binary) often 'remains firmly fixed in our collective imagination as the most recognizable and most desired family form.' Krull points out, however, that by 2006 only 17 per cent of census families fell under Statistics Canada's 'nuclear family' classification. Most Canadians, then, do not live in nuclear families, and yet the idea of a family remains important to our identifications. Krull argues that while families do exist and do matter, we should understand that family diversity is the norm. Consequently, she contends, sociology should acknowledge that a common definition of the family will always prove elusive because 'how we understand the family is how we experience it.' Since there are many different such experiences, it does not make sense to define the family (as has often been the case in the sociology of the family) by who belongs to it; rather, the family needs to be approached by 'what it does'. And in this perspective lies Krull's call for an understanding of diverse forms of families—a recognition that each form is directly generated out of specific social conditions. The experiences of family, she concludes, are conditioned through various socio-economic processes, including those contoured by gender, class, ethnicity, workplace, and exclusionary relations.

Questions for Reflection

1. What part do norms play in structuring the relationship between individuals and the society they live in?

2. To what extent did you decide to go to university, and to what extent was this decision made for you by your social context (your class, gender, family background, age, and so on)?

3. What did Michel Foucault mean when he said that 'madness only exists in society'?

This book is chato chaotic, confused, and poorly written. FUCK

1 | Am I Free?

George Pavlich

Introduction

Many people bandy the term 'free' around as if its meaning were so obvious that it merited little further attention. After all, inhabitants of a country like Canada live in a 'free society', as part of the 'free world'. In general, people go about the business of everyday living without undue interference from the powers that be. We exercise many free choices in the course of each day—whether or not to eat breakfast, which fashion of clothing to don, whether to attend classes or work, which mode of transport to use, what route to take to-day, and even whether to protest against a ruling government on a given issue. To be sure, the number of choices we are required to make on a daily basis, as members living in a 'free society', is vast.

Over and above these personal choices, free societies provide formal guarantees for particular freedoms, such as those enshrined in the Canadian Charter of Human Rights and Freedoms. Such laws are designed to protect 'fundamental freedoms', including the freedom of religion, conscience, expression, peaceful assembly, and association. Still other laws seek to protect individual privacy from unfair intrusions by the state (or other parties) into one's personal affairs (e.g., protection of privacy legislation). These legally under-written freedoms are part of a wider democratic political system. This system relies upon citizens being free to cast votes for leaders or parties of their choice. Such freedom is key to any liberal democracy. Compromising its tenets threatens the integrity of the entire system. Equally, capitalists champion the importance of free markets for economic well-being. The emphasis on freedom is also evident in cultural contexts, with artists, writers, musicians, and dramatists fervently championing individual freedom. In these diverse contexts, we glimpse how prominently images of freedom feature in the everyday political, legal, social, economic, and cultural spheres of our lives.

It is hard to deny that we do exercise degrees of free choice, but in what sense does this mean that I am free? It certainly does not mean that I may do exactly as I please under any circumstances.[1] So perhaps we need to rephrase the question in more precise terms: in what way am I free when I exercise the choices available to (or perhaps required of) me as a member of this society? The present chapter explores this question by examining two responses that have inspired influential sociological approaches.

First, it examines a popular liberal view that individuals are 'born free', or that freedom is a natural aspect of all individuals. In this view, free individuals can only live according to their true nature when they live in free societies where formal power is held in check. Here, individual freedom is taken to be the opposite of political power; indeed, it is thought to exist only where the state's power is reigned in. From this perspective, sociology—as a science of society—could enhance individual freedom by discovering what a truly free society entails, and offer recommendations on how best to achieve it.

Against this position, we will consider a second viewpoint espoused by an influential French thinker, Michel Foucault. He challenges the main assumptions of modern liberal ideas. For Foucault, individuals are not born free; instead, **power relations** create both individuals and the particular freedoms ascribed to them. From this vantage point, who we are as individuals, our pleasures, our desires, likes, and freedoms, are all produced by power. His alternative view of freedom, individuals, power, and society has important implications for the role of sociology, especially for a critical sociology that seeks to expose the dangers of given power formations. It also offers a unique response to the question 'Am I free?'

Sociology and Liberal Images of Freedom

'Man is born free; and everywhere he is in chains.' (Rousseau 1983, 165)

In this brilliantly condensed quote, the first line of Rousseau's famous work *The Social Contract*, lies the founding assumption of modern liberal sociology's approach to freedom. Freedom is taken to be a basic natural attribute of human beings.[2] One could think of individuals born on a desert island to convey the main idea. Left to their own nature in an ideal society, without constraining interventions by formal powers, people would—according to Rousseau—grow up and live as natural, free, and sociable beings. They would freely and naturally choose social rules under which they were prepared to live. However, for him, modern industrial societies constrain people rather than free them from the shackles of past societies (hence he finds people 'everywhere in chains'). As such, individuals, who are free by nature, live in societies that do not allow them to express their natural inclinations.

Rousseau's liberal view prefaces several influential sociologists—including Marx, Durkheim, and Weber—to the extent that all sought tolerant, free societies. Let us explore this wider liberal backdrop on freedom in greater detail, before turning to Foucault's alternative view.

Freedom and Responsibility

Following from the above, a liberal response to the question 'Am I free?' is this: yes, as a human being you are by your nature (i.e., makeup) a free being. A rock does not have the ability to choose how to act—it is predetermined by its surroundings. Equally, a lion is born with instincts that largely dictate how it lives its life. It may learn hunting skills, and could be a better or worse hunter; but instincts require it to hunt for survival. Lions cannot be held responsible for their actions, for they do not make free moral or political choices. If a lion eats a zebra, we do not say that it is immoral (implying that it can be held responsible for its actions), for it is following instincts. Similarly, an acorn does not decide whether or not to grow into an oak tree. None makes strictly moral choices; they do not have a capacity to rationally choose how to exist, or to decide on the most ethical ways to behave.

From this perspective, human beings are distinct because they are born with a **free will** and an ability to make rational decisions on how to live out their lives. They are not completely controlled by basic instincts, or environments, but can choose life courses from a range of possibilities. Such choices include physical things such as how to grow (through diet, exercise, etc.), whether or not to reproduce, but also extend to questions about the sorts of people they want to be (reliable, compassionate, selfish, courageous, etc), what careers to pursue, and so on. As such, within certain biological constraints, people are born with an ability to choose particular life paths. Freedom is therefore part of our special makeup—it is our distinguishing essence.

Before and after World War II, a group of influential philosophers associated with so-called existentialist ideas expanded upon this view. Most notably, the work of Jean-Paul Sartre (1964 [1938], 1970) and Albert Camus (1991 [1947]) described the cold, harsh realities that face us because of our unique makeup. Their work insists that no matter what situations we find ourselves in, no matter how constrained or seemingly hopeless, we are always in doomed to be free.[3] Consider the case of a downtrodden person who is horribly exploited by a master. One could think of past times where 'masters' who 'owned' slaves often treated them very poorly. Let us say further that one unfortunate case involves a slave who is tied up and about to receive another lashing from her or his master. Even when so restrained, the person on the receiving end is free to respond in different ways, to imagine the situation in different ways—as a painful example of injustice, as a good reason for plotting revenge on a master, as part of the inevitable fate of a slave, or perhaps to let the mind wander in a dream world of sumptuous feasting, etc. Any number of possibilities could be entertained. For existentialists, this provides evidence that human beings are always and inescapably condemned to be free. Our lives are inevitably and irreconcilably undetermined, and hence free. Therefore, foreshadowing existential thought, Rousseau notes that 'to renounce liberty is to renounce being a man, to surrender the rights of humanity and even its duties' (1983 [1762], 170).

The idea of being condemned to freedom is beautifully characterized by Jean-Paul Sartre's philosophical novel *Nausea* (1964 [1938]). This book chronicles the life of an ordinary man who is forced to confront a life of freedom. As the story unfolds, Sartre shows how being condemned to freedom comes with awesome responsibilities. We may chose freely, but we are also responsible for the choices. Sartre describes the sheer burden of choice and responsibility in a world that is ultimately meaningless. Because we are free, we are free to make meaning; but—and here is the catch—we can never be certain that the choices we make are the best, right, just, fair, or correct ones. That imposes an awful anguish over our lives, an existential angst, because we make choices never knowing whether they are ethical ones. And then we are held accountable for those choices. As we recognize this grave situation, this terrible fate, we are struck with awful feelings of anxiety, a pitiful nausea. We try to overcome that nausea by doing everything in our power to deny our freedom, by trying to hide behind the semblance of doing things out of necessity (i.e., not having any choice).

This thinking has been incorporated into sociology in various ways, including in the 1970s through an existential sociology (see Douglas 1970a; Douglas and Johnson 1977). This approach worked out of the assumption that we are free to choose the social meanings that we do. It focused attention on the social effects of individuals being condemned to freedom. Closely related to this approach was a so-called ethnomethodological approach in sociology. It analyzed the logic of the 'methods' (methodology) that people (ethno) use to create meaning in the ever-changing social horizons in which they find themselves (Garfinkel 1967, 1986; Hilbert 1992).[4] Despite their differences, these various sociological approaches assume that individuals are fundamentally free, and note that such freedom includes an ability to create meaning.

Power and Freedom

'Being free stands opposed, classically, to being in someone else's power, being subject to the will of another.' (Ivison 1997, 1)

Rousseau offers a characteristically liberal critique of modern society by suggesting, as noted before, that in society people are 'everywhere in chains'. He worries that individuals have been trapped in power networks that restrict their free nature. In a characteristically liberal move, power is seen as the opposite of freedom: where there is freedom there is no power. Conversely, where power operates unhindered, where it constrains absolutely, there freedom is no more.[5] No doubt, this formulation implies a very specific conception of power; namely, power is identified with political institutions that limit individual freedom.

This image of power is perhaps most clearly developed in Thomas Hobbes' (1989 [1651]) famous work *The Leviathan*. Hobbes accepts that individuals are born with absolute freedom, and are thus potentially able to do anything within their grasp. With such absolute freedom, they can choose to help one another, but they can just as easily decide to kill one another to maximize their self-interests. In a 'state of nature', in a natural condition where individuals are absolutely free to do whatever they please, Hobbes describes a horrific 'war of each against all' so that life is 'nasty, brutish and short'. However, as egoistic and rational beings who pursue pleasure and turn away from pain, who pursue their self-interests, individuals band together to form a 'social contract'. In this contract, they promise to yield selected freedoms to a sovereign power (the state). In turn, they receive protection and the security to live life without the constant threat of death, terror, theft, and so on. This sovereign has absolute power to enforce the social contract enshrined in formal rules, called laws.

This intriguing and important analysis presents a view of power as a way of restricting, limiting, constraining, and checking individual freedom. Power is possessed by a sovereign (state, parliament, king, queen, etc.) who exercises power over subjects. In this framework, power limits, stops, prevents, or coerces (Wrong 1988). The implication is that where power operates, there natural freedom is limited; power and freedom are thus inversely related.

What does this mean for the question 'Am I free?' Clearly, if we hold to this view of power, then I am only ever free when power is held in check, where a sovereign power does not interfere with basic choices. In contexts where a sovereign does exert power, even if this is considered legitimate (e.g., through a democratic rule of law), my freedoms are constrained when power is exercised, where an overarching power can determine how we should act. So, we are never really free in the presence of a power over us. We need, according to this view, domains of freedom in which sovereign power is disallowed. Liberal thinkers have long pondered and tried to develop such domains, from the early images of 'public life' (Sennett 1992), to 'civil society', to images of the 'social' or 'community' as domains free from state power (Habermas

1971). Sociology has been involved with various attempts to develop free so-cieties that regulate themselves as far as possible, beyond the coercive inter-ventions of sovereign powers.

Individuals and a Free Society

This raises another question: what sort of collective grouping (society) could we imagine that limits state power and maximizes natural individual free-doms? As we have noted, a recurrent dream within sociology has been to rec-oncile the natural state of individuals with appropriate social groupings; or to put it differently, sociologists aimed to discover a free society that would trans-parently reflect the individuals that comprised it. How could this be achieved? Let us take Durkheim's (1989 [1893]) specific suggestions in his famous text *The Division of Labour in Society* as a case in point.

As a sociologist, Durkheim (1964 [1895]) does not deny that there is a biological (natural) component to 'individuals'. However, he insists that soci-ology is concerned only with that part of the individual that has to do with society. For him, people only come to exist as 'individuals', and moreover as free individuals in modern societies. The type of society into which people are 'socialized' largely decides whether they will live as free individuals or not (1989 [1893], 238–9). The 'type of society', in its turn, is determined by the ways in which labour is organized in a given context (i.e., the ways tasks are divided up and apportioned by a group—how food is collected, how children are tended, how people are educated, how decisions are made, etc). He argues, for instance, that pre-modern societies are of a type held together by 'mechan-ical solidarity' (1989 [1893], book 1, ch. 2). Here necessary tasks are relatively simply structured, strictly regulated, and sparsely divided (often between men and women, between tribal elders and others) through rules and customs. In such societies, individuals are not clearly identified apart from the roles they play as members of clans, tribes, and so on. A member of a group is not identi-fied beyond the social functions, duties and roles defined by customs, laws, etc. In context, it makes little sense to suggest that individuals are naturally free, since individuals are not clearly differentiated.

By contrast, Durkheim argues that modern capitalism—with expanding populations and industrialized forms of production—produces a type of so-ciety in which labour is divided in new and complex ways. In particular, tasks are broken down into discrete components, become specialized and require many different individuals to work in concert to get the overall job done (e.g, to get a tomato onto my dinner plate requires numerous people involved who expend labour on diverse tasks, including developing seeds, growing plants, distributing to supermarkets, selling, etc). This type of society is held together by an interdependence of function. He regards this as a resilient social 'glue' that he calls 'organic solidarity'.[6] Members of this society are required to perform specialized labour tasks, and this makes them highly dependent upon one another for their survival (e.g., a housekeeper may place her or his money in the bank, but the manager of that bank could rely on the housekeeper to prepare food; both rely on others to produce the fruit, and so on). This mutual reliance on diverse labour functions makes it possible for modern societies to develop a 'cult of the individual'. This encourages members to regard themselves (or identify) as 'individuals'—as free beings, who collectively make up society. The shift to modern societies brings with it a particular conception of freedom and individuality. It even allows the idea of individual freedom to dominate.

The assumption is that societies, like physical phenomena in the world, exist in the ways that they do through underlying laws that can be discovered via scientific inquiry. Furthermore, the aim is to obtain valid and true knowledge of how free societies really operate. Armed with such knowledge, sociologists can make recommendations to a given society on how it could improve or make progress toward a better, freer society. From this viewpoint, the role of sociology is akin to the engineer designing a bridge. Both must work on the basis of scientifically established principles of truth.

An Alternative View of Individual Freedom

We have so far examined liberal sociological views of freedom and society. We saw how some social thinkers regarded freedom as natural to individuals, but that is limited by power. Although deeply influential in sociological thinking, there are certain problems with this approach. For example, if modern society and its unique power structures create modern individuals, then does it also create the freedoms ascribed to them? Is power really then the opposite of freedom, or do liberal forms of government actually define freedom? Raising these questions has encouraged social thinkers like Foucault to develop alternate understandings of freedom, power, the individual, and society. This alternative framework also suggests a different way to understand the role of sociology.

For Foucault, freedom is never something static—always the same—regardless of where it is found. The statement 'I am free' is always uttered in a specific context. It is not independent, outside, or impervious to a given social history. That is, all versions of freedom, including those that are held so dear in Canada today, are born to a specific history. Just as it may be possible to trace your family tree, so it is possible to trace the family of ideas associated with our images of 'freedom'. Following this logic, one may use the term 'freedom' to describe our ability to shop 'freely' within the limits of a budget when visiting a local mall. But we would surely be using the term very differently from those wanting to revolutionize societies for greater individual freedom. Quite literally, the meaning of the term freedom is dependent on the context in which it is used (see Bauman, 1987, 1988). Freedom is not a universal concept with one meaning in different times and places; rather, it is very much the product of different historical horizons.

If freedom is relative to context, then we can raise two important questions. First, if the very idea of individuals and their freedom depends on historical context, then can individual freedom ever be universal? Second, is the freedom that we hold dear in Canadian society the opposite of power, or does say the state—and law—help to shape the sort of freedom available to us as members of this society?

Power's Products

Turning to the first question, Marx and Engels (1976, 20) challenge the view that individual freedom is universal. But more than this, for them, not only is freedom located in history, but so too are Rousseau's so-called naturally free individuals. If they are correct, then I am not naturally, and for all time, an individual, as common sense might dictate. Rather, social relations at a given moment in history create the very idea that we are 'individuals'. As Marx puts it, 'The human being is . . . an animal which can individuate only in the midst of society' (1973, 84). This is a profound statement: it means that each of us, with our different identities—from the clothes we wear to our images of self, from the pleasures we enjoy to the dislikes we avoid, from our most intimate thoughts to our most public expressions—are creations of a given social context. And so too is the image of freedom that we associate with our individuality.

But what specific mechanisms in society create 'free individuals'? For Foucault (1977, 1978, 1980a), the answer is clear: power relations. While this is not the place to detail his intricate and complex images of power,[7] it is nevertheless important to note that Foucault understands power as a relation—not as something that is possessed by an entity (e.g., an individual, a king, a corporate tycoon, a prime minister, a parliament, etc), and not as simply a top-down, constraining force. If anything, power relations are exercised through techniques used by historically situated subjects as they relate to one another. Such relations involve actions directed at shaping other actions through local 'clashes of will'. Power is therefore not simply repressive and constraining—it is a creative force that shapes actions through local, interactive wranglings. In

concert, such local power relations sometimes link to form overarching historical and social structures. Yet, power shapes all social relations; it also creates us
as historically specific subjects (peasants, vassals, free individuals), defines who
are 'other' (e.g., friends, enemies, etc.), and produces the meanings through
which we understand the world around us (see Foucault 1978, 92–98).

In this sense, power does not so much restrain, constrain, and limit what
individuals can do—it actually creates individuals. Foucault's deeply influential book *Discipline and Punish: The Birth of the Prison* (1977) is about many
things, but it also describes how a new technique of power—discipline—
emerged with the advent of modern societies and helped to create specific
kinds of 'normal' individuals. Discipline effectively created 'normal' individuals, separated them from the so-called abnormal, and located them as the
basic units of modern society. It is worth noting that Foucault saw disciplines
such as sociology, psychology, criminology, and education as types of knowledge that formed an important part of modern society's attempts to create
normal individuals. But his basic point is this:

> The individual is not to be conceived as a sort of elementary nucleus, a primi-
> tive atom, a multiple and inert material upon which power comes to fasten, or
> against which it happens to strike. . . . In fact, it is already one of the prime effects
> of the power that certain bodies, certain gestures, certain discourses, certain de-
> sires, come to be identified and constituted as individuals. The individual, that is,
> is not the vis-à-vis of power; it is . . . one of its prime effects. (1980a, 98)

As products of power relations, the normal individuals of modern society
were also defined as free (i.e., liberated from the yokes of past societies). But
such individuals were not free by nature; rather, liberal power relations created
individuals who were 'obliged to be free' if they were to become the 'normal'
people of modern societies (Rose 1999). In this way, modern power relations
created rather limited images of 'free individuals'.

However, Foucault goes further. He argues that at a deeper level, power
and a more basic sense of freedom imply one another directly. There is no
power relation without this kind of freedom—it is not possible for a subject
to try to shape another subject's actions (i.e., exercise power) without the subjected having a basic measure of freedom. By definition, therefore, power must
involve a degree of resistance, which implies freedom (Foucault 1982). For
power relations to exist, subjects must be free at least to resist: 'Where there is
power, there is resistance' (1978, 95).

Given Foucault's alternate formulation, in what sense might one claim to
be free? Clearly, we may deem ourselves to be free, but individuals are not

born naturally free and nor do free individuals exist outside power relations. Rather, the very claim 'I am free' must always be understood from within give historical contexts. The 'I' is a historical product of power relations in a given society, and the freedom ascribed to that 'I' is similarly created.

This approach suggests at least two issues. First, the obligation to be 'free' in a 'normal' way is required of us as subjects living in a 'free society'. But such freedom is limited. Marx and Engels (1976, 301) note of nineteenth-century individuals that they may be free to choose which religion to belong to, but are not free choose whether to be religious or not. In our times, we may choose to own various sorts of property (land, cars, TVs, iPads, etc.), but this society does not permit us to choose not to accept private property relations. I cannot—without facing significant sanction—take another individual's TV on the grounds that I choose not to believe in private property! Canada requires its subjects to be free in circumscribed ways, to perform rituals and engage the world as very specifically defined free individuals. To do otherwise is to risk sanctions imposed on those deemed incapable of making 'rational' or 'proper' free choices (e.g., children, the insane, the dangerous, etc.—see Rose 1999). Freedom in this sense is an important mechanism through which given power relations operate. Power is exercised through our claims to be free; saying 'I am free' is to endorse the 'free society' that has created both the 'I' and the 'freedoms' that 'I' hold so dear.

A second element of the limited freedoms espoused by a free society is this: there is always the possibility of resisting, of standing up to, the freedoms of a given society. The point is not that it is possible to arrive at a 'natural' state of freedom that escapes all power. However, we can use our current freedoms to imagine and work toward other sorts of freedom. But it is important to recognize that the latter freedoms will always themselves be relative to specific power relations and social formations. This is inescapable. Yet, we can escape the limits of given power formations and the types of societies they structure. If one sort of freedom supports existing social patterns, there is also another liberty that conjures different and alternate social relations, subjects, and freedoms. In this sense we might want to say that a 'free society' is never a static entity; on the contrary a free collective entity is always open-ended, always open to imagining and practising freedom in new ways. Sociology can provide an important vehicle for reflecting on current forms of, imagining new types of, and actively expressing freedom.

Conclusion: Am I Free?

This chapter has outlined an influential liberal response within sociology. Its reply is clear: yes, we are all born free, but there may be social conditions that constrain us and stifle our natural freedom. If we want to live according to our nature, then we must preserve and try to understand our lives as free beings. From this vantage point, we should try to ensure that we protect as many of these natural freedoms from being taken over and destroyed by central powers. Sociology emerges in this story as a science seeking the true nature of a free society, recommending ways to achieve this ideal.

From an alternative, Foucauldian-inspired viewpoint, our question is rather more difficult to answer. Yes, in one sense I am free, but I am free in a very limited way. I am certainly not 'naturally' free, if we mean that I exist outside of a social history. In this framework, 'I' am a creation of power relations that have fashioned me as an individual in a particular society, and the freedoms that are granted to me are neither universal nor natural. When I claim to be free I do not so much assert my freedom from power as accept a given form of power. In other words, individual freedom is not outside of power but rather one of its products, as freedom is always relative to context, and a free society embraces only finite possibilities of what it is to be free. Here perhaps we glimpse a sense of a different kind of freedom that is not tied to a given image of the individual or a free society. That is, there is a form of freedom that allows us to imagine new ways of thinking about freedom and new ways of acting as free subjects in specific contexts.

Responding to the question 'Am I free?', the preceding discussion has explored various approaches, leaving you free to decide which of these, if any, best answers the question. The point to underscore here is that in challenging everyday commonsense to make your way through the issues at hand, you begin to glimpse the practice of thinking sociologically. This text explicitly encourages you to think through questions for yourself, and this involves a freedom that should be cherished. By engaging sociology, you may not be able to say with absolute conviction that you are free or not, but you will be able to say that you have exercised a freedom to think otherwise than is normally the case. The challenge is to keep that spirit alive, and never to allow thought to close itself off as something that cannot be questioned.

Questions to Consider

1. Are we born free? What kind of society do you think is most able to accommodate your response?
2. Does Canadian society create, reflect or constrain individual freedoms?
3. Are power and freedom opposing concepts?

4. If, as Foucault suggests, we are partially governed through the freedoms we hold so dear, what does it mean to use our freedom to challenge government decisions?

5. Suppose you are explaining to someone from a completely different worldview why you take Canada to be a free society. Suppose further that the person responds by saying, 'How can all this talk and practise of individual freedom lead to anything other than selfish, egoistic anarchy with no concern for the collective good?' How would you respond?

Notes

1. This statement echoes Miller's common view that freedom 'is a claim to throw off the chains that enslave us, to live our lives as we ourselves decide, and not as some external agency decides for us' (1991, 2).

2. It is important to note that Rousseau uses the exclusionary term 'man', and at the time of his writing he does not appear to mean to include women under the rubric. As well, it would seem that men of peasant backgrounds, those who were not church nobles, aristocrats, or commoners, are similarly excluded. Quite literally, he appears not to be referring to these people in his exclusionary statement. However, subsequent liberal theorists, especially through the work of later feminist writers and socialist thinkers, broadened the idea to include all human beings (see Weedon 1999; Birke 2000; Squires 2000).

3. As Sartre notes, for human beings, 'to be is to *choose oneself* . . . freedom is not a being; it is the being of man' (1970, 151).

4. These approaches grew out of a phenomenology that tried to understand society by understanding the meanings generated by individual actors and the choices they make (Schutz 1967; Schutz and Wagner 1970; Berger and Berger 1976).

5. Elsewhere, he states, 'the larger the state, the less the liberty' (Rousseau 1983, book 3, ch. 1, 210).

6. Durkheim uses the term 'organic' to suggest that these societies are held together by their functional interdependence in much the same way as an organism, say the human body. Think of it this way: your heart has various functions (pumping blood through the body via a systems of valves) to perform, just as the lungs oxygenate the blood, the brain sends signals to vital muscles, etc. The heart, lungs, and brain all perform identifiable functions, but the entire body requires that all of these functions be coordinated to exist in a healthy state. In an analogous way, society (the whole body) is made up of many different interdependent functions (the banking system, commercial systems, education systems, etc). These functions must be integrated and coordinated for society to exist in a healthy state. Social solidarity is assured here because many functions must be coordinated for people to survive.

7. The interested reader might consult any one of many secondary sources, including Pavlich, (2011, 2000), Smart (1985), Moss (1988), and McNay (1993, 1994).

2 | Who Am I? Who Can I Become?

Dawn H. Currie and Deirdre M. Kelly

Introduction

Historically, sociologists have not shown much interest in the study of identities as social projects. As feminists[1] have argued, this neglect reflects the fact that socially dominant groups tend to (mis)take their own **identity** for a naturally occurring norm. Thus it primarily has been those designated as 'other'—women, people of colour, sexual 'deviants'—who have questioned how we become 'who we are'. Women were among the first to ask 'Who am I?' and 'What can I become?' Our need to do so reflects what Bartky (1997) calls women's psychological alienation: the social definition of what it means 'to be a woman' historically has been authored by male 'experts'. Because this alienation robs women of self-determination, we have been denied the exercise of what constitutes us as social subjects in liberal democracies. Thus, the movement by women to claim selfhood challenged not simply femininity as a seemingly naturally occurring identity but also the power of men to name our identity as women.

In this chapter, 'selfhood' refers to a specific form of identity; it informs our sense of what we 'are' and therefore what it is possible for us to 'do' and to 'become'. It captures the meaning that our social presence has for us and thus sustains a degree of predictability in our encounters with others. For adults, much of the routine work entailed in reconstituting 'self' occurs at a level below ordinary consciousness. During adolescence, however, figuring out who we are and who we want to be becomes an urgent task. As a time of physiological maturing, adolescence coincides with heightened awareness of the gendered and sexualized nature of our social identities. This awareness is not limited to the teenagers themselves, however, as much public concern surrounds especially the sexualized self-expression of teens: in reaction to what is seen as the overtly sexual dress of schoolgirls, there is much discussion about dress codes for public school. What is lost in much of this debate is what the often extravagant displays of selfhood mean to the youth themselves. Recognizing this gap, Girls' Studies emerged as a distinct field of inquiry. We locate our work within this field. In this chapter we draw on interviews with 28 girls between the ages of 12 and 16. We explore how girls talk about their social presence at school, and we refer to their identity projects as 'doing girlhood'.

Academic interest in adolescents has a long history in sociology (see, for example, Hollingshead 1949; Coleman 1961; Hebdige 1979; Shanahan 2007). For the most part, however, our everyday understanding of adolescent selfhood has been influenced by developmental psychologists, many of whom view adolescence as a time of 'stress and storm' (Erikson 1968). This view emphasizes adolescence as a time of 'risk', especially for girls: what girls risk is a lowering of their self-esteem, setting the stage for such problems as disordered eating, hatred of the female body, depression, and self-inflicted harm. Feminists link this process to recognition on the part of girls that femininity requires adoption of a subordinate identity valued for passivity and compliance (see for example Pipher 1994; Brumberg 1997; Brown 1998).

While we do not dismiss the importance of research on adolescent problems, we challenge the view of girls as victims of **adolescent femininity** through an exploration of their agency. By acting within constraints that shape their daily existence, girls negotiate their identities while making decisions about how to interact with others. However, we distinguish between 'agency' as what girls say and do and 'power' as processes that make some ways of being sayable and doable, and others not. On the one hand, girls play an active role in defining who they are and whom they want to become. On the other hand, 'doing gender' engages us with forces that do not simply shape 'who we are' but also limit our capacity to 'be otherwise'. Understanding what girls say and do requires recognition of both the pressures on youth to take up conventional ways of being and their ability to resist processes that reconstitute girls' subordination to boys. In the latter we see possibilities for social transformation.

In order to understand the personal agency of girls sociologically, our work explores the ways that girls' subjectivities are constituted through discourse. 'Discourse' refers to ways of thinking and talking that bring social reality into existence. Discourse coordinates girls' talk with 'ways of acting, interacting, valuing, believing, feeling with bodies, clothes, nonlinguistic symbols, objects, tools, technologies, times and places' (Gee 2002, 25). In our work, the cliques that characterize school cultures operate as semi-autonomous spheres of cultural production that sustain particular discourses about girlhood. These cliques, and not individual girls, are thus our unit of analysis. We begin by discussing a clique that enacted and reinforced conformity to conventional femininity—'popular' girls.

Policing Conventional Girlhood: Popular Girls

As explained by 15-year-old Emily, 'Most people don't define us for who we are but for who we hang out with.' Within this context, being identified as a member of the popular crowd was desirable; the popular crowd were the 'cool kids' who 'go out and *do* stuff' (13-year-old Vikki). In the words of GG, also 13, if you're not popular 'you're just one of those *other* people.' Because popularity is being known or recognized by classmates, and being sought after as a friend, popularity is a source of personal power. Membership in the 'popular' clique thus could be a source of conflict among girls in our study. As 16-year-olds Christine and Kate explained, 'There's so much gossiping and like backstabbing, whatever. You know, [some] people don't like [other] people. . . . [Popular girls] look down on them as if they're not worthy of walking past them, or whatever. That's just like "Eew".' Although many girls did not like this behaviour, especially when they were the target, like 14-year-old Riva most accepted the dynamics of popularity as simply 'the way it is'.

Despite the fact that the girls in our study were drawn from a broad range of schools, their explanations for popularity were consistent: 'You have to be cool. . . . like wear the right clothes and talk the right way' (13-year-old Liv). 'You know, they're all like "Oh, I'm so fat," and they diet and stuff like that. And then they just get more skinny. . . . I guess that's their whole image' (13-year-old Vanessa). According to 14-year-old Anna, to be popular 'you have to hang out with the right crowd every day, even though you want to hang out with somebody else.' And you have to 'keep up' your reputation because 'if you do even one little thing wrong, it gets talked about everywhere' (14-year-old Vera). What do these kinds of 'rules' tell us about girls' agency as a social and not simply personal phenomenon?

In our study, 'agency' refers to what girls say and what girls do. Girls' self-expressions cannot be read as simply 'choices' about 'who I am', however; rather, girls must choose between being deemed 'okay' or 'normal' by their peers rather than 'weird' or 'different' (Jones 1993, 5). For many girls, fitting in at school was a source of constant stress. They described pressure not simply in terms of avoiding negative peer labels but also in terms of their desire to keep up with the trends that made girls popular. The problem was that 'styles change all the time. Like now there is flares and then there was capris and then no tank tops and that went away and platforms was the big thing one year' (12-year-olds Sally and Marie).

Given the pressures for conformity, it interested us that some girls actively embraced identities that girls like Sally and Marie worked hard to avoid. During exploratory focus groups with young university women,[2] we were encouraged when 18-year-old Stephanie exclaimed that during high school, 'We called ourselves "geeks" and we thought it was good.' Excited by this 'confession', 19-year-old Myra added, 'Like my friends and I like we called each other geeks.... We even got our physics teacher to make buttons that said "The geeks shall inherit the earth!"' In the past, the identity as a 'geek' would have marginalized young people among their peers (Milner 2004). This willingness to embrace 'geekiness' challenges the image of girls as lacking self-esteem and turning negative judgments inward. For us, it signalled girls' ability to escape conventional identity norms and suggested that girlhood can be rewritten. Consequently we were drawn to interviews with high school girls who consciously constructed identities that made them distinct from rather than similar to the popular crowd at their school. While not intending to create a dichotomy of 'regular' and 'alternative' girls, in the discussion below we refer to these participants as 'alternative' girls.

Being 'Who You Are': Alternative Girls

Popular girls were not well liked by the girls we designated as 'alternative':

Grover: We call them 'bun' girls ... [because] they used to all wear hair buns and tight jeans and stuff like that.

Sandy: They wear these really tight tank tops. And they all look the same.... I mean it's also the way they act too. It's not just how they dress. They all act like 'Aaahhh'. Ditzy like. [both 14 years old]

Sandy complained, 'They act stupid when they're really smart or something.' For 15-year-old Zoe, 'They're always the same. Like they talk the same, they always dress the same. And it gets annoying after a while.' Agreeing, Pete (also 15) claimed, 'Their main goal in life—at least it looks like to me—is to be "cute".' Pete directed annoyance toward 'the way they live their lives through an image that kind of pisses me off. The whole "girl thing".... being skinny, pretty, makeup. Uhmm. Lots of money.... Kind of living their life for a guy.... I think it's just totally wrong to live your life like that.'

    Among other things, these kinds of comments illustrate how dress is one of the most visible, hence culturally encoded, representations of gender. It is also one of the most 'policed' aspects of girls' self-representations. While the 'ordinary' practices of looking pretty and attracting boys were accepted, signalling 'excessive' sexual agency earned disapproval. Errors could be costly: if labelled 'slut' a girl faced rumours that could be difficult if not impossible to counteract (White 2002).

Despite the stress associated with the 'right' styles, dressing for school was also seen by some girls as fun. For 'alternative' girls, the fluidity of meaning surrounding dress opened possibilities for oppositional self-presentation (Gleeson and Frith 2004). According to 14-year-old Gauge, 'They're [popular girls are] sheep and we're like penguins. Sheep [pause] all do the same things, and penguins are cooler.' However, being 'penguins' earned Gauge and her interview partner Spunk the label 'weird' among their peers. They attributed this label to the fact that their group is 'outgoing and doesn't listen to pop music'. Importantly, they rejected the rules that governed other girls' dress at school. At the time of their interview, Gauge was wearing a skater T-shirt and baggy pants, while 14-year-old Spunk was dressed in black and sported a shaggy haircut: 'I wear a lot of black and I have a lot of chains and I have a dog collar and—I don't know. I just like that kind of stuff.' Significantly, Gauge and Spunk were among the girls in our study who had taken up skateboarding, a physical activity that until recently has been dominated by boy skaters. Their case illustrates that dress does not simply signal 'girlhood' as an identity label but shapes what it is possible for girls to 'do' (Pomerantz, Currie, and Kelly 2004; Kelly, Pomerantz, and Currie 2005). For these girls, dress was an expression of resistance to the pressure for conformity and an opportunity to 'play' with gendered norms. What made their transgression possible?

In our study, the designation of popular was associated with what Connell (1987) calls an 'emphasized femininity': a form of femininity, defined at 'the level of mass social relations', that is based on women's compliance with their subordination to men and 'oriented to accommodating the interests and desires of men' (1987, 183). Emphasized femininity is the most culturally valued form of femininity, reflected in the prevailing beauty standard for womanhood.[3] In Currie, Kelly, and Pomerantz (2009) we connect emphasized femininity to Butler's notion of a heterosexual matrix: 'a hegemonic discursive/epistemic model of gender intelligibility that assumes that for bodies to cohere and make sense there must be a stable sex expressed through stable gender . . . that is oppositionally and hierarchically defined through the compulsory practice of heterosexuality' (Butler 1990: 151 note 6; also see Youdell 2005 and Ringrose 2008). While girls repeatedly claimed that popular kids had money—to buy the right clothes and do cool things—popular girls were also described as pretty, thin, and attractive to boys. For them, emphasized femininity was a route to social approval; hence their avenue to power. As feminist researchers, we were aware of the ways in which the pressure to conform to emphasized femininity is implicated in the lowered self-esteem of many girls. Given the potential risks of transgressing the norms that regulate status in peer cultures, what gives the girls we designated as 'alternative' their power to be otherwise?

Admittedly, it was our hope that participants would cite feminism as an influence for their resistance to emphasized femininity. For the most part, our desire was not fulfilled. While 15-year-old Gracie expressed pride in exclaiming, 'I am a feminist,' it was far more common for girls to distance themselves from feminism, as did Sandy: 'I wouldn't say I was a feminist. I mean, I am *for* it.' Whether embracing or actively resisting the conventions of emphasized femininity, the most forceful discourse we heard in girls' talk was that of an individualism that allowed girls to claim to be 'unique'. By **individualism** we refer to the way that alternative girls talked about 'being yourself'. Across interviews, 'being yourself' was employed to signal authenticity of self-representation. It allowed girls to claim what Gee (2000–1, 111) calls a 'core identity' that constitutes a sense of what we call 'selfhood' (albeit never fully formed or always potentially changing). As a taken-for-granted category, 'being myself' foreclosed discussion that might otherwise draw attention to the instabilities and inconsistencies that typify any individual's self-construction. For example, 14-year-old Beverly emphasized, 'I want to be known as, like, who I *am*.' Like other alternative girls, Onyx (also 14) reasoned, 'Everyone's unique, and if you change that you wouldn't be unique any more. You'd just be like wanting to be something else. And that's not *you*.'

This ability to be 'unique' rather than 'feminist' was not entirely disappointing to us. Individualism enabled some girls in our study to resist the social pressures that were so stressful for Sally and Marie. Onyx argued that 'if you keep adjusting yourself to fit in', you could lose yourself, a problem that she saw as 'the centre of teenage problems':

> Not finding yourself again. Not knowing what you're worth. Thinking that you are only good if someone else finds you to be who they think you should be. And I think this is a big time for kids our age to either go one direction or the other.

Grover's self-confidence was also expressed through a discourse of 'being yourself':

> I know who I am and I am confident with who I am. . . . I think you should just let someone, you know, express themselves the way they want to be expressed. And I am against people, you know, saying, 'You shouldn't look a certain way' like that because, you know, 'it's not pleasing', 'it's degrading', or something like that.

This search for authentic selfhood was an important theme in interviews with girls who rejected the emphasized femininity that made 'bun girls' popular. In contrast to the fakery exemplified by bun girls, claiming a 'real' selfhood enabled Grover and Onyx to position themselves outside the male-centred culture at their school. It enabled girls to claim identities that are devalued within practices of emphasized femininity. To be sure, we are not claiming that popular girls would not use a similar vocabulary. However, as practised by the alternative girls in our study, a discourse of authentic selfhood signals possible awareness of the socially constructed nature of femininity and thus opens up the search for selfhood to critical introspection:

Sandy: Well, I guess 15, 16 is like—

Onyx: The age where you separate yourself from maybe other people.

Sandy: Yeah. You're more like—I think it's more like you're independent, especially from your parents. I think you become more like—like you think the way you want to more and like, you know, you're more social. And I don't know. You just kind of know yourself better than when you were younger. . . . You know yourself and you've been around longer, so like you just make better decisions and—

Onyx: It's like between wanting to be a woman and realizing that you are one. Maybe that's what this age is all about.

This ability to reflect on 'realizing you are a woman' is important: like other girls, Sandy described 15 as 'the "breaking age" where you are trying to figure out who you are. And what you want to do. And stuff like that.' It encouraged us that despite their descriptions of life at school as complex and stressful, Sandy and Gracie celebrated girlhood as giving them freedom to explore 'who you really are' with girlfriends:

I think probably it's better being a girl because you can be like more 'who you are' because the guy, you have to—you can't really talk about things that much. And with girls, like your friends are usually really important to you. You can always talk to your friends if you want to. And I don't think that it is the same for guys. I mean, they have friends, but they can't, like call their guy friend up and be like 'Oh, I have a problem.' [Gracie]

Given that these participants both claimed that 'girls have a lot more stuff to deal with' than boys, the freedom they associate with being able to be 'yourself' is significant. In this context 'authenticity' opened up ways for girls to think about new possibilities for 'doing girlhood'. It thus gave individual girls the power to 'do' girlhood in new ways. Does it also signal the power for girls to rewrite girlhood as a social rather than a personal identity, an act we would associate with transformative agency?

Transforming Girlhood? From Personal to Social Change

How individual actions can effect social change has been a central question in sociology since its inception. Historically, sociologists framed their answers through debates over the relationship between agency and structure. In large part, debates revolved around how structures—operating through the social institutions that are the focus of sociological inquiry—determine what individuals do, how institutions are created and maintained, and what limits, if any, structural constraints have on individuals' capacity to act independently. Beginning with Durkheim, a longstanding argument has been that sociology should be concerned only with social structures as the enduring, ordered, and patterned social relationships into which individuals are born. Because these social structures predate any individual (and continue after she or he is gone), they determine the life paths of individuals—whose personal desires and actions are insignificant, sociologically speaking. One problem is that this reasoning considers social structures, not people, as sites for agency. Its critics reject a sociology within which people disappear, arguing that sociology should study the way by which individuals create the world around them (Abercrombie, Hill, and Turner 1984).

Sociologists have tended to emphasize either social structures or the agency of human actors in their explanation of social change. More recently, sociologists have attempted to offer a 'third' way of thinking about these issues. Giddens (1984) employs the concept 'structuration' to signal the mutual dependency rather than opposition of human agency and social structure. He maintains that social structures should not be seen as barriers to individual action but rather are implicated in an individual's ability to act: the structural properties of social systems provide the means by which people act, but they are also the outcome of those actions. He uses the term 'reflexivity' to refer to the way in which individuals monitor their aspirations and behaviour in response to the ongoing flow of social life (3).

Following Giddens' view, the notion of 'reflexive modernization' has become one of the most influential ideas in contemporary sociology. While the term 'reflexivity' has been taken up in various ways, writers agree that there is something distinctly new about the contemporary period of modernization that has enhanced the reflexive nature of social life through the proliferation of communication technology and easier access to knowledge. These developments enlarge our agency by expanding individuals' capacity to orient themselves in the social world: today we have the ability to reflect on and hence monitor our social presence to a degree not possible in previous societies. As a consequence, we no longer passively accept our destiny as prescribed by the traditional patterns into which we were born but instead construct our own ways of being in the world. Thus our personal histories are not predetermined, because our biographies have become personal projects characterized by mobility and flexibility as we continually reinvent ourselves. In short, these writers characterize our biographies as lifelong projects of self-production. People in post-industrialized nations are free to choose much more about their lives than was even thinkable in the past—for example, they actively choose their occupations, whether to marry and have children, to alter their sexed and racialized bodies, and so on. By claiming that gender, class, and family 'roles' no longer have a determining influence on individuals, these writers describe Western societies as 'detraditionalized' (Adkins 2002).

At first glance, these kinds of arguments may have intuitive appeal: our contemporary culture is characterized by a rhetoric of free choice embracing everything we do, from participating in democratic elections to reshaping our bodies. However, the notion of reflexive modernization is contentious among feminists. As Adkins (2002) notes, while theoretically emphasizing individual agency and power, proponents of the notion of reflexive modernization fail to illustrate empirically how and whether individuals are truly free from the constraints that accompany being socially designated as 'women'. Nor do they consider the social distribution of the resources that make the notion of personal 'choice' meaningful (Hennessy 1995). The thesis is itself gendered because men, more than women (and then only *some* men), have benefited from the kinds of 'freedoms' posited by reflexive modernization writers. Notably, women have not been 'freed' from having to subordinate their individual aspirations and biographies to the needs (and desires) of others. These feminists question whether femininity has in fact been freed from traditional constraints. With them we ask whether the alternative girls in our study illustrate how young women today reflexively control notions of 'who we are' and 'who we can become'.

Individualism and the Limits of Reflexivity

As we have seen, most of the girls in our study would agree with 14-year-old Grenn: 'You're supposed to be a certain way. The other girls expect you to be that way. You go against them, then they *hate* you.' To be sure, girls' search for selfhood entails many factors that go beyond school culture and thus are invisible in our interviews. Mothers, fathers, sisters, brothers, teachers, and numerous other people play an important role in the identity projects of young girls; this role cannot be heard in our text. What *can* be heard is a neo-liberal discourse of selfhood, a discourse that rhetorically values autonomy and self-determination. This discourse, more than the discourse of feminism, enabled girls to position themselves against conventional femininity. This positioning was accomplished by taking up 'me, myself, and I', an empty signifier in everyday discourse: 'I'm *me*, and if they [other kids] don't like me, then they can kiss my ass' (13-year-old Sara). This is not to claim that the girls who strive to win approval by remaining within the confines of emphasized femininity do not espouse selfhood through this way of talking. Rather, we hear 'me, myself, and I' as part of a struggle for girls to gain a voice independent of definitions espoused by others.

It was significant for us that during interviews the invocation of 'authenticity' did not require elaboration, as did other terms (such as 'bun girls' or 'geeks') used by girls to describe identity projects. Sociologically speaking, the seemingly obvious 'self' evoked by these girls is not an essential and transcendent form of social being but rather a historically specific and culturally limited practice of self-production (Nelson 1999). What remains hidden in girls' talk of authenticity, but nevertheless gives shape to projects of self-construction, are 'larger' economic, political, and institutional processes (Byrne 2003; Connell 2004). Once we recognize selfhood as a culturally specific way of achieving and maintaining a social presence, we can link it to the competitive individualism of contemporary consumer culture. Within this context, we should not be surprised that socially approved identity projects require the display of the 'right' symbolic capital such as clothes, makeup, and attitude. While dress and self-presentation were also important to the girls we designated as 'alternative', their identity projects were characterized by self-conscious rejection of symbols associated with both consumption and conventional girlhood. This rejection was no minor accomplishment: the pressures on girls to conform are considerable, and their actions transgressed the norms of middle-class youth culture. The question that remains is whether their transgressions signal the transformation of girlhood as a social (and potentially feminist) project rather than a personal project.

Conclusion

In the final analysis, talk about 'self' as an 'object' of introspection reminds us that, potentially, girls are able to reflect on and actively negotiate the (immediate) conditions of their gendered performances, as claimed by reflexive sociologists. The problem remains, however, that although individuality fostered reflexive thinking about selfhood, it also limited the transformative potential of girls' agency. This is because the ability to 'speak' oneself into an 'alternative' existence requires the speaker's belief in that ability; belief in gender equality was a condition for girls' self-mastery. Such a belief might render feminism redundant in their eyes:

> We're equal, as equal as we're going to get.... they feel that they don't have that much power and that's why they think they should be feminist, because they feel that men have more power. I don't feel that men have more power, and so I don't think I should have to be a feminist. [Sara]

Despite these claims, the girls easily provided examples when asked about sexism at school. Sexism was just as easily dismissed, however: 'It bothers me a little bit, but I think they're [the guys are] being jackasses. And it has nothing to do with the truth' (Sara). This kind of thinking allowed many girls in our study to claim that while feminism might have been necessary 'in the past' when women faced barriers to their self-determination, it is no longer needed. In this way, just as academic claims of 'detraditionalization' erase the kinds of pressures girls described towards conventional femininity, 'individualism' in girls' talk mystifies the operation of power in their everyday lives. Such mystification can prevent us from seeing, in the words of Marx (1975 [1852], 103) that while we make our own worlds, we do so under conditions that we have not chosen. In our (limited) study, there is little evidence that conventional gendered norms sustaining inequality no longer influence girls' thinking about 'who they can be' and 'who they can become.'

The Girls (in Alphabetical Order)

Anna, 14   Filipino Canadian; from a working-class family; lives with her mother, father, and little brother.

Beverly, 14   Chinese Canadian; came from Hong Kong when she was 10; from a working-class family; lives with her mother, father, and older brother.

Brooke, 15   white; from an upper-middle-class family; member of the popular group at her school.

Christine, 16	white; from a working-class family; into sports.
Emily, 15	white; from a middle-class family; hangs out with the skaters at school.
Gauge, 14	white; from a middle-class family; lives with her mother, father, and sister; a skateboarder.
GG, 13	'GG' stands for Ghetto Girl, her self-selected pseudonym; white; from a middle-class family.
Gracie, 15	white; from a middle-class family.
Grenn, 14	white; from a working-class family; a skateboarder and anime fan who describes herself as 'alternative'.
Grover, 15	Latina; from a middle-class family; attends a Catholic co-ed school.
Kate, 15	white; from a working-class family; into sports.
Liv, 13	white; from a working-class family; lives with her mother and sister; a cheerleader and member of the popular crowd at her school.
Marie, 12	white; from a middle-class family; wants to be a member of the popular crowd.
Onyx, 14	Chinese Canadian; from a middle-class family; her friends call her 'the seducer'.
Pete, 15	Chinese Canadian; from a middle-class family; a skateboarder.
Riva, 14	Iranian Canadian; from an upper middle-class family.
Sally, 12	white; from a middle-class family; wants to be a member of the popular crowd.
Sandy, 15	Chinese Canadian; from a middle-class family.
Sara, 14	Jewish; from a middle-class family; sports a punk/goth style; drummer in an otherwise all-boy band.

Spunk, 14   white; from a middle-class family; lives with her mother and sister; a self-identified bisexual Wiccan who just started skateboarding.

Vanessa, 13   white; from a working-class family; into computers as well as sports and dance.

Vera, 14   Chinese Canadian; from a working-class family; lives with her mother, father, sister, brother, and grandparents; into computers as 'anime freaks'.

Vikki, 13   white; from a middle-class family.

Zoe, 15   First Nations/white; from a middle-class family; a skateboarder.

Questions to Consider

1. In this chapter we explored the importance of dress for adolescent girls at school. To what extent are the girls correct in claiming that the pressure to 'look' a certain way makes life at school harder for girls than for boys? Do boys experience similar pressures? Why is self-presentation so important to youth?
2. Thinking about your experience of high school, can you remember any situations when different standards were used to assess the performance or behaviour of girls versus boys? If so, how were these different standards justified? At the time, did you agree with the practice? Has your thinking been challenged since you became a sociology student?
3. In this chapter we discussed 'emphasized femininity' as a form of femininity associated with popularity for girls. Is there an 'emphasized masculinity' that is similarly valued for boys? What performances of masculinity make boys popular among their peers?
4. Adults often explain what they find puzzling or difficult about teenage behaviour as a consequence of peer pressure. How might a sociologist discuss these concerns with interested parents/adults?
5. Select a popular film or TV show that depicts life at school. How are various groups of youth represented? Who does this film or TV show think you are? Who does it want you to be? Compare and discuss your answers with classmates.

Notes

1. 'Feminism' defies a succinct definition. In this chapter, 'feminism' signals commitment to the accomplishment of gender equity, despite theoretical and political disagreements over how to accomplish this goal. For an overview of the schools of feminist thought, see Jaggar and Rothenberg (1993), Beasley (1999), Lorber (2005), and Mandell (2005).
2. In order for us as adult researchers to better understand young women's experiences of public school, we conducted focus group discussions with young female university students before we began our fieldwork with younger girls.
3. 'Emphasized femininity' corresponds to what others might call 'conventional' or 'traditional' femininity. To clarify Connell's description, we point out the way that emphasized femininity is based on white, middle-class expectations for 'good girls'.

3 | Am I a Woman?
Myra J. Hird

Introduction

Am I a woman? This question seems to warrant a straightforward answer. Of course I am a woman. When I want to use a public washroom, I head for the door with a picture of a stick figure wearing a dress. When I complete a boarding card at the airport, I tick the 'F' box. My family, friends, colleagues, and strangers *treat me like* a woman. If I wasn't a woman or a man, how would people know how to treat me? How would I understand, relate to, and interact with others?

The aim of this chapter is to consider the importance of sex and gender—known broadly as sexual difference—in Canadian society. Let's begin by considering what it means to be sexed and gendered in Western society today. From a sociological standpoint, sex and gender *matter* (meaning that sex and gender are important) socially, economically, politically, medically, and culturally to individuals in Canadian society. As Canadian sociologist Roberta Hamilton (2004) shows, people experience different realities depending on their gender. Take work, for example: women continue to receive lower pay than men for equal work, various jobs continue to be gender-segregated, women continue to do the bulk of non-paid work in society, and so on. We could add to this by explaining how sex and gender interact with other important characteristics by which society is divided, such as race, education, ethnicity, age, sexuality, nationality, and (dis)ability. For example, as sociologists we consider the ways in which poor indigenous women with limited education experience the criminal justice system compared to the ways that middle-class, well-educated white women do.

There is another way to think about sex and gender, and that is to consider whether the category 'woman' belongs to some sort of universal reality grounded in nature. This is a much more complicated question, and I devote the rest of the chapter to exploring its answer. To tackle this consideration, we need to consider how the terms 'sex' and 'gender' have been used in society. We typically take these terms as important and indelible aspects of our personal identities, 'locked in the mysterious recesses of the body' (Weeks 1995, 47). Indeed, we tend to think of the relationship between sex, gender, sexuality, and identity thus:

sex	→	gender	→	sexuality	→	identity
(female)		(woman)		(heterosexual)		(businessperson)

In everyday language, 'sex' is defined as the anatomical differences (usually understood as genitals but may also include chromosomes, hormones, and gonads) between females and males. These differences are assumed to be both natural and unchangeable. 'Gender' refers to all of the external practices such as clothing and behaviour that correspond to socially accepted images of one or the other sex. Sexuality is typically seen as a constitutive feature of our personality, comprising our desires, our pleasures, and the sexual acts we engage in (see Chapter 4).

The **sex/gender distinction** is based upon three assumptions (Hood-Williams 1996). First, the biological distinction between women and men assumes that a distinction can be made between biology (sex) on the one hand and culture (gender) on the other. Second, it assumes that while gender is changeable, sex is immutable. Finally, this distinction depends on the idea that biology itself consistently distinguishes between females and males. By critiquing these assumptions, sociologists argue that what we think of as being a given about our identities is actually a complicated *outcome* or **product** of our understandings of the sex/gender distinction.

Dividing Sex and Gender

Individuals did not always define their sex, gender, and sexuality in the same ways that we do today (see Chapter 5). Indeed, the sex/gender distinction was a post-war Anglo-Saxon invention. A number of studies have shown that prior to the eighteenth century, women and men were considered to have the same body (Laqueur 1990; Schiebinger 1993; Oudshoorn 1994; Daston and Park 1998). As the superior form, male bodies contained the heat necessary to display the penis and scrotum externally; lacking heat, female bodies bore their penis and scrota internally. The leading medical and philosophical scholars detailed the anatomical equivalence of vagina and penis, labia and foreskin, uterus and scrotum, ovaries and testicles. Drawings, often based on dissections, depicted the vagina as an internal penis. Only as a result of considerable controversy and political upheaval did the contemporary two-sex model eventually dominate scientific discourse (Laqueur 1990).

During the sixteenth, seventeenth, and eighteenth centuries, men were defined by the characteristics of heat, strength, and rationality, while women were defined as more likely to be cold, weak, and emotional. These were characteristics of degree, and men and women could gain or lose these characteristics. This afforded a fluidity of movement across the sex continuum, with a large number of possible variations. For instance, medical literature during this time contains many accounts of individuals changing sex. Most accounts detail legal changes of women into men. They often reflect the courts' belief that a body would always attempt to become more perfect (i.e., male). Through the movement of the penis from interior to exterior, the body could express the gender characteristics that most suited the individual's disposition and behaviour. Since men enjoyed greater societal privileges, magistrates were more concerned with maintaining the sex boundaries than with determining an individual's 'authentic' sex.

This historical perspective does not demonstrate the advance of modern understandings of sex. Rather, it suggests that bodies are made meaningful through their interpretation. Discourses are already at work in any discussions of gender and sex—before they begin. Therefore, like gender, sex is socially constructed. Today, we might think that individuals are born either female or male, and that changing sex is impossible. However, just as in the past, some people today believe that people can change their sex.

The Two-Sex Distinction: Sex[1]

People with intersex conditions provide a valuable opportunity for sociologists to explore the relationship between sex and gender as well as the way that difference is socially created through meanings and categories. Cheryl Chase (1998) estimates that one in every 100 births shows what doctors call a morphological anomaly. This is observable enough in one in every 2,000 births to initiate questions about a child's sex.[2]

The term 'intersex' refers to a wide range of conditions present at birth. One is androgen insensitivity syndrome (AIS), which is most often a genetic condition in which a person born with XY chromosomes does not respond (in complete cases) to the androgen hormone, producing female genitals, undescended or partially descended testes, and usually a short vagina with no cervix. Congenital adrenal hyperplasia (CAH) refers to a condition in which the adrenal glands make higher levels of hormones that have the effect of enlarging the clitoris and labia.[3] Children who have hypospadias are born with the urethral opening somewhere on the underside, rather than the tip, of the penis. In some cases, the urethral opening is absent, and urine exits the bladder behind the penis (for a more detailed list of intersex conditions, see http://www.isna.org).

In the 1960s, John Money founded the practice of surgical sex reassign-ment of infants and children with intersex conditions in the United States, and his protocols remain standard practice today. According to Money (1985), core gender identity results from children's interactions with their parents as well as children's perception of their own genitals (282). We might expect that the emphasis on gender identity as socially acquired might lead Money to con-clude that anatomy is not destiny, especially since he is studying children with variable genitalia who nevertheless identify as either girls or boys. But instead, Money reasserts the importance of aligning sex and gender. He notes a 'critical period' of parent-child interaction that cements an earlier in-utero period when hormonal activation of the brain sets the direction of neural pathways in preparation for the reception of 'post-natal social gender identity signals' (Raymond 1994, 47). On this basis, Money argues for surgical intervention as soon after birth as possible, for the child's psycho-social well-being (Hird and Germon 2001). In other words, surgeons believe they 'merely provide the right genitals to go along with socialization' (Kessler 1990, 17).Whether genitals, hormones, or chromosomes should determine an infant's sex is debated. For the most part, the so-called abnormal appearance of a newborn's genitals initi-ates medical intervention.

Chromosome tests are used to determine the genetic makeup of an identi-fied child. If the tests reveal an XX configuration, genital surgery is usually performed without delay (Kessler 1990). When tests indicate the presence of a Y chromosome, surgery may be delayed while further tests determine the responsiveness of phallic tissue to hormone treatment. Such treatment enlar-ges the penile structure to the point at which it can pass as a so-called real penis (Fausto-Sterling 2000). The implication is that maleness is not only or most importantly defined by chromosomes or by the ability to produce sperm. Rather, it is determined by an appropriately sized penis. Consequently, infants with an XY chromosome configuration may be assigned and raised as female. If a child is reassigned as female, clitoroplasty is undertaken when the child is anywhere between seven months and four years of age and sometimes as late as adolescence. Surgeons focus on the ability of the constructed vagina to accommodate a penis. Scar tissue is often hypersensitive, resulting in extreme pain during intercourse. And because scar tissue lacks elasticity, a daily regi-men of dilating the vagina is required to prevent it from closing. Moreover, the vagina is often constructed from bowel tissue, which lubricates in response to digestion rather than arousal (Laurent in Burke 1996).

The high-profile case in which Money famously argued for the necessity of surgical intervention illustrates many of the problems with the modern two-sex model of sexual difference. David Reimer and his identical twin

brother were born in Winnipeg, Manitoba, in 1965. After a bungled cir-
cumcision during infancy, Reimer eventually found himself in the hands
of Money's surgical team, who reassigned him as female. Reimer's case
was particularly important because he happened to have an identical twin
brother. Money argued that if Reimer lived the experience of femaleness,
then culture, not nature (genes), determine gender identity. While Money
repeatedly detailed Reimer's success in living as woman, interviews with
Reimer after he became an adult reveal that this success was greatly exaggerated (Colapinto 2000). Despite Money's assurances that 'Brenda' would
live comfortably as a woman, as an adult Reimer lived with his wife, three
adopted children, and a reconstructed penis, adamant that he was a man. In
2004 Reimer committed suicide.

While Reimer and Money would seem to disagree on just about every fact
of this case, they concur as to the constitution of femininity and masculinity.
Money argued that the identical twin brother was male because he preferred
playing with cars, gas pumps, and tools, while Reimer was female because of
his preference for dolls, a doll house, and doll carriage. Reimer says he knew
he was not a girl because, among other signs, he did not like to play with dolls,
preferred standing while urinating, and daydreamed about being a '21-year-
old male with a moustache and a sports car, surrounded by admiring females'
(Colapinto 2000, 69). The various psychiatrists who eventually examined
Reimer used similar markers to define his so-called underlying masculinity.
One psychiatrist, for instance, described seeing Reimer 'sitting there in a skirt
with her legs apart, one hand planted firmly on one knee. There was nothing
feminine about her' (Colapinto 2000, 70). Paradoxically, then, at the same time
that the medical community strongly requires a biological definition of the
sex of a person with an intersex condition, the surgeons, endocrinologists, and
psychiatrists clearly employ a social definition.

A growing political intersex community identifies many of these problems: the variability of sexual identification, the a priori definition of feminine
and masculine behaviour, the phallocentric bias in sex reassignment, and the
problem people with intersex conditions often experience with belonging in
a society that demands gender differentiation. The Intersex Society of North
America (ISNA) and its associated support groups around the world lobby to
increase understanding about intersex conditions. They want to ensure that
any surgery performed is with the full understanding and consent of the individual involved.

The modern medico-psychiatric response to intersex reinscribes the normative belief that sex creates gender (Hird and Germon 2001; Hird 2003a,
2003b). This reinscription takes place '. . . in the face of overwhelming physical

evidence that this taxonomy is not mandated by biology' (Hausman 1995, 25). Thus Money refigures the natural provision of more than two sexes as an aberration—a 'handicap' and 'birth defect of the sex organs' when manifested in an individual, which surgery will 'repair' (Hausman 1995, 280). What encourages the medical community to favour intrusive surgery for anatomical conditions these doctors themselves admit present no functional or medical dangers? The authenticity of sex resides not on or in the body but rather results from a particular nexus of power, knowledge, and truth. That something as natural as sex can be or indeed needs to be produced artificially is an ongoing paradox (Hird and Germon 2001; Kessler 1990).

The Two-Sex Distinction: Gender

If people with intersex conditions raise difficult questions about the extent to which sex is derived from biology, at least they have not chosen their bodies in the way trans people are often claimed to have done. So how important is the experience of living as a woman or a man? Trans women and men claim gendered status on the basis of knowing themselves to be women even though they lack the accepted corporeal signs (vagina, breasts, beard, and so on) designated as female or male. Trans people have spent their childhood, adolescence, and often much of their adult lives within the bodies of one sex. At some point in their lives, trans people begin to live as the so-called opposite sex, often with the aid of hormone therapy and surgery.

Christine Jorgenson's sex change operation in 1953 propelled trans onto the public stage. The trans narratives of that time adhered strongly to the 'woman-trapped-in-male-body' trope. Bolin (1994) argues that this narrative was created out of necessity to forge an origin story required by the medical and psychiatric communities that regulated access to surgery. That is, medical practitioners, psychologists, psychiatrists, and trans individuals crafted a 'transsexual identity' (Billings and Urban 1982; Bolin 1994). Many trans individuals were also keen to differentiate themselves from classifications such as pedophilia. In this way, trans was emphasized as a temporary identity, a pit-stop before permanent womanhood.

Given feminists' commitment to illuminating supposedly innate feminine behaviours as socially constructed requirements of patriarchal society, trans narratives unsurprisingly raise suspicion. Janice Raymond's (1994) classic text *The Transsexual Empire* argues that there are authentic and inauthentic women:

> We [women] know who we are. We know that we are women who are born with
> female chromosomes and anatomy, and that whether or not we were socialised

to be so-called normal women, patriarchy has treated and will treat us like women. Transsexuals have not had this same history. (114)

Raymond's critique is echoed by a number of feminists. For instance, Sheila Jeffreys (1990; 2003) argues that trans women choose to 'imitate the most extreme examples of feminine behavior and dress in grossly stereotypical feminine clothing' in preference to feminists who supposedly dress 'in jeans and T-shirts' (1990, 177, 178). Jeffreys criticizes trans women for what she argues is an inability to understand that supposedly feminine behaviours and characteristics are ones that women must adopt in order to avoid societal censure. She maintains that what trans women consider individual attributes are really political signifiers of women's oppression. By adopting stereotypical clothing and behaviours, trans women, Jeffreys contends, collude with **patriarchy** and further contribute to women's oppression.

Jeffreys' suspicion about the transgressive potential of sex reassignment is grounded in a feminist perspective, but some scholars more generally share this skepticism. Those opposed to sex reassignment surgery argue that medicine colludes with society to perpetuate the cultural imperative of the two-sex system. For example, in *Sex by Prescription*, Szasz (1990) suggests that trans is a 'condition tailor-made for our surgical-technological age': the desire to experiment with new technology ensures that critical reflection on the efficacy of sex-reassignment is minimized (86). Some Canadians are skeptical as well. For instance, when Kimberley Nixon applied to train as a volunteer counsellor for female sexual assault survivors at the Vancouver Rape Relief organization in 1995, the organization refused to allow Nixon to enrol in counsellor training when she revealed herself to be a trans woman. The resulting court case went in favour of the organization that excluded Nixon. As of 2007 the British Columbia Supreme Court had refused Nixon's appeal to hear the case (Prasad 2005; Namaste 2005). The case pivots on arguments about the authentic embodiment of femaleness (Bindel 2004).

For sociologists, the problem with the authenticity argument is that despite the emphasis on sociality it nevertheless adheres to the concept of sex as real. A founder of the discipline of sociology, George Herbert Mead (1934) forcefully argued the self cannot exist without society: the continuous interactive process among individuals establishes and maintains conceptions of self by reflecting back images of the self as object. Consequently, it is immaterial whether trans people can or cannot know that they are the so-called opposite sex or whether sex reassignment surgery constitutes an ethical resolution. As Erving Goffman (1976) argues:

Our concern . . . ought not to be in uncovering real, natural expressions, whatever they might be. One should not appeal to the doctrine of natural expression in an attempt to account for natural expression, for that ... would conclude the analysis before it had begun. (7)

Goffman notes that while gender identity does not exist in any biological sense, it is often mistaken as real. So to the extent that trans people are able or want to pass as so-called real women or men, gender is revealed to adhere to particular bodies in a haphazard manner. In effect, trans people render visible the invisible signs on which society relies to produce gender. These signs are pre-established performances that trans people, like everyone else, are confronted with:

> The more closely the impostor's performance approximates to the real thing, the more intensely we may be threatened, for a competent performance by someone who proves to be an impostor may weaken in our minds the moral connection between legitimate authorization to play a part and the capacity to play it. (Goffman 1971, 66)

Or as Taylor more directly puts it, 'however strange a cross-dresser looks, a genetic woman can always be found who looks even stranger' (Taylor 1995, 6). Judith Butler (1990, 2004) makes the cognate argument that transvestism does not mimic femininity or masculinity, but rather that it reveals the social construction, or performativity, of gender.

Sociologists are particularly aware that gender is a social construct—Raymond's (1994) definition emphasizes women's identity based on social interaction with patriarchy. As such, differentiating between authentic and inauthentic narratives is a moral exercise, and calling for a return to bodies provides no more reassurance of authenticity than gender does.

Conclusion: Recognizing Sex/Gender/Sexuality Diversity

We have explored the ways in which assumptions about sex and gender work together to maintain our contemporary gender structure. Much of this structure is based on the implicit assumption that nature neatly differentiates all living organisms into female and male categories, that these categories are mutually exclusive and stable, and that the division serves evolutionary purposes: in short, that sexual difference is natural. In this final section, I offer a short foray into the wonderful diversity of living organisms.

Biology provides a wealth of evidence to confound static notions of sexual difference.[4] The majority of cells in human bodies are intersex, with only egg and sperm cells counting as chromosomally dimorphic. Most of the reproduction that we undertake in our lifetimes has nothing to do with sex. That is, the cells in our bodies engage in constant, energetic reproduction in the form of recombination (cutting and patching of DNA strands), merging (fertilization of cells), meiosis (cell division by splitting the chromosome number in half—for instance in making sperm and eggs), and mitosis (cell division with maintenance of cell number). Nor does reproduction take place between discrete individuals, as many cultural analyses would have it. Indeed, only by taking our skin as a definitive impenetrable boundary are we able to see our bodies as autonomous. Our human bodies are more accurately 'built from a mass of interacting selves . . . the self is not only corporeal but corporate' (Sagan 1992, 370). Our cells also provide asylum for a variety of bacteria, viruses, and countless genetic fragments. And none of this reproduction requires any bodily contact with another human being. Moreover, there is no linear relationship between sexual dimorphism and sexual reproduction. Male sea horses, pipe fish, and hares get pregnant. Many species are male and female simultaneously or sequentially. Many types of fish change sex back and forth depending on environmental conditions (Rothblatt 1995; Bagemihl 1999). Most of the organisms in four out of the five kingdoms do not require sex for reproduction. And some organisms have many sexes—Schizophyllum, for instance, has more than 28,000 sexes. In sum, sexual difference may well continue to be culturally significant; but as we have seen, our understanding of what sexual difference is and what it means for individuals and society as a whole has changed significantly over time. Moreover, it is problematic to base arguments in favour of sexual difference on a recourse to nature.

Questions to Consider

1. Before reading this chapter, did you know that infants born with intersex conditions in Canada are routinely sex-reassigned through hormone treatment and surgeries? If not, why in your opinion is it not commonly discussed in Canadian society?
2. Why is it commonly believed that trans people must negotiate gender in ways that from-birth women and men do not?
3. In what ways do sociologists argue that gender creates sex?
4. How does nature demonstrate sex diversity rather than sex dimorphism?
5. What would social interactions be like without gender or sex?

Notes

1. The following two sections are taken from Hird (2000).
2. Accounts differ as to the statistical frequency of intersexuality. The Intersex Society of North America (ISNA) states that one in every 2,000 infants is born with some form of intersexuality from approximately 14 different causes (Nataf 1998).
3. CAH is the only intersex condition that poses a potential real emergency risk in the newborn period. Some infants with a CAH condition do not make sufficient amounts of cortisone and/or do not regulate the level of salt (through hormones) in their bodies.
4. This section is taken from Hird (2004).

4 | Why Be Queer?

Barry D. Adam

Introduction

Is the question 'Why be queer?' yet another claim for tolerance or multiculturalism? Is it about me, a heterosexually identified person sitting back and deciding whether I will let them, the queer people, do their own thing? Or about me, a gay, bisexual, lesbian, or transgendered person pleading once again to be left alone to conduct my own life? Is it yet another affirmation of the individualist ethic that stands in for a morality of advanced capitalist societies like our own—'I do my thing, you do your thing, we won't bother each other, and thus we realize society as we know it'?

In this chapter, I would like to push against this conventional understanding in Canadian society—and perhaps not so bad a convention given the alternatives that prescribe censorship, suppression, persecution, or worse. The argument I will advance is that queerness cannot so easily be assigned as a trait of 'other' people and that looking at the world through a queer optic tells us a lot about how that world is organized and affects everyone. In short, we are all implicated in the queering of some people and not others, and queer dynamics circle back to shape who we all think we are and the spaces we accord to ourselves and others for self-expression. Queerness is in some sense inescapable: it inhabits so-called alpha males (perhaps especially alpha males) as much as it does lesbians. Why be queer? It is not so much a question of being queer or not but a story of resisting, denying, and externalizing—or allowing and embracing—things queer and all of the implications that follow.

Minoritizing, Universalizing

So, are homosexual people a minority, or is erotic and affectionate feeling for other men and women within all of us, whether a little or a lot? In this insoluble dilemma rests a large story about how people make the worlds they live in, divide them into basic categories, draw distinctions between self and other, and conflict over who gets to wrap themselves in the flag of the right and the good and who is exiled from this charmed circle (Sedgwick 1990). It is not difficult to see how all this works in societies like our own: there is a divide—on one side heterosexuals, on the other lesbians and gay men. But the question that interests both sociology and **queer theory** is why do we think that? How did it get that way? Is it true?

On the one hand, the answer to the latter question is clearly affirmative. Lesbian, gay, bisexual, and transgendered (LGBT) people have come to be identified as a people not unlike such familiar ethnicities as Italian Canadians or African Canadians (presuming that LGBT people are allowed to play a part in the national imagination at all). They are, in sum, a part of the whole yet separate. They have an identity marked out from the rest, a geography with neighbourhoods and venues of their own, cultural artifacts like festivals and magazines, and a history. And there are good socio-historical reasons why Western societies have arrived at this point. LGBT identities have been forged over centuries of change.

The shift away from agrarian production to wage labour in Western capitalist societies reorganized traditional kin relationships, diminished parental supervision of their children's choices in partners, and concentrated large numbers of people in urban environments (Adam 1996). These changes have been profound for everyone regardless of sexual orientation and have created the conditions for greater faith in romance as a determinant of partner selection, enhanced ability to create households on one's own volition (rather than living with families of origin), and greater possibilities for meeting new people in the expanding cities. These changes were grounded in opportunities afforded by wage labour with its (limited) financial autonomy, at first mainly for men and subsequently for women as they too entered wage labour. In addition to these socio-economic preconditions in Western societies, overt persecution by Judeo-Christian authorities against 'sodomy' pressed those whose emotional lives were with people of their own sex into a camp of the sexually 'other' and invented, then sharpened, a boundary that reinforces that 'otherness'.

On the other hand, the answer to the question as to whether homosexual people are a distinct minority is clearly no. The historical and anthropological record shows that the foregoing brief history of the West was not inevitable but just one of several possibilities. For example, the anthropological record reveals that at least some indigenous societies on every inhabited continent include socially valued relationships with a homosexual aspect. These relationships fall into a few major patterns typically defined by life stage, gender, status, and/or kinship (Adam 1985; Greenberg 1988; Murray 2000). One major pattern, well documented in the Americas and Polynesia, is the 'berdache', 'two spirit', or transgendered form in which gender fluidity, gender mixing, or gender migration appears to be possible for some men and a few women. In these societies, homosexual relations are part of a larger pattern in which men and women take up some or most of the social roles and symbols typical of the other gender and enter into marital relations with other people who have conventional gender attributes (Jacobs 1997; Lang 1998). A second major pattern takes the form of hierarchical, military, age-graded, and mentor/acolyte relationships in which adult men who marry women also take a romantic and nurturant role with younger, subordinate males (Dover 1978; Herdt 1984; Adam 1985; Halperin 1990). Examples of this pattern have been documented in ancient Greece, medieval Japan, pre-colonial Africa, and Melanesia.

A third pattern, sometimes overlapping with the first two, orders homosexual relationships along the same kinship lines as heterosexuality. Thus if members of a particular clan are considered appropriate marital partners (and others are deemed inappropriate), both males and females of the appropriate clan may be considered attractive and acceptable partners. There are Australian and Melanesian cultures in which, for example, one's mother's brother is considered both an appropriate marital partner for girls and an appropriate mentor (including a sexual aspect) for boys (Adam 1985). Similarly, in some societies where the accumulation of bride price is the prerequisite to attracting a wife, occasionally women with wealth can avail themselves of this system to acquire wives (Amadiume 1980), and men can provide a corresponding gift to the families of youths whom they take into apprenticeship. These kin-governed bonds have been documented in some societies of Australia, Africa, and Amazonia. These major patterns point to the fact that there is no unitary idea of homosexuality in different societies, no single role or attitude toward same-sex sexuality, and no predominant conception of social approval or disapproval.

Historical research shows that same-sex eroticism and affection tend to coalesce around four major themes in Western societies (Halperin 2002): effeminacy, pederasty or 'active' sodomy, friendship or male love, and passivity or inversion. Martha Vicinus (1992) identifies the social scripts of the 'passing woman', the 'mannish woman', the 'libertine', and the 'romantic friend' as sites in which female bonding is most often found. All of this is to say that sex between men or between women has often not been the primary category of interest but rather a practice or trait that gained visibility as part of these social forms. Same-sex attraction and bonding, then, appears to arise more often in a few major patterns and social sites, entering at times into the lives of majorities or minorities of the inhabitants of a society. Conversely, homoeroticism may be shaped by these patterns or driven underground according to the precepts and prejudices of these societies.

[handwritten annotation: equilib quantity ↑, demand shift must have been larger]

The political and philosophical traditions of the West are rooted in a so-ciety deeply affirmative of homosexual relations of the mentor/acolyte mod-el. Indeed, most of the heroes of ancient Greek mythology had male lovers; the founding of democracy is attributed to the male couple Harmodias and Aristogeiton, who slew the tyrant Hyppias in 514 BCE (Halperin 1990; Foucault 1978). Socrates, in unexpurgated translations of *The Symposium*, rhapsodizes about how the love of youths leads to the love of beauty and thus to the love of wisdom. Yet modern Western tradition has suppressed, denied, and appro-priated this homoerotic heritage, consigning it to sin, sickness, or crime. The gradual shaping and consolidation of Christian doctrines into the orthodox canon law and the propagation and enforcement of these views by the Roman Catholic church from the twelfth century onward replaced the heroic friend-ships valued by the ancients with the idea of the sodomite (Jordan 1997).

Like the traditions it suppressed, the concept of the sodomite cannot simply be equated with modern ideas of the homosexual. In ecclesiastical law, sodomy typically referred to a vague, comprehensive category of sexual practices that lack pro-natalist objectives, including non-reproductive heterosexual acts and bestiality as well as homosexual practices. The consolidation of church power through the first millennium of the Christian era included the gradual eradi-cation of indigenous European forms of sexual friendship (Boswell 1994). By the fifteenth and sixteenth centuries, sodomy became a charge pursued by the Inquisition, with varying degrees of rigour in different countries, along with its campaign to suppress Jews, witches, and other forms of religious noncon-formity. In the sixteenth through the twentieth century, Christian orthodox-ies imposed by military conquest on indigenous populations of the Americas, Africa, and Asia actively extinguished local forms of same-sex bonding as part of larger campaigns of cultural colonialism or forced these local forms under-ground. The conceptualization of homosexuality as a sinful, non-reproductive sexual act then became widely established as governments and empires acted in concert with established churches to enforce cultural and juridical domin-ion over much of the world's population in the Christian realm.

As nation-states emerged from empires in the eighteenth through the twentieth century, many of them organized their criminal codes out of the legacy of canon law, depending on the social ingredients that went into state formation and their relationship to church control. With the rise of nation-states in the context of a Eurocentric, Christian, modern world sys-tem, the modern conception of homosexuality emerged as a sexual act attributed to a class of people subject to social sanction and criminal pen-alty (Adam 1995; Stychin 1998). As the world economy mobilized masses of people in cities and as states devised more efficient systems of supervising, regulating, and policing their populations, homosexual men (and later women) began to fall into the criminal justice systems of Europe. From the early example of the fifteenth-century Venetian republic to eighteenth-century campaigns to catch and suppress organized sodomy (that is, the nascent gay world) in Britain, the Netherlands, and Switzerland, state agencies (and at least in Britain, societies for the reformation of morals as well) swept up hundreds of men and some women in its punitive nets. The legacy of this nexus of church and state-building has been the disciplining of same-sex eroticism, the categorization of its adherents as a people apart, and the invention of homosexuality as a juridical and medical category.

By the nineteenth century, gay and lesbian venues had been firmly established in the major cities of Europe and North America and became subject to occasional exposés by police, physicians, and moralists, who have bequeathed us often shocked descriptions of 'colonies of perverts'. In Western societies such as our own then, people with homoerotic interests and gender dissidents have been forged into peoples with LGBT identities—or perhaps better said, LGBT identities have arisen among those willing to stand up for the right to love and live with the person(s) of one's choice. Why be queer? It is less a question about a 'fact' than a defence of a larger world of choice, an aspiration to find a way to what feels right in relating to other people, and a discovery of innovative ways to connect erotically and emotionally.

In Canada, LGBT communities and movements have often sought to realize these aims by availing themselves of and working with the avenues afforded to citizens in a liberal democratic society. These avenues and rights have been not so much pre-ordained as struggled for, contested in court, and demanded of recalcitrant governments (Adam 1995; Kinsman 1996). In the 1950s and 1960s, when public debates centred on whether homosexuals were criminals or mentally ill, the struggle was to gain freedom from police harassment and psychiatry (Kinsman and Gentile 2010). Canada decriminalized homosexuality in 1969 (for two consenting adults in private), and psychiatry began to depathologize it, beginning in the early 1970s. In the last decades of the twentieth century, a long struggle in provincial legislatures, courts, and finally the federal government succeeded in including 'sexual orientation' in human rights law, a symbolic affirmation of the full citizenship rights of lesbian, gay, and bisexual people (but less clearly transgendered people, a struggle that continues). At the turn of the twenty-first century, relationship recognition, for example, in the form of same-sex common-law relationships in Ontario or civil unions in Quebec, had been affirmed by the courts. In 2005, the Canadian parliament extended marriage to everyone regardless of gender such that any two persons (of age) could assume the legal rights and responsibilities of marriage.

So are we not back to minority rights, some version of multiculturalism, or the concerns of a minority that by definition need not occupy the energy and attention of the majority? Sometimes it may seem so, but more often the implications are much more far-reaching.

Disciplining Gender and Affection

Homophobia (that is, anti-LGBT sentiment and practice) is scarcely a thing of the past. Indeed, it is alive and well in many places, most notably schools, conservative religious institutions, some arenas of government, and certain regions and populations. An obvious answer to 'Why be queer?' might be: 'No way. I don't want to be derided, despised, even attacked'—which leads in turn to the question, 'Why are so many resources put into keeping homophobia active'? What are the many popes, presidents, preachers, mullahs, and school-yard bullies gaining from the volley of hate that they actively lob in the direction of anyone they can label, whether they have any idea of their actual sexual orientation or not? Homophobia is more than prejudice that will simply wilt in the face of reason (Adam 1998). Consider this finding from a study of 10- to 14-year-old schoolboys:

> In many countries it is now commonplace for researchers and media commentators to voice particular concern about two features of masculinity: young men's worsening record of academic attainment in comparison with girls and their propensity for violence. . . . [V]arious studies have identified the forms of masculinity that gain most respect as involving hierarchies based on toughness, threat of (or actual) violence, casualness about schoolwork, 'compulsory heterosexuality' and a concomitant homophobia. . . . As a result, boys and young men are forced to position themselves in relation to these issues, whether or not they wish actually to be violent or disengaged from schoolwork. (Phoenix, Frosh, and Pattman 2003)

Homophobia is not just anti-LGBT activity then; it functions as a whip to keep everyone toeing a particular gender line. What is striking from a national survey of bullying in Canadian schools is the sizable proportion of students suffering gender-related and homophobic harassment that are not in fact lesbian, gay, bisexual, or transgendered themselves (Taylor and Peter 2011). It operates particularly forcefully among men and boys, demanding a strict conformity that few can ever believe they have finally and comfortably attained. It works as a policing mechanism, both among males policing each other and as a vigilance over oneself. It is comprehensive and demanding, disciplining presentation of self, manners, and gestures. It prescribes the things in which one can legitimately take an interest, forcing other interests into the closet. If doing well in school becomes one of those supposedly insufficiently masculine things to do, then there are many boys convinced that they must sabotage their own potential on the altar of toughness. Of course, homophobia also regulates relationships among males, limiting warmth, affection, and mutual support. It even prescribes what one can wear, eat, drink, say, or dream of lest one fall vulnerable to the charge of being a 'sissy'. It is ubiquitous and relentless: the epithet 'that's so gay' has become one of the most widespread insults in Canadian schoolyards today despite the fact that it almost never refers to anything that is characteristic of gay worlds or sensibilities

So, is homophobia an essentially male dynamic? Traditionally, masculinity and femininity have not been simple mirror images of each other. Girls and women have usually been afforded more leeway in gender in that many accomplishments and activities associated with men can also be done by women without impugning one's integrity as female. Feminism as well has developed and consolidated a strong critique of the disadvantages of strict conformity to feminine gender requirements, defined them as a form of oppression, and pointed out how they have inordinately limited women's access to employment and opportunity. Nevertheless, women are far from immune to homophobia. Opponents of the women's movement were quick to try to paralyze it by charging that feminists were 'just a bunch of lesbians', and the movement did some soul-searching before deciding that it was the gender whip of homophobia that was the problem, not lesbians in the women's movement. Anti-lesbian ideologies and practices typically aim to thwart women from making their own choices and asserting their independence (Rich 1989). Today, the heightened visibility of things gay and lesbian has amplified anti-lesbian homophobia in everyday life. As Taylor and Peter (2011) found in its survey of schools, girls also increasingly suffer the verbal and physical violence of homophobic bullying.

By now it should be evident that homophobia does not act alone but operates like and often together with a number of other 'isms' like sexism, racism, able-ism, and classism. All of these practices share similar tactics through which people perceived to be vulnerable are picked out for special persecution. It is not surprising then to see that studies of prejudice find that those who rank highest in measures of homophobia are precisely the same people who are more likely to score highest for racism and sexism (MacDonald et al. 1973; Henley and Pincus 1978; Morin and Garfinkle 1978, 31; Adam 1978, 42–51; Larsen, Cate and Reed 1983; Bierly 1985; Herek 1988; Britton 1990; Seltzer 1992).

The link between homophobia and sexism is strong. How can males revile all things feminine in themselves and other men without affecting their valuation of women as a whole? These 'othering' dynamics of homophobia can mesh with racism and able-ism in that schoolchildren of colour or different abledness can be particularly vulnerable to being labelled and minoritized (Taylor and Peter 2011). That neither Hamed Nastoh nor Azmi Jubran were gay in sexual orientation did not stop them from being gay-baited and gay-bashed throughout high school (Ramsay and Tremblay 2005; Teeter 2005). Nastoh committed suicide at the age of 14 in 2000. The response of the Surrey school board, responsible for the school that he attended, was a refusal to permit any anti-homophobia curricula in Surrey schools. A ruling in Jubran's case by the British Columbia court of appeal in 2005 upheld the finding of a human rights tribunal that school boards cannot shirk their responsibility to make schools a safe place for students.

Schoolyards are just microcosms of larger social forces. Conservative religious organizations have frozen homophobia into religious doctrine and do not hesitate to avail themselves of human rights legislation guaranteeing religious freedom in order to promote homophobia at the same time that they actively seek to deny the same human rights protection to LGBT people. The Canadian same-sex marriage debate drew together the conservative and fundamentalist wings of a wide range of religions from fundamentalist Protestants to the Roman Catholic hierarchy, along with conservative Jews, Muslims, and Sikhs. At the same time, some adherents of all these faiths have organized to oppose conservative leaders because they understand all too well how the dynamics of 'othering' can and do hurt them as well and that the prerequisite for a peaceable society with social justice is an end to the politics of exclusion. At the United Nations, the recognition of basic human rights for LGBT people was long held hostage by a powerful bloc composed of the United States (as successive Republican governments remained captive to the Christian right), the Vatican, a set of Islamic states, and assorted dictatorships (Barris 2005). This same bloc stands in the way of the advancement of women in wresting control of their own reproductive potential from patriarchs and governments.

There are homophobia hot spots associated with governments as well. In the United States, the most notorious instance was the military with its active and official policy of exclusion (Scott and Stanley 1994). Not until the Obama administration assumed power did the discriminatory 'don't ask don't tell' policy finally come to an end. In Canada, it is censorship imposed by several layers of official regulation—from Canada Customs and Revenue regulations to obscenity law, bawdy-house law, and provincial film classification—that falls heavily on the small cultural institutions of the LGBT community (Cossman et al. 1997; Weissman 2002). There are as well more subtle forms of homophobia—as when LGBT lives are closely policed and thrust into a 'closet' because everything LGBT people do is supposedly about 'sex' and therefore must be kept secret. Same-sex courtship, romance, partnership, home-building, mutual support, and communication through the arts are not always allowed the same public manifestation accorded to that of others but rather are often subject to warning labels and restrictions.

Conclusion: Queer = Freedom

So, why be queer? By now it must seem as though there are rather a good many reasons not to be, but I want to argue that most of us have a great deal to gain by throwing off the ugly taskmaster of homophobia that dictates who we must be and dare to want to be.

Is there something about a queer viewpoint on the world that is interesting, insightful, and beneficial to all? If there is a 'gay sensibility', it is not shared by all LGBT people, and it may be appreciated by many who are not gay. If it does exist, it is not easy to define, since LGBT people have at least as many viewpoints and disagree with each other as much as anybody else. Even so, there is in the arts and literature of LGBT communities something of a tradition of critical awareness, irony, and 'camp' that understands the pomposity and dead weight of the moralists and bullies who take themselves too seriously and seem to have nothing better to do than try to run other people's lives. There is a long tradition of laughter that extends from gay bars to philosophical texts in response to a machismo that believes in itself, dogmatic righteousness, and gunslinger swagger. After a century, the plays of Oscar Wilde and Noel Coward still delight as they slyly send up the pretentiousness and absurd officiousness of social worlds trying to act the way they are 'supposed' to. Philosophers such as Wittgenstein, Barthes, and Foucault have stood out in their interrogation of the hidden assumptions and power dynamics of Western modernism. While their stance might not be linked to their homosexuality, one still might argue that their experiences gave them a vantage point on the world from which these underpinnings became more visible (Halperin 1995). Some of the most fundamental texts that puncture the ostensible 'naturalness' of gender also benefit from the queer optic (Rubin 1975; Butler 1990; Butler 1993b), as do some of the humorous texts that deflate puffed-up gender defenders (Simpson 1994).

Why be queer? Or more precisely, why tolerate the tyranny of homophobia? One can only wonder at the deformation of male character caused by the taboo on all things 'feminine'. Gentleness, style, aesthetics, dance, even intellect fall under the searchlight of homophobia as it casts its chill over ever wider territory. The emotionally crippled male has become a virtual icon of women's literature and psychology as women try to cope with the 'stiff' consequence of male gender disciplining (Faludi 1999). At one time, Englishmen could kiss each other with impunity; then sometime around the sixteenth century, this act too began to fall under 'suspicion' (Bray 1982). Now, according to the New York Times, a lot of men dare not even sit next to each other in a theatre, eat together in a decent restaurant, or talk honestly with each other about their deepest concerns without triggering a fear of suspected same-sex intimacy (Lee 2005). Fortunately, there remains considerable cross-cultural variation in inter-male gestures of casual affection: men from Morocco to China can walk arm in arm or hold hands in public without fear of reproach. But will Western gender panic contaminate their relaxed approach to affection, or will we in the West begin to learn something from them?

Homophobia also places women on a gender tightrope when they dare to enter traditionally masculine realms. The high rate of expulsion of women from the US armed forces is a case in point: the image of women carrying out the demands of military service soon attracts the homophobic gaze, since the gender whip requires that military women act both as 'women' and as 'men' simultaneously (Scott and Stanley 1994). That raises the question as to whether increasing equality for women disrupts gender or stimulates a wave of gender policing (or both). As long as the entry of women into more and more male-identified fields makes the male pretence that men alone are capable of doing these jobs appear increasingly ridiculous, there is hope that gender discipline will collapse of its own absurdity. But at the same time, there are signs that the easy expression of intimacy among girls and women is falling under 'suspicion', pressing them toward homophobic male standards of coldness.

The truth is that there have never been firm boundaries dividing sexual orientations in the lived experiences of most people. Studies of sexuality repeatedly reveal considerable behavioural bisexuality, experimentation, fluidity, and change over the life course. Some of these ambiguities have been recognized in schools in the form of gay/straight alliances that challenge homophobia without requiring members to declare an identity allegiance. But we are still left with the question: why is so much energy put into labelling other people 'gay' and drawing the boundaries that enforce a dictatorship of gender conformity? Why be queer? Challenging homophobia has the potential to make everyone much more at peace with themselves—even lesbians and gay men who themselves are hardly immune to the demands of gender. Still, LGBT people are necessarily on the front lines of resistance to homophobia, often the pioneers who innovate new kinds of relationship

(Weeks, Heathy, and Donovan 2001; Adam 2004; Adam 2006) and challenge the boundaries that reserve jobs for one gender or the other. A little more queerness in a lot more people might expand everyone's horizon of personal expression and opportunities.

Questions to Consider

1. What social and historical conditions led to the formation of people identified as gay, lesbian, bisexual, or transgendered?
2. What forms do same-sex bonds take in different societies around the world? What does this say about common notions of homosexuality?
3. How does homophobia affect nearly everyone regardless of sexual orientation?
4. Has the fear of things queer stunted the growth and expression of men and women?

5 | How Are Emotions Social?

Stephen Katz

Introduction

This chapter explores one of sociology's most important questions: 'How are emotions social?' In so doing, I examine some of the theoretical and methodological approaches used by researchers who explore the **sociology of emotions**, illustrated by the critical examples of gendered feeling rules, **emotional labour** in the workplace, and the history of romantic love. As students of sociology are aware, we are constantly bombarded with cultural messages to 'go with', 'trust', and 'follow' our feelings as if they were the deepest, most natural, and most authentic part of ourselves. However, Deborah Lupton notes that, 'as an outcome of the association that is commonly made between emotions and authentic selfhood, we often use our perceptions of the emotional self as rationales for explaining why we behave in certain ways' (1998, 91). Further, emotional experience, however personal and individual its forms of expression, only becomes meaningful in relational and social contexts of interaction and exchange. We know this because if feelings are expressed at the wrong time, in the wrong place, or in the wrong way, we react instantly with embarrassment, defensiveness, fear, or upset. Certain contexts also permit or evoke specific emotions, such as crying at movies or being 'sexy' in singles' bars. Disneyland counts on adults as well as children instantly feeling playful once inside its gates. Shopping malls promote whimsy and spontaneity (to buy things, of course). Funerals produce sentiments of sadness and loss. Fashion tells us to be 'cool' or 'hot'. Video games elicit states of excitation and loss of control. Talk shows capitalize on the performance of personal confession and narratives of recovery. Courts of law expect dispassionately presented accounts. Thus a central goal of emotional research is to explain why certain emotional expressions are tethered to particular social contexts. To pursue this goal, sociologists who study the emotions are challenged to make them accessible to sociological research in methodologically rigorous ways, particularly in locating the emotions between macro-social public realms and micro-social private realms. In these ways, sociologists are inspired by a 'social imagination' in the sense of the term proposed by C. Wright Mills (2004), as that which 'enables us to grasp history and biography and the relations between the two within society' (3).

The Emotions in Sociology

While the classical sociologists did not treat the emotions as a main focus of their work, their writings include significant questions about the emotional conditions of modern society. Karl Marx wrote about 'alienation' as a personal consequence of the exploitative capitalist labour process whereby labourers create commodities for exchange and profit by others rather than for their own use. Max Weber saw the spiritual development of the Protestant 'ethic' as an affective regime of self-governance essential to the entrepreneurial 'spirit' of capitalism. Weber was also mindful of the disturbing inner experience of the 'disenchantment of the world' that arose with modernity. Émile Durkheim emphasized that solidarity and sacredness were both objective social facts and subjective emotional states. Georg Simmel investigated the emotional reactions to modern urban life, such as the blasé attitude of boredom and sensory overload (see Kashima and Foddy 2002). To summarize the emotions in classical sociology, Chris Shilling (2002) posits two theoretical traditions: 'order and the emotions' and 'action and the emotions.' The concern for emotional order was an element of the French sociological tradition of Auguste Comte and Durkheim, who believed that political, educational, and religious institutions could shape and guide human emotions in positive, civilized, and collective ways. The concern for individual emotional action was an element of the German sociological tradition of Weber and Georg Simmel, who believed that the industrial and bureaucratic constraints of modern society would limit opportunities for individuals to express their 'true' emotional selves. The questions posed by these two traditions still endure today, as we struggle to balance emotional liberation with constraint and to distinguish between healthy and deviant emotions.

It is also crucial to understand that the emotions and passions in Western culture have been defined largely in contrast to the supposedly superior human faculties of reason and rationality. According to feminist philosopher Alison Jaggar (1989), the emotions, characterized as impulsive and uncontrollable, arouse suspicion in scholarly work geared to unbiased objectivity. However, it is impossible for researchers to control for all subjective influence since beneath the veneer of claims to research objectivity lie the various biases, prejudices, ambitions, strategies, and compromises that constitute knowledge-making. Indeed, where their contributions are acknowledged the emotions provide rich and creative resources in social research, as anthropologist Renato

Rosaldo (1989) discovered in his fieldwork with the Ilongot people of the Phillipines. For years Rosaldo unsuccessfully attempted to understand how the Ilongot people's experience of anger and grief could lead to headhunting rituals, until he was stricken with his own emotional grief after the death of his wife Michelle Rosaldo and 'began to fathom the force of what the Ilongots were telling me about their losses through my own loss, and not through any systematic preparation for field work' (1989, 8).

Western culture's great divide between objective reason and subjective emotion goes beyond epistemological and methodological issues of research to configure systems of social difference and inequality. Think about how constructed categories of gender, race, and class are aligned to emotional stereotyping. For example, conventional feminine emotions are represented as naturally weak, uncontrollable, unreliable, and irrational, as opposed to masculine emotions of strength, control, reliability, and rationality. Stephanie Shields (2002) maintains that anger, however volatile an emotion, in the hearts and minds of men can appear as calculated, reflexive, and vindicated because it, along with aggression and assertiveness, is an acceptable and privileged emotion accompanying male entitlement to social power. Where women are more marginal to social power, their perception of anger is that it is neither legitimate nor rewarding. And if they do express anger, women are often stigmatized as being hysterically out of control, or advised to internalize and manage their anger (rather than learning to express it better), or treated for bio-psychological problems such as hormonal imbalance, depression, or menopause.

Jaggar also argues that female anger can also serve a feminist purpose, however, because anger is one of many socially inhibited emotions that can become an 'outlaw emotion' against the imposition of mainstream gendered **feeling rules**. For instance, a woman interrupted and laughed at by a man in a classroom may feel intimidated or embarrassed. Rather than obligingly accepting and hiding such feelings (as appropriately feminine), if the woman became angry at being shut down she could use the occasion to resist and transform taken-for-granted expectations. Thus outlaw emotions, Jaggar (1989) asserts, 'may provide the first indications that something is wrong with the way alleged facts have been constructed, with accepted understandings of how things are' (9). In other words, critical thinking and action in sociology involve a radical curiosity about how we are made to feel and how we might feel otherwise.

Emotional Labour and Feeling Rules

In the 1980s the sociology of emotions emerged as a distinct subfield, largely because of the innovative research of Arlie Russell Hochschild, a sociologist at the University of California at Berkeley, whose book *The Managed Heart: The Commercialization of Human Feeling* (1983) was a seminal study of the exploitation of 'emotional labour' in the workplace. Emotional labour involves a worker's management, evocation, and potential commodification of particular forms of emotional expression in order for her or him to satisfy the feeling rules of a specific job or social role. Hochschild (2003) says that a feeling rule is different from other kinds of rules because it does 'not apply to action but to what is *often taken as a precursor to action*' (98–9). In examining the emotional labour of Delta airline stewardesses, *The Managed Heart* provides a critique of the predominantly female service economy and the detrimental emotional consequences of its conflation of private and public worlds (an issue expanded upon in Hochschild's *The Second Shift: Working Parents and the Revolution at Home* (1990) and *The Commercialization of Intimate Life* (2003). Another good example of emotional labour is modelling and the contradictory job requirements made of models who must appear to be energetic, friendly, and personable, even while they work in uncomfortable and physically harassing conditions. As Mears and Finlay (2005) observe in their study of the modelling profession, a model's own feelings become subservient to the needs of their clients and photographers; hence skilled emotional management and role-playing are just as important to a model's career success as bodily discipline, dieting, and fashionability.

The demands of emotional labour in the service industry parallel the rise of a corporate culture preoccupied with human productivity and growth; organizational metaphors of team and family; efficiency models of quality control and customer service; and labour loyalty based on subjective qualities of flexibility, enterprise, leadership, and adaptability. One of the giants of the new corporate culture is Walmart, where author Barbara Ehrenreich (2001) worked in Minnesota in order to learn first-hand how poorly paid service workers survived. Ehrenreich discovered that despite the store's positive corporate aura and daily team-building motivation exercises, many Walmart workers or 'associates' live in semi-homeless conditions, experience extreme disciplinary surveillance on the job, and must cope with the disruptions of frequently changing shift-work patterns. Sennett and Cobb wrote about the dignity of workers in *The Hidden Injuries of Class* (1972), a pioneering study of the emotional costs of class inequality. Similarly, Ehrenreich admires how Walmart workers emotionally respond to their exploitative conditions and lack of freedom by developing alternative badges of accomplishment, honour, and dignity in the face of the power over them. The customers or 'guests' who regularly shop at Walmart are also often poor women with little control over their own lives and express their emotional frustration by throwing clothes around and making a mess—female rebels fed up with their own lives of toil and childcare and denied access to the real prosperity of consumer society. For both the workers and the customers at Walmart, therefore, as in other areas of the service economy where emotional labour is an exploitable resource, the struggle over social status includes an affective dimension of resistance that comes from the feeling worlds of economic impoverishment and political marginalization.

The Social Making of Emotions

While emotional labour is a telling example of the social nature of emotions and the value of an imaginative approach that connects biographical to social processes, this section asks about the historical development of emotions. Where do the meanings, feeling rules, and social roles associated with particular emotions come from? For instance, depression is one of the most publicized emotional problems today and attracts extensive psychological, biological, pharmacological, neurological, and behavioural research. Depression is also part of an everyday vocabulary and mixes easily with commonsensical talk about feelings of sadness, anxiety, stress, disappointment, and confusion. Rom Harré and Robert Finlay-Jones in 'Emotion Talk across Times' (1986) take a longer view of depression by looking at the 'obsolete' historical emotion called 'accidie'. Since the beginning of early Roman Christianity 'acedia' (as it was initially called) was a term applied to the emotional state of being spiritually lost, weak, and miserable. Its cause, especially for religious persons, lay in the lack of joy and conviction when fulfilling spiritual tasks. Thus, treatment for acedia required spiritual counselling and encouragement. When 'acedia' became 'accidie' in the Middle Ages, it grew as both a moral and emotional problem.

However, in late medieval and Renaissance societies, melancholy emerged as a second related emotional condition whose symptoms included sadness, laziness, forgetfulness, and gloominess, leading in extreme cases to suicide. Medicine at that time involved a diagnostic system based on balancing bodily fluids or humours: blood, phlegm, yellow bile, and black or blue bile. Each humour was aligned to a specific feeling, colour, season, and position of stars and planets. An excess of yellow bile could create the condition of cholera, whose orange skin tone was associated with anger. Too much phlegm could result in lethargy. Melancholy was blue and characteristic of nighttime, autumn, and chilliness. In 1586, when Robert Burton wrote *Anatomy of Melancholy*, melancholy was known as a condition that could afflict everybody; indeed, it was seen as part of the human condition itself and gave the sufferer reflexive opportunities, as Burton says 'to be more exact and curious in pondering the very moments of things' (quoted in Harré and Finlay-Jones 1986, 224).

Melancholy was an aggregation of feelings appropriate to the personal dilemmas of early modern life, whereby sadness and confusion along with intellectual insight were thought to be the emotional counterpart of the enterprising spirit of the Renaissance as it broke with the religious bonds and certainties of the past. Today we do not suffer from the spiritual idleness and lethargy of accidie, or from the humoural imbalances and seasonal effects of melancholy. We do suffer from depression as a mood disturbance, however, and trace it to biological (neurological disorder, serotonin malfunction), psychological (experiences of isolation and abuse), and social (unemployment, poverty, marginalization) determinants. Thus clinical as well as cognitive therapies are prescribed. Yet accidie, melancholy, and depression have an intriguingly similar feeling base, which as historical research documents has woven its way through the experience of self as some emotional states become obsolete and others take their place with new authority and legitimacy. If we approached other emotions in the same way—according to their supposed causes (spiritual, medical, psychological, neuroscientific), places of emergence (the body, the mind, the soul, the brain), authority figures (the priest, the physician, the therapist, the psychiatrist, the pharmacologist) and forms of expression and discourse—we might also discover the social conditions underlying our own emotional states and their connection to worlds that seem so different in time and space.

A related sociologically relevant emotion linked to depression is self-esteem, which sociologist John P. Hewitt (1998) thinks of as a 'myth' because we *believe* in self-esteem despite the scattered nature of the scientific research. Self-esteem has become an explanation system for who we are and why we succeed or fail. As an emotional meter ('high' or 'low' self-esteem), it is a powerful metaphor trumpeted alike by motivational speakers, industrial leaders, exercise and diet experts, education reformers, and self-help proponents who advocate assertiveness and recovery. Whereas self-esteem originally referred to the honourable recognition of a person's accomplishments earned over a lifetime, today it means a person's 'feeling good' about himself or herself. The fact that the meaning of self-esteem has historically changed in these ways prompts Hewitt to look for the social reasons why self-esteem has become internalized as a kind of master emotion today. Further, he questions whether self-esteem programs in schools do stimulate successful performance and if not whether it is realistic to expect such programs to resolve the educational problems of students that are likely due to social inequality, school underfunding, and issues of housing and employment. As Hewitt (1998) says, 'The chorus of voices in praise of self-esteem merely drowns out the voices of others who argue that it is the social system itself that produces and perpetuates inequality' (95).

A critical understanding of the social development of every emotion can potentially broaden a world of discovery about what it means to be human in contemporary society. For example, stress as analyzed by Gillian Bendelow (2009) is a key to understanding modern society's problematical relationship between mind and body. Susie Scott's (2006) study of shyness and its recent retranslation into 'social phobia' points to the process of medicalization within models of public health. New applications of emotional intelligence testing for critics such as Diane Reay (2005) and Eva Illouz (2008) create interesting forms of emotional capital in schools, the workplace, and therapeutic culture. However, it would be impossible in a critical discussion of the sociology of emotions not to include love, our culture's most cherished yet elusive emotional aspiration.

What Is Love?

Love is really a multi-faceted emotion articulated by the central image of the human 'heart', by which we become attached to others, God(s), nature, pets, nations, children, and self. Our popular culture and media float endless messages encouraging us to do 'anything for love', including dying for it. Of the many facets of love, it is romantic love that looms so large as the purest form of emotional truth. However, as John Gillis claims (1988), the experience of love in Western societies has dramatically changed over the last four centuries. From the sixteenth to the eighteenth centuries, the body and its fluids, movements, and actions were seen as the seat of emotional expression and force. The body was emotional, and through it love was ritualized less as a kind of drive than a public script to be acted out in the presence of others. The signs of romantic love, such as holding hands, kissing, and embracing, had weighty social meaning because they demonstrated a person's affections. Since love was a physical essence, magical charms, potions, certain foods and herbs, divining, and fortune telling could all affect it. If marriage followed the proper enactment of the script of love, then marriage too was a public project involving family arrangements. Thus the experiences and expressions of romantic love were far less gender-differentiated than they are today because they were not based simply on private intimacy. But the magic of love has certainly not disappeared, as the advertisements for aftershaves, perfumes, diamonds, pearls, and of course chocolate indicate with their extravagant promises of instant attraction and romance.

In the nineteenth and early twentieth centuries, love became an emotion associated with deep, pure feeling. The social conventions of the new middle class degraded bodily expressions of emotion as dangerous and vulgar and reduced physical love to sexuality. By the mid-nineteenth century, wedding convention dictated that women should be dressed in white and veiled to symbolize feminine purity. Not surprisingly, this was also the period when homosexuality and lesbianism were constructed as deviant and unnatural and non-Western peoples portrayed as promiscuous and uncivilized. Most importantly, discourses on love were imbued with scientific gender-specific theories of sexual difference, pathologies, needs, and drives. For women, the enforced personal search for and expectation of love became the sentimentalized route to a new femininity characterized as soft, weak, vulnerable, and delicate (Cancian 1986). Today the world of Harlequin novels, soap operas, and Valentine's Day and anniversary celebrations continue to remind us that women are supposedly so preoccupied with romance that they accept sexually passive roles. The emotional progression from dating to falling in love to marriage is akin to the human maturation process itself and part of the architecture of the modern soul. This is obvious in the cluster of troubling love-related emotions such as jealousy (see Clanton 1989). Indeed, love is so powerful a social aspiration that it can create a discrepancy between what is expected of us and what we actually feel, as is the case in weddings, where romantic emotional levels are often pushed so high that they require careful management by the bride and groom (Hochschild 1998).

Conclusion: Other Ways to Feel

This chapter has emphasized that the hallmark of the sociology of emotions is its capacity to map the structures that give emotional work its meaning and at the same time critique the social order in which emotions are hierarchically embedded. Even in our postmodern world where virtual environments and electronic technologies can make emotions seem spurious and experimental, and relationships fractured and fantastical, emotions still constitute a realm of social meaning that ground the self in thoughtful feeling and reflexive action (see Bargh, McKenna, and Fitzsimons 2002). However, the chapter has framed the social and historical importance of the emotions within normative contexts of normal selves. In conclusion, we ask what can be learned about the emotions by thinking about people who are judged as deficient in or lacking emotional attributes. For example, autistic children used to be considered mentally retarded, and people with Alzheimer's disease (AD) have always been regarded as non-existent selves, bodies without minds. If we looked at autism and AD in other ways, what might they tell us about the emotional possibilities of different selves and other ways of being human?

Since neurologists Leo Kamer and Hans Asperger first began researching autism in the 1940s as a disorder located in the brain, the image of autism has been one of a rogue brain bypassing the protective emotional mantle of the self. The research on autism shows that brain, mind, and self have a unique relationship that produces the obsessive behaviours and intense vulnerability to environmental stimuli that we know to be autism's main features. In his collection of writings in *An Anthropologist on Mars* (1995), Oliver Sacks explores how neurological disorders such as autism provide new prospects as well as problems to those afflicted with it. Included in his book is the story of Temple Grandin, a professor of veterinary biology at Colorado State University in Denver. Grandin is internationally renowned for engineering new humanistic livestock facilities and slaughterhouses—and is also autistic. Her own writing (Grandin and Scariano 1986; Grandin 1995; Grandin and Johnson 2004) and speaking engagements have been tremendously helpful in bringing autism to public awareness. While she has no problem communicating with and emotionally connecting to cows or dogs, Grandin has many emotional problems dealing with people, with whom she has learned to build a 'normal' presentation of self to express the emotional cues and behavioural codes others expect of her. When Sacks visited one of Grandin's slaughterhouses, he saw how human creativity can derive from the fixations and obsessions with detail, patterns, and routines that are typically autistic. The poetics, imagination, and emotions of 'normal' selfhood may appear to be absent in autism, but understanding people like Temple Grandin reveals that autistic persons are greatly concerned with their place in the outside world and at the same time forming a sense of self as an expansive and compensatory resource to secure inner life in relation to that outside world.

As with autism, it is claimed that Alzheimer's disease (AD) is on the rise, but also potentially misunderstood (Whitehouse 2008). Many of us know people or family members with AD and are aware of the tragic suffering that comes with the loss of their cognitive and emotional abilities. In the later stages of AD, it is not unusual to wonder if there is a person still 'there' at all—someone who still feels, laughs, cries, and experiences pain and joy. Like autism, AD is a recent medical category, discovered in 1907 by German neuropathologist Alois Alzheimer, who considered it a very rare form of pre-senile dementia. In the 1960s and 1970s, AD was expanded to encompass other cognitive and behavioural problems, including senility itself. Today, AD is part of a disease movement, with millions of dollars invested in the promise of treatments aimed at reversal.

Outside medical research, what does AD tell us about the sociology of emotions, especially as losses of self, memory, language, and emotional expression appear to be its main characteristics? Tom Kitwood (1997), a British social psychologist who, along with others whom he influenced such as health researcher Pia Kontos (2004), advocate a radical 'person-centred' approach to self in AD, even if it is emotionally expressed through non-linguistic means such as body language. Likewise, gerontologist and dramatist Anne Basting organized storytelling workshops for people with AD in her project *Time Slips* (2001; http://www.timeslips.org; see also Basting 2009). After collecting 100 stories, Basting understood them not as partially remembered narratives or as data for reminiscence therapy, but as stories with an artistry and spontaneity that do *not* rely on memory. Indeed, the *Time Slips* stories are less about dementia than about emotional expression, including humour and creativity where the expression of self happens relationally—between persons—rather than individually. As with autism's unmediated emotional self, the Alzheimer relational emotional self should lead us to suspect that there are other kinds of selves out there, waiting to tell us even more about how thin the line is between what we feel, what we are supposed to feel, and what is possible to feel.

This chapter, by looking at the emotions in terms of their special histories, cultural contexts, and social meanings, is not denying the private life of intimacy or the power of emotional experiences as life-shaping events. Rather, the bold potential of the sociology of emotions is to illuminate the emotions as signposts to our understanding of the social making of our interior lives. In the words of philosopher Gilles Deleuze, the emotional self could be considered a type of *folding* (1993): a dynamic shaping and pleating of subjective worlds as they interact with the external imperatives for living in time. As such, there is no separation of inside and outside, because the self is the 'inside of the outside' (Deleuze 1988, 97), both uniquely biographical and collectively sustained by the social imperatives that define successful living. In such worlds, we also find our critical agency to challenge social imperatives and conventions, as much by feeling as by thinking our way through them.

Questions to Consider

1. What does the sociological study of the emotions teach us about the relationship between private and public realms?
2. How can we say that emotions have social and historical meanings when they are felt as so deeply personal and intimate?
3. Where do dominant feeling rules align to prevailing relations of power, inequality, and social difference?
4. Where do specific social contexts evoke and regulate the expression of specific emotions?

6 | What Does Mental Illness Mean?

Erin Dej

Introduction

The term 'mental illness' conjures up many different images. Maybe it reminds us of the self-help section of our local bookstore and its promises to solve our relationship problems or to help us self-actualize. Perhaps we think of our mental health initiatives at school or work that offer counselling services and seminars on how to find balance in our lives. It might evoke images of a close relative who may be diagnosed with depression. Often, though, when we hear the words 'mental illness' we think of someone who is very sick, who behaves strangely, who makes us uncomfortable, who maybe even scares us, and who does not fit in with everyday society.

In this chapter we rethink what we know about mental illness. We consider where our modern notion of mental illness comes from and the techniques and practices used to promote this way of thinking. Finally, we explore the anti-psychiatry and mad movements, both of which offer an alternative perspective on mental illness.

How Do We 'Know' Mental Illness?

The Medical Model

Scientific psychiatry developed in the nineteenth century as a medical approach to understanding madness by concentrating on the body as the site of mental distress. Tuke and Pinel are credited with the development of the modern-day asylum and its scientific methods of treatment (Everett 1994; Cockerham 2003). Renowned philosopher and historian Michel Foucault (1988) is critical of the claim that Tuke and Pinel's developments were scientific; he argues that they were moral in nature. Foucault notes that, beginning in the nineteenth century, psychiatrists became experts on mental illness and used this authority to impose moral judgments on others. According to Foucault (1988 [1964]), many of the techniques place responsibility on individuals for their distress. As psychiatry grew more powerful, psy-experts developed. 'Psy' refers to psychiatry but also to psychology and other disciplines related to these areas. The links psy-experts made with medicine allowed the discipline to gain credibility and to use neutral and objective language (such as 'etiology', 'symptoms', 'treatment'), regardless of its moral basis.

The use of psychiatry to explain differences in behaviour informs the broader literature on deviance. When we decide that certain attitudes, behaviours, or actions are 'normal', this means that others are 'abnormal' (Downes, Rock, and McCormick 2009). When we use psychiatry to classify some people as sick and/or bad we are making claims about what we consider 'normal'. Using this classification also assumes that anyone who acts outside this continuum of normality not only is abnormal but is biologically different from everyone else (Pfohl 1994).

Psychiatry is now part of the medical model. Mental distress is regarded as an illness—that is, a problem arising from a biochemical disorder, genetic predisposition, or virus (Tew 2005). Psychiatrists study the brain, where chemical changes are thought to create syndromes. The medical model looks for a single, technical explanation for a problem and often ignores the social circumstances that bring about distress or a crisis (Goffman 1961). As Laing (1971, 24), a founder of the anti-psychiatry movement, claims, 'This [medical] model, when applied to a social situation, helps us to see what is going on about as much as do dark glasses in an already darkened room.' That is not to say that those who subscribe to the medical model do not consider external circumstances; but in order to maintain the model's connection to physical medicine, environmental factors are often thought of as simply triggers to biochemical changes in the body. Even in cases where there is little physical evidence to support a purely biological connection, a medical approach prevails (Cockerham 2003; Rogers and Pilgrim 2010). For example, although post-traumatic stress disorder (PTSD) is considered one of the few mental illnesses grounded in the social/interpersonal context (Becker 2004), the psychiatric literature suggests that there is a psychological and biological predisposition to PTSD that is triggered by a traumatic event (Keane, Silberbogen, and Weirerich 2008).

Psychiatry's connection to the medical model is evident in the *Diagnostic and Statistical Manual (DSM)*. The DSM was created in 1952 and is used to classify the various mental disorders for the purposes of diagnosis. The aim of the DSM is to provide stability and consistency to psychiatry; however, critics suggest that the DSM is used to gain influence over the public, the media, and the government by presenting psychiatric diagnoses as scientific and research driven (Caplan 1996; Kutchins and Kirk 1997) and by hiding the moral and political influences involved. Claims of deviancy are necessarily caught up with issues of power and politics (Pfohl 1994).

The addition, and later removal, of homosexuality from the DSM is an example of the manual's value judgements that hide behind the claim of scientific rigour. Homosexuality was listed as a mental disorder in the first DSM, but was removed in the early 1970s, a move that Kutchins and Kirk (1997) note involved little scientific discussion. Beginning in the 1960s, meetings of the American Psychiatric Association (APA), which produces the DSM, were inundated with protests about the validity of categorizing homosexuality as a mental illness. In 1974, members of the APA voted to remove homosexuality from the DSM. Afterwards, a new diagnosis, gender identity disorder, was added to the DSM, which some argue is a way to maintain homosexual behaviour as an illness (Zucker and Spitzer 2005; Conrad 2007).

The Targets of Mental Illness Diagnosis

Despite these criticisms, the medical model prevails—partly because psychiatry does not attempt to cure mental distress. Unlike physical medicine, psy-experts only claim to manage symptoms (Russell 1995; Rogers and Pilgrim 2010). As Bean (2008) argues: 'Its acceptance has also been assisted by the law of repetition: if assertions are made with sufficient regularity, and by people of high status, eventually they will become accepted' (8). The medical model survives in psychiatry not because it is necessarily useful but because of its coupling with key players in the medical and pharmacological fields. One of the most compelling critiques of the psy-discipline is the evidence suggesting that some groups are more likely to be diagnosed with mental illness than others. Among these groups are women, the poor, and racial minorities.

Critical scholars widely acknowledge the overrepresentation of women in the mental health system. Women are more likely than men to be diagnosed with personality disorders such as eating disorders, generalized anxiety disorder, obsessive compulsive disorder, or borderline and dependent personality disorder (Russell 1995; Holmshaw and Hillier 2000). Women are also more likely to be prescribed psychotropic medication (which acts on the mind) and given electroconvulsive therapy (ECT) (described below) (Ussher 1991; Holmshaw and Hillier 2000).

There are a number of hypotheses about why women are diagnosed with mental illnesses more often than men. Women who do not conform to traditional notions of femininity—what it means to be a woman—are more likely to be diagnosed with a mental illness. For example, women who are competitive, aggressive, or independent may be labelled with any number of personality disorders because these traits are devalued in women, although they are considered acceptable among men (Russell 1995). Even when women conform to stereotypical notions of 'womanhood', they may become involved in the mental health system for being overly sad, fearful, or dependent. As Holmshaw and Hillier (2000) note, women are caught in a Catch-22 situation in which either adopting the ideals of femininity or resisting them can lead to a mental illness diagnosis. Finally, there are some broad diagnoses that are gender specific to women and that may be applicable to any number of women. For example, premenstrual dysphoric disorder (PMDD) was added to the DSM in 1993. PMDD is described as a severe form of premenstrual syndrome. Critics of PMDD suggest that the diagnosis can be used on any number of women to discredit them and that describing it as a mental rather than physical illness reveals a moral judgement (Caplan 1995).

Psy-experts rarely recognize poverty as the cause of distress. Approximately one in three homeless people in Canada are labelled mentally ill (Davis 2006); however, we have to question the connection between homelessness and mental illness. Just as the psy-literature depicts women as more fragile than men, Bresson (2003, 312) argues that it is politically beneficial to equate mental illness and homelessness because it makes individuals responsible for being 'fragile' and 'vulnerable' rather than the social environment from which they come. Similarly, Snow et al. (1986) suggest that the very nature of homelessness, and the most common responses to being homeless (inappropriate dress/appearance; depression; agitation; unresponsiveness, etc.) are considered symptoms of a mental illness. Although it is important to recognize the distress many individuals living in poverty experience, the mental health system may not be the most adequate or helpful response to the problems they face.

People of colour are also overrepresented in the mental health system. Research from the United States shows that white people are significantly more likely to perceive African Americans as aggressive, unintelligent, and lazy. Given that psy-experts are predominately white, these assumptions may lead to institutional racism, characterized by a collective failure to provide the same type of care to people based on their race (McKenzie and Bhui 2007) and to explain the disproportionate number of mental illness diagnoses for certain racial groups. Constatine (2006) finds that people of colour who experience racism on a daily basis may develop coping mechanisms such as becoming suspicious of others or feeling a sense of persecution. These characteristics can be considered symptoms of paranoid personality disorder or schizophrenia. Moreover, members of a racial minority experiencing distress are also less likely to receive support and counselling than are white people (Constatine 2006). As we can see, the complex connection between gender, class, race, and mental illness helps us to think critically about who is diagnosed with a mental illness and how the mental health system may be perpetuating stereotypes as well as a method of managing certain populations.

What Happens to People Labelled Mentally Ill?

Several strategies informed by the medical model are used to treat, manage, and control individuals diagnosed with a mental illness. We will review the most popular techniques: hospitalization, ECT, and psychotropic medication.

Once referred to as asylums, institutions for individuals diagnosed with a mental illness are generally accepted as a way to control individuals deemed to be a danger to themselves or others. Goffman (1961) referred to these as 'total institutions' because people's daily lives are completely controlled and these actions are justified in the name of science. Faith in hospitals as institutions of care has, in some cases, led to an abuse of power—for example, in using patients as uninformed research participants for medical experiments, especially for new forms of psychotropic medication (Stenfert, Kroese, and Holmes 2001). Although deinstitutionalization (discussed below) reduced the number of people incapacitated in mental hospitals, involuntary commitment continues as a technique for managing the mentally distressed, especially for individuals linked to the criminal justice system and those designated as the 'most dangerous' (Cockerham 2003).

Electroconvulsive therapy (ECT) is likely the most controversial form of treatment today. ECT involves sending an electric current to the brain in order to induce a seizure and is used to treat depression, schizophrenia, and mania (Kimball 2007). ECT is used twice as often on women as on men (Ussher 1991), perpetuating the overrepresentation of women who are diagnosed and treated for a mental illness. ECT is generally accepted amongst psy-professionals (Everett 1994; Rogers and Pilgrim 2010), but some activist groups protest against ECT with slogans such as 'fry eggs, not brains' (Frese 1997). One psychiatric survivor says of ECT: 'Shock treatment, when you strip off all the pretensions, is cruel, and no amount of expression of good intentions will make it otherwise' (Phyllis quoted in Burstow and Weitz 1988, 54). Despite these personal accounts condemning ECT (Burstow 2004; Crossley and Crossley 2001), and the scientific research raising doubts about its usefulness (Kimball 2007), ECT continues to be promoted and used as a method of treatment.

The most common form of treatment is the use of psychotropic medication, referring to medication designed to have an effect on the mind (Davis 2006). Chlorpromazine was introduced in the 1950s as a medication to reduce hallucinations among individuals diagnosed with schizophrenia. It continues to be used today for a variety of diagnoses (Cockerham 2003). Since that time, many new types of psychotropic medications have been prescribed to individuals diagnosed with a mental illness, often as the only form of treatment. The widespread use of medication has had a dramatic effect on how individuals diagnosed as mentally ill are managed. Relying primarily on psychotropic medication leads to a depersonalization of treatment, in that there is significantly less contact between doctor and patient, and there is less interest in dealing with the nature of the distress itself (Rosenhan 1973). Pfohl (1994) suggests that psychotropic medication is a method used to chemically control individuals for an abundance of deviant thoughts or actions and has led to the development of Big Pharma. 'Big Pharma' refers to large pharmaceutical companies that yield a great deal of economic and political power. The overreliance on psychopharmaceuticals for everything from anxiety to shyness and sadness (Conrad 2007) has reinforced the notion that distress is a biological problem and misrepresents medication as a cure rather than as a way to manage symptoms (Cockerham 2003; Rogers and Pilgrim 2010). In fact, the overwhelming use of medication is often cited as one of the most significant catalysts to deinstitutionalization.

Deinstitutionalization: Ideas and Reality

The 1960s witnessed an increase in criticism of how all sorts of social institutions, including mental hospitals, were run. People became skeptical about experts and called for less structure and less state intervention. The policy of **deinstitutionalization** was the most dramatic shift of all the changes (Cohen 1985).

The central tenet of deinstitutionalization was a call for people in distress to receive assistance in the community rather than be locked up, often involuntarily, in a hospital. Deinstitutionalization 'involved a shift of the sites and responsibility for treatment and support from institutional to community settings, and has been associated with a fragmentation of mental health service delivery' (Wilson 1996, 71). The community was seen as a humane alternative to mental hospitals, and the diversion of individuals who would otherwise be institutionalized was based on the idea that people diagnosed with a mental illness should have their basic rights protected, where possible (Stroman 2003; Davis 2006).

What Went Wrong?

Although the decision to deinstitutionalize individuals diagnosed with a mental illness occurred in the 1960s, the impact of the movement was not felt until later. In Canada, for example, although the capacity of mental hospitals was reduced by 70.6 per cent between 1965 and 1981, the number of beds in the psychiatric ward of general hospitals increased dramatically. It was not until the 1990s that this number decreased as well (Sealy and Whitehead 2004).

The promise of deinstitutionalization was that people in distress would receive supports in the community (Wilson 1996, 73). These goals were not achieved. The resources meant to bring about a smooth transition from the mental hospital to community integration were either not present or were inadequate. Davis (2006) suggests two reasons for this. First, there was a lack of coordination between care providers and individuals seeking services. Many patients coming out of the hospital ended up on the streets, but the supports were often not located in the same areas as the people who needed them, were only open during the day and not at night, or did not have the staff consistency necessary to build relationships in the community.

Second, different service providers did not communicate with one another and therefore could not coordinate the types of services offered. Service organizations had trouble getting started or maintaining their position. Although generally members of the community agreed with the idea of moving toward community support, they campaigned against having mental health services in their neighbourhoods. This is an example of the 'not in my back yard' (NIMBY) syndrome. In turn, many individuals released from the mental hospital into the community were upset because they felt abandoned by the communities that were meant to be there for them. Many also felt like they were taking a passive role in their recovery and that they were being managed rather than treated. As Rogers and Pilgrim (2010, 198) claim: 'The inhumanity of the asylum has simply been replaced by the negligence of the community.' This statement exemplifies one of the most negative effects of deinstitutionalization: transcarceration. 'Transcarceration' refers to the move from one institution to another (Arrigo 2001): People previously placed in asylums are now being housed in prisons, nursing homes, general hospitals, homeless shelters, etc. (Stroman 2003). Although deinstitutionalization did not unfold as planned, it does represent a more social way of thinking about mental illness.

The Development of the Mad Movement

Anti-psychiatry

Among those most vocal about deinstitutionalization in the 1960s were those identified as anti-psychiatrists. The **anti-psychiatry movement** was largely made up of psychiatrists who were critical of their own discipline. Doctors such as Szasz, Laing, and Cooper questioned the moral judgments that they saw as the real basis of mental illness diagnoses. The anti-psychiatrists studied mental illness as a social construction; they recognized how individuals' personal and social circumstances affected their behaviour and focused on how that behaviour is understood by others. For example, Szasz (1989, 16) coined the term 'problems in living' to describe the personal difficulties that interest the psy-discipline. He adds that mental illness is in fact an individual's 'struggle with the problem of *how* he should live (emphasis in original)'. Szasz's assessment of problems in living is consistent with our example of homosexuality being labelled a mental illness until the 1970s. Until that time, many considered homosexuality a problematic way to live.

Although the anti-psychiatry movement lost momentum by the 1980s, some psychiatrists, scholars, and others still identify as anti-psychiatrists. This movement challenges us to reconsider how mental illness is understood. Anti-psychiatrists ask how we know what we know about mental illness. They use intellectual critiques of mental illness (Ussher 1991), and many call for the abolition of the mental health system as we know it. Anti-psychiatrists are critical of forced treatment and the institutionalization of individuals identified as mentally ill. The anti-psychiatry movement built a foundation for the mad movement, and its proponents often work with contemporary anti-psychiatrists (Burstow 2004).

The Mad Movement

Mad activists began to organize collectively in the 1980s throughout North America and Europe (Rogers and Pilgrim 2010). As people labelled mentally ill began to move out of hospitals and into the community, they were able to talk openly about their experiences of the mental health system, organize collectively, and stop relying on critical psychiatrists to speak on their behalf. Since that time, the movement has had varying platforms and priorities. The **mad movement** moves beyond the intellectual debates of the anti-psychiatrists (Dain 1989; Rogers and Pilgrim 2010) and is committed to direct action, including protests against laws allowing involuntary commitment, ECT, and forced treatment (Stroman 2003; Beresford 2005). As the movement developed, activists began running community-based mental health services such as outreach programs and crisis intervention services (Stroman 2003; Rissmiller and Rissmiller 2006). The mad movement takes up the challenge presented by the failure of deinstitutionalization to establish resources in the community and help people in distress.

Although activists define themselves in different ways, the mad movement can be loosely divided between survivors and consumers. Survivors (otherwise known as ex-patients) reject the medical model (sometimes this means rejecting psychotropic medication) and focus on user-controlled alternatives. Consumers (otherwise known as clients) find fault with, but generally accept, the medical model and try to reform the system and to include consumers in mental health decision making[1] (Burstow 2004). Although these differences may cause tension between some activists, the mad movement has a number of common goals that reflect the views of both consumers and survivors: self-determination, empowerment, using narratives, and recovery.

Self-determination entails promoting the dignity of those labelled mentally ill. Cook and Jonikas (2002, 91) define 'self-determination' as 'clients' rights to be free from all involuntary treatment; to direct their own services; to be involved in all decisions concerning their health and well-being; and to have meaningful leadership roles in the design, delivery, and evaluation of services and supports.' For mad activists, self-determination is a human right, not a privilege; it allows people to manage their own lives and well-being (Chamberlin 1990).

Empowerment is closely related to self-determination. McLean (1995) defines 'empowerment' as connecting the personal and the political by refusing to place responsibility on the individual for the social conditions that lead to a mental illness diagnosis. Empowerment can mean taking power over one's life through assertiveness, gaining self-esteem, taking an activist role, etc. (Cohen 2005). For consumers, empowerment can also mean being knowledgeable about all treatment options and making informed choices about the types of mental health services one receives (Chamberlin 1990).

Rather than relying on what psy-experts say about mental illness, the mad movement uses the narratives of individuals who are diagnosed with a mental illness to inform what they know about mental distress and to resist the dominant view of the medical model (Crossley and Crossley 2001). Using narratives allows mad activists to 're-story' (Pollack 2005) the collective experience of the mental health system, and individuals' personal understanding of their history and self-identification by validating their experiences and finding others with similar stories. Burstow and Weitz's (1988) book uses poetry, essays, and journals from psychiatric survivors/consumers to showcase the experiences of individuals in the mental health system and to fight the oppression of people labelled mentally ill.

Finally, recovery is the ultimate goal for people in the mad movement. It encompasses individual success from the personal, social, and structural impediments to mental wellness. For the mad movement, recovery may be anything from someone's changing attitudes or feelings, developing a social network, finding employment, contributing to the community, etc. (Cohen

2005). Recovery is not synonymous with a 'cure'; instead, mad activists focus on coping strategies, individual satisfaction and dignity, being functional, and having self-determination (Cook and Jonikas 2002). With these goals in mind, the mad movement adopts strategies to achieve recovery, such as receiving so- cial support, participating in social activism, hypnotherapy, self-help groups, and having good physical health (taking vitamins, proper nutrition, exercise, etc.). These tactics may be used on their own or in conjunction with psycho- tropic medication.

Conclusion

In this chapter, we have considered some of the different ways we can think about mental illness. First, we studied the creation of modern psychiatry and its links with the medical model, beginning in the nineteenth century. The medical model is built upon the principles of objectivity and scientificity, but in fact the definition of mental illness is fraught with moral and subjective judgments, as seen through an analysis of the DSM. Moreover, we looked at how the categories of gender, poverty, and race are disproportionately repre- sented in the mental health system.

When someone is diagnosed with a mental illness, there are various treat- ments endorsed by the medical model. We looked at the use of hospitalization, ECT, and the most popular form of treatment, psychotropic medication. The use of medication is so prolific that large pharmaceutical companies, known as Big Pharma, have a strong presence in economic and political issues.

The mental health system underwent an enormous transformation in the 1960s as deinstitutionalization took effect. The goal of deinstitutionalization was to provide treatment in the community so that individuals diagnosed with a mental illness could retain as many human rights and privileges as possible. In reality, however, not enough resources were relocated to the community and many former patients were left without support, sometimes leading to homelessness or involvement with the criminal justice system.

The call for rights was central to the anti-psychiatry and mad movements. The former was popularized in the 1960s by psychiatrists who were critical of their own discipline. The contemporary movement is made up of consum- ers and survivors who are also critical of the mental health system and seek alternative ways of thinking about mental illness and providing relief from distress.

From this analysis, we can reconsider the assumptions that come with the medical understanding of mental distress. Kuhn (1970) notes that there are different paradigms that inform how we come to know something. When we learn new information or look at what we know from a different perspective, we may realize that a new paradigm is necessary to make sense of what we see. There is always potential to see something differently, and we have to be critical about how we have come to know mental illness. The medical model is not the only way to explain and support people in distress. Indeed, if we are open to new ways of thinking about distress, we are likely to empower people and help those in need without using oppressive tactics.

Questions to Consider

1. What are some of the assumptions you make about people diagnosed with a mental illness? How can we combat these stereotypes?
2. Can you name alternative strategies for recovery other than the ones mentioned in this chapter (hypnotherapy, eating healthily, etc.)?
3. In your view, what impact can the mad movement have on the way we think about mental illness? What are some of the challenges the movement faces?
4. The word 'mad' in mad movement is used to reclaim the term by those who are diagnosed with a mental illness and to redefine its meaning. What do those in the mad movement mean when they say 'mad'? How is language used to resist the medical model?

Note

1. There is much disagreement about the meaning of the term 'consumer', as it suggests a sense of choice in a private system, which is not an accurate representation of the public mental health system (McLean 1995; Rogers and Pilgrim 2010).

7 Does 'The Family' Exist?

Catherine Krull

Introduction

To address the question of whether the family exists, we first need to understand what we mean by the word 'family'. The image that first springs to mind for many people is that of a legally married heterosexual male/female couple and their biological children. Despite growing family diversity in Canada, this nuclear family structure, centring on the male breadwinner/female caregiver binary, remains firmly fixed in our collective imagination as the most recognizable and most desired family form (Bibby 2004; Nelson 2006).

The assumption that the nuclear family structure is both ideal and representative of Canadian family life has been incredibly powerful. Public policies, laws, government benefits and pensions, national censuses, access to contraception and reproductive technologies, and the structuring of employment and schools have all been shaped and impacted by this hegemonic idea. As a normative rule, non-nuclear family forms become viewed as subordinate, deficient, or even flawed—terms like 'broken families', 'adoptive families', 'step-families', 'single-parent families', 'gay, lesbian, bisexual, transgendered [GLBT] families', 'voluntary non-kin families', 'childless families', and 'other-mother families' make sense only if understood in reference to the normative, nuclear ideal (Krull 2011,11). As such, Canadian family diversity is often read as a criterion of family decline and the deterioration of the institution of marriage, an interpretation of difference often used to justify and necessitate public scrutiny and surveillance. Any assessment of the condition of Canadian families necessitates an understanding of the underlying assumptions and complex legacy of the 'traditional' nuclear family.

Situating the 'Traditional' Family

Although the 'traditional' nuclear family form is often mistaken to be both timeless and universal, its pervasiveness as an ideal form is much more recent. Moreover, the idea that families have only lately undergone change is also inaccurate—'many of Canada's "new" family forms have always existed but some have done so in the margins, in the shadows, or during specific historical and economic contexts' (Albanese 2010, 5). Changes that produced the North American nuclear family began 'at different times in different classes, meant different things to families occupying different positions in the industrial order, and did not proceed in a straight line' (Coontz 2010, 39–40). Some changes—like the development of **the male breadwinner model**, which separated home and work along gender lines, and a restructuring of many households to include only the husband, wife, and their biological children—coincided with industrialization. Furthermore, it was not until the 1930s that nuclear family relationships were considered the centre of emotional bonds; before this time, emotional bonding between kin members (siblings, cousins, parents, uncles, aunts, etc.) and close same-sex friends were considered equally important.

Family change has never occurred without public reaction: 'Commentators in the 1920s hearkened back to the "good old days", bemoaning the sexual revolution, the fragility of nuclear family ties, women's "selfish" use of contraception, decline of respect for elders, the loss of extended kin ties, and the threat of the "Emancipated Woman"' (Coontz 2010, 42). Although the moral panic over 'family decline' subsided during the Depression and the Second World War, it re-emerged with a vengeance after 1945. Of primary concern were rising divorce rates, falling fertility rates due to delayed births, and the aggregate number of middle-class women in the paid workforce (Milan 2000; Saccoccio 2007). Post–Second World War government efforts, the media, and professionals did much to reinforce the idea that women's proper place was in the home as wives and mothers. Closure of government-sponsored daycares, interminable propaganda advocating that 'maternal care was the most appropriate care for children', and the appropriation of motherhood by professionals did much to reproduce the so-called natural division of labour (Luxton and Corman 2001, 48). In the late 1940s and throughout the 1950s, the average annual income of women was 50 per cent less than that of men's, despite women's higher education levels (Lowe 2006, 12). For those women who had a choice about whether to engage in paid work, low wages reinforced the idea that women's proper place was in the home. Academics were also culpable in exalting the nuclear family structure and the gendered division of labour as progressive, inevitable, and ideal (Bradbury 2000, 2005; Krull 2011). As renowned sociologists Parsons and Bales (1955) argued, 'The importance of the family and its function for society constitutes the primary set of reasons why there is a social as distinguished from purely reproductive differentiation of sex roles . . . the male adult will play the role of instrumental leader and the female adult will play the role of expressive leader' (315–41).

Canada's media was also replete with advice columns and radio talk shows instructing women how to be 'good' mothers and wives. Women could purse their own interests, according to *Chatelaine* magazine, as long as they did so in the name of motherhood: '[T]he accomplished woman should also know a little about everything, since her destiny and that of her children are tied to the fate of the world' (quoted in the Clio Collective 1987, 303; see also Spencer 2006). Television shows, such as *Leave It to Beaver* and *Father Knows Best*, also reinforced the idea of the happy well-adjusted 1950s nuclear family; in these shows, fathers were exalted as successful breadwinners and mothers applauded for having embraced their self-sacrificing role as family care-workers (Krull 2011).

Government and employment policies, influenced by the media, academics, and other professionals, were incredibly successful. The die had been cast in the public imaginary: adult men were natural breadwinners, while the modern woman was fundamentally a wife and mother. Within a few years, less than 5 per cent of Canadians believed it acceptable for mothers to be employed outside the home. Accordingly, the percentage of women remaining single dropped significantly, marriage rates soared, and the average age of marriage decreased by two years so that more than 40 per cent of women were married by their twenty-second birthday (Baker 2001, 92; Spencer 2006, 226). An unprecedented baby boom ensued and, by 1959, women were having an average of 3.9 children (Ambert 2006b, 9). Not surprisingly, the education gap between men and women dramatically increased and divorce rates plummeted to only 1 in 20 marriages (Owram 1999; Milan 2000). As domesticity and consumerism sky-rocketed, there was for many a sense of stability and a renewed faith in family life, all of which diminished the earlier perceived threats of family decline (Lowe 2006).

Not surprisingly, the 1950s have been discursively constructed as the golden era of the traditional family. However, the relative stability and optimism of this decade was anomalous, aggrandized over the ensuing years, and certainly not experienced by all Canadian families; gross inequities existed across racial, class, religious, age, sexuality, (dis)ability, and gender lines. The adversity suffered by many families often occurred in silence, which only marginalized them further (Luxton and Corman 2001, 40). Knowledge or suspicion of an individual being gay were grounds for firing, many public schools segregated African Canadians, and concerted government efforts were aimed at rupturing Aboriginal families. But marginalized groups were not alone in being negatively affected by the privileging of the nuclear family model. Difficulties experienced within many middle-class nuclear families were obscured because it was simply not conceivable that ideal families could suffer from 'alcoholism, substance abuse, spousal abuse, child abuse, poverty, mental illness, stress and marital problems. . . . But, at the time . . . airing dirty laundry was considered shameful' (Lowe 2006). And since family matters were private, many struggled with problems in silence. This was particularly true for women who, because of their subordinate status within families, restricted access to resources, and isolation in their homes, were cut off from any potential support from friends and the community. Moreover, accompanying a 'superficial glorification and institutionalization of middle-class mothering' was an intense moral regulation of women (Albanese 2010, 11). Overshadowing the 1950s was the insecurity fostered by the advent of the Cold War and the polio epidemic—for the latter, there was no universal health care or vaccine;[1] polio not only killed or disabled many children, it left numerous families financially stricken (Lowe 2006, 4).

Legacy of Privileging the Nuclear Family

Despite evidence to the contrary, the 1950s continue to be referred to as the 'golden age' of the family: 'During a period of social insecurity and disruption, arguments supporting plurality can easily appear to promise chaos while those calling for a return to the 'traditional family', however mythical it may be, appear to promise stability and security' (Luxton 1997, 11). Neo-conservative narratives bemoaning family decline and advocating a return to traditional family values have infused Canadian politics for some time. Proponents of this view argue that the rise in divorce, single parenthood, cohabitation, same-sex marriage, and feminism, coupled with rising individualism and weakening religiosity, are responsible for eroding family values and placing children at risk (Walker 2003, 407). The rhetoric of strengthening nuclear families and the traditional values of marriage was the foundation of the Family Coalition Party's platform in the 2007 Ontario provincial election, which ran a record number of candidates in 83 electoral districts and won more than 35,000 votes. Likewise, Alberta's previous minister of finance and enterprise and former political science professor, Ted Morton, tried but failed to pass Bill 208, which sought to prevent human rights complaints against teachers and marriage commissioners who do not accept gay marriage (McLean 2010, 2006). Morton also maintains that 'social scientists are finally recognizing the social and economic value of the traditional family and the moral infrastructure that it helps to sustain' (Morton 1998).

Idealizing the traditional nuclear family in this way reinforces the fallacy that families operate as independent, self-contained units that satisfy the needs of their members and is ideally suited for raising children. The evidence, however, is to the contrary. Paid work by both parents is a necessity and not a choice for most two-parent families. As such, the majority (85 per cent) of parents are employed and non-family members are often involved in child-care (Hansen 2005; Iacovetta 2006; Vanier Institute of the Family 2010d). Furthermore, marriage does not guarantee stability, as evidenced by high Canadian divorce rates (Le Bourdais and Lapierre-Adamcyk 2004, 937–8), and healthy adjusted children are just as likely to be found in non-nuclear families (Smart and Neale 1999; Walker 2003; Strohschein 2007). Privileging the nu-clear family also places a higher value on children who are genetically related to their parents, which explains a booming reproductive services industry de-spite numerous Canadian children waiting to be adopted; adoption is clearly viewed as an 'inferior way of forming a family' (Satz 2007, 525).

Contrary to research demonstrating that marriage, mothering, and fath-ering have dissimilar meanings for different communities and, as such, are highly contested categories (Smith 1987; Collins 2000, 1990; Das Gupta 2000; Baines 2004; Nelson 2006; Baines and Freeman, 2011), non-normative Canadian families continue to be scrutinized and even penalized. The history of residential schools, the **Sixties Scoop**,[2] and existing child welfare practi-ces are but three examples of colonial and paternalistic government initiatives intended to force conformity that resulted in ravaging Aboriginal families, communities, and cultures (Das Gupta 2000; Krull 2006; Baines and Freeman 2011). Recently, the federal government admitted its culpability: 'We now rec-ognize that, in separating children from their families, we undermined the ability of many to adequately parent their own children and sowed the seeds for generations to follow. . . . The government of Canada sincerely apologizes and asks the forgiveness of aboriginal peoples for failing them so badly' (Prime Minister Stephen Harper, quoted in Curry and Galloway 2008, A1). Despite such apologies, federal policies undermining Aboriginal families continue, evidenced by a child welfare system in which approximately 40 per cent of foster children are Aboriginal—more than 8,000 Aboriginal children (about 5 per cent of all Aboriginal children) have been removed from their homes across Canada (Canadian Press 2008; Krull 2010). And the state not only inter-feres with how certain parents care, teach, and safeguard their children; it also determines who legitimately belongs to a family. Even after liberal changes to Canada's immigration policies, the nuclear family model continues to be used as a standard in deciding which family members can immigrate to Canada.

Although Ottawa has been involved in family life for more than a century, only a fragmentary set of programs and policies exists, rather than a com-prehensive national family policy. The state has tended to limit its involve-ment primarily to situations of child abuse, child neglect, and limited family financial resources; and even in these situations, intervention has varied by gender and across different income and cultural/ethnic groups (Baker 2010). The constitutional impediment to developing a cohesive national family policy is that different levels of government—federal, provincial, and territorial—have assumed different responsibilities. Ottawa focuses primarily on income support, while provincial and territorial governments primarily concentrate on welfare assistance, child protection, and other services, all resulting in significant regional variations (O'Hara 1998; Krull 2010). Embracing a neo-liberal agenda that individualizes family/work pressures and difficulties, the different levels of government have typically relied on surveillance techniques to identify those who are deserving of state support. Child welfare and child care benefits are cases in point. Little (2011) argues that in blaming adults for poverty and unemployment, the neo-liberal state has 'embraced a discourse calling for the alleviation of the child poverty and promoting social policy that separates children's needs from that of their parents. . . . Poor mothers are raising poor children, and it is the mothers' poverty that must first be addressed . . . not increased surveillance mechanisms for poor mothers' (203–4). It is not surprising that poverty rates remain high despite an aggressive national campaign to eradicate child poverty (Krull 2010). Clearly, neo-liberal agendas tend to privilege nuclear families, particularly white middle-class two-parent ones, while targeting and even penalizing non-normative families.

Canada's Family Diversity

The ideal nuclear family form not only has had dire consequences for many Canadians; it also does not reflect how most Canadians live as families. Only 17 per cent of all census families[3] were classified as nuclear families in 2006 (Statistics Canada 2007), which corroborates observations from the Vanier Institute of the Family: 'Even when you look at families today, who may on the surface have the appearance of looking like those stereotypical, traditional families of the past, there's probably many, many ways in which those families are quite different' (Canadian Press 2007). The institution of marriage has also become less prevalent. Whereas married-couple families comprised 80 per cent of all family forms 20 years ago, they only account for 69 per cent today; similarly, the percentage of common-law couple families has increased from 7 per cent to over 15 per cent (Statistics Canada 2007). And even when the 2005 Civil Marriage Act (Bill C-38) was passed, legalizing same-sex marriage, only 17 per cent of same-sex Canadian couples opted to marry (Statistics Canada 2007). Not only are there fewer marriages, particularly in Quebec,[4] but marriages no longer endure as they once did. Approximately 38 per cent of marriages are terminated by the thirtieth wedding anniversary, while the percentage of repeat divorces—people divorcing two or more times—has tripled in the past three decades (Statistics Canada 2005).

Given the waning popularity of marriage and the wider acceptance of divorce, the percentage of children living with married parents in the same household has significantly decreased over 20 years—from about 81 to 66 per cent—and the number of lone-parent households, especially female-headed ones, has been steadily rising. Additionally, the number of lone parents never legally married grew exponentially between 1950 and 2006: from 2 to 30 per cent (Statistics Canada 2005). Stepfamilies have also changed. In the past, they typically resulted when one spouse died and the other remarried; today, stepfamilies generally result from remarriage following a divorce or the dissolution of a common-law union. In Canada, stepfamilies account for 12 per cent of all couple families with children, and 46 per cent of these are blended families, which include at least one child from one or both previous unions and one child from the present relationship (Vanier Institute of the Family 2010b). Adding to family diversity is the significant increase in education levels: one-half (Vanier Institute of the Family 2010c, 7) of Canadians between 25 and 64 years have either college or university education. As such, young adults leave home, marry, or cohabit and have children at a later age. Increased education levels have also altered gender roles in both the home and the workplace (Vanier Institute of the Family 2010c, 7).

Concurrently, the birth rate has decreased by more than 50 per cent and the average number of children per woman has dropped to well below the requisite 2.2 for population replacement (Lowe 2006, 3). For the first time in Canada, more families are composed of couples without children than those with children—43 and 41 per cent, respectively. Paradoxically, children live with their parent(s) much longer, often into their twenties (Turcotte 2006), and the transition to adulthood is taking longer to complete (Clark 2007). And it is not just that Canadians are opting to have fewer or no children. How they can become parents has also radically changed as surrogacy, sperm banks, in vitro fertilization, transnational and trans-racial adoption, and implanting frozen embryos have become more commonplace.[5] Moreover, how Canadians parent is also changing. According to the Vanier Institute of the Family (2010d, 8), '[T]he division of labour in parenting has become a more complex process with more role ambiguity, more emphasis on negotiation of roles, and more fluidity in the way that parents respond to the demands of everyday life.' Fathers have become much more involved in doing care-work for their children (Doucet 2011, 2006a, 2006b, 2004). Between 2001 and 2006, the percentage of fathers taking parental leave from their paid work increased from 38 to

55 per cent (Statistics Canada 2007); and between 1986 and 2005, the percentage of men reporting that they did some housework increased from 54 to 69 per cent—although among women, it is 90 per cent (Statistics Canada 2006c).

Thirty per cent of women and 22 per cent of men also do some form of eldercare and, given that disability has been increasing, related to an aging population, the number of Canadians doing elder care is expected to rise (Statistics Canada 2006c). Yet, younger family members caring for senior family members is less prevalent than the reverse situation (McDaniel 1997, 2003; Rozanova, Northcott, and McDaniel 2006; Mandell and Wilson 2011). Multi-generational bonds have become an increasingly important resource to many Canadian families, perhaps 'more important than nuclear family ties for well-being and support' (Bengtson 2001, 5; see also Collins 2005; McDaniel 2001, 2002, 2008; Pahl and Spencer 2004; Roseneil and Budgeon 2004; Stacey 1996, 2004). Approximately 6.3 million grandparents reside in Canada. Of these, almost one-half are under the age of 65, and many are still employed; the majority provide valuable assistance—both financial and care-work—to their families (Vanier Institute of the Family 2008). Skip-generation households are also becoming commonplace: more than 56,000 Canadian grandparents, two-thirds of whom are grandmothers, are the primary caregivers of their grandchildren (Statistics Canada 2004a) and approximately 44 per cent of Aboriginal grandparents are involved in raising grandchildren (Baines and Freeman 2011).

Created families or **fictive kin relationships** are also becoming important as families are progressively separated by geographic distance. Created families function in ways similar to many other families in terms of caring and supporting one another. The major difference is that fictive kin are chosen: '[T]hey are free of many of the more formal role prescriptions which govern families relations' (de Vries 2010; cf. Maupin 2007, 3, who distinguishes between 'logical families' and 'biological procreative families'). Although more Canadians are choosing to live within created families, family sociologists warn that using the language of 'family' to define and legitimize these alternative social units might obscure their uniqueness and importance (de Vries 2010).

The more than 200 ethnic groups in Canada have also contributed to the multitude of ways in which we live as families. Approximately one in five Canadians is foreign-born, the highest proportion reported in 75 years (Statistics Canada 2008). As the permeability of national boundaries has increased due to globalization and transnationalism, families divided by borders have become common, although their transnational experiences varies by gender, age, ethnicity, country of origin, and occupational class (Dreby 2006; Krull 2011). For instance, one study found that transnational Chinese families in Vancouver exemplified how 'social relationships can operate over significant distance, spanning national borders, and reducing the importance of face-to-face context in personal interaction' (Waters 2002, 118). However, this is not the case for all transnational families. In comparison to non-immigrants, immigrants are more likely to earn significantly lower incomes and have difficulty finding employment and housing (Lowe 2006, 6). In responding to global market demands for low-wage female domestic and service labour, numerous women from developing countries have left their families to take on low-pay domestic work abroad. The consequence has been new forms of marginality (Young 2001; Lan 2003; Dreby 2006; Krull 2006), an international division of gendered reproductive labour (Salazar Parreñas 2005, 2008), and new mothering arrangements as these workers try to care for their own families from a distance (Hondagneu-Sotelo 2007; Mandell and Wilson 2011). Clearly, care-work remains 'gendered, raced, and classed in its norms and expectations, in its involvement and intensity, in the relationship of caregivers to care recipients, and in its effects on individuals and social arrangements' (Mandell and Wilson 2011, 30).

Modifications in market work have affected Canadians differently. The male breadwinner–family wage model of 48 hours for 48 weeks for 48 years, often associated with the ideal nuclear family, no longer reflects the majority of paid-market work (Siltanen and Doucet 2008, 98). Whereas 67 per cent of 1950s family households had a single earner, only 14.4 per cent have one today (Lowe 2006; Vanier Institute of the Family 2010d: 5). Globalization has changed the kinds of jobs and sectors in which Canadians work. A growing number of Canadians are also working in part-time, temporary, or self-employed jobs that offer low pay, little or no job security, and few benefits. Intensifying pre-existing employment inequalities, most of these jobs are held by women, who make up almost 75 per cent of the part-time workforce: more than 60 per cent in part-time or part-time self-employment and approximately 70 per cent of part-time shift work (Siltanen and Doucet 2008, 98; Vanier Institute of the Family 2010e, 1). Shift workers also 'report lower levels of satisfaction with their work–life balance than regular nine-to-five day workers and are more likely to report role overload—that is, having too much to do and not enough time to do it' (Vanier Institute 2010e, 1). Women remain overrepresented in certain occupations, have fewer opportunities but more workforce constraints, receive less pay than men in all occupations, and remain responsible for the majority of unpaid household and family care-work (Siltanen and Doucet 2008, 105; Baker 2010; Bezanson 2010; Vanier Institute 2010e; Mandell and Wilson 2011;).

Since 2008, Canada has been experiencing the 'great recession', which has further entrenched inequalities and family conflict by differentially impacting families as well as individual family members (Bezanson 2010; Duffy and Pupo

2011). One-half of the alarming 486,000 job losses between October 2008 and July 2009 were suffered by young people between ages 15–24; men aged 25–54 lost twice as many jobs as women in this age group (Tipper and Sauvé 2010, 2) primarily because of a marked decline in demand for manufactured and industrial products, particularly in the automobile-related sectors (Bezanson 2010, 9). Many of these jobs have been replaced by 'jobs with poor characteristics', precarious part-time and temporary work filled mostly by women (Duffy and Pupo 2011, 101). By the end of the third quarter in 2009, average household debt to income ratio increased to an unprecedented 145 percent, and the average household debt reached $96,100 (Tipper and Sauvé 2010, 2). Of course, some families are experiencing these burdens more intensely than others: 59 per cent of employed Canadians would have trouble making ends meet if their paycheque was delayed even one week (Tipper and Sauvé 2010, 4). Critiquing neoliberalism—Canada's economic response to this crisis—the argument is that

> the great recession, then, creates a crises in social reproduction for families who must find new ways to respond at the household level to the varied needs of members, often without adequate resources. . . . These crises—which ultimately affect our collective social and human capacities and capabilities . . . have left families increasingly vulnerable (Bezanson 2010, 6–7).

Neo-liberalism has disproportionately affected women, especially those marginalized and/or most dependent on the state, such as low-income mothers (Little 2011, 199). The great recession has substantially exacerbated the disparity between families in poverty and those with resources; indeed, the richest 20 per cent of Canadians took home 44.2 per cent of total after-tax income, whereas the poorest 20 per cent's share was only 4.9 per cent (Canadian Center for Policy Alternatives 2011; cf. Sauvé 2011). Also telling is the 86 per cent increase in the number of Canadians using food banks (Canadian Council on Social Development 2008, 6).

More positively, the new economy is facilitating a trend 'toward gender convergence' in both paid work and care-work. As already noted, women have for some time taken on greater economic responsibilities and, more recently, men are becoming more involved in domestic and care-work. The 'traditional patriarchal male—the boss, breadwinner, and head of the household—will likely find difficulty in fitting into either the new economy or emergent families and communities' (Duffy and Pupo 2011, 112). Some scholars predict that young adult men may even become more involved in their families and communities and less committed to their employment given this climate of employment insecurity (Rubin and Brody 2005; Duffy and Pupo 2011).

Conclusion: Families Exist and They Still Matter

Families exist and they matter; and, importantly, there is just not one kind of family—that reflecting the supposed golden ideal of the 1950s. If Canadians today are asked what 'the family' is, there would be as many responses as people asked. The reason is simple: how we understand family is how we experience it. While agreeing that a typical family is mythical, the majority of Canadians also maintain that family is the most important thing in their lives; moreover, they prefer to live as families. What has changed in the past half-century is the multitude of ways that Canadians understand the meaning of this institution. However, there tends to be an incongruity between personal experiential understandings and the ideal traditional nuclear family so deeply rooted in culture and memory. In the end, family cannot be defined by who belongs to it but, rather, by what it does.

Family diversity does not necessarily imply choice. One does not choose to be an impoverished single mother or traverse the obstacles that immigrant families often experience. Of course, choices about how we live as families do exist; many people can choose with whom to cohabit or marry, whether to have a child as a married or single parent, whether to move to a different country, and more. Class, ethnicity, age, education, gender, sexuality, support networks, geographic region, access to resources, and other factors determine and shape our choices. While the nuclear family still prevails in the public imaginary as the ideal form—despite growing diversity in how Canadians choose to live as families—the concomitant deinstitutionalization of marriage and the tendency of Canadians to move in and out of different family forms throughout their lifetime indicates that the links between traditional and non-traditional families are fluid, not closed.

Moreover, the perception that work and family are incompatible spheres that need to be reconciled or balanced is premised on the male breadwinner/female homemaker traditional family model (Krull 2011). Opting for one or the other part of the equation speaks to the dilemma of 'choice' between professional employment and family; a long-familiar frustration is that both cannot be done well or can only be accomplished with the most skillful of balancing acts. Many conceptions within family and work literature—reconciliation, balance, conflict, integration—begin with the notion of a division in need of reconciliation. 'Choice' presumes equality, leaving socially generated inequality obscured. Despite the multiplicity of family types, workplaces, and political institutions today, the traditional family model persists, reinforcing the widely accepted conception of separate family and work spheres. Not surprisingly, for some time the household work/paid work dichotomy has produced feminist critiques centring on the dearth of effectual government policies facilitating family care work with the economy of employment.

Thus, families need better government support; but Canadian family policies have not only been in short supply, they also have not adapted to the changes that have taken place over the past few decades. Parents, especially women, do not need direction on how to balance work and family; they need options that increase their choices so they do not have to choose between family care-work and paid work. Policies that aid all parents in incorporating family and work are essential. Alternatively, we can continue denying, resisting, displacing, and holding to a singular ideology of the family by not providing social and economic conditions that make life for diverse contemporary families viable, let alone dignified and secure. The rest of Canada can learn from Quebec, which has taken the lead in terms of implementing comprehensive family policies geared toward assisting parents in balancing paid work and family responsibilities, promoting parental employability, and reducing poverty—such as its universal, inexpensive 24/7 childcare program, and the 2004 Act to Combat Poverty and Social Exclusion. As a result, Quebec's child poverty has decreased by 50 per cent, children's test scores have improved, and the province now boasts the highest percentage of mothers who are in the workforce (Canadian Council on Social Development 2008; CUPE Ontario 2008; Krull 2010). While Quebec's family policies remain the most innovative and ambitious in the country and provide North America's only example of an integrated approach to family policy, the rest of Canada has yet to even develop a comprehensive poverty reduction plan.

There needs to be an acceptance of the fact that families are crucially important to Canadians, but also that families are varied as social units and that their survival is connected intimately to the economy and workplace. In other words, the family cannot be defined by who belongs to it but, rather, by what it does. How Canadian society understands this situation and responds to the dissimilar needs, strengths, opportunities, and challenges confronting families must be at the forefront as we move through the twenty-first century.

Questions to Consider

1. Why has the concept of the 'traditional' nuclear family been so pervasive in Canada since the 1950s? What implications has this had on gender equity? On family policy? On marginalized families?

2. Neo-liberals argue that the rise in divorce, single parenthood, same-sex marriage, cohabitation, and feminism, coupled with increasing individualism and a weakening in religiosity, are responsible for eroding family values and placing children at risk. Discuss.

3. What is problematic with the notion that family care-work and market work have to be balanced? How does the concept of 'work-life balance' fit with a neo-liberal agenda?

4. In what ways should the state be involved in our families? Why is it problematic for anti-poverty campaigns and policies to focus primarily on eradicating child poverty?

5. What value lies in having a variety and diversity of families in Canada?

Notes

1. Hospital insurance and the Diagnostic Services Act appeared in 1957, but it was not until 1966 that universal health care via the Medical Care Act was created (Lowe 2006, 5). The polio vaccine, government-issued by the late 1950s, was not readily accessible to the public until 1962, when the Sabin vaccine became licensed in Canada (Rutty 2002).

2. The Sixties Scoop was a government initiative that involved child welfare authorities taking Aboriginal children from their homes, communities, and cultures—without permission and often forcibly—and adopting or fostering them out to primarily non-Aboriginal families.

3. A census family is composed of 'a married couple or a common-law couple, with or without children, or of a lone parent living with at least one child in the same dwelling. A couple can be of the opposite sex or of the same sex' (Statistics Canada 2007, 10).

4. Quebec also has the highest cohabitation rates in the country; approximately 30 per cent of all couples live common-law compared to 12 per cent in the rest of Canada (Statistics Canada 2007b).

5. Access to the array of reproductive choices differs across gender, class, sexuality, age, and race (Davis 2001; Bartholet 2005; Fogg-Davis 2005; Roberts 2005; see also the edited volume by Haslanger and Witt 2005). Moreover, reproductive technologies have been used primarily to reproduce normative understandings of family rather than to radicalize them (Throsby and Gill 2004; Baker 2005; Cornell 2005; Haslanger 2005; Spar 2006; Satz 2007).

PART II

Imagining the Social

Part II shifts the focus of our discussion from examinations of self-identity to concerns around the concept of the 'social'. Recall that the term 'social' refers to a subject terrain that emerges when we focus directly on collective relations in and of themselves—without reducing this terrain to individual or psychological matters. More specifically, the essays in this part question what that social may be, offer suggestions on how to address it (as well as why it is important to do so), and examine the concept's contemporary relevance.

In the opening chapter, Annette Burfoot responds to the question 'What is social reality?' She immediately rejects the idea of social reality as something stable, fixed, or absolute, arguing instead that it is a dynamic, shifting set of cultural constructions. These constructions materialize only because of context-specific cultural meanings, and so the idea of social reality is best understood through an analysis of culture. Thus she focuses on cultural studies as 'a relatively recent approach in sociology that both enriches and exposes what we understand as social reality and how we define it.' To understand how culture produces social realities, Burfoot suggests that we tap into insights gained from the ways in which the discipline of cultural studies has developed over time. She highlights its focus on culture, cultural products, and cultural production, which it approaches through various theoretical perspectives, including psychoanalysis, ideology ('the socio-political organization of ideas'), semiology ('the study of signs and symbols'), and discourse analysis ('the illumination of how meaning-as-power flows through our taken-for-granted parlance or way of speaking'). Each of these approaches throws a different light on the cultural creation of social reality.

Chapter 9, 'What's "New" about the New Media Landscape?' asks important questions about media in Canada and the rest of the world. Daniel Downes describes a shift during the past 25 years from old to new media. Old media is characterized as coming from a single source (a newspaper publisher for instance) and delivering singular-focus content with the aim of creating a common experience among its audience. One of the main features of old media is that the direction of communication moved from media outlets (governments and corporations) to a mass audience that did not interact with or control the media's content or form. Old media was also concerned with communicating middle-class values to its audience. As technology, industry (for instance, phone and television cabling), and regulations developed and converged, old media shifted to new, characterized as digital and interactive. With the invention of the Internet and social-networking tools such as Facebook and Twitter, media 'users'—members of the public—are able to take a much more active role in media, shaping both its content and form. New media targets a much more diverse and fragmented global audience. And precisely because new media content is created by anyone who posts a blog or contributes to an Internet site, new media sources are less professional and authoritative than old media. Concerns about the negative influence of the media on attitudes and behaviours continue to be voiced and debated. Whereas society was concerned about young people sitting with strangers in a darkened movie theatre in the 1930s, today the concern is about young people's access to uncensored material on the Internet. Sociologists are interested in the dramatic shift from old to new media and its implications for social structures and relations.

In Chapter 10, R.A. Sydie addresses the perception that social theory is 'abstract, difficult, and of dubious relevance to everyday life'. In responding to the question 'Is social theory useful?' Sydie begins by noting that early social theorists (e.g., Martineau, Durkheim) formulated theories about the 'personal troubles' as well as the societies of the time. They did so with the aim of developing harmonious and peaceful social formations. Their theories served this aim, not as irrelevant abstractions but rather as direct explanations of everyday practices designed to point the way toward better relations with others. Yet we all theorize whenever we try to make sense of our practices. What distinguishes sociological from everyday theorizing, however, is its commitment to critique. Sociological theory is useful because it raises basic questions about the very foundations of everyday social relations, and it does so with the aim of undoing specified negative (unjust, unequal, tyrannical, etc.) conditions. Theorizing demands a self-questioning social theorist who understands the precariousness of being simultaneously creator and creature of the social relations criticized. With this in mind, Sydie explores how various modern social theorists developed universal explanations of 'order and progress' when offering theories of modern society. She examines how current (postmodern) conditions have undermined modern social theory, including its emphasis on homogeneous, universalizing images of progress, knowledge, and society. This undermining has demanded new approaches to the concept of society—to address the challenges that racial, ethnic, cultural, social class, age, ability, sexuality, and gender diversity bring to the assumption of a national identity, for example—and opened the way for new forms of social theorizing. However, Sydie is clear: 'The important point that should guide the social theorist if she is to play a useful and important role as a public intellectual is that she should not simply diagnose the critical issues of our time but also offer a critique and thus reveal the way in which personal troubles are public issues.'

'Does the past matter in sociology?' Rob Beamish asks in the next chapter. His formulation of C. Wright Mills' sociological imagination takes as a starting point the personal troubles that Canadian sprinter Ben Johnson faced by having his Olympic gold medal stripped away because of steroid use. Beamish then locates this event within the wider social history of the Olympic Games to reflect on the powerful social pressures that Johnson faced when deciding to take steroids. This historical approach to sociology demonstrates just how complex the issues surrounding performance-enhancing substances are at the level of world-class sport; it also challenges the simplistic condemnation of individual athletes. Specifically, this chapter makes clear that without a lucid historical sense of the development of the Olympic Games, many important social factors that led to Johnson's personal troubles would be overlooked. For example, Beamish's analysis shows how such issues as increasing commercialization and professionalization have significantly eroded Olympics founder Coubertin's vision of the games as an arena for amateur sport. Further, the Nazis confirmed the political, symbolic, and propagandistic utility of the games in 1936, a facet of the Olympics that continued to be developed and exploited throughout the Cold War. Such historical developments shed light on the kind of broader pressures imposed on athletes to perform. In this context, we can better understand Johnson's decision to use a performance-enhancing substance. That is, his biography and problems are located within a wider social history that generates demands on athletes quite at odds with the fraternal public image of the Olympic Games. And it is precisely because the past matters in sociology that we can provide a macro-analysis of such micro issues.

In Chapter 12, Nob Doran responds to the question 'What do official statistics tell us about ourselves?' He does so by narrating his own intellectual journey through various social theories used to examine the status of official statistics. The chapter expressly challenges the common-sense view that official statistics provide an objective, impartial representation of different aspects of society. It outlines two levels of critique directed at this view. On a micro level, Doran describes how ethnomethodological approaches in sociology alerted him to the subjective, everyday decisions that statistical researchers must inevitably make when creating statistics, especially the founding categories (e.g., suicides, homicides) to which purportedly impartial statistical methods are directed. Rather than leading sociologists to accept social statistics as impartial knowledge, this approach directs them to examine the everyday social relations that produce particular statistics. Doran argues that Dorothy Smith's feminism and Marxism-inspired formulations improve on this approach by adopting a more macro perspective and focusing explicitly on how power creates official social statistics. Doran further argues that part of this power includes the experiences an individual has in her or his life—experiences shaped by societal structures such as the uneven division of labour and racialization—that influence how individuals 'decode' texts.

As Lois Harder makes clear in Chapter 13, despite a vocal minority's criticisms of the welfare state, Canadians continue to demand publicly funded social programs and to assess governments partly on their ability to provide effective social services. In effect, they have responded in the affirmative to the question 'Is social welfare viable?' However, she argues, this endorsement does not capture several important recent changes to the very idea of social welfare as well as its provision. Harder outlines the unique history of social welfare in Canada before turning her attention to the attack on Keynesian social welfare precepts that emerged in the 1980s (especially in the area of social assistance), launched by groups aligned with a neo-liberal ideology. This assault was mounted from within a rapidly changing socio-economic context and alongside a protracted constitutional crisis. Advocates of neo-liberal thinking sought to reduce the state's role in regulating markets, families, and communities and called for a thriving private sphere. When directed toward social welfare, this approach called for a system overhaul that emphasized private (consumer) 'choice' and 'responsibility'. Harder highlights how such thinking helped to bring about significant changes in social welfare: policies such as the National Child Benefit show the extent to which social welfare is directly involved in shaping individual and social identities, 'integrating citizens into the prevailing mode of economic production', and legitimating particular forms of government. These policies indicate that the viability of any vision of social welfare (whether Keynesian, neo-liberal, or otherwise) is dependent on how it reinforces social relations between individuals, families, markets, and the state.

In the final chapter in Part 2, 'Who Governs Whom in Canada?', Dawn Moore addresses one of the book's recurring themes: governance—or the ways in which people's thoughts and actions are part and parcel of the ways in which they are controlled and governed. The chapter recognizes that we are all governed by a complex interface of formal, informal, local, and general control techniques. These techniques include 'formal laws and rules, social conventions, guidelines, suggestions, timetables, family obligations, our expectations of ourselves, nature, and so on.' Much of the chapter is devoted to a careful examination of specific examples of governing in the Canadian context. For instance, Moore examines the case of Robert Latimer, convicted of murdering his 12-year-old daughter, who had a serious disability. She contrasts the formal law governing this action (first-degree murder) in the Criminal Code of Canada with the conflicting social conventions around morality—specifically, the right to die because of prolonged suffering versus the right to life independent of the quality of that life. Moore's examination demonstrates the limits of Durkheim's 'collective conscience' theory as a way of understanding how our society is regulated. Through other examples, including various legal cases, the chapter elaborates upon and develops the sociology of governance.

Questions for Reflection

1. Do different cultures co-exist within Canadian society? If so, how?

2. To what extent do you think Canadian norms about appropriate behavior are middle-class norms?

3. To what extent do you think individuals are held responsible for societal norms?

8 | What Is Social Reality?

Annette Burfoot

Introduction

Since the inception of sociology, the question of what is real in the social world has both excited and hampered the study of society and the meaning of social relations. Émile Durkheim (1952 [1897]) sought statistical ways of identifying, measuring, and predicting social 'realities' such as one's matrimonial state and its effect on suicide rates. C. Wright Mills (1959) with his 'sociological imagination', established a link between personal problems (like losing your job and feeling very depressed as a result) and social or more widespread issues (for example, an economic recession or socio-technical change). In both cases, the question of what constitutes social reality is fundamental.

For Durkheim, there appeared to be some relationship (a positive correlation) between men being married and lower suicide rates. Is it then a social fact that in order to be happy as a male in our society you need to be heterosexual and married? Today many challenge such assumptions as social facts. We also look at society from more varied perspectives, including perspectives that generate different social realities by asking different questions based on different assumptions. So the reality of higher than average suicide rates among young homosexual males may be presented more along the lines of Mills' sociological imagination as an individual anguish that results not from a failure to meet heterosexual norms but as a result of widespread homophobia. The facts have changed; social reality has shifted. And how has that happened?

This is where a sociological analysis of **culture** can add to the mix because it gives us even more avenues to explore rather than unearthing new social facts along the same old paths, such as Marx's structural paradigm based on predictable class formation and a critique of capitalism as a relatively steady state. We can question how social realities are constructed beyond a structural and scientific model of exploration, reporting, and experimentation of social facts (as if they were fixed things); we thus engage in the critical study of complex socio-cultural relations that generate social facts through dynamic and fluid processes. In this chapter, we will examine **cultural studies** as a relatively recent approach in sociology that both enriches and exposes what we understand as social reality and how we define it. We will first examine cultural studies through the history of the sociological study of culture since there have been important changes and fiery disputes as to what constitutes cultural studies itself. Several key arguments continue today, and we will see that, rather than weaken the field, as some argue, they enrich it as well as the discipline of sociology. We will conclude with the state of cultural studies today with particular attention to what is happening here in Canada.

Back to the Future: Cultural Studies from the Sociology of Culture

It might seem logical to approach a history of cultural studies from 'the start', normally situated in the late nineteenth century, when culture became the subject of philosophical and political debate. However, we shall start with the most recent approaches and work our way back. This strategy will move us from the material with which we have the most experience to material that may be more difficult to grasp or locate in experience. It will also help to explain how we arrived at the current situation. What follows begins by looking at several important trends—namely, trends that engage concepts and issues of social marginalization in culture. We then move to the establishment of cultural studies as one of the first and most successful interdisciplinary studies in contemporary academia. This leads us to the early youth studies and popular culture studies in the UK that helped to establish the Centre for Cultural studies at the University of Birmingham. We will examine how current cultural studies arose from approaches (theoretical and methodological) established by the Birmingham school and has been developed by its critics. Current theories and methods serving cultural studies, such as discourse analysis, material culture, and visual culture (to name just a few) also emanate from well-established subdisciplines, including many sociological ones.

A good deal of attention has been paid to the study of the culture generating and surrounding hip hop (Rose 1994; Potter 1995; George 1998). This music genre, perhaps more than any other, illustrates the problems of producing culture from the margins, a social location that is typically understood as the space farthest away from the site of political control (or the ideological centre). In the case of hip hop, poor urban black kids from the streets of various New Jersey cities began a form of musical ballad that combined chanting, singing, and lecturing in a street-like dialect familiar to their specific lifestyles and experiences. It also had a particular look that included oversized jeans intentionally worn provocatively low-slung and unhemmed, the material constantly dragged and torn, thus literally taking apart the then-current designer-jeans couture. The hip-hop look also included status-seeking emblems such as chains, some golden, with diamante-encrusted logos, often stolen from high-end luxury cars like the Mercedes. Lyrics spoke, and continue to speak today, directly to young black men about the oppression of blacks in the United States and often evoke a frustrated and militant response to this oppression. 'Gangsta rap' is a subgenre of the musical form that illustrates this well as a true gangsta not only wears the deed of having killed someone as a badge of honour but also lives the result of continued police and other forms of racial harassment. Such experiences of alienation have also been exported outside the North American context to Africa. In a study of the popularity of Tupac Shakur, an American hip-hop musician slain by another, Jeremy Prestholdt (2009) finds that young men and boys caught up in the brutal civil war in Sierra Leone identify with the artist, which helps them to alleviate their particular traumas.

In tandem with rebellious lyrics, the hip-hop look was meant to alienate, parody, and criticize a dominant white culture while advancing a raw new street-based black one. It was a cultural practice from the margins. Logos were taken by the artists and their fans, often in rampant shoplifting, from prestigious designers such as Hilfiger, Polo, DKNY, and Nike to feed the hip-hop look. Then something else happened. Designers realized the profit potential of their logos appearing in a cultural venue that was being picked up and mass marketed as an exciting new sound and look to all of the United States and beyond, not just to black communities in the US northeast. Rappers who triggered the trend in the 1980s also started what Naomi Klein calls 'cool hunting' or logo appropriation (Klein 2000). For example, in 1986 the rap group Run-DMC featured their favourite brand in the song 'My Adidas' (rap is commonly understood as the cultural precursor of hip hop). Now consider what happened when—initially reluctant to sponsor the group since rap was then seen as culturally insignificant in the popular music world and politically problematic because of its militant message and blatant criticism of the dominant culture—Adidas executives attended a Run-DMC concert:

> At a crucial moment, while the rap group was performing the song ['My Adidas'], one of the members yelled out, 'Okay, everybody in the house, rock your Adidas!'—and three thousand sneakers shot in the air. The Adidas executives couldn't reach for their checkbooks fast enough. (Christopher Vaughn, quoted in Klein 2000, 74)

Pilfering from the apparent dominant culture in the form of logo appropriation was then 'blown up' by hip hop during the late 1990s and the early years of the new millennium. But as Klein points out, the companies whose logos are 'hunted' and displayed in now highly popular hip-hop videos and concerts enjoy a very profitable return in this newly defined youth market. Designers for companies such as Nike appropriate the appropriated look, reproduce it on a massive scale, and sell it back to the communities that created the look. Is this a successful cultural production from the margins, or is it cultural appropriation for profit?

Rinaldo Walcott (2000), a Canadian academic concerned with black culture in Canada, raises another issue associated with racialization and music—namely, national identity. He examines the Canadian rapper Devon (Devon Martin) and his 1989 album *It's My Nature* as an example of a common ground marked by racialization of blacks beyond national boundaries. Walcott describes this territory in terms of Devon's open criticism of the Los Angeles and Toronto police forces in his notorious and successful song 'Mr Metro' (written after he was stopped by Los Angeles police just for being near the scene of a crime). He reveals how blacks throughout North America are associated more with criminality and violence than with any national identity and in fact are denied the advantages of citizenship.

In rap and hip-hop cultures, there are also issues of gender. Not only have women had a very difficult time in becoming recognized artists but the representation of femininity can be highly problematic, especially in terms of sexual objectification. Lyrics are typically sexually explicit and follow various sexist narratives—for example, David Banner's 'Ain't Got Nothing' (2005) portrays a 'brother doin' bad' who has no money but wants sexual contact with a black woman on demand. The tone is aggressive and the message is clear: why should the man have to pay for sex, especially when he has been beaten down by a white-dominated society? Often lyrics in rap and hip-hop music refer to sexually appealing black women as sex workers: 'hos'. And to those who watch music videos in general, it is no news that the images accompanying many hip-hop songs include scene after scene of highly sexually objectified young black women (and occasionally white women) as props and as the necessary signs of the black man having 'made it'. These women are trophies alongside collections of fast cars, golden chains, and diamante-encrusted logos. So for black women, hip hop may not be the means of cultural celebration and resistance to dominant culture that it can be for black men.

Some female hip-hop artists, such as Ciara and Missy Elliot, address these problems in their work. One example is Ciara's song '1, 2 Step', written with Missy Elliot. Besides being an exaltation of music and dancing and an acknowledgment of the roots of hip hop in jazz (another popularized cultural form appropriated from blacks by the dominant white culture), the song also articulates a young black woman's enjoyment of her sexuality as it toys with the popular black culture stereotypes. Just as she seems to acknowledge her fame as out of her control ('so retarded'), Ciara knowingly flaunts her 'goodies' at the boys. She may not be able to control the sexual objectification of black women, but she can acknowledge and exploit her own objectification (Ciara and Missy Elliot, 2004).

The Rise of Popular Culture from Youth Studies

Before race became complicated with gender within cultural studies, much attention was paid to the process of masquerade in terms of femininity (assumed to be white; see Doane 1982). Madonna was the primary icon of this process, although now you can substitute Lady Gaga with much the same results. As video became the dominant vehicle for delivering popular music in which the role of femininity was chiefly a highly objectified sexual backdrop, Madonna began to perform what was initially deemed outrageous. An Italian American raised as a Roman Catholic, she sported huge crucifixes and made a video (for the song 'Like a Prayer') featuring a sexual rapport with Christ. She emphasized her sexualized attributes to the point of not only of wearing her underwear as outerwear but also extending her bras into exaggerated cone shapes. Madonna's videos and live performances became legendary for breaking the boundaries of moral decency (with acts such as apparently masturbating on stage and including so-called deviant and relatively explicit sexual practices in videos such as 'Like a Virgin', which was banned from television). The successful popularizer of cultural studies John Fiske (2010) argued that Madonna masqueraded femininity and by doing so offered resistance to cultural domination or hegemony. And each time Madonna challenged socio-cultural norms (a woman popularizing and arguably resisting the sexual objectification of feminine sexuality), young women and girls picked up on these signs of resistance and paraded them as well. This interaction between a popular cultural icon and fans (consumers of culture) also became an object of study.

The work on masquerade was inspired by feminist film critic Laura Mulvey, who exploded onto the scene with her article 'Visual Pleasure and Narrative Cinema' in 1975. Here she argued that there was an intended 'gaze' or way in which the person viewing the film was constructed by the film itself. Using psychoanalytic theories, Mulvey also argued that this gaze is typically male or that culture is constructed around masculine desires. So when viewing a film in which women appear as sexually objectified, we can understand that this look is manufactured to satisfy a male audience. Mulvey's argument was not meant as a technique for distinguishing sexist films from the rest but for demonstrating that the dominant culture was constructed according to a male gaze. Mulvey's article, now considered a classic in cultural studies, has inspired a great deal of work in how cultural domination functions and in the exploration of modes of resistance such as the role of masquerade (recognizing the male gaze, turning it inside out, and parading it as such. See Doane 1982). It has also led to contemporary considerations of race and sexual orientation, such as those considered above, and complicates the concepts of the 'other' and cultural resistance.

The question of consumer-controlled culture has been present since the start of cultural studies. In the 1950s, British and American sociologists and anthropologists became interested in a new social subgroup—namely, youth (Mannheim 1952; Bernard 1961; Brake 1980). These were the post-war years (soon after the Second World War), and Western economies were on the rise, especially in the United States. Some argue that the inception of the study of youth culture was related to increased leisure time and a rise in numbers of young people, commonly assumed to be young white men with little to do but 'hang around' and cause trouble and concern for those from dominant social groups. Popular cultural representations can be found in the American films *Rebel Without a Cause* (1955) and *West Side Story* (1961). The academic study of such youth groups as culture began in the United Kingdom where the dominant critical sociology was class analysis. Scholars such as Stuart Hall, a founder of the University of Birmingham's Centre for Cultural Studies in the late 1960s, applied principles from class critique (chiefly Marxism) to the study of youth culture and popular mediums of cultural expression, including television and advertising (Hall 1959; Hall and Whannel 1998). At that time, Marxism was the chief critical theory in the UK. Fundamentally concerned with the social and political organization of labour and capital, culture within the Marxist arena of critical thought was seen as the logical, intellectual appendage of the ruling (capitalist) class. In other words, those who controlled capital (the stock of valuable accumulated goods designed to contribute to further production of goods) controlled cultural production. In the original social science of Marxism, culture did not figure prominently: it was class consciousness (being aware of how one was oppressed in one's class position), not cultural control, that would lead to social change (revolution). Consequently, Hall received a great deal of criticism from his colleagues for his arguments that culture could be a site of social change according to the principles of Marxism and that cultural change helps to get rid of class-based oppression.

Theoretical Underpinnings of Cultural Studies: Post-structuralism

By now you should be getting the picture of cultural studies as both a multi-disciplinary and an interdisciplinary enterprise that helps us to understand social reality. In addition to Marxism and political economy, cultural studies also builds on a host of other theories and criticisms directed at social change. The objects of study—culture and cultural products as well as cultural production (or the process of culture)—lend themselves well to psychoanalysis (particularly Freud's theory of the unconscious), ideology (the socio-political organization of ideas), semiology (the study of signs and symbols), and post-structuralist discourse analysis (the illumination of how meaning as power flows through our taken-for-granted parlance or way of speaking; see this book's introduction).

In order to understand how cultural studies developed existing theories of social change within post-structuralism, it helps to examine some principal components of Freud's theory of the unconscious. Sigmund Freud (1856–1939), founder of psychoanalysis, was medically trained and specialized in nervous diseases. His great work, *The Interpretation of Dreams*, was published in 1900 and introduces his theory of the unconscious as a topography for understanding the psyche. Freud used dreams to enter into the patient's unconscious mind to determine anxieties and fears hidden and disguised there. He describes the manifest (obvious) content of the dream as that which the patient presents. The latent (hidden) content is the underlying issue (fear, anxiety, pain, etc.). To find the underlying issue for interpretation—to use dreaming to release the underlying issue such as great fear or anxiety—is 'dream work'. It is this type of work that relates to cultural studies, but instead of analyzing individual dreams, cultural studies scholars investigate the common imagination or popular cultural representations to find underlying or latent meaning. For example, Freud's theory of the unconscious places a great emphasis on sexual repression and fetishism. We cannot reveal our true (sexual) desires openly, so we find other avenues such as transferring the desire to another object (a fast car, for example). Because of the frustration of not being able to express the true desire, the object becomes a fetish or part of a ritualized expression. Laura Mulvey used concepts of this psychoanalysis to develop her theory of the male gaze. She described how women's bodies on film screens were sexual fetishes of heterosexual masculine desire. Thus Freud's psychic categories and the creation of the unconscious are used to understand the operation of potent cultural images and often to dissect or find the underlying (latent) meaning in (manifest) images within a broader socio-cultural context.

One of the ways in which Marxism is brought into cultural studies is through the concept of **ideology**. This is the term that Marx used to describe how class consciousness was obscured for the benefit of the ruling classes, and it can be related to the type of repression raised by Freud. Marx's chief focus was not on ideology but on large-scale social and economic change. However, ideology was picked up in cultural studies, particularly the way it was re-worked by people such as Louis Althusser, who argued that the personal and the political could not be treated separately (as did Marx). Althusser (1918–90) was a French communist philosopher and Marxist theoretician who ex-tended Marx's theory of political/economic state structures to other areas of society and in an innovative way: ideologically (1971). Althusser distinguished what he called 'ideological state apparatuses' (ISA) from repressive forms of state control (the threat of physical violence by an army, for example). Here we can see how Althusser activates Freud's concepts of desire, repression, and representation at a socio-political level. And this is the way that Althusser's ideology was used in early cultural studies.

As Freud's dream work demonstrates (1966 [1913]), images are powerful vehicles of human desire. Although not directly related to Freud's psycho-analysis, a science of the study of signs and symbols—semiology—was de-veloped shortly afterwards. Roland Barthes (1915–80) is best known for analyzing popular images, including ads, and connecting them to politics as a cultural expression, particularly in the form of sign-based myth (1972 [1957]). The semiology developed by Ferdinand de Saussure (1983 [1916]) provides a technique for reading beyond the obvious or manifest image to a deeper or embedded meaning (much like Freud's dream work). Basically, the equation reads as follows: signifier (the image presented) > (points to or signifies) signi-fied (what the image represents) = the sign (embedded meaning). Applied to our earlier example of hip-hop culture, the formula would produce: diamante Mercedes logo worn by young black male hip hop artists > success = African Americans making it in a white-dominant culture. Barthes also moved beyond this approach to a second level of meaning in the social production of signs: myth. Here he refers to a broader and political context of the sign: for example, we could read the gangsta rapper as sign of centuries of racial tensions in the United States.

Finally, let us look at one of the more difficult concepts used widely in cultural studies: discourse. As employed by the French philosopher, historian, and social analyst Michel Foucault (1926–84), 'discourse' is a complicated con-cept and means much more than simply 'what is said'. Like Althusser, Foucault argued for a relocation of power away from the large macro-sociological struc-tures such as class, referred to by previous sociologists and other social critics.

Foucault claimed that power resides in multiple relations of force rather than in social institutions and structure or in any individual, groups of individuals, or characterization of individuals (1980a). This renders problematic any claims of cultural dominance by gender, race, or sexual orientation—which is not necessarily a bad thing. Foucault spent a good deal of time tracing the history of ways of knowing about certain things, including mental illness, sexuality, and criminality. He focused on the use of language in these studies (hence the use of the term 'discourse') and how not simply words but entire vocabularies and grammars (ways of putting things properly) guide power relations and the consequent treatment of people as normal or deviant. Thus the problem is not with racial or sexual difference but with the discursive production of race and sexuality, especially in terms of how difference is spoken.

Sociology of Culture

Before cultural studies emerged as a discipline in academia and before post-structuralism, culture was the focus of much debate during the first half of the twentieth century, particularly in the context of its growing social role as a result of emergent means of mass production and the growth of a cultural industry. One important strand in the debate came from the so-called Frankfurt School of social theory (critical theory), with Theodor Adorno and Max Horkheimer (1979 [1944]) in particular worrying about culture and its ideological use by fascist and then capitalist interests.

Keep in mind the times in Europe, where these sociologists lived and first began to work: fascism was on the rise and was soon followed by a world war (see also Chapter 11). In that context, culture was used for the first time on a massive scale for political ends. In fascism, this technique is referred to as 'propaganda' and functions as a method of stupefying the public through popular means to advance a political cause. According to Adorno, a similar argument could be made about the popular music of the time, which was disseminated through sheet music and the gramophone, then radio and cinema. In contrast, a contemporary of Adorno, Walter Benjamin, also focused on the technological shift in cultural production and dissemination and the concurrent rise in the social role of popular culture, but saw political possibilities there. He did not adhere to the notion of the masses as cultural dupes—people who could be easily led by those who controlled popular cultural production. Although he was very critical of fascist propaganda and the aestheticization of politics (the emphasis on 'looking good' over political content), he also found a rich ground for study in terms of art, authenticity, and the populace in 'the age of mechanical reproduction' (1968 [1936]). The

Canadian communications guru Marshall McLuhan—famous for the expression 'the medium is the message'—focused on the mass media, especially television (1994 [1964]). Adopting a position somewhere between Adorno's and Benjamin's, McLuhan characterized various modes of mass communication for popular consumption as either 'hot' (books, radio, and film) or 'cool' (television) and thus indicated their respective socio-cultural value: hot meant an interactive relationship between the product and the consumer, and cool indicated a passive one.

Among the first to study culture socially and critically are Mathew Arnold (1822–88) and F.R. Leavis (1895–1978). Both Arnold and Leavis were educated in English literature at highly respected universities (Oxford and Cambridge respectively) and became well-known cultural critics. They were considered arbiters or judges of what was culturally valuable, which was informed by their education in classical English literature and modern equivalents. Arnold (1999 [1875]) defined culture as 'sweetness and light', the 'creative power of genius', 'real thought', 'real beauty', and 'the best that has been thought and said about the world'. Leavis (1999 [1930]), one of modern English literature's most famous critics, also pointed to changing times as a threat to what he understood as culture in terms of 'the consciousness of the race'. He identified a social crisis spawned by mass production and standardization of writing by the press and talked about the 'surrender' of intellect to base emotions in the rising new industry of cinema. Further, he characterized much of cultural production in the early twentieth century as a levelling down to the common denominator. 'This [twentieth] century is in a cultural trough,' he claimed, 'and the situation is likely to get worse before better' (1999 [1930], 19). This limited and elitist view of culture and its social role was radically challenged by subsequent critics and scholars of culture, particularly in how mass and popular culture were reconstituted as significant to social progress.

Conclusion

There are some who argue that cultural studies today has become too focused on popular culture. Others still automatically characterize popular culture and its mass distribution as sociologically and culturally insignificant. There is still great hesitation today, for example, in allowing cultural studies programs and courses into universities and colleges, since it is assumed that studies of, say, rap and hip hop could not possibly be worthy of serious academic attention. But despite the difficulties in finding an academic home, cultural studies does continue, and evolve—for example with visual culture (Sturken and Cartwright, 2009). Visual culture refers to the shift from written text as the central focus in studies of culture, especially classical studies (remember that Arnold and Leavis, both literary critics, argued that it was in literary culture that the best of society was to be found), to the visual. The visual culture approach works instead on the assumption that we have become (again, since mass literacy is a relatively new phenomenon) an image-based society. Everything from signage in international airports to medical imaging is analyzed within typically critical and sociologically progressive theoretical contexts. Technoculture, the social study of the convergence of technology and culture associated initially with Constance Penley and Andrew Ross (1991) takes new forms in explorations of social media alongside examinations of racial and class-based stratification (Diners, 2011).

At this point you may have a better idea of what cultural studies is than what culture is. This is not necessarily a bad thing. After more than 100 years of studying the concept, there is simply no nice pat definition of culture available. We have seen how approaches to culture have varied from laments for a passing golden era of high art to a complex celebration and critique of everyday life and its cultural manifestations. Very important sociological issues have been raised throughout this century of study, and many continue to be raised today, including: how culture is produced and who or what controls that production; how we talk about culture—as images, as signs and myth, as ideology, as discourse; how we mediate or understand our world, especially discrimination or social stratification, through culture and our places in it in terms of who we are and who we are allowed to be; and how things such as the social expectation of heterosexuality can be challenged and changed culturally. Such issues also implicitly address the question 'What is social reality?' because what we take to be reality in social contexts is directly contingent on cultural relations.

Questions to Consider

1. How can popular culture, such as songs, perpetuate social inequality?
2. On the other hand, how can popular culture, such as songs, provide a voice of resistance from socially marginalized groups?
3. How does gender discrimination figure in marginal cultural productions such as rap and hip hop?
4. Can you find an example of a cultural production that is produced by and remains under the control of its consumers?

9 | What's 'New' about the New Media Landscape?

Daniel Downes

Introduction

This chapter explores the significance of media technologies and media institutions in contemporary Canadian society. The chapter will describe the characteristics and transformation of what I shall refer to as the 'old' media. Several frameworks for thinking about the media will be presented and a number of questions will be raised about the content, operation, and structure of the media. Finally, I will examine changes in our experience of media as digital technologies and the Internet become prominent tools for public communication.

The Context of Mass Communication

Most of the technological innovations we live with today have been developed in the last century and a half. That is an extremely short period of time when measured against the history of human civilizations and culture. Many of the communication devices we use and the interactions we pursue did not exist even a decade ago. For example, each of the following is an invention of the years since 2000: YouTube, Facebook, Twitter, Google Earth, WikiLeaks. Along with new forms and channels of communication, today we have access to the historical archive of media content. In principle, much of the texts of sound recording, radio and television broadcasts, cinema, and publishing are available through digitization in ways that were precluded by earlier technologies and patterns of information dissemination. This situation both deepens and flattens our experience of mediated culture. What are some of the consequences of a media environment that has grown so vast and so quickly?

Mass communication describes the process of creating shared meaning between mass media and their audiences. The term refers to the process by which a complex organization of professional communicators, using varied and expensive technological infrastructure, produce and distribute standardized, public messages aimed at a large, scattered, and heterogeneous audience. Mass communication involves hundreds or thousands of people and there is no immediate feedback between receivers and the source of a message. Newspapers, magazines, radio, television, and film are all examples of mass media.

In general, the old media are mass media. They presume a single content distributed to a large audience at the same time. The goal of mass communication is to create a common experience, thereby fostering homogeneity in its audience. In Canada, we have a long history of thinking about physical transportation networks, information technologies, and communication institutions. This interest has appeared in a set of recurring and related questions about the roles and responsibilities of the media, including how new technologies (from the Canadian Pacific Railroad to the information technologies of radio, television, and the Internet) can be used for the project of nation-building and fostering a sense of national community. With regard to the content in Canadian media, the recurring question is whether such content reflects us. Indeed, debate is often centred on what we can or should do about the abundance of US content carried by Canadian media outlets. As media companies are social institutions, how should the balance between freedom of expression and the rights of such companies to pursue their own interests be weighed against the perceived power of media to exert political, social, or economic influence? Finally, these issues raise the question of the role of governments: what, if any, role should government play in regulating the operation or structure of the media?

Mass communication in Canada helped to develop a national consciousness by creating shared experiences for readers, listeners, and viewers. But it has increasingly become a force of economic growth and competitiveness. Vipond (1992) argues that by the end of the nineteenth century, mass media played a mediating role as one of the principal institutions by which individuals were brought into the transition from traditional to modern forms of society. She suggests that the media played an important role in educating rural migrants who were now living and working in cities, as well as new immigrants to Canada who were encouraged, through the media, to adopt a set of middle-class values that seemed natural through their repetition in the media (Vipond 1992). The saturation of Canadian-owned media with US content is the result of tensions between two Canadian idea systems. On the one hand, Canadians have fostered a myth of communications promising that a new technological system will bind us together. Charland (1986) argues that the very idea of an English Canadian identity was created through such various 'national' experiences as the CPR and later, the broadcasting system. This rhetoric ideologically constituted those people living in Canada *as* Canadians. As historian David Taras (2001) puts it, the challenge of broadcasting in Canada 'was to counter American influence by creating a distinctively Canadian mass media culture, one that would generate its own stars, its own memorable and popular programs, and its own allegiances' (120–1). The role of media in creating a national community is clear in the early work of John Grierson (he would later head the National Film Board of Canada), who recognized the power of representing working people in film in ways that would maintain the status quo (Nelson 1988). On the other hand, we share with our American neighbours an ideology of liberal individualism, which influenced the kind of media industries we created and their attendant values (Vipond 1992).

What questions did the old media raise? Does scarcity of some sources of information (or some viewpoints in the marketplace of ideas) lessen the depth of content, or does it in some way diminish the range of common experiences we have as members of our society? Does the commercial origin of much media content influence that content? If it does, then in what ways? How can we detect and study the influences that shape the kinds of content we use to construct social reality? Further, because people often assume the link between media content and social identity, we raise issues about control and ownership of the media. The question arises, how do we structure the media, and how do we place controls on content to achieve desirable social goals? Indeed, in Canada, it is often assumed that the ownership of the means of communication has a greater impact on society than the media content itself (Hardin 1985; Raboy 1990).

Approaches to Media Study

In general terms, the study of mass media focuses either on the content or messages of mediated communication or on the media as social institutions. Researchers have evaluated the effects of media messages on audiences or, by investigating media institutions, they have analyzed how the media operate and how the media are structured.

Media Effects

The first approach to the study of media concentrated on the effects of media messages. Early studies assumed that media messages exerted powerful influences on those who experience them (Blumer and Hauser 1939). The basic question from this perspective is, 'Do the media have the power to shape, change, or determine the attitudes, values, and, perhaps most importantly, the behaviours of individuals?' At various times in the past 80 years, opinion has swayed from the assumption that the media can influence behaviour so that messages have direct, strong effects, to a more limited view of the influence of media messages that suggests that media content simply reinforces pre-existing opinions, beliefs, and values held by audience members (Lazarsfeld, Berelson, and Gaudet 1944; Berelson 1959; Trend 2007). If media messages are powerful stimuli that can influence our behaviour, government restrictions on certain types of objectionable content might seem reasonable. If, on the other hand, media messages are limited in their ability to influence audiences, then the media should be allowed to provide their audiences with whatever content the people want. Both approaches to **media effects** can be found today.

Fear that the media have a powerful influence on people leads to moral panics arising out of actual or perceived responses to media content. Dr David Walsh, in an interview for CBC's *the fifth estate* (CBC 2009) supports the view that violence in video games can have a negative effect on young people. When Walsh claims that the computer divides the family, he echoes earlier fears: that the radio threatened the family during the 1950s because teenagers started to listen alone in their rooms instead of with the family in the living room, or that in the early days of cinema, youth were vulnerable to bad influences of viewing movies without adult supervision —in the dark, in a room full of strangers.

By contrast, a special issue of *Maclean's* magazine (2008) on the subject of Internet porn, argues that parents ultimately have the power and responsibility to monitor their children's Internet use rather than calling for government intervention. Video-game violence and Internet pornography are certainly problematic and socially undesirable forms of media content. Why, then, is such media content readily available?

When people argue that governments should regulate objectionable media messages, they are arguing that media messages are powerful and that at least some media messages are dangerous. Further, when people call for the Canadian government to regulate the media industries in Canada, the issue raised is whether *we* are shaping the kind of identity we want or whether that identity is unduly influenced by outside sources (in the Canadian context this raises questions of cultural nationalism, cultural dependency on American culture, and the role for media regulation). Are we telling enough 'Canadian' stories? Once again, if messages can influence our behaviour, and, if the media do shape identity, a society needs controls over the production of content.

How the Media Operate

The second approach we can take to the study of media institutions is to ask how the media operate (for examples of this approach, see Tuchman 1980; Schudson 1991; Herman and Chomsky 1988). What are the internal and external influences that help determine the information disseminated and the tone the media take on particular issues. We can also focus our attention on the newsgathering functions of the media (surveillance of the environment and correlation of relevant information). In this way, we can ask how well the news media perform. Are they reliable or biased? Is there a clear distinction between news, opinion, and promotion?

In 2006, after more than three years of research and hearings across the country, the Senate of Canada released a report on Canadian news media. Their report, the third such federal study in 35 years, urged the government to curb media concentration. One of the targets of the report was CanWest, which was, at the time, the largest integrated media company in Canada, owning the *National Post*, 13 dailies in major cities and 23 papers in smaller cities, Global TV's 11 stations, a handful of radio stations, and an Internet site.

When CanWest bought its newspapers from Southam News in the late 1990s, the new owners alienated journalists by spiking columns that disagreed with the political views of the owners, attempted to centralize the production of editorials, rewrote stories and, ultimately fired the editor of the *Ottawa Citizen* for publishing a story on the scandal that was to become 'Shawinigate', along with an editorial calling for then–Prime Minister Jean Chretien to resign (McDiarmid 2006).

The CanWest owners' involvement in the editorial and journalistic practices of their newspapers is called 'operational' control. The owners are actively involved in the editorial or news-gathering practices of the papers. Another kind of control that owners can use to shape news coverage is called 'allocative control'.

How the Media Are Structured

The choices made about media content by editors and media owners illustrate one of the ways that content is shaped. However, the way the media are organized (as private, commercial businesses, as public institutions, or as global conglomerates) also shapes their relationships with society. Commercial media institutions are corporations that own and operate media outlets for profit. The commercial orientation of the media means that the media must optimize revenue while they minimize production and operating costs. Commercial media create new content or purchase content from media producers in other countries in order to build audiences whose attention is sold to advertisers who offset the cost of programming and are the primary source of revenues for the media outlets. The commercial pressures that media face can have odd, long-term effects on the cultural life of a society (for examples of research that explores the structure of the media, see Bagdikian 2000; Kunz 2006; Mosco 2009).

In the age of broadcast media (what critical theorist and historian Mark Poster [1995] calls the 'second media age') communication was something that was done to us, usually by large, institutional communicators who had specific reasons (sometimes economic, sometimes political) for distributing a standardized message to the largest possible audience. There are practical reasons for this process. For example, in the case of both radio and television in the United States, the media developed as networks rather than as individual stations competing with one another. The networks gave advertisers access to large, national audiences, for which the advertisers paid high prices. This revenue allowed the networks to produce programming (sponsored by advertisers) that could be sold to stations (in the United States and Canada) more cheaply than locally produced content (Starr 2004). The networks came to dominate broadcasting for most of the twentieth century. However, the development of media industries based on advertising and commercial programming has created the possibility for media companies to shape their content to satisfy commercial needs or pressures.

Take for example, the Bill Moyers essay 'Society on Steroids' (Moyers 2007). Moyers argues that baseball has changed from a national pastime, a national symbol of sporting identity, to a commodity governed by economic and broadcast requirements. Steroid use is tolerated even if officially frowned upon because the game is a spectacle rather than a sport and players feel immense pressure to out perform one another and the stars of earlier generations. Moyers analogizes the situation in baseball to the spiritual or moral climate in the United States, where greed and short-term profit are more important than the integrity of sports or politics. The same case could be made about pressures to allow violence in junior hockey in Canada because it trains players who want to play professional hockey. In both cases, it is the operation of the media as purveyors of spectacle that subtly changes the nature of our cultural activities.

In addition to studying media messages, operation, or structures, students of communication also pay close attention to changes in the media landscape. In particular, we are changing our media consumption habits as we turn to the Internet as a source of information and seem to be losing faith in the traditional media to provide us with reliable information.

A 2009 survey conducted by the Pew Research Center for the People and the Press reported that nearly two-thirds—63 per cent—of Americans believe that news stories are often inaccurate. In contrast, in 1985, only 34 per cent of respondents believed stories were frequently inaccurate. In addition, the study found that 74 per cent of respondents thought the media were biased (that news stories tend to favour one side of an issue over another) (Bauder 2009). The study also showed that more Republicans than Democrats felt that the US media were biased, and that while television was the dominant news source, the Internet had surpassed newspapers as a source of national and international news. Reporting on the results of the survey, Bauder (2009) proposes several reasons for the loss of faith in the reliability of the press, including financial pressures, partisanship, and the effects of competition with the Internet as a source of information.

According to a Pew poll of December 2010, Americans were watching less television and continued to use the Internet for national and international news. For the first time, a population group—those under 30—were using the Internet more than television for news (Pew Research Centre 2010).

In Canada, a similar trend is occurring. Canadians between the ages of 30 and 49 are using the Internet as much as television as a news source. Further, significant numbers of Canadians are online. Figures for 2007 show that 95 per cent of 15- to 24-year-olds, 85 per cent of people 45 to 54 and 70 per cent of those between 55 and 64 regularly use the Internet in Canada (Dewing 2010, 1). However, in contrast to the American studies, Canadians seem to trust the media as a source of information more than do their neighbours to the south. Reporting on news coverage of the 2006 federal election, Ray (2008) observes that Canadians tend to recognize the difference between opinion columns and news coverage in daily newspapers. They find opinion columns biased toward particular political viewpoints, but, contrary to the US data, they feel that, in general, news coverage is pretty neutral across the board.

From these studies, a number of general assumptions and conditions of the mass media can be distilled:

- The media are somehow expected to provide unbiased, or at least balanced, coverage of issues and, for a variety of reasons (financial, political, social) they are not succeeding as they have in the past.
- The media are commercial organizations, and commercial pressures can affect how they function or operate. For example, a reference to the effect of a 'budget squeeze' on the practice of fact checking in newspapers refers to the economics of news reporting and publishing. In particular, the issue is the allocation of resources (where money gets spent in the organization) and the effect of those decisions on the practice of journalism and the reliability of the content produced.
- Some forms of media are perceived as more or less reliable than others as sources of information. Reference to the 'torrent' of information and the

implied de-professionalization of journalism as a result of blogs, cable TV, etc. affect the profession and the public's perception of journalism.

- The Internet challenges the old media (either negatively because audiences are drawn away from the old media, or in a more positive manner as a corrective to the failures of the older mass media). New media afford the opportunity for people to correct errors and scrutinize the media— hopefully improving the overall quality of the press. This assumption is an expression of the view that the Internet is a more democratic form of communication than was the process of mass communication.

Why do governments investigate the media? Often the reasons have to do with fears that the media, or certain media companies, are becoming too powerful or that those who control the media may unduly influence the content. Questions that have been asked about the media in Canada over the years have focused on the issue of concentration of ownership, concerns over whether the media should be publicly or privately owned or controlled, and the origins and nature of media content (are the programs we watch or listen to Canadian or American, or does media content threaten harm to some segment of the population?). Government commissions on the media have had a mixed impact on the nature of the Canadian media system. In some cases (commissions on broadcasting and the arts include Aird in 1929, Massey in 1949, and Fowler in 1957), the answer is to the question of whether the government should regulate or influence the operation of the media in the interest of society is yes. In each of these cases the questions raised by the commissioners had to do with the nature of broadcasting in Canada. On the other hand, for commissions on the press, (Davey in 1969, Kent in 1980, and the Senate Commission in 2006), the answer to the same question is no. The reports filed by these commissions did little or nothing to change the patterns of ownership and media concentration that have been characteristic of Canadian (and international) media since the 1960s.

What Happened to the Old Media?

During the 1980s and '90s, the functions traditionally performed by the mass media became overshadowed by their need to entertain (Postman 1985). Television's traditional network audiences were drawn by the growth of cable content and the mass audience dwindled except under certain extraordinary contexts like the O.J. Simpson trial or the funeral of Princess Diana. Businesses became global in desire, if not reach. Similarly, multilateral trade agreements created the economic and regulatory latitude for global business to emerge and thrive. Technologies such as the computer became central to the information and communication industries in the 1990s, initiating a period of convergence.

Convergence

During the 1990s, technological convergence through the application of computers to the production, distribution, storage, and reception of information made a number of laws and regulation applicable to the media industries seem old fashioned and, at times, ridiculous. For many years, in Canada, cable companies could not enter the phone business even though they provided cables to the home that could carry television signals as well as phone traffic. Similarly, the phone company was not allowed to use the phone lines to bring television into the home. In particular, since the same process of digitization was used to create text, sound, still images, and moving images, as well as to distribute these messages, it made little sense to structurally separate content-providing industries (such as radio or television stations) from distribution industries (such as the telephone company or cable television companies), which had been the case in Canada (see Ridout 2003 for a discussion of shifts in telecommunication policy in Canada).

During this period, the organizations that produced and distributed information and communication content also began to converge. Industries that were formerly separate converged into large multinational information and communications entities. Further, by the end of the 1990s it seemed that Canada needed large industrial actors to compete with an increasingly globalized information and media sector. Thus, in Canada, like other countries, mergers and acquisitions among the media and telecommunication sector created giant conglomerates.

Finally, laws and public policies governing the media, career opportunities in media and public sectors, social and personal issues arising from media consumption, and even theories of the media and their role in society changed to reflect the fact of convergence. Under the banner of technological convergence, media companies argued that earlier industrial regulation no longer applied to the emerging information industries. They complained that governments were too slow to adapt to the speed at which the information society was becoming a reality (see Barney 2000).

Fragmentation of Audiences

The pressures facing the traditional media players during the late 1980s and throughout the '90s became apparent through the decline in audiences. It was not so much a loss as a fragmentation of audiences, who looked to other sources for the media content they wanted.

Since then, the traditional television networks have tried a number of things to recover their audience. The focus on reality TV is an attempt to consolidate the 18- to 34-year-old demographic by integrating the viewing experience with cellphone use, phone use, online discussion groups, etc. Online, viewers are able to see raw material and extras not aired as part of regular programs. The networks use new media to create interest in their content: Internet advertising promotes programming; online games keep viewers interested in crime shows such as *Homicide: Life in the Streets* or *Lost*; and gimmicks more deeply involve viewers—for example, the fictional writer Richard Castle posts comments on Facebook and Twitter between seasons of the television series (*Castle*) in which he is a central character.

Another strategy used by television to recapture audiences was the development of reality television geared to global markets. During the early 1990s, reality TV was the only format of television production that was not deficit financed. According to Ted Magder (2009), there were several reasons for this success: prepackaged formats became popular as the basis for program production, product placement and brand integration became a source of revenue for program producers, TV programs became springboards for multimedia exploitation of creative property, and the importance of European program suppliers in the US market grew. Global television formats are one successful response to the changes facing the traditional media over the past 20 years.

Technological Adaptation

The broad effect of the Internet on the traditional media has been to give them a common technological infrastructure. This has forced them to compete against one another as never before. The Internet has lowered the cost of entry into the media market, and anyone can now create media content. We see the effects of this shift in the challenge blogging poses to traditional newspaper reporting; in the movies (think of the viral marketing campaign used to create a buzz around the *The Blair Witch Project* and the 'Are you serious?' viral campaign to promote Christopher Nolan's *The Dark Knight*); and in the way YouTube challenges television by providing a medium for people to watch both traditional TV content and new forms of video created specifically for the Internet.

The convergence of computers, telecommunications, and mass media systems is bringing about some fundamental changes in the way the mass media function. Mass media sources are becoming more numerous and, at the same time, less professionalized or authoritative. Their ability to act as gatekeepers that set the agenda for public discussion is also being diminished. Messages are customized for smaller and more specialized segments of the audience, sometimes more accurately described as 'communities', who use personal forms of address than as audiences. The media narrowcast to these segments rather than broadcast to a homogeneous audience. Audiences are likewise becoming smaller and less anonymous than they were formerly. The media know more about their audience members, who, in turn, have a greater range of effective means of providing feedback to the producers of media content—and even of participating in the creation of that content. For some, this is a sign that the audience is becoming more powerful as we move away from a notion of the passive mass media to interactive media (Straubhaar and LaRose 2000, 28).

However, a number of factors have contributed to a bumpy transition for the media in this century. The Web has challenged conventional television as a delivery source (by allowing the downloading of programs through torrents, providing old media content on YouTube, etc). Viewing habits have changed to the extent that television no longer orders people's evenings, and therefore no longer provides reliable audiences for advertisers. As an alternative to network broadcasting, the Web has yet to provide a reliable audience to advertisers.

Characteristics of New Media Systems

In her important study of digital culture, *Hamlet on the Holodeck*, author Janet Murray (1998) identifies four qualities specific to our experience of digitally mediated content. First, computer programs are responsive to our input, so a digital environment can change the way our experience unfolds in response to the commands we enter through the keyboard, mouse, or other device. Murray calls this 'interactivity'. Second, digital environments are 'immersive': a user has the ability to change the nature of the interactions she or he has in the digital media with ease. The digital environment is 'responsive' and compliant.

The third, 'navigational', component is evident in applications such as Facebook or a complex website like Wikipedia. We know where we are in the digital space on the computer screen by engaging in the interactive process of navigation. When we enter commands on the keyboard, or move the mouse across a pad, a visual marker—the cursor—moves to specific locations on the screen.

Finally, digital media is often 'encyclopedic'. When we watch television, we watch a particular episode of a specific program broadcast at a specific time. In the digital environment, however, we can access the entire series, as well as production information and biographical details of the actors, and we can interact with other viewers. More importantly, there is so much information in a digital environment—more information than we can use in a single visit—that we can forget its constructed nature. Murray suggests that new forms of interactive media will take advantage of these properties.

So, how are the characteristics of digital communication distinct from those of traditional mass communication described earlier? First, regarding the production of information, in the new media landscape the distinctions between professional, organized communicators and amateur or individual communicators are increasingly blurred. We still consume content provided by media organizations, but we also create information—emails, user profiles, accounts on electronic shopping sites, videos, etc. Some people even engage in activities that resemble the work of traditional media practitioners—blogging, for example. Many argue that such user-generated content undermines the authority and popularity of professional media content (Keen 2007).

Second, traditional distribution networks, which were technologically and, often industrially specific to a particular medium, have been challenged by the common infrastructure of Internet and mobile communication devices. Now, different forms of media content reach us through the same devices. However, we can understand the Internet as a site of tension between different philosophies regarding the production and distribution of content. For many years, the Internet could be understood as an environment of 'generative' technology: people identified problems with the technology and solved them, thus creating an environment of innovation and the sense that the Internet expanded due to individual efforts. From the generative perspective, computing devices can be modified and software or programming can be created to fulfill a variety of needs by any number of creative individuals or companies. On the other hand, with the rise of mobile devices such as the iPod, and smart phones, a competing view of the Internet has emerged that treats computing devices as 'tethered appliances' that require a user to obtain all software and content from the company that provides the hardware. From the perspective of tethered appliances, the new media environment more closely resembles the old media environment in which a relatively small group of people or companies have access to the means of mass distribution (see Zittrain 2008).

Wu (2010) argues that all media systems have a life cycle that begins with chaos and amateur experimentation and develops towards oligopoly and centralized control.

Jonathan Zittrain (2008) sets up a complex debate about the kind of Internet we desire. On the one hand, an open network that allows for innovation and unexpected developments also opens the door to abuse, vandalism, piracy, and attack—this is the dilemma of an open architecture that requires a particular set of values to operate successfully. On the other hand, reliability and security are linked to closed networks that can be regulated for optimal performance. He writes:

> Internet users are again embracing a range of 'tethered appliances', reflecting a resurgence of the initial model of bundled hardware and software that is created and controlled by one company. This will affect how readily behavior on the Internet can be regulated, which in turn will determine the extent that regulators and commercial incumbents can constrain amateur innovation, which has been responsible for much of what we now consider precious about the Internet. (8–9)

Third, whereas in the age of mass media technological mediation required industry-specific technologies, digitization has provided a common infrastructure for the traditional industries. Other forms of mediation (regulation and national laws) have also been challenged as countries work to harmonize copyright and other intellectual property rules.

Finally, audiences have been recast as users and participants rather than just recipients. The old media economy focused on the production and control of distribution. Radio and television networks sold the attention of audiences to advertisers who subsidized or paid for programming. In a real sense, the media turned audiences into commodities. In the new media environment, however, we turn *ourselves* into commodities through the very acts that seem, on the surface, to give us a power and independence not experienced in traditional mass communication. As we exchange messages and information about ourselves on sites such as Facebook and LinkedIn, we participate in **social media** in which our interactions themselves are the content and raw material for both the sites and third parties to turn into information commodities.

However, whereas the traditional media packages audiences into commodities for advertisers, in the new media economy we do much of that work ourselves. Our online activities generate data about ourselves as we surf the Internet, visit websites, and engage in online and transactions. Nick Couldry argues that participants in reality TV shows (the mass media version of online gaming) engage in a kind of Foucauldian process of governmentality. They are overtly shaped into contestants and celebrities as much as implicated in the process of self-fashioning. Couldry (2009) writes that 'what develop[s is] not so much a self [as] a *media self* (83). Further, the music business actively requires us to present media selves 'that it can operationalize, package and promote. Record companies and management firms no longer want to invest in the uncertainties of grooming talent so much as they want proof of success and, significantly, by wanting to be in the media we affirm the continued importance of the media' (Downes 2011). According to media scholar Alison Hearn, 'in a promotional culture, at some level, we all must generate our own rhetorically persuasive meanings and become "commodity signs", . . . whereby our values and commonly used symbols are colonized by the market and put to work to *sell*' (Hearn 2009, 42).

These new online activities of media consumption, surfing, and social networking have been criticized (as has media content in the past) for the ways they dull our critical faculties. Often, writers highlight negative changes that have arisen from the adoption of new forms or tools of communication. Such critiques are often attacks on contemporary media. For example, Nicholas Carr's (2008) article 'Is Google Making Us Stupid?' raises a number of issues about the power and influence of media. He is not the first to criticize media in this way (see Postman 1992).

Carr begins with some observations about his own experiences of mediation. Where once he used to read and contemplate, using the Internet as his main medium of information has changed the way he thinks—skimming on the surface of a vast sea of information. He concludes that we may be in the middle of a sea change about how we think. Google is the example he uses of a company that is using the computer to do the work of the mind. Whereas McLuhan (1964) described the 'global village' of mass communication as a prosthetic extension of the human nervous system, Carr worries about the success of just such an imagined prosthetic.

For Carr, life moves too fast for us to sit back, contemplate, and digest the torrent of information at our fingertips. The barrage of media images gives us what media scholar Todd Gitlin has called 'feeling lite'—media is all about conveying feeling, creating a reaction or an emotional response rather than presenting reasoned argument or facts for deliberation on issues. In the end, for such critics, the contemporary media environment generates a perfect condition for political disengagement (see Gitlin 2002, 166 and Hedges 2009).

To recognize that there are particular characteristics—or specific forms of—communication, or that there are specific characteristics of different media, or that different media operate in distinct ways is not the same as making the simply claiming that specific forms of individual behaviour, social organization or human experience are determined by social, economic, political, or technological conditions.

Is there a counter-argument to Carr's perspective on new media? Yes. Johnson (2005) argues that today's popular culture is actually making us 'smarter' by teaching us new skills: games that force us to probe and telescope; television shows that require us to make sense of stories that unfold over extended periods of time; software and games that require us to take actions and participate rather than sitting back and watching as we might have done in the past with movies. For Johnson, these aspects of contemporary culture demonstrate a more than 30-year trend toward increasing complexity.

A recent study reported by the BBC suggested that children who use a variety of communication tools are more likely to read and write than their classmates who use fewer communication tools and prefer settings such as face-to-face interactions or telephone conversations (Kleinman 2009). According to the 2009 UK study conducted by the National Literacy Trust, children who engage in a variety of forms of communication activities have stronger core literacy skills than students who neither blog nor use social-networking sites. The BBC reported that there is a strong correlation between technology use and wider patterns of reading and writing.

While the BBC story reported that primary school teachers are reluctant to encourage children to use computers, the teachers do recognize that there might be benefits in incorporating children's passion for texting into teaching/learning methods (Kleinman 2009). Most significant in this report is the recognition that we have to learn new forms and techniques of communication and new forms of **media literacy** or 'mediacy' to adapt to new social realities. This is a much more compelling insight than the simplistic argument that our old literacy skills are on the decline because of new media.

Conclusion

With more Canadians using the Internet and digital media than ever before, it is possible to argue that we are regular participants in a new media landscape. The old mass media have gone through a process of technological, industrial, and regulatory convergence over the past 25 years. Audiences have fragmented and migrated to new sources of information, but have also become 'users' and content providers in the new media environment.

Questions to Consider

1. In what ways do the mass media shape our sense of social or national identity? Do new media systems such as the Internet have the same effect?

2. Can you think of examples to support the idea that media content might have an effect on human behaviour?
3. How does the structure of the media affect society?
4. In what ways has the Internet challenged the way we think about the media?
5. Why is media literacy important in an era of digital and mobile communication?

10 | What Use Is Social Theory?

R.A. Sydie

Introduction

Theory is the 'act of viewing, contemplating, considering' and it usually involves some imaginative interpretation of what is referred to as 'data', which for social theorists is the raw material of everyday life. Social theory is 'first and foremost a *way of thinking* about the human world' (Bauman 1990, 8: emphasis in original).

The term **theory** often generates negative reactions because it is assumed to be abstract, difficult, and of dubious relevance to everyday life. This is ironic because the founding mothers and fathers of social theory regarded their theoretical work as critically relevant and significant to finding solutions to the problems of everyday life. Harriet Martineau (1983 [1869], vol. 2, 335) defined social theory as the science of the discovery of social laws and therefore the 'eternal basis of wisdom' for the development of 'human morality and peace'. Émile Durkheim also maintained that abstract theory would not be 'worth the labour of a single hour if its interest were merely speculative' (1989 [1893], xxvi). As a result these early social theorists saw the theoretical X as an essential explanatory part of any practical Y.

What Is Social Theory?

The key element in the development of social theory was the conceptualization of **society** as an autonomous entity, separate from its individual members. For nineteenth-century theorists, it seemed clear that the social was different from, and in contrast to, nature, and that modern society was equally different from traditional or primitive societies in other parts of the world. For classical social theorists, the new concept 'society' was the object of scientific investigation that would provide solutions to the various social problems that modernity had produced. Most classical social theorists were from Western, largely European or North American societies, and they assumed, on the basis of 'evidence' from ethnographic and anthropological reports, that the West was modern and the 'rest' were primitive or backward. In this light, social theory was seen as a vital contribution to social progress for Western societies and as the means to bring primitive societies into the modern world under the benevolent guidance of Western 'experts'. Consequently, Saint-Simon wrote in 1814, the 'Golden Age of the human race is not behind us but before us; it lies in the perfection of the social order' (136).

It was the clear scientific eye of the social theorist that would provide the directions for the perfection of the social order. Without necessarily agreeing with the specifics of Marx and Engel's predictions for a new social order and how it might be achieved, classical social theorists generally endorsed the notion that the 'philosophers have only interpreted the world, in various ways; the point is to change it' (Marx and Engels 1947 [1846],199). Social theory was to break out of previous philosophical or abstract modes of thinking about the world and produce tangible scientific facts that would provide the basis for social change and the establishment of 'human morality and peace' that Martineau predicted.

While the optimism of the early theorists has been considerably modified in current theoretical work, social theory nonetheless remains committed to addressing the pressing social issues of our time in the hope of alleviating the various troubles that affect individuals in their everyday lives (Smith 1978). It is how these troubles can be understood theoretically that generates different solutions for social change. Many of our current public problems may seem to be similar to those addressed by the classical social theorists, but the social, political, economic, and physical contexts are often profoundly different and require somewhat different theoretical perspectives. For example, the former distinctions between modern and traditional (primitive) break down in the wired global world we inhabit in which even subsistence farmers carry cellphones. But the imaginative interpretation of the raw material of everyday life that was the foundational method for classical social theory remains the same today, because theory is 'first and foremost a way of thinking about the human world' (Bauman 1990, 8).

For classical social theorists, the solutions to modernity's problems varied, but they were framed by a confidence that theorists could produce objective and hence irrefutable knowledge about the social world as opposed to past philosophical, religious, or ideological constructions of social reality. As Comte (1975, 37) remarked, by discovering the invariant laws governing the social, the theorist could determine 'what is, what will be, and what should be' so that past theological or metaphysical abstractions and fantasies by which theorists had explained the social world could now be rejected. The 'real' nature of society would be revealed and humanity freed to pursue 'Order and Progress' through positivist social science.

Theoretical thinking is therefore not merely contemplative; it also involves some imaginative interpretation of what can be called data—which for social theorists is the raw material of everyday life. Now we all make sense of our world in a theoretical manner and make decisions about our conduct and responses to our world based on those theoretical suppositions, most especially if we are encountering problems. For example, in the 1960s Western women began to question the assumption that their supposedly natural destiny as adults was to be wives and mothers. Betty Friedan's book *The Feminine Mystique* (1963) discussed the sense of malaise that women (especially North American, educated, middle-class women) felt about the social pressures to realize their 'femininity' solely in their roles as mother and housewives. She called the malaise the 'problem that has no name' because women did not articulate their personal troubles. Women blamed themselves for their discontent, feeling that there was something wrong with them, especially because the suburban American woman was the 'envy, it was said, of women all over the world' (13). This seemingly personal problem that produced a sense of personal failure eventually became, through informal discussions and grassroots organizing among women, a collective issue that coalesced into a mass movement for women's liberation. As women realized that they were experiencing a common problem, they began to theorize the reasons for their situation and their discontent. Their collective theoretical analysis of the problem was summed up in the slogan 'the personal is political'. That is, the ostensibly individual and personal problem was revealed as a political, ideological formulation of gender power relations that oppressed women for the benefit of men. The outcome of feminist theorizing about women's position and relationships in society was a radical rethinking of how power operates, how it structures gender relations, and what constitutes the political.

Theory is useful in making sense of the world. But if theorizing is something that all of us do, then what special claims can social theorists, or any other specialist, advance in respect to their theoretical efforts? What sets social theory apart from our everyday sense-making? The answer lies in the distinction between criticism and critique. In the example above, women may have criticized the causes of their discontent, but the theorist does not rest with finding fault or venting frustration, trying instead to produce a critique. Critique goes beyond mundane criticism to ask 'What is the evidence?' and, most importantly, 'How might it be different?' The theorist examines the social and cultural context in which this discontent arises and the how it affects the lives of others in order to understand how to make a positive, constructive difference. That is, the 'sociological imagination' of the theorist translates 'personal troubles into public issues' (Mills 1959, 187).

What Do Theorists Do?

Social theorists explain and interpret seemingly personal troubles to make sense of the social world and provide signposts as to how to affect change. Dahrendorf (1973, 58) suggested, 'Two intentions were the godparents of sociology. The new discipline was supposed to make the fact of society accessible to a rational understanding by means of testable assumptions and theories' and 'to help the individual toward freedom and self-fulfillment.' It was the clear, scientific eye of the social theorist that would both provide theoretical directives for the perfection of the social order and advance individual happiness. The problem is that the two intentions often produce antithetical results. The perfection of order can just as easily constrain rather than promote the freedom and happiness of individuals. It is this dilemma that confronted classical social theorists in their examination of modern society.

For the classical social theorists, the critical public issues of modernity were capitalism, industrialisation, urbanization, secularism, bureaucratization, excessive individualism, and alienation. In particular, the alienating nature of modern life seemed to be inevitable given the demands of a capitalist, industrial social structure. Rationalization and objectivity are essential to the success of capitalist modernity, but they are Janus-faced, offering an illusion of individual freedom but only as long as individuals control themselves and fall in line with the regimented demands of modern capitalism. Max Weber (1904–5) observed that capitalism involves the objective, impersonal pursuit of wealth 'stripped of its religious and ethical meaning' and that this in turn produces 'specialists without spirit, sensualists without heart' (182). This rational, regimented treatment of people and things eliminates 'respect, kindness and delicacies of feeling'. But if capitalists who are interested only in the pursuit of wealth are 'reproached with callousness and brutality' they reject the accusation, claiming they are only acting with 'logical consistency and pure impartiality' and not with any 'bad intentions' (Simmel 1990 [1900], 434).

Unfortunately, it was often the work of the social theorist that contributed to the fulfillment of the first of the two intentions described by Dahrendorf. The facts that social theorists provided enabled state bureaucracies to produce more sophisticated, alienating, and constraining social structures and conditions that invariably ran counter to the discipline's second intention of providing for human freedom and self-fulfillment. The bureaucratic structures of modern states are designed to be efficient and effective means for the objective application of rational legal rules for the pursuit of good social order and progress. But those same bureaucratic structures ensure that any idiosyncratic needs and desires of individuals in the pursuit of their personal freedom and happiness are controlled, regimented, and/or denied. Modern states are about 'red tape'—about setting rules, about administration, management, surveillance, and supervision of all individual citizens. And it is the social theorist, as the expert, who provides reliable information as to how to prevent any deviance from the social norms, any breaching of the rules, anything 'haphazard, erratic, unanticipated and accidental' from occurring (Bauman 2000, 76). This is not to say that social theorists deliberately set out to preserve or augment the powers of the modern state, but the work of many who insist on the scientific status of their task in providing objective knowledge of society is useful to policy-makers and politicians seeking to control populations. The social theorist as scientist reveals the 'what', 'why', and 'how' of social problems, but as scientist, the theorist cannot appropriate the role of the politician or administrator and determine what should be done to resolve these problems.

Complicity with modern institutions of power and authority was not overtly duplicitous on the part of theorists. On the contrary, co-operation was often provided with the best of intentions. For example, the abstract population surveys and classifications sorted by age, sex, class, race, etc., produced by social theorists concerned with poverty and inequality, provided the impersonal, 'objective' basis for the bureaucratic management of a welfare state that would ostensibly solve those problems. But many individuals involved with welfare state bureaucracy often find that the statistical category to which they are assigned does not seem to fit the realities of their lives and their specific needs. Social theorists are alert to the dangers of co-option, especially by undemocratic, authoritarian regimes, but the social engineering of state bureaucracies is necessarily dependent on the research of social theorists. As a result, the second, emancipatory intention of using the theorist's expertise to advance the freedom and self-fulfillment of individuals may well be contradicted by the implementation of their research findings.

Classical social theorists produced useful analyses of the nature of modernity, but the reviews and results of social theory as a science of society have been mixed. The social problems identified as characteristic of modernity—capitalism, industrialization, bureaucratization, excessive individualism, alienation, and secularization—remain problematic, generating personal troubles and producing public problems, but how they are manifested and theorized has changed. For example, the extremes of wealth and poverty have increased as capitalist enterprises have consolidated their global reach, seemingly indifferent to any coherent control or regulation by governments. Industrialization is a global phenomenon and one that has often sidelined the former industrial powerhouses of the West only to introduce horrendous working conditions for many industrial workers in the southern hemisphere. The presumed disinterested objectivity of 'pure' science is challenged by various problems in the aftermath of discoveries. For example, drugs developed from medical breakthroughs may generate unexpected, often dangerous, side effects. Engineering innovations may result in unforeseen problems of environmental degradation. And confidence in science is challenged when it is revealed that top scientists have 'cooked' their results. The social problems caused by excessive individualism and alienation, of central concern to classical theorists of modernity, remain and are exaggerated by the simulated, wired, abstract world we inhabit, where, for example, 'friends' are only encountered on screens and an enemy can be depersonalized as a blip on the computer and easily erased. Racial and gender inequities persist and have generated genocidal conflicts. Secularization, regarded as the inevitable result of modernity, has not materialized in quite the manner foreseen by classical theorists. On the contrary, in the most powerful, capitalist, liberal democracy—the United States—religion remains a critical determinant in all dimensions of social and political life. In addition, the fundamentalism that affects all religious denominations has become a decisive and divisive factor in global politics.

It is not surprising, therefore, that there is considerable skepticism about the social theorists' hope that a reformed, scientifically based modernity can usher in a golden age of order, progress, happiness and self-fulfillment. One theorist even contends that current '[t]heory discussions have little bearing on major social conflicts and political struggles or on important public debates over current social affairs' (Seidman 1991, 132). Nonetheless, the explanatory capacity of social theory remains important precisely because of the abstractions of social power and the sense that social problems seem to be inevitable, intractable, and beyond individual capacities for change. The theorists' task is to tackle such problems, guarding against the ethical dangers of a 'pure' science that may dispense with the 'real' and make it easier to condone or ignore inhuman actions. As Mills (1963) pointed out, it is the ethical dangers of abstraction that 'hides' the humanity of individuals affected by 'efficient, rational, technically clean cut' actions. Such actions are 'inhuman acts because they are impersonal' (238).

In the present day, modernity is no longer an issue for some theorists. We are now 'postmodern' and therefore we confront a different social universe that requires different ways of explaining the social. But what is postmodernity? Can it present a more positive future for all individuals? And what is the use of social theory if we are postmodern?

Postmodern Social Theory?

The confident assertion that scientific knowledge can act as a progressive force for the freedom and emancipation of humanity by revealing the 'truth' about social and political reality is, according to postmodern theorists, a delusion. In fact, truth claims need to be treated skeptically because they are invariably claims to power (Foucault 1977). For example, one of the truth claims advanced by many social theorists (as well as scientists, theologians, and medical practitioners) well into the twentieth century was that women were unfit for intellectual pursuits. Among the several reasons advanced for this 'truth' was the claim made by many physicians that 'the physical organization and function of woman naturally disqualify her for severe study, and an education essentially popular and largely ornamental is alone suited to her sphere' (Rothman 1978, 27–8).[1] Unalterable physical and mental difference was the 'truth' of gender. As a result, patriarchal power was biologically ordained, immutable, and inevitable. But it has become clear that sex is not a biological binary that separates women from men at birth, and that gender is a variable social/cultural designation.

The postmodern perspective contends that all knowledge is contingent. Plurality, diversity, difference, complexity, and hybridity replace confident universalizing classical theories, the 'grand narratives' that claimed to produce the truth about the nature of social life. But if social theory has to abandon its generalizing, universalizing ambitions (Featherstone 1988), what remains? How can the theorist claim any authority to speak about the social when such reflections are regarded as simply variants on language games or culturally specific notions, none of which can claim any privileged status? More troubling is the question of the sincerity of the postmodern position. The assumption of Western intellectuals in the past that their modernity gave them the authority to speak of or, more arrogantly, for primitive, traditional others may have been rejected, but can we be sure that current postmodern theory is not another variant on this old theme? For example, can the subsistence farmer in Africa or the exploited garment worker in South Asia understand their world as a postmodern space in which individuality is prized, life-style choices and playful consumption are the order of the day, and contingency is embraced as making life worthwhile? Or is this another Eurocentric/North American universalizing theoretical stance?

Whatever the answers to these questions, it is clear that it cannot be business as usual for social theorists (Bauman 1992, 54). The critical point is that social theorists can no longer claim that the classical concept of 'society' is the basic, fundamental theoretical concept. The classical concept was always

tacitly tied to the idea of the **nation-state**. Although it may have been recognized theoretically that nation-states were not closed entities, most theorists continued to confound society/nation-state as the framework for analysis.
In addition, the primary models of society that theorists used were Western
democratic states. It was the use of 'society' in this way that enabled social
theorists 'to speak of social laws of regularities, of the *normative regulation*
of social reality, of *trends* and *developmental* sequences' (Bauman 1992, 60;
emphasis in original). As indicated above, it was this conflation that made
social theory useful to nation-states, especially Western nation-states in their
control over the 'less developed' or 'less advanced' sectors of their own or other
'uncivilized' societies.

The nation-state/society is a porous concept and global social order today is governed more by the needs and dictates of transnational corporations,
NGOs, and international consortiums and agencies. In addition, nation-states
no longer need to employ the old coercive, disciplinary practices of modernity to ensure order and legitimacy. Social order and citizen compliance can
be secured more easily by seduction (Baudrillard 1983). Coercion and control can be exercised through persuasion, impression management, and image
manipulation. Seduced by consumer culture, bombarded with infomercials
and slick advertising, and tempted by the constant creation of new 'needs', the
satisfaction of which is guaranteed to transform the self in new and desirable
ways, citizens have great difficulty in finding ways to articulate their personal
troubles as public issues.

Seduction, however, is limited, if only because there are multiple sectors
of power that compete for the affections of citizens. Furthermore, people are
not robotic dupes. For example, the 'crisis' of voter apathy, or, more realistic-
ally, voter cynicism, is partly explained by voters' realization that elections do
little to alter the fundamental mundane, practical problems of everyday life
(Habermas 1975).[2] The crisis is largely one for political elites whose legitimacy
is rendered questionable when it rests on poor voter response, although consistent poor responses may have the paradoxical effect of forcing political attention on pressing social problems in the hope of regaining voter confidence.

While the self-enclosed notion of 'society' is difficult to sustain, and global
forces tend to generate a fatalistic approach to solving local, national, or international problems, social change is not always a top-down process. Most of
us still identify ourselves as citizens of a nation-state, and the continued proliferation of grassroots pressure groups indicates that not everyone is a solitary, postmodern individual, lost in the crowd, feeling 'unimportant, lonely
and disposable' (Bauman 1990, 68).[3] Problems that may seem overwhelming,
constraining, and even inevitable can yield to citizen pressure. As a result,

social theory is still needed to convert personal troubles into public issues by helping to make sense of the abstractions of social power and how the various forces that appear so constraining are developed, maintained, and might be resisted and changed. It is the social theorists 'special business' to help us to make sense of what seems to lie outside 'the scope of everyday practices' (Smith 1987, 161).

And So What Is the Use of Social Theory?

The classical narratives of social theory may no longer hold up, but the 'post' of postmodernity does not necessarily indicate a radical rupture with the social and political issues addressed by those narratives. If postmodernity is understood as 'after' rather than 'anti' modernity, this 'clears the ground for new political and social strategies which embrace difference, pluralism and the incommensurability of culture and values' (Turner 1990, 12). The important point that should guide the social theorist if she is to play a useful and important role as a public intellectual is that she should not simply identify the significant issues of our time but also offer a critique and thus reveal the way in which personal troubles are public issues that can result in the formation of solutions to these issues. Social theory must claim the 'right to expose the conceit and arrogance, the unwarranted claims to exclusivity of others interpretations, but without substituting itself in their place' on the understanding that the choices made about 'how to go on' in this world are not waiting to be revealed but must be worked for (Bauman 1992, 214). Social theorists still need to 'engage (and enrage) the public', recognizing that they will never win a popularity contest among those who claim power and privilege (Agger 1991, 185). In the complex, risky, global world we inhabit, the 'vocation of the social theorist is . . . to be *positively*—as opposed to negatively and nostalgically—analytical and critical' (Robertson, 1990, 57; emphasis in original).

Conclusion

There is as much need for social theory today as there was in the past. The confidence in the discipline's first intention—making the facts of society accessible to rational understanding—may have been reformulated by a healthy skepticism about scientific claims, but this needs to be balanced by the recognition that scientific theory and practice is still a necessity—all the more so because it is currently under siege by a religious zealotry that hinders the pursuit of the second intention—helping individuals realize freedom and self-fulfillment. It is the second intention that forms the critical, ethical basis for the social theorist's goal when reflecting on current problematic public issues and suggesting solutions.

Questions to Consider

1. How do concepts of community, social solidarity, and social class remain important in explaining social issues in the twenty-first century?
2. How do media reports of non-Western conflict encourage the perception of 'otherness' among those participants?
3. How do social locations affect judgments made about terrorist troubles and help perpetuate social problems?
4. How does the Western significance attached to autonomous individuality affect Western feminist approaches to the problems of non-Western women?
5. Can there be a common set of humanist values in a postmodern, global world?

Notes

1. University or college education was especially dangerous to women because of the 'periodical *infirmity* of their sex' which, on a monthly basis, 'unfits them for any responsible effort of mind, and in many cases of body also' (quoted in Rothman 1978, 25; emphasis in original).
2. It should be noted that the issue of voter apathy seems to be a problem for Western nations. Newly enfranchised citizens in many parts of the world, such as Afghanistan, have had high and enthusiastic voter participation.
3. For example, the collective euphoria expressed by Canadians over the 2010 Winter Olympics was an occasion for the expression of national, patriotic pride for many citizens and certainly for the Canadian athletes.

11 | Does the Past Matter in Sociology?

Rob Beamish

Introduction

With 48 blazing strides, run in under 9.8 seconds, Ben Johnson became the world's fastest human, capturing gold in the men's 100-metre sprint at the 1988 Seoul Olympic Games. Within 72 hours, following a positive test for the banned steroid Stanolozol, Johnson was stripped of his medal and vilified as a cheater (see CBC 2005). Do these events matter now? Why did Johnson take steroids and why are they banned? Have the Games changed since 1988? Because the Olympics are such a major, global phenomenon, these are important questions for many sociologists; they also demonstrate why the past matters.

To understand the events in Seoul and their significance today, this chapter begins with the historical context within which the modern Olympic Games were initiated, their fundamental principles, and the social forces that subverted those principles. Critical to understanding the contemporary relevance of the events at Seoul are the symbolic power of the Games, their commercial value as a media spectacle, and the quest to push athletic performance to the very limits of human possibility. Ironically, rather than resisting the modernizing forces in Europe, the Games became a spectacle that fed directly into the dominant social forces that shape the values of today and create the controversy around the use of performance-enhancing substances in world class sport.

Reviving the Ancient Olympics

The transformation of Europe from a feudal to a market-based society led to new and very different ways of thinking about the world, conducting one's affairs, and carrying on everyday activities. But not everyone thought well of the changes. French aristocrat Baron Pierre de Coubertin was deeply troubled by what he regarded as a catastrophic spiritual and moral decline in Europe. At the close of the nineteenth century, Coubertin initiated a far-reaching, innovative educational program that he hoped would return Europe to its 'traditional values'.

Drawing upon the ancient Greeks' belief that character is developed through the body and not simply the mind and the 'muscular Christians' practice of using traditional English games to build character and moral virtue in young boys, Coubertin believed that sport, appropriately structured, could play a pivotal role in revitalizing the moral and spiritual fibre of Europe (Coubertin 2000, 294–5, 532, 308). Coubertin's image of sport was inspiring:

> The athlete enjoys his effort.[1] He likes the constraint that he imposes on his muscles and nerves, through which he comes close to victory even if he does not manage to achieve it. This enjoyment remains internal, egotistical in a way. Imagine if it were to expand outward, becoming intertwined with the joy of nature and the flights of art. Picture it radiant with sunlight, exalted by music, framed in the architecture of porticoes. It was thus that the glittering dream of ancient Olympism was born on the banks of the Alphaeus, the vision of which dominated ancient society for so many centuries (2000, 552).

Coubertin's Olympics would immerse European youth in a sacred event renewing the spiritual vitality of the participants' souls. He wanted the Games to create a 'spirit of chivalry' in which '"brothers-in-arms", brave energetic men [are] united by a bond that is stronger than that of mere camaraderie, which is powerful enough in itself.' Forged in the cauldron of competition, the Games would create strong, morally sound leaders for Europe (2000, 588, 581).

To reach his goals, Coubertin and the members of the first International Olympic Committee (IOC) excluded professional, win-oriented athletes from the Games. Open only to amateurs during the first 74 years of the twentieth century, Olympic Games' participants tended to come from the social elites because these men had the means to financially support themselves while training in sport.

Immediate Challenges to Coubertin's Project

If the modern Olympic Games were designed to reverse the slide of Europe into the moral abyss of industrial capitalism and its crude materialist philosophy, Coubertin quickly discovered that his project could not escape the realities of the market economy. For example, to launch the Games Coubertin had to rely on wealthy businessman George Averoff's financial largesse to renovate the ancient stadium in Athens, which hosted the first modern Olympiad (Guttmann 2002, 15–16). More important, rather than combating the modernist thrust of capitalist society, the IOC had to hold the Paris, St Louis, and London Games (1900, 1904, and 1908 respectively) in conjunction with world's fairs, which celebrated technology, science, and the ethos of modernity—the forces Coubertin blamed for the demise of Europe's spiritual values.

Three further divisive forces that have plagued the Olympics were also present from the outset—nationalism, professional athletes, and the 'cult of victory'. Preparing for the inaugural 1896 games, Russian, British, German, American, and French officials all criticized the IOC's amateur restriction. Using the Olympics to demonstrate national strength in international competition, each country wanted to use the best athletes possible. Paying lip service to Coubertin's ideals, European leaders were really interested in the symbolic value of winning on the world stage and the pursuit of national interests rather than international harmony.

The disjuncture between Coubertin's principles and the real world of international sport, even at the turn of the twentieth century, was particularly evident in the IOC's conflict with the Fédération Internationale de Football Association (FIFA). Soccer, Europe's premier sport, was excluded from the initial games because the best players in the world were all professional and thus ineligible. When the IOC tried to include soccer in the 1928 games, only 17 teams could meet the eligibility requirements. FIFA asked the IOC to relax its rules and let professionals play or allow amateurs to be compensated for the time lost while at the Games. The staunchly amateur International Association of Athletics Federation (IAAF) pressured the IOC to reject FIFA's proposal, and soccer was excluded again.

Recognizing the value of an international spectacle, FIFA established the World Cup in 1930. It was the direct antithesis of the Games, involving the best players in the world in a tournament in which winning was all that mattered. Overtly commercial and fostering national rivalries, the World Cup was a direct competitor that celebrated everything the Games condemned. By 1936, compromise was possible, but for the IOC the stand against FIFA was significant because it was only on the IOC's own terms that the world's most popular sport entered the Games.

The Nazi Olympics

After 10 Olympiads, additional social forces were pushing the Games farther away from Coubertin's ideal. Ironically, perhaps, it was nationalism and international politics that were among the most significant—a point that was made crystal clear at the 1936 games, at which Nazi Germany demonstrated the full symbolic power and political importance of the Olympics.

Following World War I, Europe was slow to involve Germany in its international affairs, but as the new German Republic established itself, European leaders warmed to greater German participation in European activities. The IOC's decision to grant Germany the 1936 games symbolized that change.

Although the IOC gave the Games to a liberal democratic regime, Adolf Hitler took power in 1933. With no other host available, the IOC could not revoke its commitment. Hitler was actually ambivalent about the Olympics and considered declining them, but Joseph Goebbels, head of the Ministry of Public Enlightenment and Propaganda, saw them as a unique opportunity to project specific images of Nazi Germany domestically and internationally (Teichler 1975).

The Games were just one part of an ongoing, multi-faceted program of Nazi political propaganda. Prior to the Berlin games, the Nazis had routinely exploited the newly emerging technologies of mass communication. Hitler's speeches to vast rallies relied on state-of-the-art public-address systems, and were broadcast on radio and shown in movie theatres across Germany. The Nazis' propaganda events combined dramatic music and the tightly choreographed movement of hundreds of performers inside imposing neo-classical-styled stadiums before thousands of spectator/participants. The Nazis blended music, choreography, drama, and neo-classical architecture into captivating, emotionally draining experiences (Speer 1969; Clark 1997).

The Nazis used their 1934 party congress in Nuremberg as a test run for the 1936 games, and Leni Riefenstahl, the most innovative filmmaker at that time, perfected techniques in Triumph of the Will for use in Olympia, which celebrated the 1936 games (Sontag 1980). At both events, and in Riefenstahl's carefully cropped and painstakingly constructed film 'documentaries', the movement of hundreds of people in enormous geometric formations symbolized the power and order of Nazi Germany. Hitler's entrance through the wide aisles of the assembled throng and his climb to an elevated podium represented his emergence from the people and ascendance from the rank and file to Germany's top position—Führer of the German Volk. Riefenstahl edited both films so that the viewer's attention shifts continually from the massed ranks or spectators to the Führer, to the enormous swastika banners in the stadiums. One cannot miss the message—'ein Volk, ein Führer, ein Reich' (one racially pure people, one leader, one empire).

Nazi ideology celebrated and glorified youth, strength, struggle, and conquest, emphasizing genetic and racial endowment in the Darwinian struggle for the survival of the fittest. Coubertin's Olympic Games already celebrated nature, power, and struggle. The Nazis carefully wove the ideology of racial supremacy into the Games' existing aesthetic, and although some felt that Jesse Owens' victories undermined Hitler's political objectives, the Führer's message was clear to sympathetic German viewers. With 33 gold, 26 silver, and 30 bronze medals (the US won 24, 20, and 12), Germany topped all nations, symbolically placing it once again among the most powerful nations in the world.

Olympic Principles and the Reality of Cold War Sport

Following World War II, the 1948 London games were modest in scale, but the 1952 Olympics in Helsinki were far from low-key. Although Canada, Britain, France, and the United States were allies of the Soviet Union in the fight against Germany, tensions between the capitalist West and the communist East arose immediately after the war. Helsinki was the first battleground in which the world's two new superpowers, the US and the USSR, would confront each other. The Cold War was underway.

With its scholarship athletes trained and developed within well-funded college programs, the United States had a long history of Olympic success. Joseph Stalin, Secretary-General of the Communist Party of the Soviet Union, made it his primary post-war objective to surpass the capitalist nations of the world in everything, including sport (Riordan 1977, 161–2). To that end, the USSR initiated a nationally coordinated development program for Olympic sports. It created an infrastructure of high-quality facilities, professional coaches, scientific training programs, and physiological, bio-mechanical, and psychological research in the pursuit of improved athletic performance, as well as financial incentives for successful athletes (Riordan 1977, 162–4; Senn 1999, 85). By the late 1940s, Stalin was ready to compete directly with the West and sought formal admission to the Olympic movement. Admitted for the 1952 Helsinki games, the Soviets shocked everyone by jumping to an early lead, where they remained until the final day when the Americans finally edged them out for first place in the unofficial medal and point standings. The drama once again demonstrated the Olympic Games' tremendous political significance.

Attracting little attention at the time, the USSR's performance in weightlifting had a crucial impact on the Olympic movement. Watching the Soviets win three gold, three silver, and a bronze, US weightlifting coach Bob Hoffman believed the Soviets were enhancing their performances artificially (Todd 1987, 93). During the 1954 world weightlifting championships, Hoffman and American team physician John Ziegler became convinced that the Soviets were using testosterone to assist their weightlifters.

With the assistance of Ciba Pharmaceutical Company, Ziegler developed the synthetic steroid methandieone (or Dianabol), which he gave to American weightlifters to level the playing field (Ryan 1976, 516–17; Goldman 1984, 94). 'The news of anabolic steroids spread through the athletic community like wildfire,' Bob Goldman (1984, 94) noted, and drugs became the focal point of conversations among athletes and in the sport press. By the early 1960s, steroid use was widespread among athletes in weightlifting, shot put, discus, hammer throw, and other strength events (Yesalis and Bahrke 2002, 53). While the use of steroids was significant, more important was the approach to sport their use indicated. After the Helsinki games, the cold, calculated, scientifically assisted pursuit of victory and national honour emerged as the key force guiding the serious competitors and nations at the Olympics. They would be increasingly dominated by instrumental reason—a term that describes the process where one calculates the most efficient means to a particular end without regard to the broader context of action and decision making.

Although steroids would become the most vilified performance-enhancing substance, it was cyclist Knud Jensen's death, allegedly due to an amphetamine overdose at the 1960 summer games that showed how ominously the all-out quest for victory loomed over the Games.

Political interests were not the only social force behind the increasingly instrumental approach to athlete performance; the Olympics were becoming a commercial success and the training and development of athletes was becoming more professionalized. From a commercial perspective, the USSR-US confrontation made perfect television drama. Spectators around the world could experience events as they happened. Merchandisers saw the Games attracting increasingly larger audiences that could be targeted for sales. As the Olympics proved themselves as a television spectacle, the networks were willing to pay millions of dollars for exclusive broadcast rights. But political drama alone was not enough: US (or at least Western) athletes had to win, and world records had to fall. Those results would occur only if Western athletes trained as rigorously as the Soviets, who were supported by a state-funded system of scientifically based athlete development. Western athletes needed financial support and a scientific infrastructure. Under-the-table performance fees supported the best high-performance athletes as training became more intense. By the 1970s, world-class sport had become a full-time commitment.

All of these forces set in motion a spiral that extended its reach with each Olympiad. While many in the IOC felt it was time to abandon amateurism as a requirement for participation, in 1962 IOC president Avery Brundage realized a 20-year-old dream by incorporating Rule 26, the amateurism code, into the Olympic Charter.

Enshrining amateurism in the charter would not eliminate performance-enhancing substances or the use of instrumental reason, so the IOC established a medical committee to study drug use in sport. The committee recommended that the IOC denounce drug use, introduce testing, and have athletes pledge that they were not using performance-enhancing substances (Todd and Todd 2001, 67). Over the next three years, the medical committee developed the first list of banned substances and added Rule 28 to the Olympic Charter to enforce the ban.

Rule 28 demonstrated two important points about how the Olympics were evolving. First, for Coubertin victory at the Games was always secondary to character development, but in the post-war period, winning—by any means possible—increasingly characterized the Olympics. Rule 28 was designed to curtail some of the ways athletes pursued all out victory. Second, Rule 28 was aimed at the growth of scientifically assisted performance enhancement in general. The cult of victory and the instrumental rationality of sport science were two sides of the same coin, and neither had any place in Coubertin's original vision of the Games. The IOC hoped that new rules would stop the trajectory towards the unrestricted pursuit of Olympic gold. Unfortunately for the IOC, the US and the USSR were not the only nations that wanted to demonstrate national strength through international sport.

Cold War Sport: East German versus West German

At the end of World War II, Germany was divided into four sectors, each occupied by one of the allied victors—Britain, France, the US, and the USSR. The Soviet sector was in the eastern half of Germany and became the German Democratic Republic (GDR) under the political leadership of Walter Ulbricht. Like Stalin, Ulbricht recognized that sport provided an excellent vehicle for building national pride in the new socialist society. Just four years after the end of the war, and before the GDR was admitted into the Olympic movement, Ulbricht began to build what would become the world's most successful centralized sport system.

Ulbricht established the State Committee for Physical Culture and Sport (Staatlichen Komitees für Körperkultur und Sport, or STAKO) and gave it a clear mandate: create a world-class sport system (Spitzer, Teichler, and Reinartz 1998, 38–43). STAKO began by concentrating athletes in centralized facilities. It focused on specific sports such as track and field, swimming, and gymnastics, in which a single outstanding athlete could win multiple medals—in contrast to team sports like hockey, in which 22 athletes could win only one medal for the nation.

Following the Soviet example, the GDR opened children's and youth sport schools, which implemented carefully designed developmental programs for child athletes as they moved from primary or junior elementary schools to senior elementary schools (Röder 2002). STAKO ranked athletes to motivate them and determine the level of coaching they would receive and the competitions they could enter.

In the immediate post-war period, the GDR and the Federal Republic of Germany (FRG) were excluded from the Olympic Games. In 1952, the IOC admitted the FRG to the Olympic movement, but because the IOC would only recognize one National Olympic Committee (NOC) per country, the GDR remained excluded. Under pressure from the USSR, however, the IOC relented and recognized an East German NOC, although it would permit only one German team to enter the Games. Official recognition revitalized the East German system (Gilbert 1980; Hoberman 1984, 201–7).

Due to its superior industrial and financial strength; larger population base; and well-supported voluntary, club-based sport system, the FRG dominated the combined German Olympic team in the initial period. By the early 1960s, however, as world-class sport became more intensely competitive and athletes had to make an increasingly full-time commitment to sport, the FRG's German Sport Federation (Deutscher Sportbund, or DSB) recognized that it had to make significant changes to stay competitive. The DSB thoroughly revised West Germany's high-performance sport system (Lehnertz 1979, 50).

Two decisions in the mid-1960s had monumental impact on the FRG and GDR in particular and the world of high-performance sport more generally. The first was to allow separate German teams from 1968 onwards. The GDR could compete head-to-head with the FRG while also demonstrating its strength in comparison to the world's two leading sporting nations—the US and the USSR.

Second, in 1965 the IOC granted the 1972 games to Munich, West Germany. The GDR immediately recognized that this meant it could defeat the FRG on its own soil. To maximize their chances of victory, Ewald initiated an extensive, high-level, classified laboratory research program, funded by the state, to produce the most scientifically advanced system in sport supporting the use of steroids (see Franke and Berendonk 1997). While not the sole reason and likely not the primary one behind the GDR's success—the financial investment, number of full-time coaches, attention to detail, and extensive recruitment of athletes were all superior to those of other nations—the tight community of world-class, high-performance athletes on both sides of the Iron Curtain knew about the widespread use of banned substances in the GDR. If they were to keep things fair and equal, some athletes, coaches, and sports leaders faced some difficult decisions.

The prospect of embarrassment on its own soil spurred the West German DSB to institute its own high-performance sport system. The program drew heavily from the East German model to produce a well-funded, rationalized sport system. The new plan included national team coaches, high-performance training centres, elite sports schools, talent identification, a sport and athlete ranking system, and improvements to overall athlete development (Lehnertz 1979, 37–52; Bette 1984, 25–8).

There were two outcomes from these developments in East and West Germany. First, the East German system, modelled on the Soviet high-performance sport system, became the blueprint for the West German system, which in turn shaped the Canadian system when it was granted the 1976 games. Canada's system then became the model for Australia and ultimately the US high-performance sport systems (Beamish and Borowy 1989; Beamish 1993; Green and Oakley 2001). The Munich games, with the two Germanys competing head to head, accelerated the development of centralized high-performance sport systems aimed at national aggrandizement through Olympic medals.

Second, nationalist political ambition was intensified as the main driving force behind the developing high-performance sport systems on both sides of the East-West divide. High-performance sport became increasingly professionalized as training and athlete preparation relied more and more on instrumental rationality.

The Rest of the Road to Seoul

Enshrining amateurism in the Olympic Charter in 1964 did nothing to alter the trajectory of the Games (see Killanin 1976). Faced with that reality, a joint IOC-NOC commission recommended in 1970 that the IOC replace the 'amateur code' with an 'eligibility code'. IOC President Brundage complied by changing the designation of Rule 26, but the new code was more restrictive than ever. Despite the new rule, top world-class athletes continued to receive state subsidies in the East or under-the-table fees in the West. Following several embarrassing incidents, in 1974 the IOC brought Rule 26 in line with the reality of world-class high-performance sport, allowing athletes to receive compensation for their athletic performances (Killanin 1976, 151; Senn 1999, 136). It was now absolutely clear that the athletes competing at the Games would be pursuing the direct antithesis of Coubertin's original goal. With IOC approval, the Games would now feature the world's best athletes competing for Olympic gold, financial rewards, and national prestige. The Olympics had become an overtly commercial enterprise generating profit rather than future world leaders.

Although the IOC had opened the Olympic Games to professional athletes, concerns over performance-enhancing substance use remained. In 1967, the

IOC drafted its first list of banned substances (Todd and Todd 2001, 68). It is important to note that although steroids entered the Games in 1952 and were banned 15 years later, the IOC did not test for them until 1976. Over that 24-year interval, the Games had completely shifted to the all-out pursuit of gold-medal performances, and the shattering of world records and steroid use became widespread (Todd 1987; Connolly 1989; Dubin 1990; Francis 1990; Franke and Berendonk 1997; Todd and Todd 2001; Yesalis and Bahrke 2002). From 1988 to the present, the use of an ever-growing array of performance-enhancing substances has continued.

Conclusion

Does the past matter for a sociological understanding of Ben Johnson's performance in Seoul? Definitely. First, history puts the race into its proper context. Johnson used steroids within a system that was, and remains, very different from its public profile. Although victory was marginal to Coubertin's original, lofty goals, the Olympic Games developed differently, and by 1974 the IOC had jettisoned its founding principle (Beamish and Ritchie 2004).

The Olympics' political importance was a decisive factor in Johnson's victory in Seoul. The Nazis had demonstrated the propaganda value of the Games, and from the first 'superpower' confrontation in 1952, the US, USSR, GDR, and other nations had used the Olympics to symbolize national superiority.

A historically informed study of the Games reveals that performance-enhancing substances have a long history in Olympic competition, and their importance grew after 1952. The decision to hold the 1972 Games in Munich provided the GDR with the opportunity to upstage the FRG on its own soil, leading to an extensive state-funded program involving steroids. The GDR's politically motivated, instrumentally rational approach to Olympic sport created the context within which the Seoul games were contested.

Almost 25 years after the first use of steroids, the Olympics were essentially an open competition. Rather than undermining the Games, athletic performances that continually pushed back the limits of human performance enriched the IOC, advanced national political agendas, and turned the Olympics into a multi-million-dollar media spectacular, produced by professionalized, high-performance athletes. Extensive, well-funded, high-performance sport systems, combined with multinational commercial interests, have created a spectacle in which it is not surprising that performance-enhancing substances are so widely used.

For sociologists, all of these points put Johnson's decision to use steroids in a light in which outright moral condemnation is hard to justify. Johnson and other athletes in Seoul competed in the midst of powerful historical forces that induced many of them to place a gold-medal performance above all else. Some (or many) took chances—risked using substances for which they might get caught—to keep the playing field level, to win Olympic gold, to enhance their nations' prestige, and perhaps to gain substantial financial rewards. After dedicating the best years of their lives preparing for Seoul, their decisions are not surprising.

Has anything changed substantially since 1988? Olympic sport remains a fully professionalized and commercialized undertaking. Athletes still pursue performance maximization with single-minded determination. Olympic victory is even more dependent today on the scientifically assisted pursuit of the outer limits of human performance. The performance demands at the world-class level today are so extreme that ergogenic aids have become central to the regular practices of athletes in numerous sports. As a result, even though the World Anti-Doping Agency (WADA) pursues 'the drug cheats' with increasing fanfare, it is continually undermined as politically motivated instrumental rationality is woven ever more deeply into the lives of world-class high-performance athletes.

Why, one might ask, does this matter? Despite all the resources that the IOC and WADA invest in banning performance-enhancing substances, athletes in the modern Games will continue to use them—of that there is no doubt. Under the current policies, the underground use of steroids and other powerful ergogenic substances places the health and safety of athletes at undue risk. Athletes are not monitored properly by medical specialists, the substances they use are often of unknown quality, the full impact of those substances is still not fully known. As a result, Kayser and Smith (2008) and more than 30 scholars who formally supported their argument have cogently argued that, for a number of reasons, the IOC and WADA should adopt a position of harm reduction rather than repression and prohibition (see also Beamish 2011).

First, under harm reduction policies, athlete testing would continue but it would be aimed at determining the health impacts of various substances rather than the presence of drugs. How particular substances, at specific dosages, affect athletes' short- and long-term health could be closely monitored. Those results would allow sport scientists to systematically gather robust data on the long-term health effects of various performance-enhancing substances. This vital information simply does not exist at present.

Second, the open use and monitoring of substances would allow sport scientists to determine the extent to which different training regimes and practices—those with and without substances—actually influence athletes' performance. Do certain substances really enhance performance significantly? If so, in what sports and how? Are there better alternatives? These two steps would allow athletes, coaches, scientists, and medical professionals to replace the truncated, scientific knowledge base currently used with reliable data on training, performance, and health so that athletes could make genuinely informed decisions about how they would develop their athletic talents and performance capacities.

Third, a harm-reduction strategy for performance-enhancing substances in sport would be consistent with the broader social attitudes toward a variety of personal and performance enhancement practices. At present, despite the growing use of drugs, surgery, and technology to improve personal appearance, performance, and quality of life, high-performance sport prevents athletes from using the most up-to-date and effective drugs to overcome injuries, recover from increasingly demanding training regimes, or simply enhance particular elements in the execution of athletic skill and prowess. Within the current context of world-class sport, not allowing the use of all the most advanced technology and knowledge puts athletes' health at risk in far too many ways—and that is avoidable.

Finally, not only does the current policy of proscription put athletes' health at risk—clearly an outcome that goes against the principles of public health—but the vast expenditure of resources on such a tiny fraction of the population, when so many other areas of public health are starving for funds and other resources, makes no sense whatsoever from a public-health perspective. Knowing the history of the use of performance-enhancing substances in sport, the extent to which they are used, and the failure to repress their use provides a critical basis from which one can assess the existing ban from the perspective of policies employed in public health. Knowing the past gives knowledge about the present to plan for change in the future.

Questions to Consider

1. Are Coubertin's original aspirations for the Olympic Games still evident today?
2. How did the Olympics change during the twentieth century? Why are the 1936 games and the 1974 change to Rule 26 particularly significant?
3. What are the key social forces that shape high-performance sport?
4. Did Ben Johnson cheat? Explain.

5. Are there other events in Canadian social life that you can identify in which understanding social change over a period of time makes what seems to be a straightforward issue—Ben Johnson cheated—into one that is much more complex?

Note

1. Writing in the 1890s, Coubertin was interested only in male athletes.

12 | What Do Official Statistics Tell Us about Ourselves?

Nob Doran

Introduction

My recollections of my first term in the honours social science undergraduate program at the University of York, England, are strongly marked by the sociology seminars I attended as supplements to the weekly lectures given to the whole first-year cohort. The first seminar topic was entitled 'In what ways do sociological explanations differ from common sense ones—indeed do they?' And it was here that I was first introduced to a world of scholarship completely different from anything I had ever experienced before. Whereas the formal lectures often took for granted the factual nature of official statistics, these seminars exposed me to an alternative approach that documented how these statistics and the type of sociology that used them (I later found out that it was called 'positivist sociology', signifying that it was a form of social science modelled on insights from the natural sciences) were integrally based on the mundane, common-sense assumptions that tacitly informed their compilation.

More important, this academic insight seemed to fit with what I already knew about the official statistics development process. Growing up on a Luton 'working class'[1] council estate[2] and frequently hearing of encounters between acquaintances and police officers, as well as having had one or two of them myself (over issues like cycling without a light or cycling the wrong way down a one-way street), I was aware that it was common knowledge that official statistics relating to crime and delinquency were compiled from the everyday practices of police officers. They decided to apprehend some people formally while dealing with others informally. And from sociology seminars such as these (which seemed to better explain my experiential world than the emphasis on the factual nature of official statistics that I was receiving in the formal lectures), I went on to discover other related critiques of official statistics. Although I did not know it at the time, these critiques had first emerged in the 1960s and early 1970s. By the time I entered university, they were not uncommon. Moreover, the points they were making helped to change the way that sociology understood itself and also changed the way that I understood myself. So let us take a look at some of the studies that intrigued me in those early days of my intellectual and scholarly formation.

Everyday Knowledge versus Official Statistics: Learning from Ethnomethodology

My first seminar reading (Douglas 1970b) had already alerted me to this alternative intellectual route. But I went on to discover other insightful analyses from similarly trained scholars. Douglas himself had written a book (1967) on the problems involved with the official statistics on suicide, but it was from Atkinson's work (1971, 1982) in this area that I probably learned the most.[3]

Drawing on his own empirical research, Atkinson proceeded to demonstrate the mundane, taken-for-granted, common-sense knowledge that competent coroners use on a daily basis in order to make their decisions about how an unexpected death should be recorded. According to Atkinson, suicide is 'essentially a socially rather than a naturally defined form of behavior' (1971, 168). Thus researchers need to examine how social definitions are produced in everyday social life. When Atkinson examined the coroners' practices, he discovered that interpretive decisions resembled certain predicaments that judges face in courts of law when weighing evidence (1971, 174). That is, competent coroners use an array of informal common-sense methods to help them come to a verdict regarding unexpected deaths.

For example, coroners will weigh considerations such as the following: the presence or absence of a suicide note (suicide notes are commonly understood as being good indicators of a suicide), the mode of death (certain ways of dying, such as hanging, are commonly understood as indicative of suicide, while others are routinely treated as probably not indicative, such as road deaths), the location and circumstances of death (an overdose taken in the middle of the woods, for example, is more likely to be understood as suggesting a suicide than an overdose in bed), and the life history and mental condition of the victim (coroners routinely assume that certain biographies are indicative of suicide).[4] But—and this was the crucial point—there is no mathematical formula for precisely determining how these different clues should be put together to unambiguously determine that an unexpected death was in fact a suicide. Both the layperson's reasoning about suicide and the coroner's reasoning employ informal methods. Each weighs and sifts through evidence before coming to a decision for all practical purposes, based on the information available.

Other early and influential studies that examined the ways in which official statistics were produced included Cicourel on fertility (1967, 1973), Garfinkel on suicide (1967), Sudnow on deaths (1967), Cicourel on juvenile delinquency (1968), and Cicourel and Kitsuse on educational decision making (1963). Other studies examined the mundane methods used to produce other socially relevant but not necessarily official statistics. For example, MacKay's (1974) work examined the everyday methods used by teachers to produce supposedly objective scores for children's reading abilities from the standardized tests they administer. Garfinkel's (1967) work included an examination of the mundane common-sense methods that went into the production of quantitative studies of psychiatric admissions (see Sharrock and Anderson 1986, 44–7, for an interesting Canadian example).

Although different in their substantive areas of investigation, most of these studies shared a common theoretical perspective. They pointed out a radically new direction for empirical social research. In contrast to the conventional sociology of that time, this school of **ethnomethodology**, as its founder Garfinkel named it,[5] prioritized quite different concerns. As has already been shown, it posited that official statistics could not simply be accepted as social facts to be utilized for positivistic analysis. Rather, these statistics were 'practical accomplishments' (Garfinkel 1967) produced by the routine yet often tacit and taken-for-granted methods employed by their compilers.[6] And it was this concern with 'sense-making' that became central in the ethnomethodological perspective.

In fact, the ethnomethodologists invited other sociologists to study this process of sense-making and to make it a central feature of their analyses. And in order to prioritize the study of people's sense-making activities, older sociological conventions had to be radically altered. Garfinkel, for example, argued that it was no longer tenable to treat the 'social actor' as a 'judgmental dope'. Rather, he or she must be treated as a 'practical, rule-using analyst'. In other words, the dominant sociology of that time had tended to see the individual as acting in accordance with a certain normative system (internalized through the socialization process and providing him or her with a set of norms to choose to follow).[7] In contrast, the ethnomethodologists drew attention to the interpretive rather than the normative basis of social life. For them, we all are social actors living in an eminently practical world where rules act more like signposts.[8] As laypeople, we are constantly analyzing and interpreting our surroundings in order to make sense of what is going on around us while simultaneously acting in that social world.

From this engagement with the ethnomethodological approach, I learned some early and very valuable lessons—not just that official statistics are compiled from the mundane, common-sense assumptions about how our social world routinely works (which are then tacitly put into practice by, say, coroners) but a number of foundational theoretical lessons as well. Perhaps most important, I learned that the social world can only be known from within (Turner 1974, 204–5) and that the sociological researcher cannot escape using his or her own 'cultural competence' in order to make sense of his or her everyday world. Just as native speakers of English (or any other language) make sense of each other because they are constantly using a socially shared language (yet this is simply taken for granted by everyone involved), sociologists could also benefit from seeing social life as being structured like a language. And this view had consequences for future research. Just as linguists might study language systematically to show the underlying linguistic patterns taken for granted by native speakers, and just as anthropologists might study a foreign culture to display the meaningful pattern that culture has for its own members, the ethnomethodologists proposed to carry out somewhat similar analyses in the study of the mundane social world that we all routinely share.

Yet despite the force of these early ethnomethodological arguments, I nevertheless felt that the approach still lacked any explicit discussion of features that seemed quite integral to everyday life. Questions of power and conflict were everyday features of my life and the social world in which I lived; yet ethnomethodologists rarely paid attention to these key aspects of social life. Fortunately, in my early intellectual formation I did find some writers who took these questions of power in the everyday world quite seriously. And I learned the most from a feminist scholar—Dorothy Smith.[9]

Everyday Power Relations within Official Statistics: Learning from Feminist Scholarship

I was first formally exposed to the work of Dorothy Smith in my second or third year as an undergraduate. I was introduced to an analysis (Smith 1978) in which she built on her existing ethnomethodological skills to display the 'common sense practices' by which a group of friends routinely came to agree that another friend of theirs, K, was becoming mentally ill.[10] However, Smith's intent in that pioneering paper was not just to document these common-sense practices but also to argue that they worked as mechanisms for excluding someone (1978, 50–2) and as strategies for freezing someone out of a relationship (1978, 25). And as I was soon to find out, this concern with how people get excluded became a central theme in much of Smith's subsequent work. In fact, much of the rest of her career is devoted to developing a feminist sociology called **institutional ethnography** (Smith 1987), which analyses exactly how women have been and still are excluded from what Smith calls the 'ruling relations' (1999, 73–95).

But it was not long after this first encounter with Smith's work that I discovered her own powerful critiques of statistics (1974a, 1975). They were not
only insightful but promised an understanding significantly different from the
analyses developed by the ethnomethodologists. What she especially wanted
to draw attention to was the transformative power of certain official discourses
on everyday experience such that people's (especially women's) subjective experience, their lived 'actuality' (1974b, 257–66) as she soon began calling it,
gets excluded, marginalized, or discarded. And official discourses, such as statistical ones, play a significant part in this process.

Smith's early work in this area isolated three related targets for analysis:
first, the statistics routinely produced by (certain) sociologists in their empirical research; second, the official statistics routinely used but not necessarily
produced by sociologists in their research; and third, the prevailing official
statistics concerning the relationship between women and mental illness. She
deals with the first two issues in her groundbreaking article 'The Ideological
Practices of Sociology' (1974a), and the third in an article published a year
later. In this early work, it is apparent that Smith had learned much from
ethnomethodology but now wanted to move in a more critical direction. And
for this she looks to Marx for help. That is, she combines the ethnomethodological insistence that ordinary people's taken-for-granted, common-sense reality constitutes a paramount reality[11] (on which all other realities, even social
scientific ones, are parasitic) with Marx's concept of 'ideology'. This allows her
to claim that social sciences like sociology are concretely engaged in ideological work. Let us examine her claim more closely.

For Smith, social science and ideology should be opposing terms: we need
to be able to differentiate them. And just as Marx in his day was able to examine the science of economics and show its ideological nature, Smith subjected
sociology to similar scrutiny.[12] For Marx, this necessitated critically analyzing
concepts that nineteenth-century economics took for granted: the division of
labour, exchange, competition, and so on. Specifically, he examined the historical and institutional structures that produced such concepts. So whereas
economics viewed its concepts as natural—as being outside of any history or
institutional structure—Marx insisted on relocating them in their specific social and historical contexts. And as a consequence, he showed that these concepts were ideological. A century or more later, Smith wanted to follow Marx's
method, arguing that if we want to get beyond ideological knowledge we have
to pursue analysis through the concepts of the existing social sciences (economics, sociology, etc.) to their other side—to the 'practical activity of actual
living individuals' (Smith 1974a, 42). It is only through such a process that we
are able to pass from ideology to knowledge.

But whereas this (1974a) article pointed out the ideological nature of the statistics produced by sociologists themselves, another article a year later (1975, reprinted 1990a) focused on the ideological nature of official statistics (at least those on mental illness). Here Smith elaborates the exact nature of her critique of official statistics on mental illness but also clarifies an explicit feminist focus on women's shared experiences and culture. Moreover, her feminist approach is distinctly influenced by her ethnomethodological training. As she points out in the article, whereas other feminist scholars have critiqued the official (US) statistics on mental illness primarily in terms of their accuracy, Smith wants to do something quite different.[13] Building on her prior work on ideology, she wants to show how the statistics are worked up in the first place so as to produce a certain 'reality' of mental illness, a reality that is taken for granted by professionals but that has been compiled by the transformation of the actual lived experience of women.

Specifically, Smith says that we cannot divorce mental illness from the practices of psychiatry that produce it. And building on her earlier claim that 'the actualities of living people become a resource to be made over into the image of the concept' (1974a, 51), she shows how something similar is at work in the social production of 'social facts' such as mental illness. For example, a psychiatric diagnosis of depression that focuses on a 'withdrawal of interest . . . a slowing of mental and physical activity' may act as a set of instructions for a physician to select out of the actual everyday experiences of someone only those particulars that can match this abstract description. In this process, according to Smith, the psychiatric grid is 'specifically inattentive to the actual matrices of the experiences of those who are diagnosed' (1990a, 129). Thus Smith gives us this account written by a working-class woman experiencing the 1930s Depression years:

> This constant struggle with poverty this last four years has made me feel very nervy and irritable and this affects my children. I fear that I have not the patience that good health generally brings. When I am especially worried about anything I feel as if I have been engaged in some terrific physical struggle and go utterly limp and for some time am unable to move or even think coherently. This effect of mental strain expressed in physical results seems most curious and I am at a loss to properly explain it to a doctor. (quoted in Smith 1990a, 128)

Smith goes on to say that this account and this woman's life could quite easily be converted into a case of depression.[14] Yet the woman herself makes no mention of mental illness. Instead, as Smith points out, 'she speaks of arduous work, commitment to sustaining children, exhaustion, perhaps of fear and anxiety, of an unbearable load that is daily borne. She shows us strength rather than illness' (1990a, 129). Yet this 'lived actuality' is discarded in the psychiatric working up of the case. And this point is of crucial importance because, as Smith discovered when she talked to other women who had been labelled mentally ill, 'the threat of invalidation or discounting recurs again and again in experiential accounts' (133). In other words, the problem with statistics on women's mental illness is not so much their accuracy but rather their power to invalidate or discount the experiences of the women who have been so labelled.

Class-Based Experiential Knowledge versus Official Statistics

Not only did Smith's work advance the original insights of the ethnomethod-ologists with regard to our understanding of social statistics (official and otherwise) but her concern with how the everyday is infused with issues of power, control, and authority suggested an important redirection of those original critiques. Nevertheless, I was not totally satisfied with Smith's own theorizing on this subject. Although I had been impressed with her redirection of the ethnomethodological insights, I found her utilization of a rela-tively straightforward Marxism rather difficult to digest. Specifically, Smith has always preferred to use Marx's own work rather than that of later Marxist scholars in developing her feminist theory; yet for me it was unclear to what extent Marx's own descriptions of working-class exploitation could still be productively used a century or so after his death.

I had been brought up in a (supposedly) working-class home, with my father working in manual jobs all his life, including 23 years in a car factory (I lasted three weeks there). Yet I was also a product of the British welfare state (which among other things introduced the possibility of a university education to students like myself), so the classic texts of Marx that I was for-mally taught at the University of York seemed almost as foreign to my lived experience as the introduction to the positivist sociology that I had also ex-perienced there. Moreover, the lack of reception that my burgeoning ethno-methodological interests met from most of the lecturers at York alerted me to the everyday power relations inherent within academia. So it might not be too surprising to hear that I left York feeling a certain degree of frustration with the academic enterprise. Unfortunately, my struggles at the micro level were also being matched by macro-level developments. That is, I graduated into the aftermath of a socio-economic and political crisis, the severity and global effect of which only became clearer over time. Yet its effects on my life and employment prospects were immediate and dire. With the thoroughgoing implementation of 'Thatcherism' underway, I escaped to Canada to improve my employment prospects by taking an MA and waited for things to improve. Thus my life experiences meant that I could not have the easy attraction to classic Marxist texts (such as *The German Ideology*) that Smith had, despite the appeal of much of her micro-work. So I had to search further afield for some other way of figuring out not only my original welfare state/working-class up-bringing but also the rapidly changing macro-social world that was now push-ing me in completely unexpected directions. And eventually I found a critical approach that resonated with my own situated experience (Doran 2004) in a way that Marxism had never been able to do, despite all its explicit attention to the 'working class'.

Nevertheless, the fundamental insights regarding official statistics that I had learned in my earliest days of university life have stayed with me. In fact, much of my own empirical research has built on these ethnomethodological and feminist insights, and has developed them in interesting ways. The ethno-methodologists taught me to always contrast experiential knowledge with offi-cial knowledge, while the feminists taught me to examine the process by which official knowledges transform experiential knowledge. But by beginning from a classed experience and not just a gendered one, I have come to realize that this latter process is not simply one of marginalization, but that it also involves **codification** (Doran 1994, 1996, 2008), and cultural 'incorporation' (Doran 2001, 2003) as well.

Codification is accomplished, in part, via the collection of statistics that reframe and transform an emerging, embodied cultural voice into an official discourse with quite different concerns and priorities. For example, when the embodied, cultural voice of working-class children first emerged in the 1830s, these 'factory children' articulated a shared demand that their health be pro-tected. They were the first generation to grow up working in factories, and their common-sense, paramount reality was that factory life was destroying their health. But, within a decade, that experiential voice had been codified. Official statistics started getting compiled on factory life, and these statistics began suggesting that accidents (rather than health) were the major problem within factories (Doran 1996). In other words, the factory children's experien-tial concerns with their health were quickly displaced onto a narrower concern with 'accidents'. But not only were these factory children's shared concerns dis-placed by this process, their actual voices were replaced as well. The factory inspectors with their official reports and statistics were listened to by parlia-mentarians and law makers; the young workers' own voices no longer even appeared at this level of official discourse. Their shared experiential concern with health was codified into the official, but disembodied, textual concern with accidents instead.

Conclusion

To conclude, this chapter has been concerned with displaying the importance of a critical awareness of official statistics. But I have not been content with simply suggesting that these statistics may be inaccurate in some way or another (as the ethnomethodologists implied). Rather, I have also tried to show what these statistics do. As Smith documented, official statistics have tended to disqualify (women's) voices, and I have learned some important lessons from that research. But because my lived experience was powerfully influenced by growing up in a 'working-class' family, and not just a patriarchal one, my own work has gone beyond this feminist concern with disqualification to explore issues of codification and incorporation as they have emerged at particular points in our history. Whereas the current critical scholarship on official statistics is increasingly going in a historical direction, few of these analyses juxtapose the official knowledge created by these statistics with the experiential knowledge that is transformed in that process.[15]

Finally, what has also been implied throughout this chapter is that anyone's (including your own) receptivity to scholarly material does not just depend on its persuasive ability or on the claimed accuracy of its analysis; it also depends on the situated embodiedness of you, the reader. Although sociologists have been rather slow in recognizing this fact, it is now being realized that how we as readers 'decode' any text depends on the personal experiences that we bring with us to the reading experience. In other words, your understanding of your own age, class, gender, ethnicity, etc., will affect how you decode any text. But what is equally important for you as students to realize (especially as you are now in the very process of becoming educated about your self and your social world) is that we invent and create our 'educated selves' through this process as well. What I have tried to do in this chapter is to make that process more explicit by attempting to show how I decoded the texts that I encountered in my education and what I learned (about myself and my societies) in the process.

Questions to Consider

1. What does it mean to think of a suicide statistic as a 'verdict' rather than a 'social fact'?

2. When Smith looked at the statistics on mental illness in women, her focus was not on their 'accuracy or otherwise'. What was her focus?

3. Both the ethnomethodologists and the feminists suggest that the social world can only be known 'from within'. How do their analyses exemplify this claim?

4. This chapter is continually concerned with the contrast between experiential knowledge and official knowledge. How does the style of writing (the chapter takes the form of a biography) contribute to this?

Notes

1. When I was small, Luton was a large industrial town that had been extensively surveyed by sociologists interested in examining the changing fortunes of the industrial working class (Goldthorpe 1968, 1969; Goldthorpe et al. 1968). So when I went to university I discovered that sociologists generally labeled families like ours 'working class'. Today, there is little industry left, yet Luton is still being surveyed. Recently, it came top of the list of 'crap towns' in the UK (Jordison and Kieran 2004).

2. Although I know of no easy cultural equivalent to the 'council estate' in Canada, I have heard terms like HLM (habitation à loyer modéré) used in French culture and 'the projects' used in US culture to describe superficially similar phenomena.

3. In part, this may have had something to do with the fact that Atkinson's work on the interpretive foundations of suicide seemed to suggest a serious problem for positivist sociology, especially in the format pioneered by the academic founder of the discipline, Émile Durkheim.

4. As one of Atkinson's coroners (1971, 181) stated with regard to a suspect's life history: 'broken home, escape to the services, nervous breakdown, switching from one job to another, no family ties—what could be clearer?'

5. This was in part because he wanted to stress the similarity between this type of research program and studies like ethnobotany or ethnomedicine. Just as the latter were concerned with examining lay (ethno-) understandings of botany or medicine, ethnomethodology was concerned with examining the lay understandings of the social world that people ordinarily use in their everyday activities. That is, it was concerned with showing the lay methods that people use to make sense of social life (Garfinkel 1974). For a contemporary discussion of the name and its utility, see Francis and Hester 2004, 198–214.

6. This concern with studying different aspects of social life as 'practical accomplishments' can be succinctly demonstrated through an example. Garfinkel encouraged his students to go home and act like a lodger or a boarder in their own homes for an hour or so. What this experiment vividly demonstrated was the usually tacit work that goes into the 'practical accomplishment' of routine family life. When the students slightly adjusted their routine methods (behaving politely, talking formally to their parents), they produced a quite different understanding of family life. Frequently, the routine orderliness of family life was temporarily but seriously threatened as parents desperately tried to 'make sense' of what was going on.

7. This normative approach was heavily influenced by the structural-functionalist sociological perspective developed by Talcott Parsons (1902–79). From this perspective, one might see norms as being routinely installed in children so as to give them the energy and directions for acting in socially appropriate ways in the future. More formally stated, these norms act as 'potent energizers motivating lines of effort and striving, on the one hand, and as bases for selecting and integrating courses of action, on the other' (Gouldner 1970, 191).

8. Wittgenstein, a philosopher who has had a tremendous influence on many sociologists and ethnomethodologists, drew attention to this understanding of rules. Signposts may suggest a route

forward, but they do not compel us to follow this route. For example, you may choose instead to
take a more scenic route, or you may choose to follow a different route, perhaps one that is less
congested at that time of day. See Wittgenstein (1953, 80) for more details.

9. Of course I also learned a tremendous amount from other feminist scholars throughout my entire intellectual formation, especially writers whose critiques targeted the power relations inherent
in the world of social sciences (e.g., Smart 1976, 1989; Harding 1986; Haraway 1988; McRobbie
1980; Hartsock 1987). Yet Smith's ethnomethodological attention to the specific, empirical ways in
which power gets constituted has not only remained a constant source of inspiration but provides
a specificity sometimes lacking in other critiques.

10. In this powerful analysis, Smith systematically documents how a story written by one of the friends,
Angela, to show how K became recognized as mentally ill uses a number of 'common-sense' methods to produce itself as a plausible account of someone becoming mentally ill, an account that any
competent reader would tend to agree with after an initial reading.

11. A good discussion of this progression can be found in Smith (1987, 69–78). Here she makes clear
her debt to the pioneering work of Schutz on these issues. See Schutz (1962) for further discussion.

12. What Smith means by sociology here remains rather imprecise, unfortunately. However, the context suggests she is focusing on one of the contemporary positivist versions that had emerged at
that time in response to perceived problems with both the structural-functionalist and Marxist
interpretations of social life.

13. That is, although she begins by showing the problems involved in reading statistics as some type
of representation of reality, she really wants to show this type of reading, even by feminist scholars,
may be missing something more fundamental. Thus she cites several feminist scholars who examined the statistics on women and mental illness and proposed to explain the high rates either in
terms of women's oppression (Smith 1990a, 109) or in terms of women's roles in modern industrial societies tending to produce higher rates of mental illness than among men (112). Yet in both
cases these arguments are based on the examination of statistics that show higher rates of mental
illness for women. Now, although Smith does point out that the Canadian numbers do not seem
to support the types of conclusions that the American feminists Chesler, Grove, and Tudor make
(and she gives some reasonable suggestions as to why the numbers might be counted differently by
different analysts and in two different countries), her real aim is to move beyond this conventional
paradigm, which simply wants to frame the issue in terms of the accuracy (or otherwise) of the
statistics. Instead, she wants to focus on the social organization of these statistics.

14. In another article (1990b), she shows the mundane techniques by which this social process is carried out.

15. The early genealogical, governmentality, and state-formation writings (Hacking 1982, Rose 1991,
Curtis 2001, Corrigan and Sayer 1985) were all instrumental in drawing scholars' attention to the
historical construction of official statistics at the macro level. And these works were especially useful for displaying the connection between forms of knowledge and forms of governing. Moreover,
recent research in this area seems to be furthering this general line of inquiry (Haggerty 2001;
Rusnock 2002; Bayatrizi 2008a, 2008b, 2009; Saetnan, Lomell, and Hammer 2011; cf. MacDonald
2010). In contrast, because my own research has been more influenced by Donzelot's (1984) historical work on statistical thinking (due to its explicit concern with issues of class) and Smith's
prioritization of embodied experience, my research has gone in a decidedly different direction.

13 | Is Social Welfare Viable?
Lois Harder

Introduction

The question of social welfare's viability is, at its heart, a question of the how we think about the relationships among citizens and between citizens and the state. Why is the state interested in social well-being? What responsibilities should the state have for the well-being of the people it governs? And if well-being matters to the state, should the state attend to people's needs through public services, or should it encourage the market, charities, families, or individuals to ensure that people are adequately educated; cared for when ill, young, or elderly; and have adequate income to sustain themselves? Finally what are the consequences of how we choose to define and address issues of social need?

In Canada, only a few voices advocate for complete individual responsibility for citizen well-being. Most of the discussion focuses on the purposes and means of providing welfare and the correct proportions of the welfare mix— that is, what the optimum division of responsibility should be among the state, market, community, family, and individual in providing for people's needs. In effect then, Canadians have decided that social welfare is viable and should survive. We continue to demand publicly provided social programs, assess the quality of our governments at least partly in terms of the services they provide, and expect that legislation and state action will reflect and enforce the (contested) social norms that shape our interactions. But the statement that welfare is viable obscures some profound changes in social welfare provision. It is these changes and the shifting political and social context in which they emerged that will be the focus of this chapter.

Although state-provided social services have existed in some form in Canada since the nineteenth century, the high-water mark of social welfare came with the programs developed in the years following the Second World War. The war was a watershed moment. It followed a decade of severe economic depression in which many people who wanted to work simply could not find jobs. In turn they had no wages to spend in the market and thus there was no demand for goods. The war effort put an end to these difficulties, but politicians and policy-makers feared that post-war military demobilization might bring about a return to the pre-war economic scenario. Some political leaders also worried that a failure to provide for their citizenry might intensify worker unrest and increase the appeal of the communist alternative. This prospect needed to be avoided not only because of its economic effects, but also because of the political and social consequences that were likely to arise if the heavy sacrifices of soldiers and their families were not acknowledged and rewarded. Immediately following the war, there was also a social climate of solidarity. People had worked together in pursuit of a common cause and thus the idea that the people—through the agencies of the state—were responsible for protecting each other from a variety of social, economic, and political risks had an intuitive logic.

This general social tenor provided fertile ground for the ideas of John Maynard Keynes, the architect of post-war economic management in industrialized countries. Keynes asserted that in times of economic downturn, national governments should establish social programs to ensure that people would still have enough money to purchase goods, thus sustaining individuals and families and keeping economies functioning. In the **Keynesian welfare state**, governments were to finance this intervention by increasing taxes in times of economic growth and by deficit spending in times of economic slowdown.

Flash forward to the present and we find a more unsettled approach to the governance of economies and social life. Beginning in the late 1960s, globalizing economies, transformations in labour markets, and changing family formations disrupted the basic assumptions on which the Keynesian social welfare structure was built. Between 1980 and the financial crisis of 2008, Canada, like its Western counterparts, fully embraced a new approach to governing, known in academic contexts as neo-liberalism. Neo-liberalism was a response to the perceived failures of Keynesianism, particularly high levels of public debt, declining economic competitiveness and a 'culture of entitlement' through which an overly generous welfare state was said to have created a passive, dependent citizenry with a weak work ethic. As a result of this perspective, the social programs of the Keynesian welfare state were reformed or simply terminated and the exchange of goods and financial transactions were deregulated (to varying degrees), while the idea of solidarity or collective responsibility was replaced with an emphasis on the competitive individual who was to address his or her needs in the market. The 2008 financial crisis did not shake this emphasis on individual responsibility, but it did undermine the belief that markets could reliably ensure the health of national economies.

Indeed, in the immediate aftermath of the crisis, a range of prominent think-ers asserted that neo-liberalism had encountered its 'Berlin Wall moment' (Peck, Theodore, and Brenner 2009, 96–9). In other words, the financial col-lapse of many of the world's large banks, investment firms, and some national treasuries indicated that regulation *was* necessary and that the state did have a role to play to ensure some stability in the financial system. The leaders of the world's major economies thus agreed that the Keynesian prescription of fi-nancial stimulus provided the means to recovery. Subsequently, however, debt crises in a number of European countries refuelled neo-liberal arguments re-garding the dangers of overly generous welfare states.

Defining Social Welfare

But before we interrogate these shifts in greater detail, and thus provide a con-text for the issue of social welfare's viability, we need to understand what is meant by our central term. Social welfare describes programs that fall into three major categories: education (primary, secondary, and post-secondary), health (hospital care, doctor visits), and income supports (old age and disabil-ity pensions, unemployment insurance, and social assistance). Indeed, we are familiar with social welfare in a variety of guises—for example, student loans, minimum wage laws, and health insurance.

Some social welfare programs are delivered as *direct services*. For example, children attend primary and secondary school; sick or injured people go to clinics and hospitals. Other programs are provided *indirectly*—that is, through the tax system. The tuition and textbook tax credit and Registered Retirement Savings Plans operate on this basis. Rather than governments setting up a pro-gram or a bricks-and-mortar institution, recipients are reimbursed or credited for having purchased a service in the marketplace. Indirectly provided social programs may reduce the tax owed by eligible citizens or provide funds to people who meet relevant criteria. A low income, for example, entitles people to the goods and services tax credit, paid quarterly, and low-income families with children receive the Canada child tax benefit every month.

Our eligibility for social welfare is also determined on a variety of bases, generally categorized as *universal, contributory,* and *means-tested*. Access to health care in Canada, for example, is considered a universal entitlement available to all Canadian citizens and permanent residents regardless of one's income. Employment insurance (EI) and the Canada/Quebec Pension Plan (CPP/QPP) are contributory social programs in that all workers and employers pay a portion of their earnings into these schemes. However, due to eligibility criteria, contributions do not guarantee access to benefits when people need them. Finally, means-tested programs are provided to people who can demonstrate that they lack sufficient economic resources to meet their basic needs. Perhaps the most notorious means-tested program is social assistance or what is commonly understood as 'welfare'. Indeed, social assistance was a key site of neo-liberal policy reform in most Canadian provinces. That said, arguments concerning the state's role in providing for citizen well-being have taken place in a number of policy areas.

The Keynesian Welfare State

Keynes' ideas were adopted in Canada, but they had to be modified to the country's unique circumstances. Keynes' program relied on relatively closed national economies that would enable national governments to heat up or cool down levels of demand in order to mediate fluctuations in the market. Since the arrival of European settlers, however, Canada's economy has been open and export-driven, and thus particularly susceptible to demand from international markets. The second difficulty was the degree of decentralization in Canada's federal system of government and particularly the fact that constitutional jurisdiction over one of the most important tools for implementing Keynesian prescriptions—social policy—lies with the provinces. This is not to say that the federal government has no role in social policy. For example, a constitutional amendment enabled the federal government to administer unemployment insurance and pensions, and it makes regular use of the tax system to provide indirect social programs. Ottawa has also regularly used its spending power as an incentive to encourage provinces to adopt particular programs and standards. Nonetheless, provincial agreement is a prerequisite for federal social policy initiatives.

The tension surrounding jurisdictional control over social policy points to one of the key rationales for social welfare's survival: the role of social programs in demonstrating to voters that their governments are actually doing something for them. Citizens want to be able to see what their tax dollars are buying them, and social programs fill this role. Moreover, in providing for the well-being of citizens, governments are engaged in articulating a sense of common identity, a sense of 'we-ness' that builds solidarity among citizens and can help to shore up support for a particular provincial (or federal) administration. The capacity of social programs to perform this role is powerfully demonstrated in Quebec, where a succession of provincial leaders, whether federalist or sovereigntist, have staunchly defended that province's constitutional autonomy in this domain. They insist that social programs are integral to the articulation and protection of Quebec's distinctiveness within Canada.

If Keynes' ideas around economic management required some adaptation to the Canadian context, his assumptions about an appropriate family form were more easily applied. Grounded in the prevailing idea that men and women had distinct roles, part of Keynesian policy included the payment of a family wage to workers. Men's salaries were to be relatively high in order to enable them to provide for their wives and children. In turn, women would attend to the caring needs of the family, with some support through social programs. Critics have pointed out that recent immigrant and racial minority families were often excluded from this vision due to wage discrimination (O'Connor, Orloff, and Shaver 1999, 111). Further, the apparently natural two-parent, single-earner family had to be reinforced through law. For example, women's participation in the labour market had been actively encouraged during the war years when the call to arms drained industrial and agricultural workforces of their male employees. After the war, in an effort to free up industrial jobs for returning veterans, new tax measures were implemented that severely penalized families in which both spouses had incomes (Prentice et al. 1988). As well, employers were allowed to refuse to hire married women, and women did not have the right to demand the same wage as men when they performed the same work. Divorces were difficult to obtain; women could not establish bank accounts or acquire credit without their husbands' permission; and sexual assault laws did not recognize rape within the context of marriage as a crime.

The Crisis of the Welfare State

The Keynesian model of social welfare was always subject to debate and contestation, but its viability did not seriously come under dispute until the 1980s. By this time, globalization challenged the capacity and desire of governments to protect national economies, while pressures to reduce public spending and to encourage citizens' involvement in their own governance increased the appeal of decentralization. Further, the political urgency of shielding people from social risk had diminished as memories of the Depression and the Second World War grew hazy and the triumph of capitalist economies over their communist alternatives became ever more certain. Instead, the pressing issues were what to do about government deficits, stagnating economies, rising unemployment and inflation, and (depending on one's political bent) moral decay.

With regard to social welfare, Anglo-American governments and their supporters focused on the expense and the consequences of social programs. This focus was maintained regardless of the ideology of the governing party. Although social welfare was originally envisioned as a means to offset social risks, detractors argued that it had engendered grave misuses of programs, undermined people's willingness to work, and created a dependent citizenry. As well, a number of societal shifts and legislative reforms spurred on by feminists as well as by anti-racism and anti-poverty advocates sparked a policy backlash. Initiatives such as pay equity (equal pay for work of equal value) and employment equity laws (which sought to improve the representation of women, disabled people, visible minorities, and Aboriginal peoples in large government and corporate workplaces) were resisted or withdrawn on the grounds that their implementation was too expensive and (erroneously) that they valued quota fulfillment more than merit.[1]

The most vicious rebuttal of Keynesian social welfare was reserved for the terrain of social assistance. Citing an upward trend in the number of benefit claimants, a number that did not diminish substantially during the economic recovery of the late 1980s, and borrowing from the anti-welfare rhetoric of the United States, Canadian governments implemented a series of measures to reduce benefits, tighten eligibility criteria, and detect fraud. Governments measured the success of their reforms in terms of caseload reductions—the number of people removed from the welfare rolls—but invested little energy in determining what became of people who, already in dire financial straits, could no longer count on public assistance. The Alberta government's (short-lived) policy of giving social assistance recipients bus tickets to British Columbia, for example, was indicative of this lack of concern (Peck 2001, 218).

After the Welfare State

Although vigorously resisted, the resolution of the 'crisis of the welfare state' was ultimately determined to lie in the neo-liberal strategies of privatization, marketization, decentralization, individualization, and familialization (Brodie 1997). The **neo-liberal welfare state** sought to reduce the role of the state in the private sphere—the market, the community, and the home—and, where necessary, to resituate responsibility for public services to the level of government that would be most responsive to the needs of specific communities. Neo-liberals argued that a reinvigoration of the private sphere in all of its dimensions would create a 'virtuous circle'. Less regulation of markets and increased emphasis on the provision of social services through the market rather than through the state would encourage greater responsiveness to people's needs. Competition would keep costs low while encouraging innovation. A revitalized market would generate jobs, resulting in less need for social programs (although it was also important to reduce the generosity of income support programs to ensure that workers would be available and willing to work, thus driving down wages through competition in the labour market). Fewer social programs would reduce the costs of governing, thereby contributing to more robust national accounts, reduced taxes, and an enhanced climate for investment. People would be required to live by their wits, thus further stimulating innovation and competitiveness and encouraging the most talented and hard-working people to reach their potential rather than being held back by cumbersome and stifling state regulation and de-motivating levels of taxation.

The growing popularity of this set of ideas formed the context in which the question of social welfare's survival was raised. Reconfigured social programs would require a rethinking of the relationship between citizen and state, a rethinking that can be seen in the shift in terminology—a shift from 'security' to 'choice' and 'responsibility'.[2] Neo-liberals (and indeed progressive reformers) asserted that people should be free to select services that best suited their needs and to pursue interests that would contribute to self-development. The possibility of making poor choices was a necessary component of this freedom, as neo-liberals believed that the possibility of negative consequences would inspire people to take their decisions with greater care. When neo-liberal reformers turned their gaze on the family and its role in assuming formerly state-provided services, responsibility emphatically trumped choice. Feminist critics of neo-liberalism have been particularly attentive to this development (Jenson and Sineau 2001; Lewis 2001). They observed the degree to which reduced hospital and long-term care budgets have translated into an increased reliance on the labour of family members. Work that had been performed by trained medical professionals became the task of a wife, mother, or daughter, whether or not she had the skill, time, or desire to assume these caring tasks. This assumption effectively fell back on 'traditional' as well as Keynesian ideas about the gendered division of labour despite the fact that wage rates and social policies no longer supported the male-breadwinner family model.

The New Social Welfare

Persuading voters that a neo-liberal reconfiguration of Canada's social policy regime was worthy of their support required a careful plan of attack. While it was true that many people were displeased with elements of the Keynesian welfare state, they did not necessarily see the resolution to their concerns lying in greater reliance on the private sphere. Moreover, the neo-liberal reform effort also had to proceed carefully around programs that had most successfully articulated a collective Canadian identity. For example, the idea that ill health can befall anyone regardless of his or her life choices and that a robust public health care system is the most important defining feature of the Canadian identity (true in both Quebec and the rest of Canada) suggests that the old notions of collective identity and mutual obligation remain resilient in the face of neo-liberal alternatives (Brodie 2002, 69; Soroka 2007). Still, the neo-liberal marketing plan has had some notable successes. Canadians have generally accepted the characterization of post-war social programs—particularly income support programs—as passive, overly generous handouts that provide too soft a cushion. Canadians have been persuaded by proposals for the creation of an active citizenry, providing a springboard into the job market and a hand-up in times of need. The language of activity, encouragement, and expectations feeds into a sense that citizens need to become more responsible for their own well-being rather than blaming 'the system' for their troubles.

In the 2000s, the original slash-and-burn approach of neo-liberal social policy reform took on a slightly gentler tone. European governments as well as the Organisation for Economic Co-operation and Development (OECD) raised concerns regarding the negative social consequences of strict neo-liberal policies. The language of social cohesion, social exclusion, and social investment began to emerge. And while this language was not as prevalent in Canada, Canadian policy-makers did shift their energies from cutbacks to policies that focused on strategic investment. As Denis Saint-Martin explains, the new social policy language emphasized opportunity and the future (2007, 284–5). The emerging regime was dubbed the **social investment state** and its key figure was the child (Jenson and Saint-Martin 2003; Wiegers 2007). The innocence of children and their obvious dependency made them a suitable object for governments that needed to demonstrate their commitment to citizens but had embraced neo-liberal individualism. But even more importantly, children were seen to represent the promise of what is to come and they provided a useful distraction from the discomfort of the present.

In this spirit, the federal Liberal government implemented the National Children's Agenda. One of its key programs was the income-tested National Child Benefit (NCB), which had already been introduced in 1997. Provided to families with children, the benefit is offered on a sliding scale—the more income you earn, the lower the benefit. The program also includes a supplement (and potentially provincial programs) for families with very low incomes that is designed to encourage families to remain off of social assistance. As well, the Liberals also began to invest in early childhood education and embarked on a series of negotiations with the provinces to increase access to child care. But in a fascinating example of the continued resiliency of ideological debate, once the Conservative Party was elected in 2006, it promptly cancelled these agreements (but maintained the NCB) and implemented the Universal Child Care Benefit Program (UCCB). In its universality, this program appears to swim against the tide of neo-liberal reform. On the other hand, it did replace a more expensive child care initiative. But the UCCB also provides a strong indication of the Conservative government's preferred family form and the party's effort to negotiate between neo-liberalism and moral conservatism. As the program is most generous to families in which one parent remains out of the workforce to care for preschool children, it provides a larger benefit to two-parent, single-earner families that are sufficiently wealthy to enable one adult to withdraw from paid work. Since its value is low ($100 per month, per child under age six—which is taxable and thus reduced for income earners), the benefit cannot reasonably be claimed to meet its purported objective of 'providing choice in child care' (Battle 2008). It does, however, represent a modest investment in the future while also tipping its hat to the family values of the past.

Conclusion

In this discussion of social welfare, I have argued that the question of its ongoing viability is a product of a particular historical moment in which the fiscal crisis of the state became the focus of public policy. However tempting the elimination of public responsibility for personal well-being might have been to some neo-liberal ideologues, a full-scale public withdrawal from the care of citizens was never really in the cards. The role of social policy in legitimating governments, in integrating citizens into the prevailing mode of economic production, and even in articulating a national identity has made social welfare a key instrument of governance.

These general claims about the significance of social welfare should not, however, blind us to the very significant differences in the way that social welfare is conceived and the dynamism in its purposes. The Keynesian social welfare system, as we have seen, established social programs that buttressed the specific workings of Canada's post-war economy, reinforcing the single-breadwinner, two-parent nuclear family with its gendered division of labour and building a sense of national identity. However, as political struggles were undertaken and economic structures shifted, this arrangement began to weaken, creating a crisis and subsequently a new neo-liberal attempt to articulate the relationships among citizens (as individuals and in families), the market, and the state. Under neo-liberal social welfare prescriptions, a globalized (or in the Canadian context, North Americanized) economy is supported by active labour market policies, including a more competitive labour market, enhanced choices for service provision, and increased personal responsibility for forming and maintaining the ties that bind—whether these be at the level of family, the community, or the nation. What these changes demonstrate is that the viability of any specific social welfare order, whether envisioned by post-war Keynesians or contemporary neo-liberals, rests on whether it establishes a mutually reinforcing and supportive relationship among the individual/family, the market, and the state. It seems to me that some attempt to articulate a more or less coherent framework for these relationships will continue to be a feature of governance for the foreseeable future.

Signs of stress are apparent in the neo-liberal social welfare regime. Concerns about the adequacy of private service provision, the inability of low-wage work to provide an adequate income, the inattention to work-family balance, and the consequences of budget reductions on public services are matters of growing public concern. How these concerns will be addressed is, again, an open question. Perhaps we will soon find ourselves asking, though this time in a new context, whether neo-liberal social welfare is itself viable and can survive.

Questions to Consider

1. What was the social and political context in which the question of social welfare's survival emerged?
2. How has Canadian social policy changed from the Keynesian welfare state to the neo-liberal era? And how does the social investment state fit in?
3. The chapter argues that during the Keynesian welfare state period, social policy was important in articulating a Canadian national identity. Is this still true? Why or why not?
4. Why were social assistance programs singled out as the area of social policy most in need of reform?
5. Why are children so important to the social investment state?

Notes

1. For a discussion of the federal government's unwillingness to abide by the terms of its own pay equity laws, see Fudge (2002, especially 115–24). Regarding employment equity, see Bakan and Kobayashi (2000). Employment equity laws in Canada required employers to hire job candidates from the four identified groups when there was no demonstrable difference between the equity candidate and the person from the non-targeted group. Quotas were not part of this system, although it was expected that the representation of women, members of visible minorities, disabled people, and Aboriginal peoples would increase.

2. The terminology gets a bit complicated here. 'Neo-liberal' refers to a person or policy that advocates private over public provision. The term invokes the idea of 'liberal' in its original eighteenth-century form, which promoted the individual over the collective and the institution of rights as a means of protecting individuals from the incursions of the state. Both Conservative and Liberal

governments in Canada have been characterized as 'neo-liberal' since the 1980s. The term 'neo-conservative' adds further complexity to the mix. Neo-conservatives are distinguished from neo-liberals at the level of morality. Whereas neo-conservatives and neo-liberals generally agree on issues surrounding the freeing up of markets from state control, they part company when it comes to the state's role in legislating morality. Neo-conservatives, for example, tend to support restrictions on abortion, advocate for the prohibition of same-sex marriage, and uphold traditional notions of the nuclear family, preferably with a stay-at-home mother. To the extent that neo-liberals weigh in on these debates, they generally tend to advance the opposing position.

14 | Who Governs Whom in Canada?

Dawn Moore

Introduction

For Canadians, the answer to the question 'Who governs whom?' in our country may seem obvious: we are governed by our various levels of government (federal, provincial/territorial, municipal). However, while it is true that these bodies are responsible for our legal regulation, if we think more broadly about governance, we see that it is carried out by a variety of people in different ways. **Governance**, simply put, includes all the different ways in which people are encouraged to behave in certain ways (and not in others). In order to understand the complexities of governance, it is helpful to start by looking at some of the different ways theorists have tried to explain how and why we follow rules and codes of behaviour (both formal and informal) as well as who benefits from different kinds of governance.

What Are the Different Ways We Can Think about Governance?

The Collective Conscience and Forms of Solidarity

Émile Durkheim, as noted in this book's introduction and elsewhere, was one of the first Western thinkers to argue that society exists independent of nature and is influenced and shaped by uniquely social forces. For Durkheim, the question 'Who governs whom?' was not as important as the question 'What governs whom?'. The 'what' for Durkheim was morality. Durkheim argued that societies have what he called a **collective conscience**—the shared morality or the set of values that everyone in a society holds in common. The whole point of governing in a society, according to Durkheim (1989 [1893]), was to reaffirm and protect the collective conscience. For example, a society has a shared value that murder is wrong. When a murder happens, it offends that value and threatens the collective conscience—as though the murderer is saying 'I don't care about the shared values of this society—I am challenging them.' At this point, according to Durkheim, governance kicks in. The society responds to the murder because murder is wrong according to the collective conscience. The murder serves a function because it allows the whole society to get together and reaffirm its collective belief that killing other people is not okay. In punishing the murderer, the society can act out this belief.

The case of Robert Latimer serves as a good example of how we can use Durkheim's idea of the collective conscience to understand responses to Criminal Code infractions in Canada. Latimer was accused and eventually convicted of killing his disabled daughter Tracy, who suffered from acute cerebral palsy. The case wound its way to the Supreme Court of Canada (SCC) as Latimer defended himself by framing his actions as a mercy killing—qualitatively different from the kinds of killings interdicted under the Criminal Code definition of first-degree (or premeditated) murder. Latimer argued, and eventually partially convinced the courts, that what he did was an act of compassion that was not worthy of the harshest penalty available in Canadian law (a life sentence with no parole eligibility for 25 years).

How does the notion of the collective conscience help us to understand the case of Robert Latimer? In looking at this case, Durkheim would tell us that it has a certain functionality. The question of whether or not an individual has the right to take another individual's life in order to end suffering is an essentially moral one. Latimer's actions give society a chance to revisit the moral questions that arise out of such a situation. Does mercy killing merit the same punishment as killing based on revenge? Does mercy killing merit any punishment at all? Does one person have the right to decide when another person's life should end? In opening up both the public and legal debate on these questions, Latimer's case allowed Canadian society to re-evaluate its stance, examining the collective conscience. In the end, the courts, in what many would argue was the best reflection of public opinion at the time, offered a softened response to Latimer that suggested that his crime was not as heinous as some but still maintained that what he did was wrong both morally and legally. So the case of *R. v. Latimer* was a chance for Canadian society to reaffirm its collective conscience around the notion of mercy killing.

Of course, this is not what actually happened in the Latimer decision. There never was and never will be a collective voice of Canadians who feel the same way about the Latimer case. The press coverage over the eight years it took for the case to wind its way through the courts shows a country divided on the issue, with citizens arguing all sides of the debate. The fact that there was not a collective and single voice of Canadians responding to the Latimer case illustrates a common criticism of Durkheim's ideas: it is difficult to imagine a society in which a collective conscience might exist. Given the diverse nature of our society, it is inevitable that large numbers of people will disagree with each other on moral issues. Canadian law is full of examples of this. Canadians have differing opinions on abortion, the decriminalization of marijuana, the death penalty, the use of fetal stem cells, and so on. While it is true that when these morally loaded cases arise they do give Canadians a chance to revisit the issues and engage in public debate as well as raise the potential for law reform, the results of the debates are not likely to reflect any sort of collective conscience.

Let us turn to another way of thinking about governance in order to determine whose will gets reflected in attempts to make and change law.

Ideological Domination

Another way to examine how governance happens in Canada is to look at how different groups are governed. There are many different ways in which we can define different groups in Canadian societies. Groups might be defined on the basis of age, ethnicity, sexual orientation, and so on. In terms of governance, many social scientists are interested in how the question of social class organizes people into groups that are then governed differently.

The idea that people are governed on the basis of their social class is most famously attributed to Karl Marx (1970 [1859]), who argued that the economic structure of a society dictates who gets to be in control in that society and who does not. Marx was writing about society just after the Industrial Revolution. While Marx's ideas continue to have considerable influence on how people think about issues of governance and power, many social thinkers who came after Marx felt that his sole focus on economic structure was overly simple and did not accurately reflect the complicated structures of governance in capitalist societies. One theorist who took Marx's ideas and embellished them in an attempt to reflect these more complicated issues was Antonio Gramsci.

Gramsci's (1992) biggest concern was what he called **ideological domination** or ways of thinking and governing that kept some people on top to the disadvantage of everyone else. According to Gramsci, capitalist European and North American societies were governed by pervasive ideologies or ways of thinking that came from and benefited the ruling class. This ideological domination served to make sure that one group of people and their way of governing stayed in power.

According to Gramsci, there are two different ways by which ideological domination can happen. First, people can be coerced. As noted above, there are many examples of societies governed through brute force and oppressive laws. The European 'witch craze' of the Middle Ages, the colonization of the Americas, the genocides perpetrated by the Nazis and Khmer Rouge, the anti-Communist 'Red Scare' in the United States, and most recently governments' response to the 'Arab spring' of 2011 are all examples of regimes changing the ways in which people think and act through the use of fear, intimidation, and violence.

Ideological domination does not always occur through such coercive and brutal means. There are many subtle ways by which people can be governed such that they give their consent. For example, even though there is no law dictating that we behave this way, we all tend to address certain people (doctors, judges, heads of state, religious leaders, and even university professors) by their formal titles and surnames, while expecting that these people will respond to us using our given names. This practice immediately affirms that the people with titles are more powerful than those only addressed by a first name. By continuing to follow the convention of using titles, Gramsci would suggest, we consent to a power structure that subordinates us. We consent to this power even though it offers no benefit to us and we face no formal punishment if we fail to conform.

Discipline and Normalization

As noted in Chapters 1 and 12, the practice of governing individuals and populations is not always as overt as those described above. In *Discipline and Punish*, the French intellectual Michel Foucault (1977) noted that governance often comes in extremely subtle forms. For Foucault, **discipline** is governance on a subtle and ubiquitous scale. To be governed by discipline means to be governed thoroughly on an individual level. Foucault suggested that military training was the ideal example of this kind of governance. As in prison, the strict regime of the military training camp means that a person's every action is tightly regulated. Mealtimes, bedtimes, rest times, training times, means of travel (marching in step), conversation (addressing superior officers by correct rank title), and even hygiene and dress are all regulated through military training. The idea is to create a perfectly trained soldier who will behave in exactly the same way as every other soldier without having to be forced to do so.

There are three characteristics of this kind of power. First, discipline involves *hierarchical observation,* which means that someone (or something) is watching. In the military, we see hierarchical observation in the form of commanding officers who watch over their trainees' every move, ready to correct an error in uniform or failure to complete a task in the proper sequence. Prisons have hierarchical surveillance in the form both of officers watching over prisoners directly as they go about their days (and nights) and also through the architectural design of the prison. One of the most popular designs for prisons, particularly when governments first started to build them in the eighteenth century, was borrowed from Jeremy Bentham. He called his model for a prison the 'Panopticon' (Foucault 1977). Canada's oldest prison, the Kingston Penitentiary in Kingston, Ontario, is designed on exactly this model.

The Panopticon looks like a wagon wheel with a central hub and 'spokes' in the form of cell ranges coming out from the middle. The central hub is the guards' tower, designed so that guards can see down each of the cell ranges and control the locking and unlocking of all doors (including cell doors) without ever having to leave the central hub. In addition, the hub is designed so that it is impossible for prisoners to know whether or not a guard is watching them. The term 'Panopticon' (derived from the Greek words *opticon*—'observe' and *pan*—'all') literally means 'see everywhere'. While guards can see out, prisoners can not see into the hub. The Panopticon is still used as a basic design for prisons because it allows for constant surveillance of prisoners by very few staff. Because prisoners never know for sure whether or not they are being watched, the expectation is that they will behave themselves simply because the possibility of being watched by someone in authority always exists.

Our urban spaces contain various versions of the Panopticon that we encounter every day. Technology has brought us surveillance cameras, which have become standard features of the decor in banks, shopping malls, and government buildings. More and more urban centres in high-crime areas are also equipped with surveillance cameras as a way of curbing criminal activities. The idea behind the use of these cameras is exactly the same as that of the Panopticon. People are more likely to behave themselves if they think they are being watched, regardless of whether or not the cameras are actually recording anything or if anyone will actually view the surveillance tapes. This kind of watching is a passive and subtle form of governance. No one is actually doing anything to anyone, but people still monitor their own behaviour as if someone were watching them.

The second characteristic of discipline is that it *operates through the use of norms.* A norm is a generally accepted idea of how a person ought to be. The importance of the norm as a tool of governing is made very clear by Foucault in his analysis of norms and madness. In another well-known text, *Madness and Civilization* (1988), he suggests that many of our ideas about insane behaviour come out of scrutiny of behaviours that can just as easily be understood as deviating from a particular norm. Foucault called this kind of governance **normalization**, referring to the ways in which certain ways of being are made 'normal', making alternate ways of being 'abnormal' and thus subject to governance. For example, until 1973, homosexuality was considered a form of mental illness: its symptoms and treatment were detailed in the *Diagnostic and Statistical Manual*—the handbook of psychiatry. People revealed as homosexual could be institutionalized as a way of 'healing' them (see Chapter 4). At the beginning of the 1970s, the Ontario legislature was deeply involved in attempting to 'cure' the homosexuality of prison inmates because it saw same-sex relationships within prison as indicators of an individual's higher chance of reoffending or committing additional 'deviant' acts.

Most people now accept that there is nothing sick about or wrong with people who are attracted to members of the same sex. The designation of homosexuality as a psychiatric illness was much more about the fact that people who engaged in homosexual activities went against the norm of heterosexuality deeply ingrained in our society. People eventually started to challenge the idea that homosexuality was an illness by showing that homosexuality is common and that people engaged in same-sex relationships are as 'normal' as anyone else in society. Canadian law is now moving more and more toward embracing same-sex relationships as part of the norm of Canadian society. In the cases of *M. v. H.* as well as *Egan and Nesbitt v. Canada,* the Supreme Court of Canada (SCC) recognized that same-sex couples were entitled to benefits similar to those of opposite-sex couples (such as Canada Pension Plan survivor benefits) and also liable to the same obligations (such as spousal support and equal division of a shared home on dissolution of a relationship). The most recent SCC decision concerning the normalization of homosexual relationships in Canada was the *Same-Sex Marriage Reference,* in which the Court said it was illegal to exclude same-sex couples from the existing definition of marriage.

The third aspect of a disciplinary regime is that *the consequences for failing to adhere to expected or prescribed behaviours are also varied and subtle.* Those caught through panoptic surveillance transgressing prison rules of conduct by, for example, passing something to another prisoner may have privileges such as seeing visitors or receiving mail taken away. Students caught skipping school and therefore failing to adhere to a set schedule might be given a detention or have their parents called in to meet with the principal. If you are rude to your friends, engage in offensive behaviour, or gossip behind other people's backs, you might find yourself ostracized, gossiped about in turn, or made fun of. The point is that the consequences of failing to comply with the governance structure in a disciplinary regime are not necessarily punitive in the sense that the criminal law is punitive. Instead, these consequences come in the form of what Hunt and Wickham (1994, 21) describe as 'micro-penalties and rewards'.

Who Has the Right to Govern?

Governance can take place in all manner of relationships and can be understood from a wide variety of perspectives. But how does it actually happen in

Canada? What does the law tell us about who gets to govern whom and how these relationships are meant to work?

On the broadest scale, governance in Canada is divided among different forms of government. With some overlap among jurisdictions, the federal government, for example, is in charge of a wide range of areas, including international relations, income and excise tax, the Criminal Code, national defence, the environment, treaties with the First Nations, fisheries, air travel, immigration, and employment. The provinces are meant to deal primarily with education, highways, health care, social services, liquor laws, casinos, utilities, and drivers' licences. Municipal governments are in charge of local by-laws, pet licensing, parking laws, city streets, property taxes, fire and ambulance (and, in some cases, police) services, and some social services.

Canada also has forms of indigenous governance. The Constitution Act of 1982 recognizes Aboriginal rights as outlined in the various treaties struck during colonization. This acknowledgement also includes the right of Aboriginal communities to govern themselves. Notions of self-government are becoming more and more central to the ways in which the Canadian government deals with First Nations peoples. In large part, the increased move toward self-government is a bid by the Canadian government to rectify the wrongs done to Aboriginal peoples throughout colonization and in its aftermath. The involvement of European governments in Aboriginal affairs has historically been disastrous for Aboriginal peoples, resulting in the loss of life, health, safety, culture, land, autonomy, and children. Aboriginal communities work toward self-governance because they want to be able to dictate their own affairs and shape their communities independent of the Canadian government, and models of self-governance vary from community to community. Communities that have adopted a self-governance model do not exist outside of Canadian law: they are still governed by legislation like the Criminal Code and the Child Protection Act. The administration of these laws, however, and the establishment of other forms of law and governance often fall to the local government. Band councils, for example, can be responsible for a wide range of governing practices, including the issuing of licenses, policing of communities, enforcement of Aboriginal laws and running of Aboriginal courts, health care, education, family matters (such as adoption, marriage, divorce, and child protection), hunting and fishing regulations, housing, social services, and resource management. In many cases, Aboriginal communities will work in conjunction with non-Aboriginal governing bodies in order to fully administer all the different forms of governance within the framework of limited resourcing. Aboriginal communities that have established their own policing systems, for example, may have one or two officers who do the day-to-day work of policing (dealing with traffic violations, responding to small-scale crimes, crime prevention work, and public education). However, if a major crime such as a murder occurs, these small police services often simply lack the resources to deal with the crime adequately. In these situations, the local band council will often seek the assistance of a larger police service such as the RCMP, which may come into the community for a specified period of time to assist with the investigation.

In Canada, then, the formal right to govern is assigned through legislation to various levels and forms of government. The result is that a good deal of power is given to a small number of people. How do we make sure that our governments do what they are supposed to do? How do we make sure that they do not abuse their powers?

How Do We Control the Right to Govern?

The democratic structure of Canadian governance is one way through which we put limits on state powers. Our federal government is made up of three different branches, which are meant to keep each other in check. The executive branch consists of the prime minister and cabinet. These are the people who are directly responsible for drafting the laws and policies used to govern the country. Most of the decisions made by the executive branch have to be approved by the legislative branch of government. Parliament is the federal legislative branch, comprising the House of Commons and the Senate. Legislators debate and vote on pieces of legislation and are expected to reflect the will of the public. Finally, we have the judicial branch, and in Canada the highest level is the Supreme Court. The Court's duty is to hear cases pertaining to all areas of Canadian law and render final decisions on those cases. It has the power to uphold, strike down, interpret, or otherwise direct amendments to laws.

The Charter of Rights and Freedoms

The Supreme Court often hears cases in which a citizen claims that a certain law or practice of government is unfair. In order to make such a claim, the citizen (or group of citizens) often appeals with reference to the highest law in the land—the Charter of Rights and Freedoms. The Charter was enacted in 1982 along with the new constitution, and it is the supreme law of the country. This means that all other laws must conform to the principles set out in the Charter, and many scholars see it as the ultimate check on governance in Canada. The Charter only applies to matters between the citizenry and the state, which means that issues of private law such as a dispute between two businesses over a contract are not governed by the Charter. It can only govern the laws and actions of a Canadian government.

The Charter sets out seven general areas of freedoms for all Canadian citizens, guaranteeing freedom of thought, conscience, religion, association, the press, expression, and assembly. It also outlines the rights of Canadians, such as the right to vote, to move about the country, to be taught in French or English, and to life, liberty, and security of person as well as rights upon arrest, rights to equality, rights to have the government function in both official languages, and the right to be protected from discrimination. Many of the legal disputes that reach the Supreme Court concern disputes around these rights.

The case of *R. v. Keegstra*, for example, involved a dispute around the guarantee of freedom of expression under section 2b of the Charter. James Keegstra, a high school teacher in a small town in rural Alberta, was also anti-Semitic and a Holocaust denier. Keegstra taught his students that Jews invented the Holocaust in order to gain sympathy. He argued that Jews are morally corrupt and untrustworthy and expected his students to regurgitate these views in tests and exams. Keegstra was charged and convicted under a section of the Criminal Code prohibiting the 'willful promotion of hatred against an identifiable group', and his case went all the way to the Supreme Court. Keegstra defended his actions by saying that the Charter of Rights and Freedoms guaranteed him freedom of expression. He claimed that because the Charter was the highest law in the land, it trumped the Criminal Code proscription of hate crimes. Essentially, Keegstra argued that he had a fundamental right to freedom of expression, which could not be overridden by the Criminal Code. Keegstra lost his case at the Supreme Court—but only by a vote of one.

The judges who voted against Keegstra reasoned that there was another provision in the Charter that allowed for the removal of any right or freedom guaranteed under the Charter if the removal of that right or freedom can be 'demonstrably justified in a free and democratic society'. This phrase comes from section 1 of the Charter, the intent being to leave room for the government's ability to create laws that do things like limit freedoms or treat people unequally. In order to enact those laws, the government must prove that limiting a right or a freedom is in the best interest of the public and the nation. We have many laws that limit our rights and freedoms in this way. The Criminal Code sets out penalties for people who break the law, penalties that include removing basic freedoms such as the freedom of movement and of association. Prisoners incarcerated in provincial prisons also lose the right to vote.

What If You Don't Want to Be Governed in a Specific Way?

Despite what Durkheim would have us believe, there are many laws and practices of governance in Canada that people simply do not agree with or do not conform to. Our governing structures and practices, both formal and informal, are constantly changing and being re-evaluated. The history of governance in Canada is replete with instances of people working to resist governing structures and change them.

One of the most famous examples is the case of *Muir Edwards et al. v. Canada (A.G.)*, also known as the Persons Case because the decision declared that women are 'persons' under Canadian law. The case was brought forward in the late 1920s by five women (known as the Famous Five): Henrietta Muir Edwards, Irene Parlby, Nellie McClung, Louise McKinney, and Emily Murphy. The women had gone to court in Canada to find out whether or not women could become members of the Canadian Senate. The law concerning appointment to the Senate stated that senators had to be 'persons', and the question these women posed to the court was whether or not women constituted persons. All levels of the courts in Canada concluded that women were not in fact persons. However, the women persisted in appealing these decisions until the case ended up in the British House of Lords (during this time Canada still had significantly strong ties to the UK, which meant that the highest court in the UK, the House of Lords, had the final say in Canadian legal disputes). The decision written by Lord Sankey found in favour of the women, arguing that women were indeed persons under Canadian law and as such could become senators. The case was a landmark for women's rights in Canada since it was the first time in Canadian history that women had gained this kind of legal recognition.

Conclusion

When we think about different ways of understanding the relations of governance, it is clear that there are a number of different perspectives we could adopt. We can understand governance through the lens of morality as Durkheim suggested. Alternatively, we could see it as a product of social inequality and domination as Gramsci did. Or we could adopt Foucault's perspective and see governance through the lens of discipline or 'micro' governing strategies.

Canada has a complicated formal system of governing that is largely informed by the Charter of Rights and Freedoms. As the most important law in the country, the Charter is used to challenge other laws and governmental practices—but it does not provide ultimate protection: the Keegstra case shows us that our Charter rights can be lawfully violated in the name of the public good. Still, people and popular movements can have an impact on governing and are capable of changing the governing structures that regulate a society. The case of women legally becoming 'persons' in Canada reminds us that people can and do resist forms of governance and work to change rules they find unfair.

Questions to Consider

1. In what ways should the right to govern be limited?
2. Is it always beneficial for a group of people to have a government? Are there any examples or situations in which government might harm people?
3. Does government only happen through houses of parliament or legislatures? Are there other mechanisms by which people are governed?

PART III

Critical Imaginations and Canada

The final part of the book turns to the critical engagement of various topics, often using theoretical concepts and substantive issues raised in the first two parts. It considers how subjects and social milieus interact in complex ways in specific areas of Canadian society. These interactions are at times enabling for subjects, and at other times disabling. And because the chapters are driven by sociological imaginations, each one asks questions concerned with critically understanding and engaging an aspect of what it means to live in Canada right now. In so doing, the chapters critically theorize the character of Canadian society itself.

Chapter 15, 'Is There Justice for Young People?', raises questions that are likely to resonate with many young people in Canada. Bryan Hogeveen extends his examination of governance to a group that the Canadian government historically helped to define as 'youth'. In order to respond to the chapter title's question, the author focuses attention on different visions of justice. This allows him to make a clearer argument about the areas in which youth justice in Canada is lacking. Hogeveen notes that current public portrayals of today's youth (for instance, those presented by the media) often associate young people with criminality and irresponsibility. These (mis)perceptions are reflected in changing approaches to youth justice. Paradoxically, however, such public perceptions continue to influence policy even though youth crime rates are declining steadily. Hogeveen provides several examples of the ways in which Canadian youth are governed through discourses of criminality and risk, indicating thereby a new regime for regulating young people that, for him, is far from just.

The next chapter tackles the question 'Should policing be privatized?' by focusing attention on a recent tendency for elements of publicly provided police services to be privatized. In fact, Curtis Clarke argues that Canadian policing has for some time been privatized, to a greater or lesser degree. This development has generated a 'plural policing environment' that radically alters how we might approach concepts about the provision, accountability, and public good of policing services. It has also problematized the role of the state in each of these domains. As Clarke points out, the idea of policing as a public good faces considerable challenges in this ethos, fuelled as it is by a neo-liberal ideology that calls for the privatization of previously state-run services and in the process blurs the lines between private and public spheres. In this respect, policing provides a useful context in which to examine the complex relationships between the state, ideology, and its citizens and to consider new ways of conceptualizing a public good (e.g. through civic coordination). This raises important questions about the role of the state in providing 'equitable policing' that holds key stakeholders responsible for public safety.

Chapter 17, 'Why Are Women Going to Prison?', asks important questions about the relationship between gender, crime, and incarceration. Kelly Hannah-Moffat provides an overview of the prevalence and characteristics of women in Canadian prisons, the reasons women end up in prison, the struggles they face when they are released, and initiatives to implement women-centred or gender-responsive punishment. She points out that although only a small minority of women commit crimes, and most of these crimes involve theft, fraud, or sex work rather than violence, women who have been convicted of a violent crime are overrepresented in prisons. Further, women are less likely than men to repeat offences, and repeat female offenders are less likely than men to escalate the severity of their crimes. The chapter goes on to provide evidence that structural factors—racialization, social class, poverty, mental illness, early victimization, being in a violent intimate relationship, and so on—are key to explaining how women end up in prison. Given that approximately 70 per cent of women in prison have children, the implications of women's incarceration extends far beyond the individual woman to her family, and to society as a whole; for instance, families and provincial agencies (such as the Children's Aid Society in Ontario) must ensure that the children of imprisoned women are adequately cared for. The chapter closes with a consideration of the multiple difficulties women face when they are released from prison, including unemployment, fractured families, and societal marginalization. It also critically examines recent attempts by the government and prison systems to adopt a gender-centred approach to women's incarceration, emphasizing the need to better understand the structural forces that lead women into crime and women's unique experiences within the prison setting.

In Chapter 18, Patricia Monture considers the question of indigenous sovereignty. Because of Monture's untimely death, her chapter appears in the second edition of this book unchanged. Her discussion raises a very important and ongoing debate that strikes at the heart of Canadian society: the place of multiculturalism and diversity. Specifically, she argues that the notion of multiculturalism generally lauded by Canadians often obscures the unique situation of indigenous peoples as the original settlers of geographic North America. Indeed, because indigenous knowledge generally stands outside the dominant structures and institutions in Canada (derived from British and French colonialism), it occupies an 'outsider' position. As such, it is restricted to commenting on (through, for instance, rights claims) the limitations of these structures rather than constructing knowledges in their own right. Moreover, Monture raises the very important and related point that a discussion of 'indigenous knowledge' itself denies the diversity of these knowledges (based on tribal affiliation, age, gender, rurality, history, and so on). In the process, it further contributes to the othering of indigenous peoples by homogenizing their experiences of living within Canada. Monture ends the chapter by asking what an indigenous sociology might resemble—one that takes on board the serious limitations of accounts of the indigenous within mainstream sociology.

On a related theme, Chapter 19, 'What Is Sovereignty in Quebec?', enlists an analysis of a macro-governance. Rather than rehashing longstanding ideological arguments for or against Quebec sovereignty, Philippe Couton offers a distinctly sociological approach that reflects on the underlying assumptions necessary to sustain these positions. One such assumption is that the natural condition for any given society is independence. Couton forcefully argues that nation-states are not homogeneous entities that can adequately speak for the diverse populations that they claim to embody. Another assumption that Couton criticizes is that societies naturally evolve to claim independent power. He argues that 'although there might be an evolutionary component to sovereignty . . . the way the issue is handled at the political level continues to matter a great deal'—as evinced, for instance, by events surrounding the adoption of Canada's Charter of Rights and Freedoms. The chapter concludes by considering the viability of post-sovereignty forms of government that do not rely on the precondition of homogeneity inherent in the modern nation-state.

Chapter 20 offers a sociological analysis of the challenges faced by individuals and communities when economies transition from being resource based to knowledge based. Drawing on her analysis of the Canadian Maritime region's economy, Jennifer Jarman outlines the region's historical reliance on a natural resource–based economy and its strategic position for trade in eighteenth- and nineteenth-century world markets. Since these early days, the region has undergone many changes, and Jarman analyzes the difficulties the region has faced, and continues to face, in reinventing itself to survive the closure of a number of major industries. With this background in mind, the chapter analyzes the effects of a new call-centre industry that is providing employment to many people in the region. On the basis of her field research, Jarman examines the contours of that industry in context. Analysis of this new development is complex. Despite several perceived problems with the industry—that it is transient, has an image problem (e.g., disturbing phone calls, 'sweatshop' labour), and involves close employee surveillance—Jarman notes that it does provide entry-level jobs at the lower end of the service economy. Moreover, she argues that 'The advantage of "lower middle jobs" is that there are a lot of people with "lower middle" levels of education and experience in the region.' The industry has thus provided significant levels of employment, but Jarman also cautions that '[i]t is highly unlikely that one industry can change the features of a regional economy dramatically.' Thus, she argues that the growth of the industry is important for Maritime societies, but its sustained social impact should not be overestimated.

Like the chapters on indigenous and Quebec sovereignty, the next chapter, 'How Do Migrants Become Canadian Citizens?', examines a fundamental aspect of the character of Canadian society. Canada has always relied on immigration to populate the country and provide economic labour that fuels the economy, builds social ties, and indeed forms the nation itself. And yet, many years after Confederation (which itself was preceded by many years of informal immigration), Canada is still struggling to come to terms with the implications of embracing the diversity of its peoples. Randy Lippert and Patrick Lalonde review the history of immigration to Canada as mired in racial and ethnic prejudice and discrimination. They further problematize the distinctions between the categories of 'migrant', 'refugee', and 'immigrant', pointing out that these distinctions are a product of the governance of the movement of people. The chapter ends by considering the specific ways in which Canada transforms certain individuals, under particular circumstances, from migrants to citizens as part of a wider practice of governing responsible citizens who will, among other things, sanction the very policies of immigration to which they themselves were subject. Since multiculturalism is one of *the* defining features of Canadian society, the chapter asks important and timely questions about being Canadian.

Chapter 22 is concerned with the sociology of the environment. It begins with the question 'How social is the environment?' As Lisa Cockburn and Mark Vardy argue, this question requires one to have a sense of the concept 'nature'— and whether or not humans should be seen as within nature or whether they somehow stand outside or apart from nature. The response to these matters greatly affects how we define environmental problems and their solutions.

The authors proceed to show that defining environmental problems, whether global warming, the invasion of indigenous landscapes by wildlife introduced by humans, or the annual seal hunt in northern Canada, is as much about politics, economics, and culture as it is about nature per se. The chapter concludes by considering a number of ways in which groups of people have mobilized through environmental justice organizations to begin to address environmental concerns. While there is much disagreement as to the most viable way forward, there is certainly increasing consensus that solutions are needed in order to avert human suffering in the future due to environmental change.

The book's final chapter, 'What Questions Has Sociology Deserted?', is a fitting end to this volume. Lorne Tepperman, a distinguished Canadian sociologist, asks us to consider some of the questions sociology asked some 50 years ago—but has yet to answer. His plea is for sociology to return to some 'deserted questions' that could be addressed with 'scientific skepticism, empirical rigour, and statistical testing'. For example, Tepperman calls for sociology to reopen discussions on Marx's concept of alienation, especially as it refers to the dehumanization of people as cogs in a capitalist machine, which in turn leads to a raft of social problems. And what about the enormously important contributions of labelling theory, which highlighted the social effects of labelling people? Although it may not be possible to avoid social labelling, Tepperman notes that sociology would benefit from a return to the study of 'conditions under which labelling has harmful effects'. Equally, he questions the wisdom of sociology apparently deserting questions regarding such key concepts as social distance, social mobility, anomie, altruism, and the idea that there may be universal features to group dynamics. Tepperman rightly urges sociology students to engage with influential figures in the history of the discipline, and to grapple with the key questions that they raised—even if some of these appear to have been abandoned. This may, he suggests, serve as 'a reminder that important sociological problems do not disappear simply because we choose to ignore them'.

Questions for Reflection

1. To what extent do you think social class, education, age, gender, and so on determine an individual's experiences in life?

2. How would you describe Canada's 'character', or what it means to 'be Canadian'?

3. What questions do you think sociology should ask about society?

15 | Is There Justice for Young People?

Bryan Hogeveen

Introduction

Is there justice for youth? This chapter confronts the regrettable conditions many youth face in Canada—especially those from the most disadvantaged backgrounds—and reaches the conclusion that there is little in the way of justice for them. First, I explore differing conceptions of justice in a section that underscores the (dis)connection between rights and justice. Next, I highlight three particularly lamentable instances of *in*justice experienced by young persons—child poverty, racism confronting Aboriginal youth, and the dislocation of girls under law. The final section examines the silencing of young people in Western society and urges us to listen to youthful voices.

What Is Justice?

Ours is an era in which war, prison overcrowding, genocide, ethnic cleansing, and vigilantism are all too often rationalized in the name of justice. But what, exactly, *is* justice? A significant problem in answering this question centres on the fundamental ambiguity of the word 'justice' itself. It can refer to the bureaucratic structure for administering the legal process. Canada boasts a federal Department of Justice, which embodies and reflects this convention. It can be used in law and legislation to imply the impartiality of the system (e.g., the Youth Criminal Justice Act [YCJA]). Moreover, 'justice' suggests a connection with law-and-order campaigns in which victims declare that they are owed retribution for pain suffered. In this context, justice being done means an ethic of punishment that delivers obvious signs of unpleasantness to offenders. This kind of justice can also reflect the public's desire to amend law, often in relation to existing but flawed legislation that seemingly promotes *in*justice. Until 2003, when the YCJA became law, Canadian youth were governed under the Young Offenders Act (YOA). Throughout the period leading up to legislative change, the YOA was consistently hailed as inequitable for not sufficiently taking into account the victims of juvenile deviance. Newspaper headlines suggested that federal young offender legislation was to blame for victimization and that tougher legislation would prevent the harm done to the injured (Hogeveen 2005).

For many, justice is intimately connected with inalienable and omnipresent rights enshrined under legislation. For example, the Charter of Rights and Freedoms (Canada 1982) guarantees Canadian citizens and permanent residents the following rights and freedoms: freedom of conscience and religion; freedom of thought, belief, and expression; freedom of association; the right to vote; and the right to life, liberty, and security of person. Nevertheless, until very recently youth did not enjoy access to these guarantees in the same way that adults did. The movement toward assigning rights to children went through three fundamental stages. It passed from a laissez-faire philosophy in which children were considered parental property, to a humanitarian and sentimental rationale of children as a separate class of partially formed individuals, to the current discourse of children as people entitled to individual rights (Covell and Howe 2001).

A turning point in rights allocation for youth occurred on 20 November 1989, when the United Nations Convention on the Rights of the Child was unanimously adopted. A convention is an expression not only of a moral stand but 'also of a legal agreement and international obligation' (Covell and Howe 2001, 20). In 1991, Canada ratified the convention, which comprises 41 articles divided into two broad categories:

1. civil and political rights, which include the right to self-determination and protection from arbitrary arrest;
2. economic, social, and cultural rights, which include the right to health care and education and freedom of religion.

According to Hammarberg (1990), human rights and protections set out by the convention can usefully be divided into three broad groups, often referred to as the 'three Ps': provision, protection, and participation. Rights of *provision* imply that youth must be afforded basic welfare, which includes the right to survival and development, education, and to be cared for by parents. Articles under the *protection* rubric ensure that children are sheltered from abuse, economic exploitation, discrimination, and neglect. Youth are also accorded the right to *participation*, which involves freedom of speech, freedom of religion, and the right of expression (Denov 2004).

Despite Canada's agreement to abide by the convention's conditions, substantial gaps remain between the state's promise and reality. One of the greatest concerns for youth advocates is the general lack of awareness among young people about the convention and the rights they are guaranteed. A study of high school students by Peterson-Badali and Abramovich (1992) found that very few youth could identify the most basic legal principles, such as the youth court's age jurisdiction (12–17). Moreover, when asked with whom their lawyer could share privileged information, many young people were certain that their legal representative was obliged to inform their parents and the judge what they revealed in confidence (Feld 2000; Doob and Cesaroni 2004). To what extent are rights meaningful if young people are unaware of their implications and how they are exercised?

Equating rights with justice is spurious at best. Rights conventions are of little utility when their intricacies are not widely known, understood, or distributed. They tend to float above relationships among individuals and provide little guidance on the ethical responsibility of one person to another. Rights discourses provide very little direction to those addressing inequality and subjugation in an unjust society. Rights and social goods are not equally distributed throughout the Canadian population. Socio-economic status and **class** play a significant role: people on the margins are grossly overrepresented in poverty and incarceration rates. Is this a just state of affairs? If working-class and minority youth have become the foremost clients of coercive state services and, at the same time, experience higher rates of poverty, it is *not* as a result of some innate propensity toward crime and unemployment. Rather, it is because they are trapped at the intersection of three transformations distinct to the **neo-liberal** organization of society that have targeted the visibly different and the socially marginal. Economic globalization, the dismantling of the social welfare net, and the intensification of penal strategies have all contributed to greater inequality and unequal distribution of scarce societal resources in favour of the affluent (Wacquant 2001). During the late 1990s, to paraphrase the title of Jeffrey Reiman's (1979) seminal work, the rich were getting richer while the poor were receiving prison. If the goal of justice is to ensure equal distribution of resources and goods to societal members, it would appear that Canada is moving in a most peculiar direction, especially as the situation pertains to young people.

Justice and the Poor?

Child poverty continues to rise as the gulf between the rich and the poor widens (Canadian Council on Social Development 2010). Apart from Germany, Canada leads the way among Organisation for Economic Co-operation and Development (OECD) countries in measures of income inequality (Organisation for Economic Co-operation and Development 2008). While the rich continue to benefit and grow their personal wealth, the marginalized and impoverished see social assistance subsidies slashed and real incomes erode. Between 1986 and 1996, as measured in constant dollars, Alberta welfare benefits for a single individual deemed employable were slashed by 42.5 per cent, while single parents with a child saw their benefits eroded by 23.6 per cent (Canadian Council on Social Development 2004). As poverty rates have continued to climb, the net traditionally put in place to soften the impact has been stripped away. Even the benefits available to ameliorate the conditions of the most vulnerable—Canada's children—are currently being clawed back by the state. For example, the National Child Benefit provides families with annual incomes of less than $22,615 with $126 per month for the first child and decreasing amounts for subsequent children. However, under a scheme initiated by the federal government, only working families are now allowed to keep the money while those most in need—individuals on social assistance and disability pensions—are denied support payments altogether (Della-Mattia 2004). Compare this with the almost $43 million per year that the Alberta government doles out to subsidize the local horseracing industry (Markusoff 2007). A growing group of destitute individuals, who require the greatest assistance, are having to scrounge for the crumbs that remain after services that the government deems more important get their cut.

Youth are hit the hardest by these changes. The Canadian Council on Social Development (2010) reported that almost 10 per cent of children under the age of six lived in low-income families, and according to Food Banks Canada (2010), despite early signs of economic recovery, food bank usage has continued to climb (children and youth under 18 comprised 43 per cent of food bank clients). Further, the council's 2003 report, *Campaign 2000: Report Card on Child Poverty in Canada* (Canadian Council on Social Development 2003a), provided convincing evidence that over a million children in this country live in poverty. These figures establish that more children are poor than in 1989, when Parliament unanimously pledged to eradicate child poverty by the year 2000. Poverty, however, is not an equal opportunity oppressor. In 2010, the council presented evidence that marginalized populations (i.e., children of recent immigrants and Aboriginal peoples) and children in lone female-parented households are at the greatest risk to experience poverty (Canadian Council on Social Development 2010). The council's 2010 report also confirmed that young people are overrepresented among Canadian food bank users and that Canada ranks poorly on infant mortality rates among OECD nations (Canadian Council on Social Development 2010). Despite persistent need, governments have been reticent to loosen budgetary purse strings to ameliorate adversity and hardship brought about by systemic poverty and the onset of the 2008 fiscal crisis.

To manage the excesses of, and fallout from, the current economic climate, state officials have resorted to pruning child welfare budgets and cutting jobs—a far cry from extending social welfare assistance to needy parents. The Children's Aid Society (CAS) of Halifax, for example, was forced in 2002 to cut a million dollars from its budget over a mere six months (Mills 2002). Funding cuts of this magnitude have serious and often severe implications because child welfare workers become overextended and managers feel pressure to reduce spending. In this desperate environment, youth in need have routinely been denied essential helping services such as treatment sessions and educational programs. For example, after the provincial government cut $1.1 million in funding, the British Columbia Ministry of Children and Family Development axed school meal programs, early academic intervention, and school-based support workers for inner city schools (Douglas 2002).

In such an overburdened system, children are being placed in foster homes that meet only minimal standards. Bob Rechner, child advocate for Alberta, stated that 'when funding for foster homes and resources are tight, it's not surprising standards may not be strictly adhered to. There are many great foster homes in this province. Unfortunately, there are some retained as foster homes that probably shouldn't be, but there aren't alternatives' (Johnsrude 1999). The solution to this problem offered by Manitoba's Child and Family Services is particularly deplorable. Confronted by a lack of adequate foster homes and insufficient funding, child welfare officials rented a floor in a hotel to house youth awaiting placement. A single, hardly qualified staff member who entertained his or her charges with television supervised them. For some youth, this was their home for more than a year. The most vulnerable children in Canadian society appear therefore to be short-changed and denied essential services as a result of shrunken social welfare spending (Blackstock 2003). It should come as no surprise that many of these youth become inmates of Canadian penitentiaries.

While Canadians favoured tax breaks for corporations and the richest segments of society, they campaigned at the same time for increased rates of incarceration for young people—the most costly (both economically and socially) mode of penality (Hogeveen 2005). This situation is particularly troubling when we consider that a great number of young people are incarcerated for relatively minor forms of deviance. Throughout the 1990s, a great number of inmates were sentenced to prison for such 'heinous' breaches of public order as failure to comply with court orders and property-related crimes (Hogeveen 2005).

More troubling still is that individuals warehoused in Canada's centres of detention are almost exclusively from the most marginal classes. Instead of distributing welfare benefits to the poor and destitute, Canadians have placed this class under the authority of the criminal justice system. While social welfare schemes were shrinking, programs that coercively targeted the poor were expanding. Consider the amount of relief that could be administered for the resources devoted to incarcerating excessive numbers of young people. Reflect on how much tuition could be paid with the $50,000 to $100,000 required to detain one young person for a year. Indeed, set against the backdrop of the type of crimes for which these youth are being detained, this expenditure seems extreme. Throughout the 1990s, when the tendency to lock up juvenile offenders was at its peak, so too was the erosion of welfare. One could interpret this as an indication that a new control regime was emerging for marginal and destitute youth, characterized by eroding social programs and a greater emphasis on punitive justice practices.

In effect, centres of detention had become the social service to which the poor and oppressed had the readiest access. With the rising cost of post-secondary education and toughening criteria for welfare eligibility, the criminal justice system might be the state service most available to the subjugated and marginalized. Canada seemed to have embarked on a path toward managing youth poverty and inequality through an integrated control complex. The system was no longer asked only to deter and punish crime; it would now regulate the lower segments of the social order and defend against the discardable, derelict, and superfluous (Bauman 2011; Wacquant 1999).

Justice and Indigenous Youth?

Throughout history, Aboriginal peoples have been subjected to intrusive and invasive modes of state-level control aimed at reform, assimilation, and subjugation (Anderson 1999; Hogeveen 1999; see also Chapter 18). Wherever the Euro-Canadian state encountered indigenous people, the Native land was quickly vacated to make way for white settlement and capitalist expansion. Among the tools of **colonialism** employed to regulate and shore up the Anglo vision of the country's founders were the North-West Mounted Police (forerunner of the RCMP), law, reserves, children's forced adoption by white families, and residential schooling. With the closure of residential schools and with many indigenous peoples now living off reserves, institutions of detention are now on the front lines when it comes to controlling the indigenous 'other'.

Government reports and investigations consistently point to a gross over-representation of Native adolescents at the most punitive end of the system (Royal Commission on Aboriginal Peoples 1993, 1996). Peter Carrington and Jennifer Schulenberg (2004) suggest that indigenous adolescents are 20 per cent more likely to be charged when apprehended than non-Aboriginal youth. Moreover, Aboriginal youth are more likely to be denied bail, to spend more time in pre-trial detention and to be charged with multiple offences (often for administrative violations) (Statistics Canada 2000; Roberts and Melchers 2003). While Aboriginal youth accounted for 5 per cent of the total youth population in 1999, they occupied 24 per cent of the beds in Canadian detention centres. More tragic is the situation confronting indigenous youth in Canada's prairie provinces. In Saskatchewan and Manitoba, three-quarters (75 per cent for Manitoba and 74 per cent for Saskatchewan) of youth sentenced to custody were identified as Aboriginal, while less than 10 per cent of Manitoba's youth population is Native (Statistics Canada 2000). No group has been more touched by Canada's appetite for youth incarceration than the First Nations. A Canadian Bar Association report suitably titled *Locking Up Natives in Canada* provided evidence that a 16-year-old Aboriginal male had a 70 per cent chance of serving at least one prison stint before turning 25. The report continues, 'Prison has become for young Native men, the promise of a just society which high school and college represents for the rest of us' (Jackson 1989, 216). Situated in the context of the racist practices and policies of the Canadian state, centres of detention are the 'contemporary equivalent of what the Indian residential school represented for their parents' (Jackson 1989, 216).

Buttressing this systematic subjugation of those considered alien to the national body is the coincident dismantling of welfare programs during a period of intensified poverty among indigenous peoples—especially children. Not only are Aboriginal people highly overrepresented among the street population, they are more likely than the general Canadian population to be living in urban poverty and inhabiting living quarters deemed overcrowded (Canadian Council on Social Development 2003b). According to Aboriginal activist Cindy Blackstock (2003), Canada's indigenous peoples would rank 78th on the United Nations' Human Development Index (HDI)—which measures poverty, literacy, education, and life expectancy. Canada itself consistently ranks first. The HDI, developed by Pakistani economist Mahbub ul Haq, has become the standard means of measuring overall well-being, and especially child welfare, through three basic categories:

- *long and healthy life*, as indicated by life expectancy at birth;
- *knowledge*, as measured by adult literacy rate; and
- *standard of living*, as derived from gross domestic product per capita.

When compared to people in the rest of the world, Canadians are well situated. But hidden among facts and figures is a long silent, oppressed, and subjugated population. Colonialism, it seems, is not an embarrassing period in the long-forgotten Canadian past. Instead it continues to rear its ugly head.

This section has offered a glimpse into the brand of justice that the Canadian state considers First Nations groups deserve. Colonialism has produced a situation in which indigenous youth are subjected to racism and inequality at almost every turn. They are poor, hungry, excluded, and criminalized. Instead of responding to these disgraceful outcomes through social welfare, the carceral/punitive continuum has been mobilized to regulate its worst aspects. The upsizing of the state's penal sector, along with the downsizing of its social welfare institutions, has constituted a carceral complex directed toward surveilling, training, and neutralizing recalcitrant Aboriginal youth who exist outside Euro-Canadian mores.

Justice for Girls?

Youth, especially the poorest and most marginalized, face pervasive discrimination, silencing, and victimization. While young people are often presented in media and popular discourse as particularly troubling, they are at the same time troubled (Tanner 1996). The latter part of this equation receives far less scrutiny than the former but is no less problematic. According to data gathered by Statistics Canada, those most likely to receive the sharp end of 'justice' are at the same time the most vulnerable to crime as well as social and economic subordination and are thus most in need of protection. Youth are highly over-represented as victims of crime. In 2009, youth between 15 and 24 were '15 times more likely than those aged 65 and older to report being a victim of a violent victimization' (Perrault and Brennan 2010). The same study revealed that girls were overrepresented as victims of violent crime, especially sexual deviance (Perrault and Brennan 2010).

Throughout history, the youth justice system has tended to neglect girls both as victims and as offenders. This is not surprising given that young girls have been highly underrepresented in crime statistics. Early criminologists and youth justice officials used this underrepresentation to bolster the view that wayward girls must somehow be defective. Discourses around female deviance embedded in traditional criminology illustrate this tendency. The founding fathers of criminology, such as Cesare Beccaria in 1778, Charles Hooton in 1939, and Otto Pollak in 1950, portrayed female offenders as a defective lot, the product of inferior breeding as well as biological and anatomical inferiority (Snider 2004). By the turn of the nineteenth century, offenders were considered mentally weak, but following the logic set out above, female 'deviants' were 'more terrible than any man' in that they were 'less intelligent, more passive, more deficient in moral sense, but stronger in sexual instincts' (Snider 2004, 232). Flowing out of this discourse were 'capricious and arbitrary status' offences—a category of offences that applies solely to youth, which if committed by an adult would not result in arrest (i.e., drinking, incorrigibility, truancy, and curfew violations)—that aimed to control female sexuality by incarcerating those who flouted norms of 'emphasized femininity', which stressed the importance of piety, domesticity, and above all monogamous heterosexual marriage (Snider 2003).

Juvenile court officials cast a wide net over what they deemed 'sexuality'. Girls did not have to be caught in the act to be admonished by state actors. Franca Iacovetta (1999) charged that parents often brought their girls to the attention of police on the basis of neighbourhood gossip. Indeed, the mere suggestion of sexual activity could initiate state proceedings against young girls. Throughout the late-nineteenth and early-twentieth centuries, girls were routinely incarcerated for such aberrant conduct as holding hands with boys or being out after dark in the wrong part of town in the company of a male companion.

Not only was girls' sexuality policed through juvenile court and industrial school intervention, race relations were also governed through state-sponsored intrusion. A familiar refrain from white Anglo-Celtic elites who dominated social, economic, and political life during the early twentieth century was that 'the nation' was in danger of decline (Valverde 1991). In the eyes of many, 'nation' was a generic term that referred to those of Anglo descent while racialized 'others' were viewed with increasing suspicion. By the 1910s, a widely accepted racial hierarchy was firmly established in Canada. This ordering was not solely structured by skin colour but also by degrees of whiteness. The mostly British upper-middle-class professionals who spearheaded **eugenics** constituted themselves and 'the nation' in opposition to immigrants from other cultures. Anglo-Celtic elites, bolstered by eugenics discourse, created a purportedly common sense racial logic that associated whiteness with the 'clean and the good, the pure and the pleasing' (Roediger 1991; Morrison 1992; Jackson 2000). It followed then that 'white' girls found associating with boys considered 'other' required training and reformation for the good of 'the nation'.

Such was the case in 1939 when Velma Demerson's father, with police in tow, stormed into the apartment she shared with her Chinese lover. The officers arrested her under the 1897 Female Refugees Act, which allowed for the indefinite detention of girls between 15 and 35 suspected of drunkenness, promiscuity, and pregnancy outside of monogamous union. Velma was 18, pregnant, and in love. Pregnancy before marriage was one thing: that her boyfriend was not white was quite another and a source of embarrassment to her father. Velma was sent to Belmont House—a female house of refuge—for being promiscuous, for being illegitimately pregnant, and for consorting with a Chinese man. There she spent six weeks working in the laundry before being transferred to the Mercer Reformatory. For her 'crimes' she was detained in a seven-by-four-foot cell with bars on the door to prevent her escape. Demerson gave birth to her son inside the institution with neither her mother, her father, nor her partner at her side. Soon after his birth, her son was taken away. Women like Velma suffered tremendously within institutional walls without having committed any crime. In recent years, Demerson has sued and demanded an apology for her suffering from the Canadian government. She has received the latter, but still awaits financial compensation (Demerson 2004).

Injustices experienced by girls continue under contemporary youth justice regimes, in part because they remain 'too few to count' within the youth justice system (Adelberg and Currie 1987). Despite some modest increase in numbers, female young offenders constitute one-fifth of all cases appearing in youth court. Their infrequent appearance before magistrates and in centres of detention helps to explain why relatively few youth justice resources are set aside for female offenders—it does not, however, excuse it. This condition is felt throughout the youth justice process as more and more female youth are subjected to institutional arrangements, risk assessment, and programming designed by men on the basis of boys' experience. Given that theoretical foundations have been developed out of male experience, females are excluded as subjects of knowledge and authorized knowers. The implications are profound. Existing theories of crime and deviance predict the greatest deviance by the most marginalized, alienated, and devalued by society. However, this condition applies to women much more than it does to men. Yet despite being devalued and alienated, girls do not commit crime at anywhere near the rate of boys (Reitsma-Street 1999). Thus it would be very useful if theoretical interpretations of juvenile criminality and the programming that flows from it reflected girls' experience. However, that has not been the case.

Voices of Youth?

Canadian institutions function to censor youth and fix them in a subordinate position. No one has to state overtly that youthful voices are less intelligent, barely cogent, and inferior to adults; it is simply understood. Indeed, pervasive discourses such as 'children should be seen and not heard' function to entrench the view that youth are somehow less than and 'other' to adults. However, this discourse is anchored in much more tacit ways. The fact that youth are not given the right to vote until they reach their eighteenth birthday speaks volumes about their silence (Mathews 2001). Moreover, when we consider the terms 'teacher', 'politician', and 'judge', we automatically assume that it is adults about whom we are speaking. But do youth have nothing of value to contribute to these important domains? It would seem not. They find themselves on the outside, invited to participate only when something is being imposed on them—without, of course, any choice on their part. This order of things does not need to be taught in schools: it just is.

According to social theorist Pierre Bourdieu, every established social order necessarily makes its own arbitrariness seem a natural condition (Bourdieu 1977, 164). In Canadian society, where traditional hierarchies based on age remain relatively stable, our order of things appears self-evident, innate, and ordinary. Or to put it succinctly, in Canadian society the great majority are fully aware of their social positions and conduct themselves accordingly. In this order there remains little room for many youth to manoeuvre into a more equitable position. It appears that the normative social order is fated to be replicated generation after generation. Those who benefit from the established order prefer not to unsettle the status quo. It is only the subordinated who have an interest in pushing back societal limits in order to expose the capriciousness of the presupposed order. Therefore, youth are left the task of unsettling the traditional norms that silence them.

In Edmonton, Alberta, a group of enterprising youth despondent over their silence has challenged contemporary orthodoxy by establishing and administering the world's only 'youth for youth' restorative justice program. A well-established definition of restorative justice suggests that it is an alternative criminal justice process whereby 'parties with a stake in a particular offence come together to resolve collectively how to deal with the aftermath of the offence and its implications for the future' (Marshall 1996, 37). In opposition to traditional youth justice processes in which adults predominate, the Youth Restorative Action Project (YRAP) was created, designed, and implemented and is currently administered by youth. It is made up entirely of young people—between 14 and 21, ranging from honours students to ex-offenders and recovering drug addicts—who consult with offenders to decide on appropriate sanctions within the frame of restorative justice. Adults are accorded no decision-making power and are almost entirely excluded from proceedings except in rare instances when they are called upon to provide clarification on technical points of law. YRAP paves the way for new discursive potentials and novel understandings that recognize the injustices and exclusions contained within established youth justice practice.

Unfortunately, YRAP is the exception rather than the rule. Youth continue to be silenced and nullified in matters that affect them directly. Only when the norms that reinforce adult privilege are exposed and the resulting social order is no longer considered inevitable can amendments be suggested.

Conclusion

Given the silencing of young people, their experiences of poverty, the racism that confronts certain segments, and the dislocation of girls in juvenile justice, we may conclude that there is no justice for marginalized youth. But what would justice look like? Given that those for whom justice remains elusive are subjugated, marginalized, and racialized populations, justice, broadly conceived, would imply an ethic of how to be *just* with/to the 'other'. The problem, however, is that universal pronouncements such as the Canadian Charter of Rights and Freedoms and the UN Convention on the Rights of the Child provide little guidance toward this end. We should therefore not be fully satisfied with such endeavours. Satisfaction with the application of conventions and charters reduces the language of justice to questions of rights and conceals the tyranny over the poor, the indigenous, the female, and the silent.

Canadians cannot be satisfied with contemporary action toward the 'other'—who are downtrodden, excluded, and intruded upon. There must be something more—something better. There is but one answer, which is to 'listen to the unspoken demand . . . [since] the beginning of all evil is to plug one's ears' (Bauman 2001a). Let there be no mistake: listening to the 'other' is just a beginning. Hearing and acting ethically toward the disempowered is something altogether different. Thus giving voice to the voiceless demand is a necessary initial foray into being just—but not its infallible guarantee.

Questions to Consider

1. What understanding(s) of 'justice' does the author suggest pervade the contemporary Canadian scene? What examples does he use to illustrate this?
2. To what does the author attribute burgeoning rates of poverty experienced in an era of opulence? Why are youth affected most?
3. In your view, what political processes silence youth? How is one group of Edmonton youth challenging this condition?
4. Are girls offered a different form of 'youth justice' in Canada?

16 | Should Policing Be Privatized?

Curtis Clarke

Introduction

> Some authors have warned of potential negative effects of this com-
> modification of policing, that is, of its packaging and promotion as a
> thing that can be traded. (Ayling and Shearing 2008, 43)

Recent quantitative and structural changes in the nature of security have re-
aligned the operational prominence of public policing and blurred the boundary between private and public providers. As Ian Loader (2000) points out,
this fragmentation of providers has ushered in a 'plethora of agencies and
agents, each with particular kinds of responsibility for the delivery of policing
and security services and technologies' (323).

The resulting transformation raises numerous questions with respect to
the role of the state, the assurance of accountable policing, and whether or
not the public interest/good can be effectively protected by the emerging network of providers. In the context of this transformation, should policing be
privatized? Or is a more appropriate question one that asks whether the state
will remain a focal point in the provision and accountability of policing? A
corresponding question would centre on how the state might formulate its
connection to policing, given the contemporary conditions of diverse providers (Loader and Walker 2001). Ayling and Shearing (2008) further suggest
that 'new forms of policing will challenge conceptions of state centrality in
the protection domain and raise questions about the extent of state regulation that is needed and about the appropriate loci of accountability and
responsibility for service providers' (44). While these are important points
from which to begin our response, formulating an effective response is not so
simple. In order to do so, we must understand how the current landscape of
policing has been transformed. To begin, let us briefly outline what we mean
by policing.

Policing: A Brief Explanation

The activity of policing is closely aligned with the previously discussed term **governance** (see Chapters 12 and 14). **Policing** is a process of regulating and ordering contemporary societies and individuals. Governance and the activity of policing are thus used as terms to 'denote governmental strategies originating from inside and outside the state' (Jones 2003, 605). This notion of governance has been woven into much of the current analysis of policing, and it expresses a broad function within a system of formal regulation and promotion of security (Jones and Newburn 1998; Loader 2000; Jones 2003; Murphy and Clarke 2005). A corresponding layer of analysis focuses on the institution or specific state agency tasked with order maintenance, law enforcement, and public safety. In this analysis, our attention is drawn to the formal structure and organizational practices of these agencies, not to the broad function of social control. In this context, policing refers to

> those forms of order maintenance, peacekeeping, rule or law enforcement, crime investigation and prevention and other forms of investigation and associated information-brokering; which may involve a conscious exercise of coercive power; undertaken by individuals or organizations, where such activities are viewed by them and/or others as a central or key defining part of their purpose. (Jones and Newburn 1998, 18)

Traditionally, many of these tasks and functions were considered the sole purview of the public police. And yet in the current era of transformation, these very tasks and functions have become the foothold of the private sector's perceived encroachment on public policing authority. These regulatory, investigative, and enforcement activities are, in fact, the site of intense debate with respect to the public/private nexus of policing, the crux of which rests on the issue of public accountability. As Burbidge (2005) notes:

> While the public police are governed by and accountable to democratically elected governmental authority and to the public, private police officers, even when performing the same policing functions as their public counterparts, are not subject to the same form of democratic governance and accountability. (67)

Although the issue of accountability remains a central theme, it is essential to note that private providers do indeed offer similar services to those provided by the public police. The fundamental concern is: how did public policing shed many of these tasks, thus creating an opportunity for private providers to

assume a level of prominence?[1] As the following section argues, the transformation was the result of broad neo-liberal governance policies and a perceived
crisis of ineffective order maintenance.

The Shifting Landscape of Policing

In the era of public service rationalization, public police had adopted various
strategies of managerial and organizational reform. Operationally, this meant
'eliminating, re-engineering, decentralizing, and privatizing' various types of
police services. The resulting elimination or downloading of some traditional
police services, coupled with an inability or reluctance to meet new policing
and security demands, created a new market for services previously provided by public police. In addition, the rapid growth of mass private property
and space, technology, and new modes of business has created a range of new
policing and security needs that could not be satisfied by the public police
(Shearing and Stenning 1982).

As a result of this unmet demand, a mix of public and private sources
increasingly provided alternative policing and security services. In the public domain, individual citizens, community groups, agencies, and police-
sponsored or 'partnered' community-policing groups are adopting various
modes of policing and protection. Governments, private companies, and
citizens who wanted more personalized and/or sophisticated policing/secur-
ity increasingly created their own in-house police and security services or
contracted with an expanding number of **private security** or hybrid public/
private policing services. Philip Stenning (2009) describes this landscape as
a plural policing environment (1). It is characterized by fragmentation and a
transfer of police services as a result of neo-liberal strategies of fiscal restraint
and decentralized governance.

The rationalization of public services like health, education, and policing
were made easier by the use of mystifying reform rhetoric that both legitim-
ated and masked shifts and reductions in traditional service, promoting them
as progressive improvements. The ambiguous but powerful rhetoric of community policing/integrated policing had been particularly effective, offering
both a critique of the modern full-service model of professional public policing as unresponsive and ineffective and a rationale for a more limited model
of public policing (Murphy 1998, 9).

The realignment of policing under neo-liberal policies required a rapid
adaptation from a service that 'bore many of the structural characteristics of
its organizational (and operational) origins in the nineteenth century' (Savage
and Charman 1996, 39). Reform had been stoked by diminished confidence

in the adequacy of public police services to achieve the outcomes desired of a modern police service and a growing demand for police services to adapt to the changing political economy of governance.

From a neo-liberal perspective, the monopoly of public policing represented a strategy of inefficiency, ineffectiveness, and lack of accountability. These alleged failings were cited to stress the need to rework or reconceptualize the police function in ways that would redefine the essential nature and scope of public police service. This critique has forced policing to grapple with the need to re-examine its role, its structure, and how it was to be judged. Unfortunately, the result of this re-examination had been a further blurring between private and public policing functions.

This is not to suggest that this transformation resulted in detrimental operational and organizational outcomes. On the contrary, many public police services are now more effective and efficient with respect to their designated mandate of order maintenance and law enforcement. What this had achieved was an increased public/private blurring, whereby certain functions were relegated to private actors (Stenning, 2009). The focus of this transformation has stifled the debate surrounding the issue of policing as a public good—because the objective of the realignment has been the elimination, re-engineering, decentralizing, and privatizing of various types of police services, not the assurance that policing would remain a public good.

A Question of Public Good

Ian Loader (2000) suggests that the provision and supervision of policing is secured through government, beyond government, and below government. Within these sites, one notes alternative models to the previously accepted state-centred responsibility of dispensing and governing security. In this context, the traditional link between the state and police is replaced with a model that connects both state and non-state nodes in the governance process (Johnston and Shearing 2003; Shearing and Wood 2003). However, the question still remains as to whether or not a diversity of security providers can be responsive to the concept of policing as public good.

For centuries, security and the state have been synonymous. Adam Smith, the dean of classical liberalism, is famous for stating that protecting citizens from harm is a duty of the government: it is a service that government must provide. Karl Marx argued that 'security is the supreme social concept of civil society' (cited in Jones and Newburn 1998, 33). Unfortunately, the backdrop to the current era of transition in policing is a governance trend toward a fragmented and pluralized network of security in which citizens may not broadly share security interests or achieve equal levels of security. This trend has undermined the importance of state-coordinated security as a fundamental public good. The provision of security has been couched in the economic rhetoric of efficiency, effectiveness, and creation of private goods rather than in terms of the public good.

Furthermore, it affirmed the importance of private interest and the pursuit of specific, self-defined 'security requirements without reference to any conception of the common good' (Loader 2000, 386). The state, with varying degrees of enthusiasm, had turned to business and the market as mechanisms to provide public goods such as education and health care. In the realm of public security and policing, the private sector was given responsibilities that in some settings effectively made it the key provider of perhaps the most basic public good: public safety. Thus the move toward satisfying self-defined security requirements did little in the way of ensuring that the private agencies performing more and more state actions were upholding any measure of democratic accountability (Valverde 1999).

In a post-9/11 world, the question we now grapple with is how the state might (re)formulate principles of accountability and regulation in order to address not only broadly shared security interests but also the governance of a disparate multi-organizational security and policing landscape. And while the emergence of this question may indicate a potential shift in governance, it does not suggest that the dichotomy between private and public interests no longer exists—nor is there a renewed appetite for a heavy-handed regime to ensure public security. What it does suggest is an evolving governance environment in which the provision of goods (i.e., public safety) may be achieved through the co-operative actions of multiple stakeholders.

Although the provision of a secure environment depends on the joint actions of various players, it also relies on the state's ability to coordinate the organizational apparatus of the integrated, multi-functional security and policing providers. Moreover, it is incumbent on the state to 'bring reflexive coherence and forms of democratic accountability to the inter-organizational networks and multi-level political configurations within which security and policing are situated' (Loader and Walker 2001, 27). One alternative would be to replace the previously accepted state-centred responsibility of dispensing and governing security with a model that connects both state and non-state nodes in the process of governance (Johnston and Shearing 2003; Shearing and Wood 2003). 'Within this conception of governance no set of nodes is given conceptual priority', and the level of contribution of each node is developed through negotiation or collaborative processes (Johnston and Shearing 2003, 147). Johnston and Shearing argue (2003) that 'by emphasizing that the state is no longer a stable locus of government, the nodal model defines governance as the prop-erty of networks rather than as the product of any single centre of action' (148). Moreover, governance is then considered the practice of shifting alliances as opposed to the 'product of state-led steering and rowing strategies' (148). The issue that these models raise is whether we have any assurances that they may serve the desired outcome of enhanced security and policing—or whether they merely represent a theoretical framework that has little operational value.

A Reconfigured Connection between State and Policing

As noted previously, some people would contend that the reformulation of the state's central position has been undermined by the downloading of re-sponsibility to corporations, municipalities, and citizens. In other words, how can the state expect to articulate a position of prominence when in fact it has previously reduced its significance in the realm of policing? This is indeed a critical concern, one that is both echoed and supported by Johnston and Shearing's (2003) assertion. And yet I would argue that the current realign-ment of policing actually strengthens the state's grip on the tiller. It is a re-alignment that 'flows from an appreciation of the status of policing as a public good' (Loader and Walker 2001, 11).

Jones and Newburn (1998) argue that it is the existence of a diverse network of providers that has forced the state to refocus its efforts to steer policing and security. Loader and Walker (2001) further argue that a 'positive (rather than pejorative) connection between policing and the state can be (re)formulated and defended under contemporary conditions' (11).

This differs from Johnston and Shearing's (2003) perception in that the state does play a central role both in coordinating collaborative alliances and in assuring accountability. Here, the joint actions of various players are both connected and coordinated by the state through reconstructed positions of governance. Within this formulation of governance, the state continues to maintain a primacy in the negotiation and collaborative processes involved in providing the public good of policing. This perspective is effectively presented in the following passage:

> Within the normative framework of the liberal democratic society, it is only the state or national government (and not the private sector) that has the cap-acity to mobilize all of the ingredients that, together, provide policing services that ensure the security and safety of the community. The state, as the embodi-ment of the values of society, is uniquely capable of ensuring public security,

characterized by a monopoly of the legitimate use of force, coordinated governance, collective provision and communities of attachment. (Burbidge 2005, 66)

To illustrate the central prominence of the state and its capacity to mobilize a
range of stakeholders, let us examine two points of connection at which the state
formulates the principles of accountability, regulation, and civic coordination:
the monopoly of legitimate coercion and the collective provision of policing.

Legitimate Coercion

While the services provided both by private and by public policing providers may seem indivisible, there remain distinct differences, differences that are
overlooked if we merely compare tasks and functions. As the following statement notes, status alone is no longer a clear determinant of difference:

Where the public police and private security are performing functions that are
to all appearances the same, their differing status becomes even more difficult
to appreciate. (Police Futures Group 2005, 3)

This debate over differences is most keenly argued with respect to the authority and legitimacy of the use of force: the monopoly of legitimate coercion. And while the use of legitimate force is indeed a site of contention, it also
serves as a mechanism by which the state reinforces its governance prominence. Since it is the state that both grants and regulates the legitimate use of
force, it therefore has the capacity to impose a range of regulatory parameters
on all providers of policing and security.[2] Max Weber (1948) argued that 'the
right to use physical force is ascribed to other institutions or individuals only
to the extent which the state permits it. The state is considered the sole source
of the right to use force' (78). One understanding of Weber's claim would suggest that as representatives of the state, the police are legitimately 'empowered
to use force if force is necessary'. It is the police who are 'equipped, entitled,
and required to deal with every exigency in which force may have to be used, to
meet it' (Bittner 1990, 256). Reiner (1993) argues, 'The police are the specialist
carriers of the state's bedrock power: the monopoly of the legitimate use of
power. How and for what this is used speaks to the very heart of the condition
of political order' (cited in Jones and Newburn 1998, 35).

These interpretations suggest that only the state has the right to deliver
legitimate violence and thus can limit the capacity of private policing providers to offer the full range of security and enforcement. The distinction to be
made is that 'private security has no powers delegated by government, other

than those possessed by any citizen, the scope of their activities is necessarily limited to civil matters. . . . it has the powers and protections granted all citizens in the Criminal Code and the delegated rights of clients who are property owners under provincial trespass and landlord tenant acts' (Police Futures Group 2005, 4). Stenning (2009) aptly summarizes this power differential in the following passage:

> While the public police are sponsored and mandated by society generally (through legislative and executive government provisions) and are accordingly given special powers, duties and immunities in serving the public interest, private police share none of these attributes; they serve no special status, enjoy no powers nor have any duty or responsibility toward the public interest, beyond those of the ordinary citizen and are assumed and expected to serve the private interests of those who employ them. (2)

Regardless of the limited statutory powers granted to private security providers, they do 'perform many of the functions hitherto regarded as the prerogative of the public police' (Burbidge 2005, 68). Loader and Walker (2001) argue that while the monopoly of legitimate coercion is indeed a central point of authority, it continues to be a 'somewhat limited basis for establishing the state-police nexus and it is in numerous ways being further undone by the contemporary fragmentation of policing and state forms' (13).

The concern that this raises has to do with the accountability of the private sector (especially regarding the use of force) since private police are not governed by the same oversight structures as the public police are. The reality is that 'while the public police are governed by and accountable to democratically elected governmental authority and to the public, private police officers, even when performing the same policing functions as their public counterparts, are not subject to the same form of democratic governance and accountability' (Burbidge 2005, 67). Stenning (2009) suggests that the regulation of private policing

> tends to reflect a business regulation model rather than a model of public service governance. Government involvement in such regulation is typically limited to settling and enforcing minimum standards of service (and sometimes qualification and training) through licensing and certification and protection of clients from fraud and malpractice. (5)

It is within this context that the state has both the responsibility and the authority to address the current governance deficit. From a public good perspective, the state must exercise a regimen in which private policing is regulated and audited and the objective of public good is ensured. Some (but not all) private security providers want more legal police powers, such as the powers of search and seizure and arrest, the use of force, and greater access to police intelligence information. However, this desire is tempered by a reluctance to become subject to the constraints and limits of public accountability, liability, and the courts. Most private security executives recognize that by having a more limited role, with limited public and legal responsibilities, they actually may have more operational freedom than public police.

While the granting of expanded legal powers to private security is a complex public policy question, one cannot ignore the implications of not moving to impose broad regulatory frameworks.[3] As the landscape of policing and security evolves, 'so should the governance and accountability arrangements with respect to the exercise of police powers that impinge on the rights and freedoms of citizens' (Burbidge 2005, 73). Examples of this policy shift can be noted in governance changes flowing from the *Report of the Independent Commission on Policing for Northern Ireland* (Patten 1999); Bill 88: An Act to Amend the Private Investigators and Security Guards Act (Ontario 2004); the *Government MLA Review of the Private Investigators and Security Guards Act* (Alberta 2005); and the Private Investigators and Security Guards Act (Alberta 2010). The challenge confronting each of these initiatives has been to achieve an appropriate balance between those who argue for a state-interventionist approach and those who support the minimalist-government approach. In other words, can the providers of policing be effectively held accountable through market mechanisms, or can accountability be achieved only through the regulatory mechanisms of the state (Burbidge 2005)? A more important consideration is how these governance frameworks might ensure 'the protection and vindication of the human rights of all' (Patten 1999, 18) and 'promote an explicit set of democratic values' (Jones 2003, 623). It is precisely because of these considerations that the state cannot relinquish its regulatory capacity or its ability to steer the provision of policing.

Conclusion

We began this chapter by asking the question 'Should policing be privatized?' but then quickly discarded it for another set of questions. It is not that the question of whether we should privatize policing is unimportant; rather, it is just that in reality we are already there to a certain extent. There is little disagreement between scholars and police leaders as to whether or not the landscape of policing has shifted significantly toward that of a plural policing environment (Stenning 2009). This is why we side-stepped our initial question and began to tease out another strand of questions that highlight concerns aligned with issues of accountability, assurances of the public good, and the function of the state in steering diverse providers. These are the issues that have monumental implications for how we as a society are governed and protected, and thus we must be constantly mindful of them. Whether or not we embrace a private, public, or hybrid model of policing, the critical question remains: can the public good of policing be maintained? The answer to this question lies in the capacity of the state to steer the process of policing and ensure that the diverse providers are held accountable to the principle of policing as a public good. Therefore, a more appropriate line of questioning is 'How will new forms of policing challenge the role of the state in providing equitable policing and how might state regulation ensure that all providers are held accountable and responsible for public security and safety?'

Questions to Consider

1. In your view, can a hybrid version of public and private models of policing effectively protect the public? What are the potential dangers of such a model?
2. If the state is no longer the exclusive policing authority, what is the relationship between policing and democracy?
3. What institutions of accountability do you think might be appropriate for the emerging policing arrangements?

Notes

1. For example, in Ontario the number of licensed private investigators and security guards grew from approximately 28,000 in 2002 to 64,000 in 2008, compared with 25,558 municipal and provincial police officers in the province (Li 2008). The most recent national survey of private policing in Canada showed a substantial difference in the number of private security personnel and that of public police officers (102,000 private security versus 67,085 public police) (Li 2008).
2. Criminal Code of Canada section 25(1), *Protection of persons acting under authority* states: 'Every one who is required or authorized by law to do anything in the administration or enforcement of the law a) as a private person, b) as a peace officer or public officer, c) in aid of a peace officer or public officer, or d) by virtue of his office, is, if he acts on reasonable grounds, justified in doing what he is required or authorized to do and in using as much force as is necessary for that purpose.' Section 27, *Use of force to prevent commission of offence*, is also of interest with respect to the authority to use force and the differentiation between public police and citizens (i.e., police/private security).
3. 'Across Canada and other jurisdictions, such as the United Kingdom, there is a growing awareness that the legislation governing the private security industry needs to be modernized. . . . In order to enhance public safety and increase the efficiency and effectiveness of the industry, these jurisdictions have focused on amendments to licensing, training and equipment. . . . Events such as Sept. 11, 2001, have reinforced the need to reform the current legislative and regulatory framework of the private security industry' (Ontario 2003, 5).

17 | Why Are Women Going to Prison?

Kelly Hannah-Moffat

Introduction

Imprisoned women are out of sight and regularly referred to as 'too few to count' or 'correctional afterthoughts'. Yet women are the fastest-growing prison population worldwide. More than half a million women and girls across the world are imprisoned, either as pre-trial detainees (remand prisoners) or after having been convicted and sentenced (Walmsly 2006). Women prisoners are still a minority when compared with men; but what is bringing women to prison, and how has the face of Canadian women's imprisonment changed given the growing numbers of imprisoned women?

The criminalization of women and their **pathways to prison** are variously explained by scholars. Some argue that the increased numbers of women in prison (as well as changes in the 'type' of women in prison) are a by-product of changes in the nature and severity of women's crime and their increased opportunities to commit a broader range of drug-related, economic, and property offences. Others contend that the increases are the result of social and structural factors, such as changes in policing and sentencing patterns. Another common argument is that the preferential or chivalrous treatment women once enjoyed has dissipated. The media and popular culture frequently portray women, particularly young girls, as more aggressive and violent and often focus on sensational accounts of heinous crimes involving women. However, empirical evidence consistently shows that women who commit crime, including women in prison, tend not to commit serious crimes, and continue to be those who have experienced social exclusion caused by poverty, racism, mental illness, and the trauma of physical and sexual violence (Gelsthorpe and Morris 2002; Balfour and Comack 2006). This chapter will provide (1) information about the number and characteristics of women in Canadian prisons; (2) an overview of the explanations of women's pathways to prison and the struggles they face upon release; and (3) a description of the concept of women-centred or gender-responsive punishment.

Number and Characteristics of Women in Prisons

Before discussing the number of women in prison, it is important to point out that relatively few women commit crimes. Women who are involved in crime tend to be involved in property crimes, usually theft, shoplifting, or fraud; only a small percentage of women are convicted of violent crimes (see Kong and AuCoin 2008), and women are overrepresented in prostitution-related crimes. Yet women who use violence are often sent to prison; consequently prison population statistics and detailed examinations of imprisoned women's (in particular Aboriginal women's) histories typically indicate that they are incarcerated for crimes involving interpersonal violence (assaults, robbery, manslaughter, and murder). This is especially true for women serving federal sentences (more than two years in custody). In 2007, approximately 320 (67 per cent) of all federally sentenced women and 119 (80 per cent) of federally sentenced Aboriginal women were serving time for a violent crime (Correctional Service of Canada 2007).[1]

Whether instrumental or defensive, women's violence must be understood within a wider socio-economic context. When placed in context, there is little evidence to support the claim that women overall are becoming more violent or aggressive. A Canadian study revealed that 9 per cent of federally sentenced women who had committed homicide as an act of self-defence were sex workers protecting themselves against assault or unwanted sexual relations by customers (Correctional Service of Canada 1998; also see Balfour and Comack 2006).

Generally, women are less likely than men to be repeat offenders, and when they do reoffend, their crimes tend not to escalate in severity (Kong and AuCoin 2008). Consequently, women are less likely than men to receive a prison sentence and are more likely to receive a community sentence of probation, regardless of the severity of the crime (Kong and AuCoin 2008). One exception is women convicted of interpersonal violence, prostitution, and drug possession crimes; these women are more likely than men to be sent to prison.

Women have consistently represented a small proportion of all offenders and of those sentenced to imprisonment. In 2008–9, women comprised only 12 per cent of offenders in provincial/territorial prisons, 6 per cent of those in federal prisons, and 13 per cent of those in detention centres on remand (Calverley 2010). Women in federal penitentiaries tend to be concentrated in Ontario and the Prairies. These regions consistently have larger proportions of women prisoners than other regions (Correctional Service of Canada 2007).

Prison populations are also racialized. The nature of **racial overrepresentation** varies by each country's demographics, but racialized individuals are clearly disproportionately imprisoned. In Canada, Aboriginals are overrepresented in all areas of the criminal justice system. For example, Aboriginals represent about 4 per cent of the Canadian population; yet they make up approximately 18 per cent of the incarcerated adult population (Babooram, 2008).[2] In 2008–9, Aboriginal women accounted for 37 per cent of women serving a custodial sentence in the provincial/territorial system, compared with Aboriginal men, who accounted for 25 per cent of men serving a custodial sentence in the provincial/territorial system (Calverley 2010). In federal penitentiaries, the proportion of Aboriginal women rose from 15 per cent in 1997 to 25 per cent in 2006. Proportionally, Aboriginal women are also more frequently housed in maximum security units of prisons (Correctional Service of Canada 2010). The disproportionate representation of minority women in prison is a global phenomenon. Sokoloff pointed out that while African Americans represent only 13 per cent of the total US population, about 50 per cent of the female inmate population is African American. Black women are seven times more likely to be incarcerated than white women (Sokoloff 2005, 129).

Explaining the changes in the number of women in prison in recent decades is a complicated and nuanced process. In Canada, women may face different forms of imprisonment, as determined by the length of sentence. If a woman's sentence is more than two years, she serves it in a federal prison, and if it is less than two years, she serves it in a provincial prison. Women can also be imprisoned while waiting for their trial (i.e., while on remand). Although federal admissions constitute only about 3 per cent of women sentenced to prison, since the 1980s women's imprisonment at the federal level has increased (Gartner, Webster and Doob 2009). Nationally, the admissions of women to provincial prisons increased until the early 1980s, remained relatively stable until the early 1990s, and subsequently declined. Remand prisoners, however, are the most rapidly increasing population of Canadian women in prison (Gartner, Webster and Doob, 2009); these women have been denied bail and are being held in prison awaiting trial. Kong and AuCoin (2008) reported that 'since 1995/1996, the number of women in remand has more than doubled and has pushed the total number of women in provincial/territorial custody up 30%' (12). This change in remand numbers is important because these women are often not yet convicted of a crime and this form of incarceration has significant costs for the accused: research has shown that these individuals can feel pressured to plead guilty; tend to live in harsh conditions with few programs; and can lose their jobs, homes, and/or custody of their children (Shaw and Hargreaves 1994; Kellough and Wortley 2002).

The increase in federal and decrease in provincial women prison populations can partially be explained by the opening of five new federal prisons for women across the country throughout the 1990s. Canada has far fewer provincial and federal prisons for women than for men. In the past, judges may have been reluctant to sentence women to federal custody because there was only one federal prison for women (located in Kingston, Ontario). This prison was fiercely criticized for its inability to appropriately and safely meet the needs of women prisoners and for the often vast distances between women and their families and communities of origin (Hannah-Moffat and Shaw 2001). Another possibility for the increased number of women in federal prisons is that women offenders and their lawyers consider federal prisons to be better resourced in terms of programs and therapeutic services than provincial prisons.

Some have suggested that the 'type' of women sentenced to imprisonment has changed over the past 30 years, but this broad claim is difficult to verify empirically due to limited data and a variety of complicating methodological factors (Heidensohn and Morris 2009). Nonetheless, the demographic characteristics of women currently housed in Canadian prisons reveal that their circumstances and experiences are largely related to economic instability, political conservatism, punitive crime control, exclusionary social policies, and the persistent decline of the social safety net that has resulted in benefit cuts and reduced health and social services, welfare, and housing (see, e.g., Hermer and Mosher 2002). Each of these factors has contributed to increased criminalization, and they affect women differently than men.

Approximately 70 per cent of women prisoners report having children, and many are simultaneously involved with family courts and children's aid societies. Many of these women are at risk of losing their parental rights because they do not have access to legal aid or advocacy. Children usually live with their mother before prison and most wish to live with their mother once she is released from prison. While mothers are in prison, their children usually live with another family member or in a foster home. Mothers have limited contact with their children; given the remote location of many prisoners, they often maintain contact with family and children through telephone calls and letters. It is common for incarcerated women to lose legal custody of their children (Arditti and Few 2006; Celinska and Siegel 2010).

Many female offenders report that substance abuse played a major role in their offence or their offending history (Shaw and Hargreaves 1994). Recent data on federally sentenced women indicate that 59 per cent of these women self-reported current or previous drug addictions and 37 per cent reported current/previous alcohol addictions (Correctional Service of Canada 2010). Studies of women prisoners have also consistently demonstrated that these women are less educated; prior to incarceration, many have not graduated from high school (Brown 2006). They are also frequently unemployed or underemployed at the time of incarceration and lack basic job skills and/ or employment experience. Single-parent status for part or all of their children's lives often complicates women's access to meaningful employment. Incarcerated women also reportedly have a much higher incidence of mental illness, childhood sexual abuse, and severe physical abuse than women in the general population (Laishes 2002). For many women prisoners, prison offers the first access to help for their problems (Comack 1996).

Pathways to Crime and Prison

Empirical studies have demonstrated differences in the motivational factors that lead to women's use of violence, involvement in drug and property crimes, and patterns of substance abuse, as well as how factors such as drug use are connected in gender-specific ways to initial and continued prostitution and other crimes (e.g., Daly 1992; Hannah-Moffat and Shaw 2001; Bloom, Owen, and Covington 2003; Moretti, Odgers, and Jackson, 2004; Blanchette and Brown 2006; Heimer and Kruttschnitt 2006). When women and men's offences are similar (e.g., assault, fraud, or murder), the context of offending and the offender's relationship with the victim tend to be different.

Research about the pathways to prison for female offenders has identified various ways in which women end up incarcerated. Many of these studies are based on an incarcerated sample, and show how a number of different life-course trajectories often result in women becoming part of the prison population. According to this perspective, gender-specific adversities work to produce and sustain women's criminality: histories of abuse, mental illness tied to early life experiences, addictions, economic and social marginality, homelessness, and violent relationships (Covington and Bloom 2006, 16). Proponents of this pathway theory argue that profound differences between the lives of men and women shape their different patterns of criminal offending (Steffensmeier and Allan 1998). The next sections will identify some of the factors that contribute to women's incarceration.

Economic Marginalization and Street Life

As noted above, women entering prison are often poorly educated: while 80 per cent of the general female population has progressed beyond grade nine, only about 50 per cent of women in prison have achieved the same level of educational attainment (Canadian Human Rights Commission 2003, 7). Traditionally, women (especially Aboriginal women) experience higher rates of poverty and earn lower wages than men and non-Aboriginals. Prior to incarceration, many women live in poverty with their children and rely on welfare or social assistance. In 2005, social assistance rates for single-parent families in Canada ranged from 27 per cent below the poverty line (in Newfoundland) to 52 per cent below the poverty line (in Alberta; National Council on Welfare 2006). Women who were employed upon entering prison generally report low-skill employment in sales and services industries, child care, and housekeeping (Correctional Service of Canada 2010). Aboriginal women are twice as likely as non-Aboriginal women to be unemployed, especially between the ages of 15 and 34. On average, Aboriginal women in large urban centres cannot earn enough money to meet their own basic needs or support a family (Statistics Canada 2006). Such economic marginalization heightens women's exposure to and involvement in crime.

When women are poor and/or unemployed, they are at higher risk of entering into street life and becoming involved in illegal markets to survive. For example, women may be forced to trade sexual services for a meal or to avoid sleeping in a cold public park when city shelters are full. Some may return to abusive relationships or high-risk environments, increasing the risk of further legal problems. Stable housing is positively associated with employment, the ability to access government benefits, good mental and physical health, and familial support. When women are homeless or marginally housed, they are more likely to become victims of physical and/or sexual violence and find it more difficult to provide for their children and secure sufficient employment.

Daly (1992) found that street life was a common pathway to female offending:

> Whether they were pushed out or ran away from abusive homes, or became part of a deviant milieu, young women begin to engage in petty hustles or prostitution. Life on the street leads to drug use and addiction, which in turn leads to more frequent law-breaking to support a drug habit. . . . Their paid employment is negligible because they lack interest to work in low-paid or unskilled jobs. Having a child may facilitate [receiving state aid]. A woman may continue law-breaking as a result of relationships with men who may also be involved in crime. Women are on a revolving criminal justice door, moving between incarceration and time on the streets. (3–14)

Unfortunately, this stereotype still holds true today. Simpson, Yahner, and Dugan (2008) found that women engaged in street life tend to have extensive criminal records, to have served a number of jail or prison sentences, and to have numerous criminal acquaintances that encourage further law-breaking (95). Johnson (2006) reported that most incarcerated women (50 to 75 per cent) have histories of illegal drug use. Substance abuse is pervasive among women in prison. Women's addictions are different from men's with respect to the types of drugs they use and their reasons for using, highlighting the need for women-specific resources (Hannah-Moffat and Shaw 2001). Women in prison often report using drugs and alcohol to numb the pain of past traumas or to cope with their immediate circumstances (e.g., working in the sex trade for economic survival). Some women make direct links between their substance use and their conflicts with the law (Comack 1996). The depletion of publically funded addiction counselling and treatment programs in the community has resulted in prisons becoming a default option for addicted women (Pollack 2009).

Violence and Formative Years

Most criminalized women have suffered multiple traumas. Several scholars have reported that violence (trauma from childhood sexual assault) is an important precursor to adult drug abuse and offending, and that woman who experience disruptive family life gravitate toward abusive adult relationships (Brown 2006; Salisbury and Van Voorhis 2009). Simpson, Yahner, and Dugan (2008) also found that many incarcerated women had experienced violence (physical and sexual) as children and adults, and that these women went on to be violent themselves. Similarly, DeHart (2008) found that victimization appeared to be directly related to delinquency and criminal activity through child corruption or perceived force, provocation, or pressure to do crime (1365; see also Comack and Balfour 2004). For example, during their formative years many incarcerated women had caretakers who provided them with drugs and alcohol, forced them to steal, or prostituted them. In adulthood, these women often use similar criminal strategies. Many use defensive violence during adulthood to stop abuse from partners or to prevent the assault or threat of assault of their children or family. These cumulative experiences of victimization can affect women's mental and physical health and their psycho-social functioning, influencing family and work life and often contributing to women externalizing their anger and using violence, which in turn leads them to their initial contact with the criminal justice system (DeHart 2008, 1369–70). Aboriginal women in the general population are twice as likely as other women to be victims of emotional and physical abuse, and significantly more likely than non-Aboriginals (54 per cent compared to 37 per cent) to report the most severe and potentially life-threatening forms of violence: being beaten or choked, having a gun or knife used against them, or being sexually assaulted (Statistics Canada 2006). Unsurprisingly, these prior experiences are also more prevalent among Aboriginal women in prison.

Early victimization (childhood sexual abuse) also increases a women's risk for future victimization (Carbone-Lopez and Kruttschnitt 2010, 373). DeHart (2008) reported that victimization can generate or intensify mental illnesses, drug and alcohol abuse, feelings of worthlessness and withdrawal, low self-esteem and shame, as well as suicidal ideation and attempts. Furthermore, abuse in the home (particularly at early ages) can push women and girls to the streets, where lack of housing, social support, and shelter spaces places them at further risk of violence, criminal involvement, and even premature death.

Mental Health Difficulties

Mental health difficulties are an area of growing concern among imprisoned women. Studies about criminalized women have highlighted the range and density of their needs. Correctional researchers report that women in prison outnumber men in all major psychiatric diagnoses with the exception of anti-social personality disorder. Gender differences also appear in the behavioural manifestations of mental illness. Women in prison reportedly suffer from about twice as much depression as men (and federally incarcerated women are three times more likely than federally incarcerated men to be moderately to severely depressed). Incarcerated women are less physically and sexually threatening and assaultive than men; instead, women prisoners tend to be more self-abusive and to engage in more self-mutilating behaviours such as slashing (Laishes 2002, 6–7). A study conducted in New Zealand found that compared with women living in the general population, criminalized women had a higher prevalence of mental disorders including schizophrenia, major depression, and post-traumatic stress (Brinded et al., 2001).

Once in prison, women require specialized services to accommodate their health difficulties. International scholars estimate that approximately 10 to 13 per cent of female prisoners have self-injured during their current sentences (Meltzer et al. 2002). Self-injury is a significant problem among women in the Canadian prison population (Shaw 1991). One study of 26 female inmates admitted to a psychiatric centre found that 73 per cent of the women had engaged in self-injurious behaviour prior to their admittance (Presse and Hart 1999, cited in Fillmore and Dell 2000). In one Canadian study of self-harming women offenders and corrections staff, interviews with offenders revealed that they used self-harming to help them cope with a variety of issues: to deal with isolation and loneliness; as a cry for attention and nurturing; as self-punishment and self-blame; as an opportunity to feel something; as a way of distracting and deflecting emotional pain; as a release and cleansing of emotional pain; as an expression of painful life experiences; and to give a sense of power and control (Fillmore and Dell 2000).

Current research indicates that the 'pains of imprisonment' are a major contributing factor to self-harm for incarcerated women (see Canadian Centre on Substance Abuse 2006; Fillmore and Dell 2000). These pains may include negative relationships with staff and other prisoners; confinement in segregation; stressful living conditions; and rigid and arbitrary rule enforcement. The high prevalence of mental health difficulties among incarcerated women is linked to their related experiences of trauma, violence, and drug use (Booker Loper and Levitt 2011) and is further complicated by the limited number and quality of community-based psychiatric services. Mental health difficulties complicate the experiences and management of women once they arrive in prison and require prison and health care systems to work together in prisons and communities to treat women and prevent future incarcerations.

Gender-Specific Approaches to Correctional Policy

Women face complex challenges: they must often deal simultaneously with multiple challenges that are not easily prioritized and disentangled. For more than 30 years, international research has demonstrated that crime is gendered and that gender matters in shaping criminal justice responses to women and in the differential effects of policies (Hannah-Moffat and Shaw 2001; Carlen 2002). There is no one-size-fits-all policy, and criminal justice organizations and policy-makers are starting to understand this fact. Many now recognize that corrections policies need to respond to gender and culture. Research conducted in Canada as well as by the United Nations stresses the importance of gender sensitivity and the need to rethink women's prisons without using the male prison as a reference point (see United Nations 2008). Acceptance of the premise that women are different but equally entitled to the protection of the law and fair treatment under the law signifies tremendous progress. Proponents of this approach argue that an effective system for female offenders must be structured differently from a system for male offenders; they claim that policies, programs, and procedures that reflect gender-based differences can make the management of women offenders more effective, increase resources, improve the rate of staff turnover, prevent sexual misconduct, improve program delivery, decrease the likelihood of litigation against the criminal justice system, and improve the gender responsiveness of services and programs.

In the early 1990s, Canadian women's prisons underwent significant restructuring in response to a renowned report by the Task Force on Federally Sentenced Women: *Creating Choices* (Correctional Service of Canada 1990).

The reform was intended to redress a long history of sexism and neglect in women's corrections by developing an alternative women-centred correctional model that focused on the unique needs and experiences of women (Hannah-Moffat and Shaw 2001; Hayman 2006).[3] It provided a conceptual template for the reform of women's imprisonment and led to the eventual closure of the notorious and degraded Prison for Women in Kingston, Ontario. Acceptance of the task force's recommendations by the federal government enabled feminist-inspired *knowledge* of women prisons and 'treatment' to filter from feminist critiques into Canadian penal policy and eventually into the managerial regimes of women's prisons.

The five principles set out in *Creating Choices*—empowerment, meaningful and responsible choices, respect and dignity, supportive environment, and shared responsibility—were integrated into corporate documents about women prisoners in Canada. Correctional officials and feminist researchers began to produce a body of knowledge about women prisoners and gender-sensitive treatment and confinement, which started to alter correctional practices. For example, increased knowledge about women's trauma and experiences with male violence informed the development of cross-gender staffing practices. Concerns about women's relationships with their children informed the development of various forms of parenting accommodation. Critiques of prison classifications systems inspired a new generation of gender-informed risk-need assessment research. Knowledge of women's mental health problems and self-injury led to the development of peer-support programs and a mental health strategy. A persuasive and comprehensive body of research about women's correctional programming has evolved from Canadian and US studies about gender-responsive correctional strategies (Bloom et al. 2003).

Correctional Service of Canada (CSC) characterizes its women-centred prisons as a human rights milestone, and its acceptance of the task force's progressive recommendations made it an international leader in women's corrections. However, CSC's commitment to **gender-responsive policy** has met multiple operational difficulties over the years, and Canada's progressive attitude has been overshadowed by ongoing public condemnation of the CSC for failing to protect the human rights of women prisoners and for ongoing gender discrimination. The initial adoption and creation of Canadian women-centred prisons was hasty, poorly conceptualized, and based on scant theoretical and empirical research about how gender should inform penal programs. The well-intentioned labels 'gender sensitive' and 'women centred' have been attached to a wide range of improvised and poorly adapted programs and managerial processes without substantial consideration of *how* gender should be operationalized. As demonstrated in the next section, even the provision of a gender-responsive template has not resulted in significant improvements in how gender has been addressed in penality. A number of well-documented operational and systemic problems remain in Canadian women's prisons (Parkes and Pate 2006; Office of the Correctional Investigator 2008; Dell, Fillmore, and Kilty 2009; Hannah-Moffat 2009).

The Revolving Door: Reintegration and Continued Social Marginality

Research suggests that women do not have sufficient access to resources in the community upon release from prison and that they face contextually different issues upon **reintegration** than men, even though their problems may be labelled the same (e.g., addiction, homelessness, unemployment, housing). The lack of services and support for women leaving prison contributes to their continued involvement in the criminal justice system and often to their return to prison. Marginalized and criminalized women have considerable needs and extremely few available resources. For example, many women offenders report concerns about the lack of opportunities for vocational training in prison, which limits their job opportunities upon release (Pollack 2009).

Upon reintegration, women face many unique challenges. International research has demonstrated that when they leave prison, women face the same overwhelming problems they experienced prior to entering the system (Richie 2001; Pollack 2009). Some of these persistent challenges include: meeting basic needs; access to safe, affordable housing; child care; family reunification; employment; obtaining identification; opening bank accounts to deposit or write cheques (e.g., for rent); and social assistance.

Safe housing is a major re-entry need for many women leaving prison. Empirical research suggests that addressing severe accommodation problems can reduce the risk of reoffending by as much as 20 per cent. When women are unable to find and maintain housing, they risk losing their children or not regaining custody of their children. Homeless women, like incarcerated women, are far more likely than their male counterparts to have young children in their care and to be dependent on public assistance. Upon being released from prison, many women are unable to secure housing and end up living in environments that are conducive to reoffending—at the same time as they are subjected to increased police surveillance. Being homeless or precariously housed is clearly not conducive to pro-social living.

Gaining sustainable employment, and in particular employable skills, is crucially linked to women's ability to meet their basic needs in the long term, to parole success, and to eventual desistence from crime. The ability of women to meet their basic needs upon release requires sustained economic independence. In short, women need access to employment or some form of income to support themselves, and in some cases their children. As noted earlier, many women report having insufficient job skills, education, or experience prior to incarceration, and encountering the same conditions upon release. Interviews with imprisoned women reveal how they are pulled toward high-risk situations and illegal activities as legal financial and housing options are exhausted (Richie 2001). When women are underemployed or unemployed and consequently cannot access safe, affordable housing, they often rely when possible on families, past social networks, welfare, and/or community agencies. Living with family can be a positive experience for some women, but for many it is not. Ongoing dependencies on friends, families, and social agencies for basic needs such as food and housing can erode women's self-esteem, dignity, and sense of self-worth (Barker 2009). Economic need can push women back into negative relationships with men and may act as a catalyst for re-entry into criminalized activities such as prostitution or dealing drugs.

Conclusion

Both US and Canadian studies have reported that homelessness and mental illness together are strong predictors of involvement with the correctional system (Gaetz and O'Grady 2006). Mentally ill persons who are homeless are particularly vulnerable to frequent involvement with the criminal justice system. Several surveys (including Canadian studies; see Mental Health Commission of Canada, 2009) have shown that, of the homeless population, those who report psychiatric illness or hospitalization are most likely to have a history of arrest or incarceration. As discussed above, criminalized women are affected by a range of emotional and mental health problems that are not well managed in the community and that pose significant challenges to their reintegration.

Sadly, many women enter prison expecting to receive treatment for drug and alcohol addictions and mental health conditions (Pollack 2009). In fact, the prospect of getting treatment has led many women who were facing shorter sentences to request federal sentences to access treatment options. However, once women enter the federal system, they quickly discover that prisons are punitively focused and that programs are not always available or helpful in addressing the factors that lead women to prison. Many women report that institutional and post-release programs did not adequately prepare them to manage their addiction in the community (Richie 2001). In addition, few resources are available to assist them after prison; women must struggle with abuse and trauma issues (vis-à-vis trust, relationships, and safety), and their access to programs and services is limited by the stigma of parole or ex-prisoner status. Although resources are scarce, an increase in resources is crucial to break the unique cycle of crime that faces women in prison.

Questions to Consider

1. Describe some of the pathways that lead women to prison.
2. What are the main characteristics of the prison populations and women in prison?
3. What barriers do women face upon release from prison?
4. How could the number of women being sent to prison be reduced?

Notes

1. Approximately 514 women are incarcerated in federal institutions/treatment centres across Canada and 567 women are held under federal supervision in communities across Canada (Correctional Service of Canada 2010).
2. According to the 2006 census, approximately 4 per cent of the Canadian population identified themselves as Aboriginal. In 2006–7, 18 per cent of adults admitted to remand were Aboriginal, as were 20 per cent of adults admitted to provincial or territorial sentenced custody and 18 per cent of adults admitted to federal custody (Babooram 2008).
3. Conditions at the Prison for Women in Kingston, Ontario, combined with a series of deaths of Aboriginal women in custody and mounting political pressure due to a potential section 15 Charter of Rights and Freedoms case, led to the establishment of the historic Task Force on Federally Sentenced Women in 1989 and its now 20-year-old report *Creating Choices*, which the Correctional Service of Canada routinely refers to as a foundational document.

18 | What Is Sovereignty for Indigenous People?

Patricia Monture

Introduction

First Nations made agreements with settlers about sharing the land. These agreements are recorded in both the oral history and the Western written historical record. Primarily in the prairie region (Alberta, Saskatchewan, and Manitoba) but also covering significant parts of Ontario and extending into the Northwest Territories and British Columbia, the agreements are known as the numbered treaties (from 1 to 11). They were signed over a 50-year period commencing in 1871 and ending in 1921, and—in view of the time frame—are often referred to as post-Confederation treaties (Burrell, Young, and Price 1975; Brown and Maquire 1979). It is important to study these agreements because they provide a way to understand the laws and governance structures of First Nations while remembering that 'change is constant and diversity is everywhere within First Nations and dominant culture communities' (LeBaron 2004 13). Acknowledging the diversity of First Nations means understanding that the concept of **indigenous sovereignty** is not homogeneous but entails a multiplicity of sovereignties.

An analysis of indigenous sovereignties often begins with a discussion of the 1982 repatriation of Canada's constitution and the inclusion of section 35(1). Section 35(1) is the most comprehensive recognition of indigenous sovereignty included in the repatriation, and it 'recognizes and affirms' the 'existing' Aboriginal and treaty rights of the Aboriginal peoples of Canada. Political science scholar Kiera Ladner (Cree) (2003) explains the trouble with this approach:

> By most accounts, Aboriginal peoples became interested in federalism circa 1982 when they became uninvited participants in Canada's constitution process. Canada's **constitutional orthodoxy** typically portrays Aboriginal peoples as 'constitutional outsiders' who became participants in Canadian federalism and modern constitutionalism as a result of the emergence of 'charter politics' or 'constitutional minoritarianism'. (167)

Ladner argues that this view of federalism is bound to the idea that Canada comprises the provinces, the territories, and the federal government exclusively. Consequently, Aboriginal peoples are typically ignored by those who study Canadian federalism. She points out that the problem with constitutional orthodoxy and reliance on Canada's 'official history' ignores the fact that the history of federalism on this continent predates European arrival on the shores of the Americas (167–9). For this reason, the constitutional events of 1982 and the protection of Aboriginal and treaty rights in section 35(1) of Canada's constitution are not the focus of this chapter. Rather, it approaches indigenous sovereignties in a historical way that respects the length of the relationship between Canada and First Peoples.

The numbered treaties are just one example of the agreements between Onkwehon:we ('indigenous peoples' in the language of the Kanien'kehaka—the Mohawk) and the Crown in the territory that is now known as Canada. Across the country, the agreements entered into did not only or always involve land. In the east, the focus was most often on peace and friendship. Treaty-making in Canada follows the pattern of colonial settlement from east to west, with the earliest agreements having been signed in the east. It should also be remembered that not all First Nations have signed treaty agreements with the Crown.[1] Treaties are not just historical documents: in British Columbia, modern-day treaty negotiation talks have been only recently established.

At the time of signing the treaties, the Crown recognized that indigenous peoples had the right to negotiate agreements with other nations, including both the settler governments and other indigenous nations (Ladner 2003, 175–8). This constituted an express recognition of indigenous sovereignty(ies), which is an acknowledgement that First Nations had their own distinctive laws, governance structures, and social orders. Thus, treaties were not the source of First Nations governance authorities. First Nations already held these rights and responsibilities at the time of treaty signing. As Ladner (2003) explains:

> The treaty was an agreement between two independent powers that recognized the autonomy of each nation and the ability of each to determine their political status vis-à-vis the other. It was an agreement that 'created shared responsibilities rather than supreme powers' (i.e., neither government was subordinate to the other), shared as well as exclusive territories (i.e., reserves) and two classes of 'British subjects'. (178)

This understanding of the treaty sees the Crown's rights as derivative and acknowledges that any right not delegated by First Nations remains with them.

Aboriginal title and Aboriginal rights (including treaty rights) are Creator-given rights, as the elders of many nations have explained. Detailed understandings of the authority to govern First Nations can only be gained by studying specific First Nations such as the Nehiowè (Cree), Kanien'kehaka (Mohawk), Dene or Anishnabe (Ojibwe), and so on. Speaking of the Nehiowè traditions of Treaty Six, the late Harold Cardinal (Cree) and Walter Hildebrandt (2000) explain:

> '*Miyo-wîcêhtowin* is a Cree word meaning 'having or possessing good relations'. It is a concept that arises from one of the core doctrines or values of the Cree nation. The term outlines the nature of relationships that Cree peoples are required to establish. It asks, directs, admonishes, or requires Cree peoples as individuals and as a nation to conduct themselves in a manner such that they create positive or good relations in all relationships, be it individually or collectively with other peoples. *Miyo-wîcêhtowin* as a concept and a term originates in the laws and relationships that their nation has with the Creator. (14)

Miyo-wîcêhtowin is just one example of the laws governing the conduct of Nehiowè people, and it is common to a number of First Nations. Haudenosaunee (Iroquois) people are taught about the 'great law of peace' or the 'ways to most live most nicely together' (Monture-Angus 1995, 1999). Anishnabe (Ojibwe) people are taught about the principles of the 'good life'. These teachings influence the ways in which indigenous peoples understand the meaning of sovereignty (Benton Banai 1979; Solomon 1990). In their 2005 report on the recognition and implementation of First Nations governments, the Assembly of First Nations affirmed this position on the nature of indigenous sovereignties when they wrote:

> In many First Nations languages, the concept of government means 'our way of life' or simply 'our life'. There are differences in First Nation and non-Aboriginal understandings of the concept of government. While some Canadians tend to see government as remote, divorced from the people and everyday life, First Nations people generally view government in a more holistic way, as inseparable from the totality of communal practices that make up a way of life. Unlike non-Aboriginal governments, First Nation governments involve relationships between families, clans and tribes rather than a relationship of strangers governing strangers. (34)

Approaching the study of indigenous sovereignty from the treaty paradigm allows one to highlight several important issues. From the standpoint of indigenous knowledge, all parties to a treaty are assumed to have prior rights. This means that it is not just First Nations who have treaty rights and responsibilities. Various Crowns, including the British, Dutch, French, and Canadian, as well as the US government, were also a party to those treaties and were accorded both rights and obligations under various treaties. This means that non-indigenous people, who follow the Crown, also have treaty rights. It is important to examine why we only hear about First Nations having treaty rights. We mostly hear about First Nations fighting for those rights, especially hunting and fishing rights. If you were to research the rights of non-indigenous people under a given treaty, you would probably not find a single article in the library. If nothing else, this demonstrates the degree to which power is an essential variable in the analysis of both historical and present-day First Nations relationships with the Crown and its citizens.

Let us take an example. In the case of Treaty Six, non-indigenous people have the right to share the land up to the depth of a plow (about six inches) (Cardinal and Hildebrandt 2000). Hence, non–First Nations have the right to their own agricultural practices. As well, non-indigenous people would also have the right to their government, language, and religious and educational practices. It is of course revealing that we do not hear about non-indigenous peoples fighting to exercise these rights (or more important, fighting to demonstrate that they possess them). This is because non-indigenous peoples exercise those rights every day, as easily as they breathe. Non-indigenous people do not even have to be aware that they have those rights in order to exercise them. Furthermore, why do students studying Treaty Six (or any other treaty territory, I suspect) come to their university classes without any background in this topic? And what does the discipline of sociology have to offer in the political, legal, social, and economic debates about indigenous sovereignty, including reconciliation with the state?

The study of Aboriginal nations in the discipline of sociology is a relatively new phenomenon. In 1974, James S. Frideres published a book titled *Canada's Indians: Contemporary Conflicts*. It was followed by the work of Rick Ponting and Roger Gibbins in 1980. Much of the early work in sociology focused on one of the following ideas or concepts: demography, Aboriginal persons and nations as 'issues', social conflict, deviance, or race and ethnicity (including the study of discrimination). As Vic Satzewich and Terry Wotherspoon (1993) conclude:

Somewhat ironically, Canadian sociologists have not kept pace with these other disciplines in the study of aboriginal peoples. While there was a flurry of sociological and anthropological studies of aboriginal peoples in the early

1970s, particularly in the context of Indian urbanization, the issue of aborig-inal/non-aboriginal relations has been placed on the so-called 'backburner' by sociologists. (xii)

These categorizations have unfortunately limited the knowledge base of soci-ologists interested in understanding the relationship between Canada and First Peoples (see Agocs 2000; Steckley 2003). Writing in 1981, anthropolo-gist John A. Price noted that he was critical of sociologists' practice of placing their knowledge of indigenous peoples within the sub-discipline of ethnic studies rather than creating a new sub-discipline of 'North American Indian sociology' (353).

As sociologists (both students and scholars) begin to consider the idea of an indigenous sociology, several important factors should be considered. First, in the preceding passage, all of the scholars cited (and this is representative of the authors who completed the early work) are men with the exception of Carol Agocs (a feminist and political scientist). But sovereign traditions among First Nations do not necessary reflect the same gendering of society that we are accustomed to studying in university. Second, it is not that such issues as dis-crimination, social conflict, and the overrepresentation of Aboriginal persons in the criminal justice system are not important to consider—they are. It is just that the approaches usually adopted are insufficient. These approaches have tended to view Aboriginal peoples as 'social problems' (Steckley 2003). They cast their gaze at individual explanations, not structural ones. As Frideres (1998) explains:

> For too long, social scientists have viewed Aboriginal-White relations through a micro model, focusing exclusively on individual actions, e.g., prejudice and discrimination. Not surprisingly, these models see solutions to the problems Aboriginal people face as being brought about through individual action, e.g., individual enhancement and individual entrepreneurship. We wish to approach the problem from a different perspective—structural. (2)

Without discussions and developing understandings of indigenous sover-eignty and governance, the studies cannot reflect who and what Aboriginal persons believe they are.

We can expect that the recent inclusion of indigenous scholars in the field of sociology in Canada will change the way in which Aboriginal nations are studied within the discipline. It is important to note that until four decades ago, Indians who earned university degrees were forced to give up their status under the Indian Act. This in part explains why indigenous scholars only began to enter academia as faculty members in the late 1980s. Of course, poverty among First Nations people and lack of success in educational systems (especially since the first exposure to formal education often came in residential or industrial schools) have also had a profound impact on the ability of First Nations peoples to succeed in the university setting. The result is indisputable: no 'Native sociology' has yet to emerge (Steckley 2003)

Challenging Myths, Stereotypes, and Discrimination

A number of myths and stereotypes about Aboriginal people must be corrected before we can engage in a discussion about indigenous sovereignties. Most people are now aware of the historical stereotyping that cast Aboriginal peoples as less civilized and less intelligent and their societies as less advanced. Historian John Tobias (1998) has studied the colonization of the Plains Cree and provides this example of how stereotypes of inferiority provided justification for the actions taken against the Cree nation by the Crown:

> The Plains Indians, and particularly the Plains Cree, are said to be a primitive people adhering to an inflexible system of traditions and customs, seeking to protect themselves against the advance of civilization, and taking up arms in rejection of the reserve system and an agricultural way of life. This traditional interpretation distorts the roles of both the Cree and the Canadian government, for the Cree were both flexible and active in promoting their own interests, and willing to accommodate themselves to a new way of life, while the Canadian government was neither as far-sighted nor as just as tradition maintains. Canada's principal concern in the relationship with the Plains Cree was to establish control over them, and Canadian authorities were willing to and did wage war upon the Cree in order to achieve this control. (150)

Both pronouncing and perpetuating stereotypes, as well as acting on those stereotypes, requires power over those stereotyped. In this discussion, it is important to note that 'power is always a factor that shapes whose cultural values are seen as legitimate, whose values are accommodated and how' (LeBaron 2004, 14).

Many people do not acknowledge how stereotypes have evolved and remain embedded in Canadian society. For this reason, the past is not the past (see Chapter 11). One current example of the problem with embedded stereotypes can be found in common political discourse, fed by both the media and conservative ideologues. Consider the view on the part of one segment of the population that the special rights of Aboriginal peoples are an affront to Canadian unity (Cairns 2000). However, these so-called special rights are entrenched in Canada's constitution (hence making them 'merely' constitutional rights, similar to the distinct rights held by francophones). Thus this view is a denigration of the constitutional rights held by Aboriginal nations and people. Such political stereotyping follows patterns common through all historical periods, particularly when it comes to inferiorizing anything indigenous.

The elders teach that one has to know where one has come from to know where one is going (Solomon 1990). Historian Ken Coates (1999) notes that

> Canadians have gradually, and grudgingly, come to accept that the First Nations occupied the land now known as Canada as much as 15,000 years ago and that a series of complex, sophisticated societies lived in the area for thousands of years. Only thirty years ago, the prevailing image was less favourable, suggesting that a tiny population of Indigenous people scratched out a meager living in a land that Europeans would subsequently prove to be rich in potential. This image served the interests of the dominant society very well, for it justified a history of conquest, occupation, and land confiscation; it also 'explained' the relative inability of First Nations people to join the Canadian economic and social mainstream. First Nations, though battered by decades of assimilationist programming, resented the unflattering portrait and struggled to highlight the richness and diversity of the Indigenous experience. Gradually, the message was heard, at least in part. (142)

The prevalence of stereotypes rather than the development of knowledge about indigenous understandings of sovereignty and developing intercultural competencies emphasizes the degree to which power has been a key variable in governance relations between First Nations and the Crown (LeBaron 2004).

The first of these embedded stereotypes is the problem of naming Aboriginal persons and nations. The Canadian constitution names the Aboriginal peoples of Canada as the 'Indian, Inuit and Métis'. No further definitions are found in the constitution. To this list we can add the names 'Native' or 'Native peoples', 'First Nations', and 'indigenous peoples'. The major problem with each of these names is that it collapses all Aboriginal peoples into a single category and creates a stereotype of sameness. In fact, Aboriginal nations are diverse groupings with unique languages, cultures, traditions, institutions (including governing structures), and laws. Since these names all result from colonial imposition, none of them is a good choice for referring to Aboriginal persons and nations.

Each of the names that has been applied to Aboriginal nations and persons is part of the colonial process. As I explained elsewhere:

> I tell this story about naming because it is symbolic. Growing up 'Indian' in this
> country is very much about not having the power to define yourself or your re-
> ality. It is being denied the right to say, 'I am!'—instead, always finding yourself
> saying, 'I am not!' (Monture-Angus 1995, 3)

The stereotypes, both historical and present-day, have profound impacts on Aboriginal persons, and it is important to acknowledge this in any sociological analysis.

The naming conundrum may be answered by deferring to Canada's constitution and adopting the term 'Aboriginal peoples'. 'Indigenous peoples' is the term generally used when the focus is international, and it is used in this chapter to refer to all persons of Aboriginal ancestry who reside around the globe. Most often, this chapter uses the term 'First Nations' instead of 'Indian'. However, 'Indian' is used when the reference is to the Indian Act, which applies only to those persons entitled to be registered (also called 'status' Indians).

The second of these embedded stereotypes is the idea that real 'Indians' come from reserves. Reserves, however, are not a good 'Indian' idea but rather a result of Canadian laws and the imposition of the Indian Act. Reserves are a colonial idea, intended to separate 'Indians' from the rest of society. Reserves have also had an internal impact on indigenous nations in that the communities' small size and defined membership, coupled with the inability to easily transfer membership from reserve to reserve, frustrates the ability of indigenous citizens to participate in the nation as a nation and not just a small community called a reserve. The reserve policy was justified through paternalism or the belief that assimilation was the best policy. Paternal ideas suggested that 'Indians' needed the protection of the state until such time as they were able to fit into the larger society growing around them. For 'Indian' people, it is much more accurate to think in terms of the territories that First Nations, Métis, and Inuit occupied. Hence, one thinks in terms of Nehiowè territory, Kanien'kehaka territory, Mi'kmaq territory, and so on.

The early belief was that Aboriginal persons in the prairies were nomadic, hunters and gathers, simple agriculturalists—or simply inferior to settlers. These ideas have been demonstrated to be false. The people who used to be thought of as inhabiting territory in a nomadic fashion are now known to have occupied those territories through their vast knowledge of seasonal and animal life cycles. Indeed, the advanced agricultural practices of many First Nations are only now being discovered. For example, Haudenosaunee women grew corn, beans, and squash in a mound. Today we understand that growing these three plants together, known to the Haudenosaunee as the three sisters, contributes to a balanced soil. Historical records have overemphasized male roles in providing sustenance for the people, often in tales of the big game hunters. More recently, the contributions of indigenous women to the people's sustenance by hunting small animals, harvesting, and agriculture have been acknowledged (Carter 1990, 28, 176–80; Peers 1996, 39–50).

The problem of stereotypes must be understood from within a much larger paradigm. Not only do stereotypes lead to both prejudice and discrimination but they are cumulatively part of a larger process known as colonialism. Colonization entails a series of complex process and actions that begins with a forced intrusion into the territories of indigenous peoples, quickly followed by land takeover. This in turn is followed by actions that deny the validity of the political, economic, legal, and religious systems of First Peoples. Later stages of the process include attacks on indigenous languages and denials of indigenous legal systems, social structures (including educational systems), and cultural beliefs and practices. The end product is dependency in multiple forms (Frideres 1998, 3–5). Writing on the impact of colonialism on present-day Aboriginal lives, I have noted:

> As I struggled with the pain in my life and in the lives of those I am close to, I became more and more determined to understand the process of colonialism and colonization. If colonialism brought our nations to this point, then undoing the damage of colonialism must be the answer. I now understand this thinking to be much too linear . . . to be helpful. It is not just the colonial relations that must be undone but all of the consequences (addictions, loss of language, loss of parenting skills, loss of self-respect, abuse and violence, and so on). Colonialism is no longer a linear, vertical relationship—colonizer does to colonized—it is a horizontal and entangled relationship (like a spider web). (Monture-Angus 1999, 10–11)

Gender has often been the vehicle by which colonial strategies have been delivered upon First Nations (Jaimes 1992, 11; Acoose 1995, 56). For instance, another historical misinterpretation is the view that First Nations women were servants of their men and indeed 'drudges' (Acoose 1995, 39). Janice Acoose (Nehiowè-Métis and Nahkawè) (1995) wrote:

> Moreover, the women in my family fit none of the white stereotypes of Indigenous women. As extremely powerful, resourceful, and dynamic women who vitally contributed to the survival of my family, communities, and nations. (11)

Stereotypes of indigenous women rooted in the larger practice of 'inferiorizing' all things indigenous continue to have devastating consequences. In

1991, the Aboriginal Justice Inquiry of Manitoba concluded that the murder of Helen Betty Osborne was based on both race and gender. Commissioners Hamilton and Sinclair wrote:

> It is clear that Betty Osborne would not have been killed if she had not been Aboriginal. The four men who took her to her death from the streets of The Pas that night had gone looking for an Aboriginal girl with whom to 'party'. They found Betty Osborne. When she refused to party she was driven out of town and murdered. Those who abducted her showed a total lack of regard for her person or her rights as an individual. Those who stood by while the physical assault took place, while sexual advances were made and while she was being beaten to death showed their own racism, sexism and indifference. Those who knew the story and remained silent must share their guilt. (98)

More recently, the Sisters in Spirit campaign (2005) launched by the Native Women's Association of Canada has estimated that 500 Aboriginal women in this country are missing and murdered. Amnesty International (2004) examined this situation and in a report titled *Stolen Sisters* concluded that 'this intersection of sexism and racism contributes to the assumption on the part of perpetrators of violence against indigenous women that their actions are justifiable or condoned by society' (17). Gender discrimination, both historical and current, has an enormous impact on the lives of Aboriginal women and interferes with our abilities to live in a sovereign way.

Understanding sovereignty from the position of indigenous people requires the ambitious challenging of history's misinterpretations and the stereotypes about indigenous nations and their citizens that have become embedded in what we think is objective or neutral knowledges. This challenging can be an unsettling experience for both indigenous people and the descendants of the settler nations. Indigenous people must confront an often-traumatic past (Thomas 2005, 238), while the descendants of settlers must confront both guilt and disbelief.

Sociological Understandings of Indigenous Sovereignty

Contrary to common belief, indigenous peoples have had a significant influence on the social structures of the world. In introducing his book *Forgotten Founders: How the American Indian Helped Shape Democracy*, Bruce Johansen (1982), a former journalist, writes of first learning about the influence of the Iroquois on the evolution of American democracy and constitutionalism from a student at Evergreen State College in Washington:

The idea struck me as disingenuous. I considered myself decently educated in American history, and to the best of my knowledge, government for and by the people had been invented by white men in powdered wigs. I asked the young woman where she had come by her information. 'My grandmother told me,' she said. That was hardly the kind of source I could use for a newspaper story. I asked whether she knew of any other sources. 'You're the investigative reporter,' she said. 'You find them.' (xi–xii)

The issue is not that indigenous ideas have not had influence; it is that the source of those ideas has not been accurately credited (see also Venables 1992, 77–8; Thornton 1998, 91–4). This can be said not only about the agricultural practices of First Nations but also about the influence of indigenous thinking on the ideas of Marx and Engels (see Engels 1972, 734).

The influence of the Haudenosaunee (Iroquois) on Karl Marx and Friedrich Engels is particularly worthy of further comment. It originated with Lewis Henry Morgan, an anthropologist who was a close friend of Ely Parker, a Seneca (one of the six Iroquoian nations). His first book (1851) was about the Iroquois, followed by *Ancient Society* (1985 [1877]), which Karl Marx read. The Iroquois intrigued Marx because of their democratic political organization and the way that they achieved economic equality without coercion. After Marx's death, Engels received his notes on Morgan's work and subsequently wrote his well-received essay on family, private property, and the state (Johansen 1982, 122). Engels described the Iroquoian state in this way:

Everything runs smoothly without soldiers, gendarmes, or police, without nobles, kings, governors, prefects or judges; without prisons, without trials. All quarrels and disputes are settled by the whole body of those concerned. . . . The household is run communistically by a number of families; the land is tribal property, only the small gardens being temporarily assigned to the households—still, not a bit of our extensive and complicated machinery of administration is required. . . . There are no poor and needy. The communistic household and the gens know their responsibility toward the aged, the sick and the disabled in war. All are free and equal—including the women. (cited in Johansen 1982, 123)

Despite the influence on these founding fathers of sociology, the relationship between First Nations and Western intellectual traditions receded into the background. This is a common pattern: indigenous practices—their foods, their intellectual traditions, even images appropriated as 'team mascots' by the colonizing nations (Weatherford 1988)—have their origins denied.

Sociological study soon focused on industrialized societies, and the study of 'primitive' societies was left to anthropology (Thornton 1998, 92). As time passed, academic boundaries continued to be drawn without indigenous influence. These boundaries began to be challenged as the numbers of indigenous students attending post-secondary institutions increased in the 1970s, a trend that continues today (Thornton 1998, 87). The demands of indigenous students on Canadian academia led to the development of a number of Native studies programs across the country (Price 1981, 354). For sociologists, the demand led to the development of some issues-based courses such as 'Native peoples in urban areas' and 'Native peoples and social welfare'. As indigenous sociologists have joined the faculty ranks in Canada, courses that examine the nature of indigenous justice systems, institutional racism, collective questions of identity, and the structure of First Nations governance traditions have been formed. Students of sociology will soon have greater opportunity to access indigenous understandings of the world, including indigenous sovereignties.

What we know as sociologists about indigenous sovereignties is limited not only by the history of our discipline but by other significant factors as well. Language sets the parameters through which humans amass knowledge, and language is bound by culture (Sapir 1929, 1949; Whorf 1956). Postmodernists point to the multiple ways in which language can be used to silence the voices of those whose lives are located at the margins (Meyer 2001; Kovach 2005, 25). In order to examine the definitions of sovereignty without being ethnocentric, it is important to consider the different structure of indigenous languages. Leroy Little Bear (Blood of the Blackfoot Confederacy) (2005) explains:

> It can be generally said that Euro-languages such as English are very noun-oriented. English is a good language for dichotomies, categorizations, and reductionist specificity. In its dichotomy mode, it manifests polarized, binary thinking: good and bad; saint and sinner; black and white; old and new; and so on. Aboriginal languages generally can be said to be action-oriented. Everything is about process, actions, happenings. It can be said that constant flux manifests itself in the language. The noun-orientation of English and the action-orientation of Aboriginal languages have led to different relational expectations, especially as regards relationships to land and treaty making. (29)

The differences in the structure of the languages of indigenous peoples and Europeans reflect the differences in the way people think about themselves in the world (Cajete 1999). Language is an excellent position from which to contemplate difference.

Care must be taken with language and concepts discussed only in English since they may not mean the same thing across cultures—and sovereignty (also referred to as self-government or self-determination) is just one example. Again, this emphasizes the need to consider power:

> When Aboriginal Peoples discuss the meaning of self-government and/or self-determination, we are forced to do it in a language that is not our own. We must express our ideas in English or in French, both of which epitomize our colonial experiences. It is almost solely Aboriginal energy that fosters the accommodations that are required to carry on both the political and legal dialogues in either of the Canadian colonial languages. This is a particular experience of colonial oppression. At the same time, the languages that were brought to our territories have benefited Aboriginal people, as we are able to more fully share our ideas beyond Indigenous boundaries. (Monture-Angus 1999, 22)

Not all indigenous scholars agree (see Alfred 1999, 55–60) on the best language to use from the list of possibilities, which includes self-government, self-determination, First Nations governance, or indigenous sovereignty. My preference is for a governance structure that provides First Nations with the opportunity for economic, social, legal, and spiritual independence. Choosing 'sovereignty' as the word to describe the goal prevents further degradation or inferiorizing of indigenous peoples and ways, thus disrupting the historically embedded pattern of oppression.

From many Aboriginal understandings, sovereignty (including the practice of good governance) focuses on community and relationships. In my language, there is no precise translation for the word 'self-government'. Kanien'kehaka (Mohawk) people would say *tewatatha:wi*. This word best translates into 'I or we carry ourselves' (Monture-Angus 1999, 36). It is governance that requires both personal and collective responsibility for living right. Haudenosaunee scholar and traditional leader Oren Lyons explained at the Montreal Conference on Indian Government in 1979:

> Sovereignty—it's a political word. It's not a legal word. Sovereignty is the act. Sovereignty is the do. You act. You don't ask. There is no limitation on sovereignty. You are not semi-sovereign. You either are or aren't. It's simple. (cited in Hill 1992, 175)

First Nations are beginning to acknowledge that waiting for federal acknowledgement of their rights is a long and frustrating experience. The message of many traditional leaders, such as the hereditary chief and former Assembly of

First Nations BC vice-chief Satsan (Herb George) (2005), is that we do not just have rights but the responsibility to act.

In a Western sense, statehood is identified when governments possess characteristics such as the ability to use coercive force (both militarily and legally), have defined boundaries and control over their territory, and command recognition from their population as well as from the international community. Alongside these characteristics, states have absolute authority over their citizens, are hierarchical, and often have an identifiable ruling elite. States require compliance with their decisions, and this is often the role that law plays in their social systems. States are sovereign nations. These are not the concepts used when an indigenous person describes indigenous sovereignty. But does this mean that indigenous peoples are not sovereign? Or does it mean that the definition of sovereignty has been inaccurately and overly narrowly defined? The result of the incomplete international definition of sovereignty is the inability to be inclusive of all peoples and states.

For Canada, indigenous scholars agree that the structural solution is not really so difficult. The Canadian state is built on the tradition of federalism—shared sovereignty between the federal and provincial governments. It includes a plural legal tradition combining both civil and common law systems. To this, indigenous scholars remind us of the agreements between the Crown and First Nations and argue for the implementation of treaty federalism (Henderson 1994a, 1994b; Ladner 2003). According to both Ladner and James (Sakej) Henderson, the treaties are the 'foundational law of Canada' (Ladner 2003, 173). It was the treaties that allowed settlers to establish governments in this territory now known as Canada. The solution lies in implementing the true order of Canadian governance and recognizing the third order, that of the First Peoples (or the treaties; see Henderson 1994a; 1994b, 60).

Conclusion

The study of social structures, including political systems, has been a core area of study for sociologists such as Marx, Weber, and Durkheim. Regarding state functions, these three sociologists studied power and authority, capitalism, legitimacy, bureaucracy, and labour. According to Weber, 'power is the business of government, a formal organization that directs the political life of a society' (Macionis and Gerber 2005, 411). Not often recognized in the study of social theory concepts such as 'democracy, nationalisms, individualism, liberty, rights and freedoms' (Brandon 1986; Ladner 2000, 35) is that these were also core concepts in indigenous knowledge systems, demonstrating that the birth of sociology truly predates the work of its founding fathers.

In the 1960s and 1970s in both Canada and the United States, Aboriginal people became more militant in asserting their rights (Mercredi and Turpel 1993; Warrior 1996; Cornell 1998). There is no reason to believe that Aboriginal peoples will cease this struggle. The Assembly of First Nations (2005) recognizes that the 'international and domestic scholars and independent experts have confirmed the link between the right of people to choose how to be governed and successful development' (12). In Canada, the Supreme Court in 1997 clearly recognized Aboriginal title in the landmark Delgamuukw and Gisday'wa decision. Legal recognition must be followed by continued political evolution on the part of the Canadian state toward supporting Aboriginal peoples' journey away from the consequences of colonialism.

Questions to Consider

1. How might indigenous knowledge be used to analyze Canadian society?
2. Does the notion of governmentality speak to questions of sovereignty?
3. Discuss the different definitions of sovereignty presented in this chapter.
4. Describe the kinds of rights that Aboriginal peoples possess in Canadian law.
5. How have sociologists contributed to the study of the relationship between Aboriginal nations and Canada?

Note

1. Because the focus of this chapter is on treaty relationships, the discussion focuses on the sovereign experiences of First Nations, not Métis or Inuit.

19 | What Is Sovereignty in Quebec?

Philippe Couton

Introduction

There are three simple and divergent answers to the question asked in the title of this chapter. The first is provided by proponents of **sovereignty** who argue that Quebec has long suffered oppression at the hand of the British Empire and its successor state, Canada, and would be better off as an independent country. The conquest of 1760 and the subsequent repression of various uprisings, the ensuing political, economic, and cultural domination of anglophone elites (even within Quebec), and the ongoing lack of recognition of Quebec society's uniqueness all point toward the necessity of independence (Bourque 2001). The quest for sovereignty is furthermore described not just as a reaction to perceived humiliations but as the collective affirmation of Quebec's distinctive culture and identity (Beauchemin 2008). Second, opponents of sovereignty conversely describe what they often call 'separatism' or 'secession' as a product of narrow **nationalism** that seeks to protect and defend a particular ethnic group at the expense of both the larger Canadian society and minorities within Quebec. They further argue that it is democratically illegitimate, violates international law, and goes against the global trend for greater diversity and pluralism (see Pratte 2008).

A third, less ideologically charged answer, often provided by social scientists, points out that as a historically and culturally distinct community within the larger Canadian political entity, Quebec lacks what many other such communities in the world enjoy: full political control over its own destiny. The sovereignty movement seeks to obtain independence in order to achieve this control, protect the distinctiveness of Quebec culture, and pursue social and political objectives with tools that are currently in the hands of the federal government. This quest for independence simply follows a global process that has seen the world divided into more or less clearly defined cultural units (nations) endowed with their own sovereign political institutions (**states**). Where this process has not come to completion for historical reasons (conquest, colonialism, etc.) in many other parts of the world (Scotland and Kurdistan, for example), groups similarly seek to achieve sovereignty by either peaceful or violent means. Like these other communities, Quebec has developed into a thriving, unique society that now wishes to achieve the last stage of a fully mature social and political entity: independence (see Venne 2001).

All three answers contain elements of truth. Preference for one depends on a variety of personal, cultural, and intellectual factors. There is certainly no right or wrong answer since each reflects particular political inclinations not amenable to simple right/wrong determinations. In any case, the point of this chapter is not to lend support to any particular viewpoint but to help disentangle the assumptions that underlie all three answers and that often remain underanalyzed. Only once these considerations are better understood can a person make a fully informed, critically minded choice about Quebec sovereignty. To this end, the rest of this chapter provides a discussion of the following key assumptions: the 'naturalness' of political independence; the concept of nation; independence as the endpoint of an evolutionary process; nationalism as an ideology; and the idea of sovereignty itself.

(Un)natural Independence

The first of these assumptions is the idea that the natural condition for any significant social group is political independence (synonymous with sovereignty). This is not always the case, although political independence remains a strong and durable aspect of modern social and political life throughout the world. A first argument against the presumed naturalness of independence is the clear lack of 'fit' between state and nation, which is a near universal dimension of most of the countries existing in the world today. Few states can legitimately claim to be the home of a single, culturally homogeneous nation (Keating 2004). That is, few political entities (states) govern a single, culturally homogeneous population (a nation), and conversely a very large number of culturally distinct groups do not enjoy a state entirely of their own. Canada is certainly one of the best examples of this as a true multinational state and one of the most diverse places in the world (Laczko 2000).[1] Quebec itself is of course just as diverse, with large Aboriginal groups, linguistic minorities, and rising immigration levels. Even some of the oldest nation-states in the world are home to sizable culturally distinct minority groups, including France, China, and many others (a few exceptions exist, notably Japan). And many of the oldest cultural groups in the world do not live in states of their own (nearly all Aboriginal peoples in the Americas, for instance). If language is one measure of the expression of a distinct culture, there are several thousand languages in the world today but only about 200 independent states.

The 'naturalness' of the sovereign nation-state is therefore more myth than reality; moreover, it is a potentially dangerous myth at that. One of the legacies of Western political history is the notion that states should encourage cultural uniformity within their populations, that they should mould the nations over which they rule in order to obtain a fit between state and nation. As Rae (2002) puts it, states are typically nation-forming states, and this process has very often been based—even before the advent of nationalism on a world scale—on 'pathological homogenization': the imposition of a single culture on the entire population. Quebec and other parts of Canada have periodically suffered from efforts at eradicating French as well as other non-English cultural traditions. The idea that most Western democracies have been and continue to be ethnically neutral (i.e., that they tend not to favour a particular ethnic group) is therefore simply untrue (Kymlicka 2000). All have promoted and continue to promote one culture (sometimes more) that is believed to be that of the nation the state governs. What nevertheless remains true is that a number of nation-states are home to several large cultural groups that coexist in relative harmony (Canada, Switzerland, and India are examples). Yet the norm remains that most nation-states tend to be the home of one dominant group from which comes the notion that political independence is the natural condition of culturally distinct communities (Italy is for Italians, Brazil for Brazilians, etc.).

In the case of Quebec, the argument is easily extended to say that Quebec should become a 'normal' country with the attributes of these other nation-states, although even strong proponents of Quebec sovereignty agree that Quebec has become less a single, homogeneous community and more a 'community of national communities', as Bourque (2001) puts it. No proper attempt to understand Quebec sovereignty can therefore rely on the putative naturalness of political independence. Quebec is not exceptional in having to share sovereignty with a larger entity. *Some* fit between state and nation is common in most countries, which does lend some support to the assumption, but even that is changing as some of the discussion below shows. On the other hand, most other existing states have been relatively free to promote a specific culture (through educational, cultural, and other policies), and Quebec understandably also wants to have this de facto aspect of nation-states at its disposal.

What Is a Nation?

The concept of nation itself is the second assumption that needs to be analyzed in order to better understand Quebec sovereignty. If Quebec is to achieve independence in the name of the dominant nation that resides on its territory

(Québécois, French-speaking Quebecers), what is this nation? Nations have attracted considerable attention from social scientists, historians, philosophers, and others, generating a large literature, including a number of classic works (e.g., Gellner 1997; Anderson 1991). There is little agreement on exactly how to define a nation, but major parameters of the discussion have emerged. First is the question of whether nations have always existed or are a fairly recent product of modern social life (or the constructionism/primordialism debate, as it is often termed). A loose consensus has emerged that sees nations as we understand them—large communities, territorially bound, sharing a common language and culture—as historically fairly recent. France, for instance, although one of the oldest countries in the world, has only truly shared a common language for the past century or so, and parts of its territory were disputed even during the twentieth century.

Likewise, the current territory of Quebec was only finalized in the early twentieth century, and Aboriginals, who have national claims of their own, populate very large parts of it. People within Quebec have only been identifying themselves as members of the Quebec nation (Québécois) since the middle of the twentieth century. Prior to this point, the dominant identity was French-Canadian or simply Canadian. But this is not very different from what has happened elsewhere in the world. Before the development of mass public education, mass media, and other aspects of modernity, most countries were marked by a high level of linguistic and cultural diversity, and most still are. The transition to greater national homogeneity is facilitated by various administrative instruments, including censuses, representative politics, mass education, and so on (Anderson 1998, 43; Laczko 2000). The process of nation-making is not unproblematic. Some have described it as the serialization or homogenization of individuals into largely constructed communities. Most national categories are, after all, the product of institutions and administrations. Quebec fits this general pattern and has only recently become a relatively unified society. Basing one's opposition to sovereignty on the recentness of Quebec nationhood is therefore not very helpful. Very few nations have any solid claims to ancient histories as homogeneous cultural entities.

One thing is clear, however: despite their relative newness, nations are tremendously resilient. Several ideological currents of the past predicted that nations would disappear. Liberals were hoping that a global, peaceful culture would emerge, while Marxists thought that classes would replace nations as the predominant form of social and political identity. Currently, a number of commentators claim that globalization is eradicating national borders and that we are about to enter a post-national world (Cohen 1996). The reality is, however, that a number of 'new' nations are emerging and a number of old ones are making new claims to autonomy. For instance, Aboriginal peoples in Canada, including in Quebec, and in other parts of the world are positioning themselves as nations and demanding some measure of self-determination. Another striking example of the resilience of ethno-national identity is its re-surgence after the collapse of the Soviet Union in 1989 (Laitin 1998). Despite the best efforts of the regime to repress or remove national minority groups for over 70 years, they resurfaced and sought their independence in the wake of the disappearance of the Soviet Union. Quebec, in other words, is certainly not alone in wanting sovereignty as a nation, and there is little reason to be-lieve that claim is irrelevant to today's world.

Evolution toward Independence?

A third and related dimension to be considered is whether or not societies, and Quebec in particular, follow a slow, evolutionary development that necessarily ends in political independence. As some of the above indicates, there is some truth to this view. The world seems to have evolved from fairly simple hu-man groupings into large empires (Roman, Greek, then British, French, etc.), almost all of which eventually split into sovereign states, some very recently. This phenomenon would also address the issue raised above: if so many cul-tural and linguistic groups have not reached sovereignty, it is simply because they have not yet experienced the full evolutionary process that leads to sover-eignty. In some cases, the process is still unfolding, and this could be the case in Quebec as well as in Scotland, Kurdistan, and many other nations.

The history of Quebec is well known and only needs to be briefly sum-marized here to further illustrate the point (see Dickinson and Young 2000 for details). Quebec emerged as Canada's second-largest and sole majority-francophone province over the past two and a half centuries. Once a French colonial possession, what is now Quebec was conquered by the British in 1760. Only about 60,000 French colonists lived in New France at that time. Over the following decades, inflows of English-speaking immigrants from the newly independent United States and from the British Isles came to outnumber francophones in British North America. New provinces emerged east and west of Quebec, most of them almost entirely anglophone. But despite these forces (conquest, English-speaking immigration), Quebec managed to survive and indeed thrive under British institutions. By the early twentieth century, thanks to a high birth rate, Quebec was more than holding its own demographically. And thanks to strong institutions both religious (the Catholic church) and secular (growing political institutions), it managed to preserve its culture and identity. By the 1960s, Montreal was emerging as one of the world's great cities (with the consecration of Expo 67 and later the 1976 Olympic Games), and Quebec was undergoing massive social and political change: the role of the church declined, while the provincial government took a more active role in a number of areas, including education, culture, health care, and so on. During this period, political parties promoting Quebec independence emerged and were successful at the polls. The logical outcome of this long history might seem to be some form of independence for Quebec, just as other countries have formed and developed elsewhere in the world, building their institutions, creating a unique culture, and achieving full independence. Quebec is in many ways in a similar position: long included in the British Empire, then in Canada, it has been attempting to evolve into a fully independent nation-state.

But leaving the argument at this level would miss several important points. First, the idea that Quebec should become an independent country is not new. Jules-Paul Tardivel, for instance, was an early proponent of Quebec independence. His 1895 novel *Pour la Patrie* summarized his political position, which failed to generate much support during his lifetime. Nationalists of various stripes have argued and struggled for independence over the past two centuries. Lord Durham's infamous 1839 report aptly summarized the situation as 'Two nations warring in the bosom of a single state'. However, the debate between sovereignty and federalism was not always as stark as it is today. A number of early French-Canadian nationalists were also staunch federalists. Earlier versions of Quebec nationalism included the work produced during the interwar period by Lionel Groulx, whose organic, traditional view of the nation was decidedly anti-liberal (Boily 2004). The notion of sovereignty only became a central aspect of Quebec and by extension Canadian politics in the 1960s, culminating in the first referendum on sovereignty in 1980. It was only during that period that the Quebec provincial government slowly constructed a large bureaucracy able to challenge some of the power of the federal government, particularly during the 1960s and 1970s, a period known as the Quiet Revolution. In this sense, however, the Quebec nation is actually the product of Canadian federalism, forcing a large number of Canada's francophones to identify with the Quebec territory and later with its institutions (Bourque 2001). Yet this might still seem to support the evolutionary view of Quebec sovereignty: only once its institutions were fully developed did the population of Quebec express strong support for independence.

There are, however, other explanations for the timing of the rise of the sovereignty movement. One is the influence of global anti-colonial struggles, and French-Canadian nationalism was reinterpreted through this prism during the 1950s and 1960s. French-speaking Canadians had long struggled for some measure of self-determination and against Anglo domination (from the uprising of the late 1830s to resistance to conscription during the two world wars), but only in the second half of the twentieth century did this struggle become a full-fledged independentist movement centred on Quebec. This new dimension of the fight drew direct inspiration from similar struggles in Algeria, Vietnam, and Cuba, among others. A second explanation is simply the emergence of a new class of politicians and public servants who had a significant stake in the developing Quebec institutions. They formed the backbone of the sovereigntist movement.

Another, more clearly supported explanation points to the tremendous influence of political events on the sovereignty movement, especially during the period that followed the first referendum. Quebec's position within Canada has been ambiguous and hybrid for at least 50 years: neither sovereign nor completely integrated (Laforest 2001, 299). But the recent nationalist movement has been particularly affected by the patriation of the constitution in 1982 and by the events that followed it. In brief, for historical reasons the process of amending the 1867 constitution of Canada had been left in the hands of the British government. Prime Minister Pierre Trudeau decided to 'patriate' the constitution, meaning to bring full control over the constitution from the UK to Canada. At the same time, Trudeau decided to add a charter of rights and freedoms to it and to provide for court-based enforcement of its provisions. This proved to be a divisive process, and Quebec felt cheated both by the way it unfolded and by the substance of the Charter, which failed to clearly recognize that Canada consisted of two founding societies. Two agreements were subsequently attempted, the Meech Lake (1990) and Charlottetown (1992) accords, both of which failed, only adding fuel to the fire. To this day a number of politicians and commentators feel that the entire process was illegitimate, possibly in breach of legal principles, and that the basic principle on which Canada had been founded was broken (Laforest 2001). The Charter was perceived to be a centralizing document that recognized a range of individual and collective rights but distinctly failed to recognize Quebec as such. It was seen as undermining provincial autonomy and weakening the ability of Quebec to be a nation (Kymlicka 1998). One of the consequences of this protracted process was dramatically increased support for sovereignty in Quebec, leading to the election of a Parti Québécois government in Quebec in 1994, a strong showing by the Bloc Québécois in federal elections, and near victory for the 'yes' side in the 1995 referendum.

The role of this divisive political process confirms that support for sovereignty does not follow a steady evolutionary path but is strongly influenced by political events. A large proportion of Quebecers, sovereigntists and federalists alike, were angered by the constitutional process and further inflamed by the bungled agreements. Support for sovereignty receded significantly in later years to the point that, in the 2003 election, the Parti Québécois lost the province to the Liberals, who remained in power in the next two elections in 2007 and 2008. The Bloc Québécois, the federal-level pro-sovereignty political party, continued to enjoy strong electoral support after its first sweeping victory in 1993, until its surprising near-total collapse in the 2011 election. This would tend to confirm that although there might be an evolutionary component to sovereignty (the development of institutions, etc.), the way the issue is handled at the political level continues to matter a great deal.

Is Nationalism an Ideology?

The fourth key assumption of the sovereignty question is the circumstances under which nations emerge and the claims that are most commonly made in their name. In other words, what is the nature of nationalism, and how does this apply to Quebec? Historians have long pointed out that nations are a product of the rise of democratic ideals. Nations are in that sense very similar to the 'people' that putatively govern in a democracy. The beginning of democracy, in revolutions and reform movements in Europe and North America, occurred in the name of the people or the nation in opposition to the ruling class (see Hobsbawm 1992). It is only fairly recently that nationalism has become associated with destructive and politically extreme political ideologies and movements (e.g., Nazism; the wars that ravaged parts of the former communist Europe in the 1990s). No single ideology is clearly and uniquely associated with nationalism, which has been a force of both emancipation and oppression—even genocide—in recent history. Simply equating the quest for national independence with narrow tribalism or claiming it is purely a liberation movement is therefore inaccurate. Just as elsewhere in the world, the movement for Quebec sovereignty has had its share of extremists (but far fewer than in, for example, Ireland; see Cormier and Couton 2004), although it has been thoroughly democratic and peaceful in recent decades.

A related and important aspect of the question is usually presented as a tension between liberal individualism and communitarianism—or to put it differently, between the idea that the ultimate source of freedom and autonomy resides in the individual and the opposite notion that it is found in the community. This issue emerges in a number of debates, not only about Quebec sovereignty but about the rights and objectives of a range of minority communities the world over (similar national minorities in Belgium, Spain, Indonesia, and parts of Africa; immigrant groups in many Western countries; Native communities in former European colonies). Debates on the issue tend to present most nationalist movements as primarily communitarian and thus as posing a threat to the core value of Western democracies: individual liberty. However, this is usually not the case and clearly not as far as Quebec is concerned (see Kymlicka 1998, 2000). There is no evidence to indicate that Quebec's aspiration to sovereignty is based on a stronger commitment to collective values than to individual autonomy. There is in fact substantial evidence that Quebecers tend to be more liberal and individualistic in their attitudes and behaviour than English-speaking Canadians—for example, in terms of respect for traditional institutions like marriage and religion. Sovereigntist parties and individuals have embraced many of these liberal attitudes. On the other hand, there is some evidence that Quebecers are more attached to their collective culture (with higher rates of domestic cultural consumption, for instance). It would therefore be inaccurate to characterize the Quebec sovereignty movement as ideologically homogeneous and either liberal or authoritarian. Like most other political movements, it contains several often contradictory trends and tensions.

Sovereignty to Post-sovereignty

The final issue that needs to be fully unpacked in order to better understand the question of Quebec's independence is the concept of sovereignty itself. We have just seen that neither nations, nation-states, nor nationalism are easily defined and understood. This is also the case with sovereignty. On the one hand, it is a key feature of the world today. We take it so much for granted that we rarely stop to think about it: the world is divided into a finite number of sovereign, independent countries over which no greater power exists. But this too is undergoing profound changes. The trend toward 'post-sovereignty'— that is, toward forms of governance that do not rely exclusively on the traditional statehood—is only in its infancy, but it is slowly unfolding (Keating 2004). A range of processes is challenging the traditional understanding of sovereignty, including international organizations. The European Union, for instance, is weakening the traditional power of the individual state to the point where a number of movements in Europe are mobilizing around a more regionalist perspective than around simple nationhood (Keating 2004). In other words, what is happening in Europe is a slow but profound reshaping of the nature and location of political authority. This is also happening on a more modest scale in North America, where part of the sovereign authority of states has been delegated to the institutions of the North American Free Trade Agreement (NAFTA). Quebec in fact has confirmed several times that it intends to remain in NAFTA in the event that it achieves sovereignty. Some have even argued that NAFTA may actually facilitate the transition to sovereignty by providing a level of political and economic stability above and beyond Canada.

Other processes are challenging the traditional sovereignty of states as well, including multinational corporations, transnational actors (immigrant groups, for instance), and global technological changes (states can do little to stop the flow of information). In a number of countries, including Canada, competing groups and institutions dispute sovereignty. Quebec is the most significant contender in Canada, but First Nations come a close second, with a number of less important groups making occasional claims (proponents of western Canadian separatism, for instance).

The most provocative conclusion of this line of reasoning is that state sovereignty no longer really matters. Whether or not Quebec achieves sovereignty will not change many of the processes mentioned above. Quebec will still be part of global networks of trade, migration, and information flows, just as Canada minus Quebec will remain connected to them. Yet this too would be an exaggeration. Both the federal and provincial governments in Canada have tremendous powers and responsibilities as yet unequalled by non-state actors. In fact, many see the state as the last barrier against the homogenizing forces of globalization, and some argue that Quebec would be better able to be a successful member of a globalizing world as a sovereign nation-state (see Venne 2001). Others point out that remaining in a larger multinational entity is the best way for Quebec, and francophones throughout Canada, to stave off the threat of globalization (Pratte 2008).

Conclusion

How does the foregoing discussion help to answer the question contained in the title of this chapter? Quebec's quest for sovereignty remains high on the list of critical, unresolved issues facing Canada. After two referendums—1980 and 1995—and several decades of active political mobilization, including electoral victories by nationalist parties provincially and federally, the question of Quebec sovereignty remains unresolved. The choice is largely but not solely in the hands of Quebecers. What matters most is that we understand all the issues at stake and how best to address them.

First, it is clear that portraying Quebec sovereignty and its associated movement and ideas as simplistic oppositions (nationalism against pluralism, etc.) is at best unhelpful and at worst politically dangerous. The movement is obviously part of a much greater global story in which nation-states have emerged as the basic unit of political reference. But there is nothing inevitable about that story in the world in general, as the trend toward post-nationalism and post-sovereignty illustrates, or in Quebec, as the ebb and flow of the sovereignty movement confirms. A range of historical administrative and political factors has influenced it. It cannot merely be characterized as a simple yearning for national homogeneity or in opposition to federalism or diversity. Nor is it simply a liberation movement: by most measures, Quebecers enjoy very similar social and political conditions as in the rest of Canada and do not suffer from any significant level of oppression.

And Quebec itself is changing rapidly. The province is becoming increasingly diverse, although it has always maintained a conflicted relationship with immigration and cultural diversity. Immigrants have historically gravitated toward English North American culture, leaving many in Quebec unsure about the consequences of immigration (as the recent debate on reasonable accommodations illustrated; see Bouchard and Taylor 2008)—to the point that some have accused governmental institutions of fostering the subordination of immigrant communities in the name of maintaining a fictitious national unity (Fontaine 1993). This accusation does not entirely reflect Quebec's recent success in the field of immigration. The province has secured nearly full control over immigration from the federal government and has been attracting more and more francophone newcomers. In 2009, over 60 per cent of the immigrants to Quebec spoke some French, more than double the 1980 proportion (Institut de la Statistique du Québec 2010). Partly as a result, Quebec culture is becoming increasingly diverse—to the point that an important intellectual current within Quebec literature and social sciences identifies Quebec as marked by its American character: it is a 'new world' society, more influenced by North American than by European cultural practices (Theriault 2002). Similarly, others have pointed out that Quebec culture is moving away from a sharp distinction between nationalism and cosmopolitanism, finding instead a more complex mode of belonging somewhere in between (Maclure 2003). The strong attachment of most Quebecers to their culture is beyond doubt. But it is also clear that today as well as in the past, sovereignty has been viewed as only one of the many options available to ensure the development of this culture.

The debate over Quebec sovereignty may take several routes in years and decades to come. Some have argued that a gradual evolution is unfolding, particularly in Europe, away from locating political authority simply at the level of the national state, and that a kind of 'third way' of handling the desire for national sovereignty is emerging (Keating 2004). Quebec may very well embrace this new trend and become one of the many places in the world that sit somewhere between traditional sovereignty and its current, already hybrid status. Canada may also follow a similar route, further sharing its sovereignty with multinational institutions and sub-state communities (Aboriginals, provinces other than Quebec, etc.). In that sense, both Quebec and Canada may follow what some have identified as two contradictory global trends: one toward increasing pluralism and multiplicity and one toward 'unmixing' and consolidation (Cornell and Hartmann 1998). On the one hand, migration and ethno-cultural diversity is on the rise in much of the world, but on the other hand, nationalist movements seeking independence from larger political units have also dramatically strengthened (Quebec, but also Eastern Europe, parts of Asia, etc.). How these forces will play out in the future of Quebec and Canada is for history one day to decide.

Questions to Consider

1. Why does a significant part of Quebec's population want political independence?
2. Is Quebec already sovereign?
3. Should all nations have the right to become sovereign?
4. Is a nation necessarily a sovereign nation?
5. Is Canada a sovereign nation?

Note

1. Canada received about 250,000 immigrants in 2008, the majority from Asia. See Canada, Citizenship and Immigration (2009) for details.

20 What Are the Challenges of Economic Transition?

Jennifer Jarman

Introduction

This chapter works within a tradition of sociology that views the economic aspects of life as important for understanding any society. The classical sociologist, Karl Marx, argued this most forcefully. The type of thought that stems from such an approach has been labelled 'economic determinism'. Marx (1948 [1848]) thought that many of a society's key structures, and most importantly, its system of social hierarchy or class structure, was fundamentally determined by the type of economic production dominant in a society. Thus a feudal society, in which wealth was created through the agricultural production from large land holdings created a system of social hierarchy of lords and serfs. This was very different from a modern capitalist society in which wealth is created largely through the operation of factories producing manufactured goods, and in which the main social division occurs between those who own the means to produce manufactured goods and those who must sell their labour power and work as employees for someone else. In both of these societies, the most powerful are those who own a resource and the weakest are those who do not. The difference is that in the feudal society the resource that is most empowering is land, whereas in a capitalist society the resource that empowers is capital. So in a feudal society it is the land-holding nobility based in rural areas that are the most powerful people, whereas in a capitalist society it is the capital-owning financiers based in urban centres who are the most powerful.

Marx's explanation of the nature of society has been very influential, but it has also been challenged by other sociological thinkers. Max Weber, another major German contributor to the development of the discipline of sociology, produced a fundamental critique of Marx's approach. He argued that while economic factors are important, they are not sufficient to explain social phenomena. Other factors, such as the religious life and beliefs of a community might be more important and might indeed be considered more significant influences on a society than its economy. In *The Protestant Ethic and the Spirit of Capitalism*, Weber (1904–5) argues that economic developments do not stem from economic causes alone, but rather from changes in religious beliefs and values which then produce changes in economic behaviour.

Much twentieth- and twenty-first-century sociology has been written starting from one of these viewpoints. Whether one ultimately argues that the economic base determines all other aspects of social life, as did Marx, or that there are complex interactions between economic and other areas of social life such as the spiritual, as did Weber, much of economic and industrial sociology shares a common perspective that economic phenomena—how a society produces a livelihood—is of major importance for understanding its social reality.

This chapter asks the sociological question, 'What are the challenges of economic transition?' Specifically, using Maritime Canada as a case study, the chapter seeks to understand who is empowered in a community when its economic base changes from a resource-based economy to a **knowledge-based economy**. Maritime Canada has long been based on agriculture and resource extraction, and commerce based upon these industries. Since the mid-1990s, however, it has become home to a thriving call-centre industry. This industry is part of the service sector and is located at the lower end of the knowledge-based economy in terms of complexity of knowledge work in the jobs themselves, education levels and requirements for employees, occupational status, and worker pay and benefits.

Debates about the knowledge-based economy started in the 1960s when American economists (Machlup, 1962) began to recognize the importance of the strategic development and use of knowledge in relationship to economic growth. This debate was extended in the 1970s to societies in general, with path-breaking contributions from researchers such as sociologist Daniel Bell (1973). It continues to this day.

Krishan Kumar (1995) provides a very nice summary of how knowledge transforms an economy:

> Knowledge, according to information society theorists, is progressively supposed to affect work in two ways. One is the upgrading of the knowledge content of existing work, in the sense that the new technology adds rather than subtracts from the skill of workers. The other is the creation and expansion of new work in the knowledge sector, such that information workers come to predominate in the economy. Moreover, it is assumed that it is the more skilled, more knowledgeable information workers who will come to constitute the core of the information economy. (223)

Based on this explanation, we can see that there are several ways that transformation in the Maritimes can occur: first, from more strategic management of the existing natural resources through the application of knowledge-based strategies in industries such as fishing and farming, and second, through the increase and development of knowledge workers themselves. This chapter focuses on the second type of transformation.

Unemployment and Underemployment in Maritime Canada

Maritime Canada is home to some of the oldest communities in North America. The Mi'kmaq have lived in the region for thousands of years, and Europeans arrived in the 1500s, discovering one of the world's richest fishing grounds in the Grand Bank. Over the past 500 years, communities have evolved: Natives descended principally from the Mi'kmaq; a black population descended from slaves who escaped from American plantations; a white population descended from English and French Acadian settlers; as well as small pockets of people from other backgrounds. The economic underpinnings of the communities living here has been the resource base—fish, timber, coal—and commerce arising from this, as well as other maritime activities such as ports, a navy, a coastguard, and mercantile fleets. Over the past 20 years, however, the fishing industry has been plagued with problems because of a combination of overfishing and climate change. The shrinking of Canada's rail system ended the need for the coal and steel industries that had provided its rails. Furthermore, trade and commerce shifted westward over the past 100 years as the rest of the North American continent developed and alternate cities arose to compete for industries such as banking and financing that had originally also started in the Maritime centres.

The Maritime region now has some of the highest levels of unemployment and underemployment in Canada, particularly in its rural areas. Furthermore, as in many places with economies that are natural-resource or agriculture-based, many of the remaining jobs in Maritime Canada are seasonal—the fishing industry, agriculture, and the tourism industry, for example. The consequence is that opportunities for employment alternate between high-intensity work and long periods of unemployment.

Today's young Maritimers do not aspire to agricultural, resource-based, or manufacturing careers. An analysis of the aspirations of young people in urban Hamilton, Ontario, and rural and urban Nova Scotia shows that youth—those in rural areas and those in urban areas, those whose parents were professional workers as well as those whose parents were working-class—are 'remarkably homogeneous' in their aspirations to 'middle-class male' careers—in other words, to service sector work (Thiessen and Blasius 2002). This explains the turn to higher education: faced with uncertain futures in the occupations their parents chose, young people are pursuing formal education instead, or in the theoretical terms of this chapter, are choosing to gain the credentials and experience necessary to enter the knowledge economy.

The Brain Drain and Maritime Communities

One of the longstanding problems in the region has been the retention of its own human capital. This process has sometimes been described as stopping the 'brain drain' or **out-migration** of workers, especially those who are skilled and educated, out of the region. Ross Finnie (2000) has shown that high provincial unemployment rates, high rates of collection of employment insurance benefits, and absence of employment income induce people to migrate to provinces where opportunities are better. Further, he shows that young people with higher educational qualifications are more likely to move than older people with weaker qualification profiles. Maurice Beaudin and Sébastien Breau (2001) report that data for 1995 show New Brunswick and Prince Edward Island losing large numbers of their new graduates; Nova Scotia actually increased its number of new graduates but not enough to compensate for the overall loss of human capital. More recent analysis, by the Atlantic Provinces Economic Council, suggests that fully 14 per cent (340,000) of the Atlantic Canadian region's population has migrated out to other provinces. Of these, 70,000 were in the age group 15 to 24 (Beale 2008, 1–2).[1]

For provincial governments, the continued departure of young educated people poses a problem. Education budgets are one of the largest categories of expenditure for provincial governments. How do they legitimize continued expenditure for students who leave the province as soon as they graduate when they must fund other areas of need, such as health care, for those who remain? If they do not invest in education, they do not build the type of labour force capable of supporting higher-level industries. If they do invest in higher education but do not have any way of retaining labour, then the investment in higher education is a loss to the region. The departure of young people also creates problems for the reproduction of stable communities. When young people move thousands of miles away in search of jobs, who looks after the older people? Even with extensive air transport networks, electronic communication, and cheap telephone rates, family support becomes very difficult when people live a great distance away. Human capital retention, particularly of young educated people, thus becomes a very important priority for both communities and governments.

The Rise of the Call Centre Industry

In the past few years, a new industry, and one which is squarely part of the 'knowledge economy', has developed in Maritime Canada. The region is now home to 25 per cent of the Canadian 'business services' industry (Akyeampong 2005, 6). Call centres began to arrive in the Maritimes in the early 1990s. Of the three Maritime provinces, New Brunswick had the most aggressive strategy for recruiting new firms to come to the region. Former premier Frank McKenna's much heralded and much criticized strategy of making New Brunswick 'open for business' involved identifying the strengths of the New Brunswick labour force and attempting to develop an industrial mix that would capitalize on this strength. Because of the heritage of both the Acadian French and the English, one of the strengths identified was a labour force containing many bilingual people. Call centres, relying heavily as they do on communication and language skills, were identified as an appropriate industry for the province. New Brunswick sent a team of recruiters into the United States to inform US firms of the opportunities available in New Brunswick and to help facilitate the location of operations to New Brunswick. The province thus had an 'active' campaign of recruitment. The result was the creation of some 6,000 new jobs by 1997 (Buchanan 2000).

The region's two other provinces, Nova Scotia and Prince Edward Island, developed their call centre strategies somewhat later. By 1998, at least 41 firms had set up operations in Nova Scotia. As of July 2005, there were at least 65 centres in the province with a total labour force of approximately 15,000. Existing operations such as Convergys have expanded their operations, growing from 800 employees in one centre to multiple centres with a total workforce of over 2,600. Tiny Prince Edward Island has adopted a similar passive strategy regarding call centre recruitment. Nonetheless, at least 11 call centres have opened their doors there with a total workforce of 1,192 in 2003 (MRSB Consulting Services 2003).

What Is a Call Centre?

A **call centre** is a specialized workplace that provides service and/or information over the telephone. Increasingly, call centres also provide web support, including email handling, fax support, and online chat. Call centres now serve many different organizations in a range of industries. In the Maritimes, these organizations include banks, insurance companies, telecommunications companies, technical help desks, marketing firms, government services, pharmaceutical companies, customer service departments, parcel delivery firms, transportation companies, oil delivery operations, ambulance services, taxi companies, and funeral homes.

Service Sector Employment versus Work in Traditional Industries

The new job growth is very much service sector work as opposed to the agricultural or industrial work traditional in the region for the past few hundred years. Above all, it is human resources that have drawn this industry to Maritime Canada. It makes no use of the natural resources available, nor is the region's geographical location particularly important. These centres could be located anywhere else in the world, given the possibilities that new telecommunications infrastructures create for firms, allowing them to connect instantly and cheaply to diverse locations around the globe.

The new job growth draws on a very different kind of skills and training than those required in the old economy. Although a small number of workers have made the transition from the old to the new economy, those in the industry are generally not people displaced from older industries. The fishers, foresters, farmers, miners, and steelworkers tend to be older males: they have low levels of formal education and live in rural areas.

The new industry has a different profile. Some of the call centre workers are indeed the children of the fishers and foresters, but they have had to make a significant transition in terms of upgrading their education from elementary to at least high school certification, and many centres require a university degree. While some call centres are in rural areas, the largest concentrations are in urban centres, which means that some workers have had to leave their communities to work elsewhere. Despite a popular image of call centre work as 'low-end' jobs, they demand higher educational levels than did the jobs of previous generations. Providing information, problem-solving, or making a sale in an environment that is strictly 'voice-to-voice' is a complicated social process. Workers have none of the usual visual cues that have governed human interactions since our species first began to walk upright. The industry thus puts a premium on people with well-developed social skills. Most of the better call centres train heavily around such attributes as voice and phone manner as well as the ability to navigate computer databases quickly in order to obtain information pertinent to the inquiry. Literacy is also important in the call centre because the teleservice representative must access and record information accurately. Thus social skills, literacy skills, communication skills such as speech and listening, and computer competency are all essential in a call centre.

Another element of the contemporary call centre workplace that sets it apart from other types of workplace is that many centres, especially those that serve multiple clients, operate in highly competitive environments. Most managers report that expectations for both the quality and the speed of service delivery have been rising steadily since the mid-1990s. Customers expect their calls to be answered on the fourth or fifth ring, hate to be placed in queues listening to music even for a minute, and want their questions answered efficiently without a second or third call-back. Increasingly, they expect the service to be available 24 hours a day, 7 days a week.

Constant employee surveillance has become a feature of most call centre workplaces. The centres usually contain large databases of valuable information, ranging from business information to information governed by privacy and data protection and security laws. The call centre industry has responded with a range of measures to protect this data, including careful selection of employees, installation of security cameras, recording of all interactions, and regular 'listening in' on employee conversations. Many industries have been forced to create tighter and tighter surveillance and security procedures in recent years—and the call centre industry is certainly one of them, creating new challenges and strains for workers and managers alike.

Assessing the Fit of the Industry for the Maritime Region

Most of the jobs created by the call centre industry are full-time permanent jobs—year-round rather than seasonal in nature as so many other Maritime jobs have been. According to Statistics Canada, 83.5 per cent of the jobs in the industry are full-time, the remaining 16.5 per cent being part-time jobs. This is a higher ratio than that in the rest of the service sector (77.3 per cent full-time and 22.7 per cent part-time) (Akyeampong 2005).

Full-time year-round employment is precisely the kind of employment that the region needs if it is to break out of its reliance on the employment insurance system. Furthermore, year-round 'shore-based' work provides a steady income over other types of work common in other industries in the Maritimes, such as fishing, the oil rig industry, or the navy or coast guard, which require people to be away for weeks or months at a time. Sociologists and anthropologists have amply documented the difficulties this creates for family life, both because of worries about dangerous work at sea and because of the difficulty of managing the intermittent presence of partners in the family environment (Binkley 1994; Harrison and Laliberte 1994).

Although the industry seems to have a clear preference for urban areas, job growth has also occurred in rural areas where communities have been suffering badly from high unemployment levels. While call centres developed first in urban centres, as urban labour markets reached saturation they moved on to smaller towns and to rural locations, giving new hope to those who want to stay in the region and find jobs there. The number of jobs being created is significant. According to Statistics Canada, the 'technology-driven fast employment growth in business support services' has benefited Atlantic Canada more than any other Canadian region (Akyeampong 2005). Figures drawn from the diverse sources cited earlier in this chapter suggest that there are now tens of thousands of workers employed in the industry on the East Coast (Jarman, Butler, and Clairmont 1997), which is important given the region's high unemployment levels compared to those of the rest of Canada.

While these jobs are not the highest-wage jobs in the economy, there is a reasonably large number of them, and given the lower educational profile of the Maritimes, they are a reasonably good fit. Akyeampong reports that in Canada as a whole, the average hourly wage rate in 2004 was $12.45 and average hours of work amounted to 35.2 per week (Akyeampong 2005, 3). This works out to an average yearly income of $22,788 for Canadian workers. While wage rates in the Maritimes may be lower than the Canadian average, the jobs compare reasonably with other jobs available in the Maritime provinces. The average hourly wage for a person in the group aged 15 to 24, for example, was $10.81 in April 2005 (Statistics Canada 2006a). So, rather than seeing these jobs as offering 'low' wages as some have done, it seems more accurate to describe them as having 'lower-middle' levels of pay. Additionally, many of the call centres provide significant benefit packages, with medical, dental, educational leave, and pension plans.

These jobs help retain human capital in the region, and furthermore they employ a group that has typically been footloose—young workers. The industry trains its employees constantly and thus plays a role in human capital development. One of the groups least likely to engage in lifelong learning or, in other words, to update their own skill sets is the group with the lowest educational qualifications to start with. Thus on-the-job training, as opposed to periods of credential upgrading outside the workplace available to those with some high school education, is likely one of the best ways for an individual to achieve improvements in skill and capability. Indeed, the industry's norms for training (optimum class size of 10 to 12 employees and one-to-one coaching) compare favourably with publicly funded institutions of higher education where staff-student ratios are much higher.

There is now a significant concentration of call centre operations in the region and a significant level of investment. As noted earlier, Statistics Canada reports that Maritime Canada now has 25 per cent of the Canadian share of business support services jobs (Akyeampong 2005, 6). This creates the possibility of economies of scale with respect to the purchase of hardware and software, telecommunications support, recruitment costs, and joint training ventures. It also creates opportunities for joint efforts to recruit new business contracts and the possibility of creating a strong base for industrial-level organizations and councils.

Despite concerns about the 'flighty' nature of the industry, the call centres have so far been remarkably stable in the region. There have been some failures, but on the whole the companies that were recruited have not only stayed in the region but expanded operations. Some have opened multiple centres—for instance, Convergys, Teletech, Sykes (formerly ICT Group), and Atelka (which has gone through multiple ownerships and reorganizations and was formerly Davis and Henderson, Resolve, and prior to that Watts Communications). While some people have predicted that the advent of self-serve web portals would eliminate the need for call centres, the centres have so far simply added web support to their service provision. Far from disappearing, calls from people who fail to navigate websites successfully have become longer and more complex.

What are the issues that need to be faced in order to adequately understand this industry? First, call centres suffer from an image problem not only because they represent unwanted intrusions into dinnertime conversations but also because they are understood as a convenient symbol of repetitive, boring, and unpleasant work. The 'sweatshop' image persists in many quarters. The industry just does not seem as exciting as those high-paying oil and gas jobs that may materialize if larger gas reserves are found off the North Atlantic coast. However, the offshore oil and gas industry has estimated that it needs a mere 1,880 employees, according to one recent study (Beaudin and Breau 2001). The cutting edge of modern scientific research and application has also been put forward as being of major importance to the region because of its fast pace of development, its potential for revenue generation, and its spin-offs in complementary areas such as aquaculture. But how many people were needed in biotechnology in 2002? A total of just 990 (Beaudin and Breau 2001). One large call centre alone can employ more people than these industries combined.

A strategy for regional economic development in a large and diverse region must include a range of solutions for different segments of its labour force. Certainly it is desirable to create $130,000-a-year jobs for oil and gas engineers, executives, and highly skilled tradespeople. The call centre industry, however, is an industry that provides jobs for people with high school degrees and bachelor's degrees. It employs several groups of workers who have traditionally had difficulty obtaining employment—namely, young people and those from rural populations.

Conclusion

This chapter uses the changing economy of Maritime Canada as a case study to try to understand who wins and who loses in communities whose economies shift from one type of economic production to another. The Maritime economy was originally based on the region's natural resources and strategic position for international trade and commerce. The region has seen many transitions—some improving the health and quality of life of its diverse communities and others threatening its survival. Now it faces major problems as its economies try to reinvent themselves after the decline of a number of major resource-based industries. The current challenge is to stem the brain drain and generate a new economy capable of employing those who want to live in the region.

The chapter focuses on a new industry—the call centre industry—that has started to provide employment to significant numbers of people in the Maritime region. This industry has often been characterized as unstable and exploitative and not a good solution for a region with economic development problems. Despite some of the industry's problems, however, it provides entry-level jobs with pay levels ranging from minimum wage to $22 an hour, with benefits including medical, dental, and pension plans. The jobs may be at the lower end of the service economy, but the Maritimes as a whole does not have as high an educational profile as that of other parts of the country. The advantage of 'lower-middle' jobs is that there are many people with 'lower-middle' levels of education and experience in the region. The track record of this industry so far indicates that it has created tens of thousands of jobs for people with high school and bachelor's degrees, which goes some way toward replacing the lost resource-based jobs in industries such as coal mining, fishing, and agriculture.

So then, what can we conclude with regard to the question of who is empowered in a community when the economic base changes, and who is disempowered? When jobs are simply lost, young people are the first to depart for better prospects, creating a skewed age structure with communities composed principally of older people. Retention strategies that focus on youth jobs are thus very important in any successful economic transition. A shift from a resource-based economy to a knowledge-based economy also requires a more educated population. This changes the balance of power within com-munities—those who are more easily able to acquire the new skills, certifi-cations, and degrees are empowered, and those who are not face the loss of their ability to earn a living and a loss of social power. In the case of Maritime Canada, empowerment is experienced by the younger generation, whereas the older generation, rooted in the a declining economy, suffers a loss of power. Furthermore, empowerment shifts to those in the region who are able to attain higher education in preparation for service sector jobs, rather than those with lower levels of education and blue collar skills.

Questions to Consider

1. How does the 'brain drain' affect the Maritime provinces? What dilemmas does this pose for those who make decisions about the allocation of prov-incial spending priorities?
2. What skills are needed for jobs in the old economy and how are they dif-ferent from jobs in the new economy?
3. How does the economy of a community influence the social structure of a community?

Note

1. Atlantic Canada includes Newfoundland and Labrador, along with the three Maritime provinces of Nova Scotia, New Brunswick, and Prince Edward Island.

21 | How Do Migrants Become Canadian Citizens?

Randy Lippert and Patrick Lalonde

Introduction

Immigration and citizenship are intimately intertwined. Though discussions of citizenship do not necessarily turn on immigration—obviously some persons are citizens by birth, descent, or adoption—immigration nevertheless tends to lead to citizenship. But how do these processes work? How do migrants enter Canada's immigration streams and then settle to begin exercising a newly acquired citizenship? The answers to these questions have particular significance for Canada, which is commonly thought of as a settler society, meaning that historically much of its citizenry has migrated from abroad. How migrants become citizens is a key question for those trying to understand settler societies, including critical sociologists who seek to understand governance, moral regulation, and related dimensions of social life.

In this chapter, we first briefly discuss the sociology of immigration as well as the sociology of governance and moral regulation in relation to immigration. We then focus on some ways of being and becoming first a migrant and then a citizen in Canada. We are especially interested in the transition from migrant to citizen, and wish to cast doubt on some taken-for-granted assumptions about immigration and citizenship as well as make the following interrelated points. First, there are several migrant and citizen categories and identities in Canada; not one of each. Second, while immigration and to a lesser extent citizenship processes are often assumed to be about ethnicity and labour markets (Satzewich 1990), they are also about governance and moral regulation. Third, these processes are thus not only more complex than typically acknowledged but are also fraught with inequalities and stimulate forms of resistance.

The Governance of Immigration and Citizenship

Immigration is a realm of longstanding sociological interest, and related research is easily found in sociology's annals. That said, the sociology of immigration is not a clearly defined field of inquiry. Attention to immigration is also evident in other disciplines, including anthropology, demography, geography, economics, history, law, and political science. The main research questions and levels of analysis in these disciplines vary, but at certain points they overlap with those of sociology. Perhaps one way to distinguish sociology's interest in immigration is that it has tended to focus on the receiving end of the migration process—that is, what happens to migrants on entering a settler or host society.

We do not wish to deny or diminish the importance of well-established areas of sociological study (e.g., Reitz 2003) or their contributions to understanding immigration processes in Canada. Yet we want to say that our specific, key question—*how* migrants become citizens—is not usually addressed there. Instead, it is often taken for granted, in part because immigration integration models are usually distinguished from citizenship policies and practices (Castles and Miller 1998, 238–43). Indeed, sociology has traditionally paid much less attention to citizenship than to immigration. However, recent years have witnessed a growing citizenship literature (e.g., Isin and Turner 2007), with some studies conducted by sociologists. This small body of work includes groundbreaking work on the varied ways in which immigrants practise citizenship in Canada (Siemiatycki and Isin 1998). One thrust of this newer literature is to suggest that citizenship is not limited to the formal legal kind but refers to a much broader set of practices and ways of being, which are beginning to be studied.

A relevant sociological perspective is called the sociology of governance (see Hunt 1999 and Chapters 1, 12, and 14 in this book). It draws heavily from the later work of philosopher and historian Michel Foucault on 'governmentality' and tends to be of a critical variety. Here **governance** means 'any attempt to control or manage any known object' (Hunt and Wickham 1994, 78). This broad concept includes laws, policies, and practices of the municipal, provincial, and federal levels of the state but also the efforts of private authorities and organizations as well as those of new forms that do not always easily fit into public or private categories. It also refers to how individuals govern themselves. Most often in this research, governance is equated to the conduct of conduct—that is, governance is about how human behaviour or action is directed or guided. As well, aspects of moral regulation are present in all governing practices (Hunt 1999, 6), and governing practices in the realm of immigration and citizenship take the form of moral regulation. The 'moral' in moral regulation refers to normative judgments (those judgments involving 'should') that a particular form of conduct or behaviour is essentially or inherently wrong or bad (Hunt 1999, 7). Such a perspective brings to light aspects of immigration and citizenship policies and practices that might otherwise be ignored. When taken together, this perspective can begin to make something as seemingly simple and automatic as migrants becoming citizens look more contingent, more complex, and perhaps more amenable to change. Such a sociology can potentially lend insight into how citizens are 'made' from migrants.

Becoming a Migrant

Immigration to Canada—that is, becoming a migrant—is non-random. It is a structured process, shaped mainly by Canadian immigration and refugee policies. Such policies presume eventual citizenship for immigrants. Immigration law and policy that regulate permanent residency may be more significant in influencing who becomes a citizen than citizenship law itself. Immigration law and policy is potentially the principal barrier to achieving citizenship and is therefore worthy of attention.

With the creation of a 'points system' in 1967, federal immigration regulations for the first time laid out in detail how immigrants were to be selected. This system was intended to end the explicitly racist practice of selecting immigrants from 'preferred' nations (Kelley and Trebilcock 1998). It used a grid to assign applicants a number of points based on a variety of efficiencies with the intent of reducing discretion on the part of state immigration officers (Kelley and Trebilcock 1998, 358–9). This development was widely heralded as a major turning point in Canadian immigration policy. This key shift has helped to bring about the result that recent immigrants—including those arriving in Canada over the past decade—are now more likely to have come from nations in Asia, especially China, India, and the Philippines, whereas the migrants who came before the 1960s were more likely to come from Europe (Tran, Kustec, and Chui 2005, 11).

The point system, while adjusted over the years, remains in place. A critical sociology would be less than sanguine about this system, in part because there is certainly room for racism, sexism, and other forms of discrimination to enter the picture (see Thobani 2000). For example, points are given for occupational skill in paid work, but non-paid and domestic work, more often the responsibility of women, does not count as skilled work (Creese and Dowling 2001). But a critical sociology also approaches such a system with reservation because of what it ostensibly is—a device to assess who would make the 'best' immigrants and eventual citizens and a means to determine the risk that those allowed into Canada permanently would be other than 'good' immigrants and citizens. Those found wanting are systematically excluded. The point system and immigrant selection more generally have a definite moral aspect to them. They entail moral regulation and are of interest for this reason.

Currently, potential immigrants pay a nominal administrative fee to the state to apply from a consulate or embassy abroad through an often-lengthy bureaucratic process. In the hope of eventually becoming landed immigrants (also known as 'permanent residents'), applicants must also pass medical and security screening. If successful, they will then travel to Canada and arrive at a port of entry. There are several streams and categories of migrants imagined within Canadian immigration and refugee policies. The four basic categories are family-class immigrants, economic-class immigrants, refugees, and other immigrants. Sociologists do not have easy access to statistics held by Citizenship and Immigration Canada revealing who applies to immigrate to Canada or otherwise enters these streams. We only know 'who gets in' and some features of the immigration process they undergo. We know, for example, that in Canada during every year from 2000 to 2010, between 221,000 and 281,000 persons became permanent residents (Canada, Citizenship and Immigration 2009a, 2010a) and that in 2010 there were approximately 60,000 family-class immigrants; 187,000 economic immigrants, including 13,000 business migrants and their spouses and dependents; 25,000 refugees; and 9,000 migrants falling into various other special categories, for a total of approximately 281,000 landed immigrants (Canada, Citizenship and Immigration 2010a).

We should note the key distinction between refugees and immigrants. Refugees are defined according to the United Nations (UN) Convention on Refugees, a 1951 international agreement to which Canada acceded in 1967.[1] According to the Convention, a **refugee** is a person who

> owing to a well-founded fear of being persecuted for reasons of race, religion, nationality, membership of a particular social group or political opinion, is outside the country of his [sic] nationality, and is unable to or, owing to such fear, is unwilling to avail himself of the protection of that country or to return there, for fear of persecution.

There are two refugee streams. One stream includes refugees selected from camps and crisis situations who may or may not precisely fit the UN definition. The second stream includes persons who make refugee claims in Canada. These refugee claimants have been permitted to enter the country but then must undergo a lengthy process involving quasi-legal hearings before Canada's Immigration and Refugee Board to determine whether they are bona fide refugees. Those found to be refugees undergo further screening similar to that applied to immigrants, and if they are successful, they are eventually landed; those deemed not to be refugees are asked to leave and if necessary physically 'removed' or deported from Canada.

At first glance, the state appears stingy when it comes to immigrant selection since state immigration officers administer the point system to decide 'who gets in'. Indeed, the Canadian public tends to think of immigrants mostly as skilled workers who have undergone the screening, even though in 2010, for example, skilled workers (inclusive of their spouses and dependents) represented less than half of all the migrants who became permanent residents, with skilled workers alone comprising only about 17 per cent of the total (Canada, Citizenship and Immigration 2010a). The remainder included refugee claimants, business immigrants, and family-class immigrants. Since at least the mid-1980s, asylum-seekers have been depicted as 'spontaneously' arriving at ports of entry to make refugee claims. Media attention and public concern have focused on the notion that these migrants have 'self-selected' (as though persecution or related oppression did not force them to flee to Canada) and therefore were not pre-screened by Canadian immigration authorities for their capacity to become citizens. However, various restrictions, including interdiction abroad and security certificates, have been implemented to reduce the numbers arriving (see Lippert 1998; Aitken 2008). Yet what is generally overlooked is that other immigrants virtually 'self-select' in that they largely buy their way into Canada as business immigrants. For entry to Canada, business-immigrant applicants are scored on a range of selection criteria, and the threshold for success is low: out of a maximum of 100 points across five criteria, an entrepreneur or investor class aspirant who scores just 35 points is accepted as an immigrant (Canada, Citizenship and Immigration 2008a, 2008b). A business-class applicant can enter as an immigrant even if he or she has no post-secondary education and speaks neither English nor French (Ley 2003, 428). In contrast to the 35-point requirement, skilled worker applicants must reach 67 of 100 points based on 6 criteria (Canada, Citizenship and Immigration 2009c). 'Self-selection' by entering the refugee determination process is often seen as negative, (Lippert 1998), whereas 'self-selection' by way of the business-immigrant process is apparently largely invisible or positive (see Thobani 2000).

State bureaucratic processes involving entitlement, such as public medical care, or welfare, inevitably involve some fraud among claimants. Immigration and refugee procedures are hardly unique in this regard. But it is interesting that the enforcement of fraud within streams also varies. Compared to enforcement targeting fraud in relation to the refugee-determination process, far fewer enforcement resources have been directed toward business immigrants engaged in fraud, in particular those who fall into the entrepreneur subcategory, a minority of whom never make investments in Canada as promised. As a 1999 *National Post* piece illustrates, a large number have failed to meet their business obligations, including 40 per cent of a sample of 7,000 entrepreneurial-class immigrants failing to open a business within the two-year period of their arrival as promised; fewer than 10 deportations resulted, however (Clark 1999). Such inequality of enforcement and the related hierarchy of migrant categories are of interest to a critical sociology.

It is important to understand that '(im)migrant' and 'citizen' are both a bureaucratic/legal category and an identity. By 'identity' we refer to a way of understanding and relating to ourselves and others. Law and bureaucratic categories within immigration and citizenship processes, including the Immigration and Refugee Protection Act and the Citizenship Act, contribute   .
to the formation of such identities. Legal status and identity overlap; law helps to constitute or 'make up' identities. The Citizenship Act, however, does not 'act' alone: citizenship laws in the West often go hand in hand with programs 'that encourage those identified as citizens to behave in particular ways, such as publicly celebrating their status, and even to conceive of their legal status as an integral aspect of their identity' (Galloway 2000, 83). In other words, it is not only citizenship law that makes citizens but much broader processes too; law is one but not necessarily the most important source of these identities. An interesting puzzle for sociologists is how migrant identities shift to citizen identities—and this is partially what our key question is about.

The notion of *governing through* immigration is gleaned from the sociology of governance discussed above: governing is seldom exclusively an instrumental effort to govern others' conduct (Hunt 1999, 6). Indeed, in this case, all manner of problems, processes, and conduct may be governed *through* immigration. This is evident, for example, in attempts to encourage economic growth through the business immigrant program, with the assumption that these immigrants will bring investment capital and entrepreneurial experience to Canada. Consider also the following two examples: the tragic Haitian earthquake of 2009 and its immediate aftermath, as well as national and continental security following the events of 9/11 in the United States.

One way that the Canadian government responded to the Haitian earthquake of 2009, encouraged by members of the public, was to expedite the existing immigrant applications of those with immediate family members in Canada through priority processing measures, including Operation Stork and other 'Haiti Special Measures' family sponsorship application procedures (Canada, Citizenship and Immigration 2010c). The disaster's horrific effects on the region's human population were, in a sense, governed *through* immigration, which is to say that increasing immigration from the region was not the primary target of this policy shift; instead, the goal was to alleviate human suffering or at least to respond to the Canadian public's calls for the government to do so.

Similarly, since the terrorist attacks on 11 September 2001 in the United States, Canada's immigration policy has changed to respond to the perceived need for greater scrutiny and surveillance at its borders and stepped up screening of immigrant applicants (Pratt 2005). The introduction of the 'safe third country' provisions renders Canadian policy more dependent on the fairness (or unfairness) of US refugee and immigration policies than before. This development is consistent with broader shifts evident in other world regions toward what is called the increasing 'securitization of migration' (Bigo 2002) or the notion of governing security *through* immigration. Since the early 1980s, many refugee claimants would enter the United States at various points and then travel to the Canadian border, to make refugee claims (the Canadian refugee-determination system is generally seen as fairer or at least more open than that of the United States). But the 'safe third country' provision forces refugee claimants to enter the US immigration system before they can enter Canada. Canada is obliged to do likewise with refugee claimants who first enter Canadian territory and seek status in the United States. The suggestion here is that terrorism (mostly in the United States) can be somehow better prevented by changing Canadian immigration policies in this way. The three targets—fostering national economic growth, reducing human misery resulting from natural disaster, and improving national or continental security—are all governed *through* immigration. The significance of these examples is simply that studying immigration (and citizenship) processes in this way is important to understanding how various aspects of society are interrelated with the governance of immigration.

Other Migrants: Sex-Trade Workers

Many migrants in Canada are not immigrants or 'permanent residents' and will likely never have the opportunity to become so, which is to say that they are not imagined within Canadian policies as potential citizens. For example, special policy provisions permit migrants to enter Canada to work temporarily as 'exotic dancers'. At many strip clubs here and elsewhere in Canada, these sex-trade workers are required to pay daily fees to the club and the disc jockey and sometimes special fees for the use of cubicles. In some cases, the women are not even paid by the establishment itself but are instead expected to charge patrons for lap dances, table dances, or sexual acts in the cubicles or 'VIP rooms' (Macklin 2003). The workers often feel pressured to charge patrons in part because of the significant fees they must pay but also because of (other) forms of coercion. The result is that these workers are particularly susceptible to sexually transmitted diseases and other physical harm. Agents play a role in demanding additional fees and may force these temporary migrant workers to give up their earnings in order that they be 'safely' deposited in a bank account in the woman's home country. Many of the temporary workers speak little English, and they are instructed by their agents not to speak to anyone in case that person is from the government (Macklin 2003).

It was noted earlier that our key question is often about moral regulation. The fact that sex workers' work permits are temporary is highly relevant. A rationale that employers and the Canadian government use to justify the program is that there are not enough Canadian women willing to work as 'exotic dancers' in Canada. As Macklin (2003) notes, 'Economic objectives operate in tandem with morality to reinforce the exclusion of sex-trade workers from permanent residence' (481). Some of these migrants *could* become citizens. But a critical sociology would be interested in how these temporary sex-trade workers are prevented from doing so—prevented from leaving their assigned places of work, going underground to work and live illegally in Canada, and later surfacing to gain legal status and become Canadian citizens. Of interest are the techniques used to govern or police these migrants to bar them from citizenship. These workers are prevented from accessing the resources (often by their private agents) that would allow them to go underground or gain permanent legal status through regular means (Macklin, 2003).

From Migrant to Citizen

'Citizenship' refers to a shared sense of belonging and is one way of being political (Isin 2002, 30). Isin (2002) defines **citizenship** broadly as

> that kind of identity within a city or state that certain agents constitute as virtuous, good, righteous, and superior, and differentiate it from strangers, outsiders, and aliens who they constitute as their alterity via various solidaristic, agonistic, and alienating strategies and technologies. (36)

In other words, the idea of citizenship may well be depend on the notion of migrants, and the latter helps to constitute or 'make up' the former. Isin (2002) notes, 'The alterity of citizenship, therefore, does not preexist, but is made possible by it' (4). Migrant categories may well be generated within citizenship processes.

National citizenship refers to allegiance to a nation rather than to some other form of community. Discussing the transition from migrant to Canadian citizen as a one-way journey is misleading. The vast majority of migrants in Canada are already citizens of at least one nation, so to suggest that they develop into citizens is seeing them only from a Canadian perspective. That said, once migrants are accepted as landed immigrants and if they are 18 years or older, have permanent resident status, have lived in Canada for three of the four years prior to applying, and speak either English or French, they can submit an application to Citizenship and Immigration Canada to become citizens. The process involves officials checking applicants' landed immigrant status and whether they have a criminal record. The applicants are then required to pass a standardized (either written or oral) citizenship test that includes questions pertaining to Canada's history, geography, language abilities, and system of government as well as the citizenship rights and responsibilities mentioned above (Canada, Citizenship and Immigration 2010b).

We know some characteristics of the process of migrants legally becoming Canadian citizens. It is known that 95 per cent of persons residing in Canada are Canadian citizens—81 per cent became citizens by birth, and 14 per cent first migrated to Canada (Tran, Kustec, and Chui 2005, 9). It is also clear that the decision to become a citizen occurs shortly after entering Canada. As well, more than 9 in 10 immigrants who came to Canada between October 2000 and September 2001 indicated their intention to become Canada citizens, which is to say that seeking citizenship is part of the immigrant identity.

Data from the 2006 census reveals that a large percentage of immigrants who are legally entitled to become citizens actually choose to do so - about 85 per cent (Chui, Tran, and Maheux 2007, 23). The 2001 Census indicates this percentage in Canada is higher than in other Western societies. In Australia the percentage is 75 per cent; for the UK it is only 56 per cent; and for the foreign-born in the US it is only 40 per cent (Tran, Kustec, and Chui 2005, 10). In other words, eligible migrants are more likely to become citizens in Canada than in similar societies, and our key question therefore may be more relevant here than elsewhere.

A critical sociology, however, recognizes that these numbers and related trends will not suffice; they do not reveal *how* migrants become citizens but only some features of those who do and of one process (i.e., the legal process) they undergo. The fact that so many migrants appear to become citizens is somewhat misleading because these numbers refer only to *immigrants* becoming legal citizens. As already shown, there are other migrants in Canada who are here temporarily and are not permitted to become citizens through regular or at least official means. Becoming a legal citizen can be seen only as a marker of a migrant's integration: 'Moving from permanent resident status to Canadian citizen may be interpreted as an indicator of integration into society in general and the labour market in particular' (Tran, Kustec, and Chui 2005, 11). For migrants, receiving legal citizenship may be perceived as the end of the migration process, but whether it is equivalent to full incorporation is doubtful. Citizenship is therefore more than legal citizenship.

Becoming a legal citizen is sometimes called 'naturalization'. Yet this term suggests that there is something non-social about the process of migrants becoming citizens—that it is automatic, 'naturally' occurring, and therefore of little interest to sociologists. Critical sociologists are typically inclined to look behind, and investigate further, any process widely claimed to be 'natural'. The movement from migrant to citizen is increasingly understood in the broad sense of gradually installing a capacity to exercise choice. In settlement, migrants' active capacities are to be nurtured and promoted. Far from being assumed to adapt 'naturally' after arriving in Canada, migrants are thought to require considerable care and moral investment—the inculcation of skills to develop into virtuous self-governing entities that exercise choice. Settlement programs thus seek to change individuals drawn from distant locales into self-regulating citizens and have long involved financial assistance and special services that promise to foster such change.

Ways of Making Citizens: Technologies of Citizenship

For critical sociologists, what is interesting is how the transition from migrant to citizen happens—that is, the technologies of settlement and establishment, of 'migrating' from migrant to citizen. The ways of making citizens of migrants vary. Ethnic pluralism or Canada's policy of multiculturalism is one strategy of citizenship that has been much discussed and debated. An eclectic but by no means exhaustive list of these strategies would include multiculturalism but also the less discussed citizenship tests and passports.

We noted earlier that citizenship tests are part of the process. These tests include questions such as:

- What are the three main groups of Aboriginal peoples?
- When did settlers from France first establish communities on the St Lawrence River?
- Which four provinces first formed Confederation?
- List three ways in which you can protect the environment.
- In what industry do most Canadians work?

The irony is that many current Canadian citizens do not readily know the answers to most or even all of these questions.

The test is also intended to determine whether a landed immigrant has acquired an adequate knowledge of French or English. If successful, applicants can then participate in a ceremony in which they take the oath of citizenship.

During this ritual, migrants sign the oath form and receive a Canadian citizenship certificate indicating citizenship status. This practice encourages would-be citizens to think of themselves as ideal citizens. The examination and oath-swearing practices are on the more obvious end of the spectrum of technologies of citizenship in that they clearly identify their aim as instilling citizenship.

Another technology of citizenship and part of the process is the passport. Canadians crossing international borders know that the passport represents the effort of nation-states, including Canada, to control the legal means of movement (Torpey 2000, 159). Yet as mundane as they may appear, a national passport is more than this. Citizens' passports and immigrants' identity cards (often known as 'green cards' in the United States because of their colour, which was at one time green) can be taken more literally. With photographs and personal information about their holders as well as a compact form that permits them to be carried on the holder's person, they are person(al) documents par excellence (Lippert 1999). Their issuance encourages holders to think of themselves as citizens of particular nations.

Resistance and Sanctuary

At this point in the chapter, it may seem as though things proceed according to plan. Migrants pay their fees and dutifully either enter immigration streams or, if deemed not to measure up in assessments, simply give up or are 'removed' from Canada. However, migrants have adopted many strategies to resist official channels and bureaucratic categories. These strategies include using fraudulent passports and other identity documents to travel to Canada, often with the help of human traffickers and smugglers (Matas 2005). A different strategy is to purchase services from largely unregulated immigration consultants who provide advice to move through selection processes faster and more successfully but who also have an unscrupulous reputation for encouraging migrants to submit false information to do so (Canadian Press 2010). A less common but often successful strategy is for migrants to seek sanctuary in local Christian churches once they travel to and enter Canada but later face deportation—a strategy that deserves a closer look.

In September 2009, Rodney Watson entered the First United Church in Vancouver's infamous Downtown Eastside to avoid deportation after being denied refugee status. He came to Canada from the United States in 2006 to avoid being deployed by the US military to Iraq for a second time (Platt 2010). Almost a year later, he still resides there and never leaves the church grounds. He is provided moral and material support by a group of supporters that includes church members and war resisters. A recent Canadian comprehensive study reveals that since the first incident in Montreal in December 1983, churches across Canada have provided sanctuary to migrants exhausted of legal appeals and threatened with deportation on 50 separate occasions (Lippert 2010). Typically, these incidents occur in a large city; involve a single male migrant; receive support from major Christian denominations, the broader community, and local political authorities; and more than 60 per cent of the time yield legal status for migrants involved (Lippert 2010). Immigration authorities typically avoid entering churches to make arrests. Sanctuary incidents have been limited to specific communities, and to date no distinctive Canadian national sanctuary movement or network has emerged (Lippert 2010).

Sanctuary is about resistance to regular channels and creation of new ones that make it possible for migrants to become citizens. It was noted earlier that the state is stingy about who can become members of our society. Self-selection is discouraged and, increasingly, so is sanctuary. This may be why on 5 March 2004, Quebec City police entered St Pierre United Church to arrest Mohamed Cherfi. Living in sanctuary for several days, Cherfi was an Algerian migrant faced with deportation who, like most sanctuary recipients before him, had failed to gain status through Canada's refugee determination process. He was quickly deported to the United States, where he was, ironically, granted refugee status in the purportedly less open and fair US system (see Lippert 2010). Moreover, the time that migrants must live inside church buildings to avoid deportation before their cases are resolved by immigration authorities has grown markedly from a mere 19 days on average during the 1980s to an incredible 686 days on average since 2005 (Lippert 2010), thus suggesting the government has taken a harsher line in response to this form of resistance.

It is significant that the Refugee Appeals Division mandated in the Immigration and Protection Act, which came into effect in 2002 and would permit appeals on the merits of a refugee claim, has yet to be implemented eight years later (Lippert 2010). Sanctuary providers increasingly point to a failure to implement it as a key reason migrants are forced to seek sanctuary in churches in an effort to eventually become citizens (Lippert 2010).

Conclusion

Our chief aim in this chapter has been to try to provide answers to the question of how migrants become citizens. The question turns out to be more complex than it first appeared, in part because there are a range of categories of migrants and citizens and ways of becoming such. As indicated by the control of temporary migrants in Canada, there are also ways of *not* becoming citizens. We have of course not fully answered the question, but we hope to have demonstrated that it is one that encourages investigation of other questions that may seem at first to have little to do with immigration and citizenship. A critical sociology provides insights into inequalities that the operation of these processes engender, the forms of resistance that recognition of such inequalities encourage, and the workings of governance and moral regulation that shape and make these processes possible. It may also reveal alternative categories and identities beyond those of migrant and citizen and that entail fewer inequalities among them.

Questions to Consider

1. Would allowing more discretion in immigration officers' decision making be beneficial to applicants and permit humanitarian needs to be considered to a greater degree?
2. What other social problems and processes appear to be governed *through* immigration in Canadian society?
3. How important is national citizenship compared to other kinds of citizenship in the daily lives of Canadians? Given the continuing far-reaching effects of NAFTA on Canadian society, will a corresponding North American citizenship soon become more prevalent?
4. Why are some migrants, while deemed good enough to work in Canada, not imagined to be good enough to become Canadian citizens within current immigration and citizenship policies? To what extent are these policies moral in nature?
5. Do you think the formation of migrant identities is logically necessary for the formation of citizen identities? Are the various migrant identities the 'alterity' of national citizenship, or do they represent an identity/category that lies somewhere between citizens and outsiders?

Note

1. 28 July 1951, 189 U.N.T.S. 137; 31 January 1967, 606 U.N.T.S. 267.

22 | How Social Is the Environment?

Lisa Cockburn and Mark Vardy

Introduction

From beer commercials to government-sponsored international trade shows, images of rolling prairies and snow-capped mountains appear as a popular way of selling goods in Canada. Judging from these marketing campaigns, one could argue that the outdoors figures prominently in Canadian cultural identity. Indeed, a recent sociological study of Canadians' environmental attitudes and behaviours indicates we do value the outdoors (Huddart-Kennedy et al. 2009). But the survey of 1,664 Canadians presents a more complex picture than a simple affirmation that nature is important to people in Canada. While 72.3 per cent of the respondents said that they valued nature, they felt they were prevented from doing more to protect it by a lack of knowledge, time, money, or societal decision-making power (Kennedy, Huddart-Kennedy et al. 2009, 156–7). Recognizing how human society negatively impacts the environment is a different, and perhaps easier, task than solving environmental problems.

The material basis of human existence, including food, oxygen, and water, comes from the environment. But humans are significantly altering, changing, and in many cases damaging nature. Environmental sociologists try to understand the relationship between society and the environment and resolve the apparent paradox wherein human societies degrade the very environments that allow us to live. The discipline of environmental sociology intersects and overlaps with a number of fields, including philosophy, ecology, feminism, the sociology of social movements, theories of social order and conflict, development studies, geography, media studies, and the sociology of scientific knowledge. In this chapter, we will explore how concepts in environmental sociology can shed light on some of the causes of environmental problems as well as working to find ways of addressing them. We will introduce some of the questions being asked by current Canadian environmental sociology, using these Canadian examples to highlight key ideas and important theories. The chapter concludes with an overview of solutions environmental sociologists have suggested to address environmental problems.

What Is the Environment?

Many people are familiar with a number of environmental problems. Indeed, the list of environmental issues and ecological disasters—such as air and water pollution, resource depletion, species extinctions, climate change—can quickly become overwhelming. Yet notice how situations labelled as environmental problems are often social in origin. For example, oil spills that contaminate oceans and beaches, killing countless animals, would not happen without the network of social practices and institutions that make oil such a sought-after energy source. Most other so-called environmental problems are similarly social in origin. In order to protect the environment, we need to cast a critical eye on society, seeking to better understand the complex relationship between humans and the non-human world.

Just as many environmental problems are outcomes of social practices, so too are the ways in which we understand what the natural environment actually is. Is 'nature' separate from humans? Or is nature something we are part of? How do we draw lines between the natural and social worlds? One of the most powerful concepts to emerge with the development of modern industrial society is that humans are separate and distinct from the rest of nature. This **nature/culture dualism** establishes a binary opposition in which nature and culture are seen as discrete and mutually exclusive categories (Merchant 1980). Yet close examination of any 'natural' or 'cultural' phenomena reveals that the boundaries between the two are not clear and are continually changing (Latour 1993). The nature/culture dualism has proven to be a double-edged sword. On the one hand, the separation of humans from nature was foundational in the establishment of the scientific worldview that has enabled us to make tremendous gains in knowledge, including our knowledge of environmental problems and the development of modern technology. On the other hand, it gives us the sense that we are separate from the web of life of which we are in fact a part (Everndon 1992). This sense of separation influences many modern social and cultural practices that have negative ecological impacts.

Catton and Dunlap (1980), two forerunners of environmental sociology, critiqued the **anthropocentrism** of putting humankind at the centre of the universe through either religious or scientific worldviews. They identify the 'human exceptionalism paradigm' as a set of beliefs that humans are uniquely distinct from the rest of existence, and that human society is exempt from ecological constraints (25). From this perspective, how lines are drawn between the natural and social worlds are issues to be critically examined. The next sections examine various ways in which environmental sociologists have questioned the causes and effects of the nature/culture dualism.

A Question of Domination and Justice

One important area of focus for environmental sociology is the role that globalized systems of production, distribution, and consumption play in environmental degradation. Drawing from the classical sociology of Karl Marx, **political ecology** argues that modern capitalism treats nature as both the source of raw resources and as a dumping ground for unwanted waste (Foster 1994; O'Connor 1998). An analysis of hog farming in Manitoba uses this perspective to examine how the Government of Manitoba developed a series of 'business friendly' policies to attract international hog farming corporations to Manitoba at a time when jurisdictions that were traditional homes of the pork industry introduced more stringent environmental policies (Novek 2003). The average number of pigs per farm in Manitoba went up from 172 in 1981 to 1,354 in 2000; in the same period, the number of pig farms went from 5,098 down to 1,430, dramatically increasing 'hog density' (Novek 2003). The 'treadmill of production' concept posits that capitalist economies demand constant growth and continually replace labour with increased mechanization and technology, which creates pressures that deplete natural resources and despoils the environment with waste and pollutants (Schnaiberg and Gould 1994). Drawing on this concept, Novek (2003) points out that while it might be profitable for international corporations to increase hog density, contaminants from the high concentrations of manure from these 'factory farms' can leak into the water table and lead to environmental problems for nearby communities.

In his analysis of the forestry industry in British Columbia, Young (2008) also takes a critical view of the role international corporations play in environmental issues. He argues that policies brought in by the provincial government after 2001 increased the profitability of international corporations while undercutting the long-term sustainability of rural communities by, for example, no longer requiring raw logs to be processed in the communities where the trees were felled. Taking a similar view in their research on local opposition to attempts to privatize the water distribution system in Toronto, Debbané and Keil (2004) argue that the movement toward privatization of water in Canada is driven in part by the global trend toward creating policies that enable the exploitation of nature for private profit. For these authors, local environmental concerns should be seen in the context of globalization and the neo-liberal push to dismantle environmental regulations (Novek 2003; Debbané and Keil 2004; Young 2008). A common theme is how international corporations pursue economic gain for their shareholders in ways that damage the environment upon which local communities rely for long-term sustainability.

An area of environmental sociology related to political ecology is **environmental justice**. Starting several decades ago, scholars in the United States noticed that environmental problems, such as high concentrations of radioactive nuclear waste and other industrial contaminants, were more likely to be located near poor neighbourhoods or in areas that were predominantly non-white (for examples see Neumann et al. 1998; Bullard 1996). They developed the concept of 'environmental racism' to describe how environmental pollution is often offloaded onto areas inhabited by already oppressed groups (Haluza-Delay 2007). In Canada, we need to pay attention to the differences Canadian culture, history, and demographics play in how environmental racism is experienced (Haluza-Delay 2007). For example, in the Canadian Arctic, dramatic changes associated with **anthropogenic climate change** are already influencing how life is lived for Inuit populations. The Inuit have lived on sea ice for thousands of years; indeed, sea ice is regarded as an extension of the land and an important site for hunting (Aporta 2009). Yet the past several decades have seen a significant decline in the thickness and extent of sea ice (Stroeve et al. 2008). Traditional ways of life for the Inuit are significantly threatened as the material basis of their culture literally melts underfoot (Ford et al. 2008; Pearce et al. 2010). Under pressure already from modern Western lifestyles, the impact of climate change means that elders are finding it harder to teach traditional knowledge to younger generations because the land and climate have become so unpredictable (Krupnik and Jolly 2002). Speaking from the perspective of environmental justice, Inuit leader Sheila Watt-Cloutier argued before the United Nations that the impact of climate change on the Inuit traditional land and culture constitutes a contravention of their human rights (Watt-Cloutier 2007).

A Question of Culture

As mentioned in the introduction, the concept of wilderness resonates strongly in Canadian identity, and not without reason: Canada's boreal forest makes up over 25 per cent of the world's remaining intact forests (World Resources Institute 2006). But when people speak about wilderness, what exactly are they referring to? Is it a physical place that meets certain objective criteria, or is it a cultural way of perceiving and interacting with nature? This is an important issue to address if we are concerned with protecting the environment.

Hannigan (2006) points out how different concepts of wilderness emerged at different times and places in history. Analyzing a specific episode in Canadian history, Sandilands (2005) documents how the emergence of the Canadian national park system was intertwined with normative ideas of race and gender;

the idea of wilderness took hold as a colonial concept that figured nature as a place devoid of humans prior to European settlement. Even today, a popular way of understanding wilderness views it as an area free from any perceived human influence, particularly permanent large-scale habitation or industrial development (Hannigan 2006). But the idea of wilderness being a place without people is problematic, as it ignores the presence of indigenous peoples. Over half of Canada's large, intact forest landscapes are found in First Nation historic treaty areas, and about one quarter of this 'wilderness' is contained in modern land claim settlements (Global Forest Watch 2006). Some authors argue that defining wilderness as places humans do not inhabit not only erases the presence of the First Nations in Canadian history but also limits our ability to solve environmental problems by preventing us from clearly seeing how our everyday actions are damaging the environment (Cronon 1998). Eichler (2000) proposes that rather than idealize nature as 'wilderness' and imagine a utopian society perfectly in balance with it, we address the unsustainable practices easily apparent in many aspects of current society.

An example of how we might start rethinking and revaluing nature is found in Foster and Sandberg's (2005) study of the role of indigenous and invasive plants in three public parks in Toronto. Indigenous species are typically understood as those that evolved in a certain area, while invasive species originate elsewhere and are often seen as an indicator of disturbed ecosystems and a threat to biodiversity. Yet, as Foster and Sandberg (2005) argue, contrary to the image of fixed zones of indigenous species, the ranges of all species are in constant flux, and many species that we now think of as indigenous would once have been classified as invasive. The Leslie Street Spit, in Toronto, is an entirely human-made landmass at the edge of Lake Ontario consisting of industrial rubble and sediment dredged from the lakebed. Over the last 50 years, it has gradually been colonized by various plants and animals, many of them invasive. Although it is still the site of dumping of certain waste materials, it is also a breeding ground for more than 40 species of birds and an important stopover point for migratory birds, and now serves as habitat for a variety of indigenous mammal, reptile, fish, and amphibian species and numerous rare plants (Foster and Sandberg 2005). Whereas in two other Toronto parks, High Park and the Don Valley Brick Works, various invasive species management plans have been implemented, at the Leslie Street Spit invasive species are not only tolerated but valued. Here, invasive species have turned a landscape that was created by humans dumping rubble and debris into a world-renowned birding site, thus disturbing cultural understandings of what qualifies as natural.

The influence culture has on the ways we distinguish between nature and society can also be seen in popular recreational lifestyles. Curious about the divide (mentioned in the introduction to this chapter) that Canadians experience between valuing the environment and taking action to reduce their environmental impact (Kennedy, Huddart-Kennedy et al. 2009), Stoddart (2011) conducted qualitative interviews with 45 skiers and snowboarders about their perceptions of the relationship between skiing and climate change. Skiing is a paradigmatic outdoor activity, but often requires a car to access ski hills, linking it to the networks of social practices, infrastructure, and technologies that make car-driving such an everyday part of modern life (Urry 2004). In Stoddart's work, we can see a complex cultural relationship in which ideas of nature are shaped by the experience of skiing, which itself depends upon the existence of highways and cars. Most of the individuals in the study were aware of the irony that one of the most significant ways they have of experiencing nature requires a form of transportation that ultimately damages it. But while individual lifestyle choices, such as carpooling to ski hills, are important, by themselves they are insufficient to respond to the complexities of climate change (Stoddart 2011). Stoddart asks whether the ski industry, which portrays itself as environmentally friendly, might lobby for policies that result in positive environmental changes if individuals were more vocal about the ways that skiing and snowboarding threaten the environment.

What Can We Do about Environmental Problems?

As we have seen, the relations between human society and the natural environment are often complex. Just as there are many ways of understanding the causes of environmental problems, there are also many ways that environmental sociologists proffer as possible solutions. Buttel (2003), for example, proposes four ways that environmental reforms might occur: ecological modernization, state environmental regulation, international environmental governance, and environmental activism. Other authors argue that the depth and complexity of environmental problems challenges the very categories of modern politics (Shaw 2004). Another complicating factor is the ambivalent role that science and technology plays in addressing environmental issues. As the remainder of the chapter discusses, whatever solutions we adopt, they are likely to be as complex as the issues they are intended to address.

A Question of Politics and Science

At what level of society—local, regional, national, or international—should decisions be made about the environment? Does protecting the natural world require compromises between individual freedoms and collective responsibilities, and if so, how can these compromises be made in a democratic manner? A growing body of literature analyzes the vulnerability and possible adaptation strategies of communities to climate change. Based on her analysis of three municipalities in British Columbia, Burch (2010) suggests that effectively responding to climate change on a municipal level requires skilled and flexible leadership in the public service, as well as shifts in public administration practices to make better use of existing public resources. When examining the ability of communities to respond to environmental changes, another crucial ingredient to consider is democratic participation involving local citizens and stakeholders, particularly in resource-based communities (Parkins and Davidson 2008). Parkins (2008) examines the potential for regional coalitions between government agencies, private corporations, and non-governmental organizations to address the mountain pine beetle infestation in British Columbia, which resulted from a series of warmer-than-average winters consistent with the type of impact expected from climate change. For several years, the beetles have been eating away at the trees on which the forestry industry and more than 30 forestry-based communities depend. The provincial government projects that about 25,000 families in these communities will lose about 25 per cent of their current income as a result of the infestation (Parkins 2008). As Parkins (2008) notes, responding effectively to a phenomenon as complex as climate change requires coordination and communication across many different levels, from the individual through the regional, national, and international. While democratic processes are important avenues to effect change, we also need to pay attention to how treating environmental problems only in terms given by either domestic or international politics—that is, either within or between individual sovereign nation-states—might ultimately limit analysis and action to certain conceptions about what politics should be (Shaw 2004). Some scholars argue that the complexity of environmental problems such as climate change requires us to rethink what we mean by 'politics' (Dalby 2003).

Environmental movement organizations play an important role linking citizens with industry and government decision makers (Stoddart and Tindall 2010). Drawing on social movement theory and media studies, we can say that environmental movement organizations 'frame' public campaign issues so that their intended audiences can relate to the issues on an emotional or cultural level (Benford and Snow 2000). Indeed, the success of some environmental campaigns has been attributed to their ability to gauge public receptiveness to specific cultural interpretations of wilderness (Hannigan 2006). The necessity of environmental organizations to appeal to the emotional or affective level in their public campaigns raises the issue of the relationship between science and environmental activism. Science is often used to support arguments for conservation; however, environmental movements must also appeal to cultural values that are non-scientific (Yearley 1992). That is, while it might be possible to demonstrate through scientific investigation that the ecology of a particular area is important to the conservation of a particular species, the value of environmental conservation—the desire of humans to protect a species or a habitat—is itself non-scientific. Furthermore, while science can be an important ally in environmental conservation, it can also increase the magnitude of environmental harms. A compelling example of the ambivalent status of science and technology in environmental protection can be seen in the Newfoundland cod fishery collapse (Sinclair 1996; Hamilton and Butler 2001). The fishery operated without noticeable effect on fish populations for over 500 years, but increasing support for scientific management of natural resources in the mid-twentieth century led to many technological interventions in traditional fishery practice. The scientific view of fisheries, given in terms of biomass and maximum sustainable yield, turned out to be incorrect in many instances, overestimating fish populations and leading to unsustainably high quotas (Sinclair 2006). Better fish-finding technology and scientifically informed changes in fishing practices allowed catches to remain high even as actual fish populations declined. In 1992, this culminated in the near complete decimation of cod populations in the North Atlantic, a collapse from which the cod have yet to recover and which radically altered social life in Newfoundland (Hamilton and Butler 2001).

The fishery collapse can be seen as an example of a worldwide crisis of resource management, demonstrating the limits of the idea that nature can be known, managed, and controlled through the rational exercise of scientifically informed strategies (Bavington 2002). Drawing from the classical sociology of Max Weber, Murphy (2009) shows how the pursuit of rationality can lead to irrational consequences. Indeed, he argues, the conceit that humans can rationally know and control nature might blind us to vast gaps in understanding and knowledge, and that this ignorance might prove to have disastrous social consequences. Based on his analysis of the 1998 ice storm that knocked out power to millions of people in Eastern Canada and the United States, Murphy points out how the living and non-living elements of the planet are interconnected in a complex manner that causes nature to act in surprising and unpredictable ways. That is, nature has complex dynamics that can 'burst through humanly constructed controls' (37). Murphy suggests that we need to develop ways of understanding the interaction between the natural and social worlds that are sensitive to the complexity of both.

Deep ecology and ecofeminism are another two branches of environmental thought that emphasize the limitations of ever fully knowing or managing the earth. Deep ecology is rooted in principles of diversity, symbiosis, complexity, and egalitarianism among all life, human and non-human (Naess 2008, 143–7), and argues that the environment has inherent value beyond that which humans may attribute to it (Merchant 2008). Ecological feminists, or ecofeminists, identify domination of men over both women and the natural world as the central problem to environmental exploitation. Although there is a lot of common ground between ecofeminists and deep ecologists, ecofeminists argue that the concept of anthropocentrism obscures the power relations among people (Merchant 2008). Ecofeminists draw attention to the links between the historical subjugation of women and of nature, noting that dualisms such as nature/culture, body/mind, and feminine/masculine were co-constructed and remain closely linked. They argue that the societal attitudes toward the concepts of 'culture', 'mind', and 'male' are valued more highly than the related concepts of 'nature', 'body', and 'female' (Merchant 1980). From this perspective, gender inequality and environmental degradation are historically intertwined, and so should be addressed simultaneously.

A Question of the Economy

Most of the perspectives discussed thus far are critical of capitalism. In contrast, sustainable development and ecological modernization are ways of understanding the relationship between humans and the natural environment that are more optimistic about the potential of the capitalist system. The term 'sustainable development' entered into popular use in 1987 with the publication of the Brundtland report *Our Common Future*, which called for 'development that meets the needs of the present without compromising the ability of future generations to meet their own needs' (World Commission on Environment and Development 1987, 43). Emerging in Western Europe in the 1970s, ecological modernization has become one of the more enduring concepts in environmental sociology, incorporating the ideas of sustainable development into analytical tools, sociological theory, and a political paradigm (Spaargaren and Mol 1992).

Proponents of ecological modernization argue we must reform our current framework of state administration, international agreements, and capitalist business models (Spaargaren and Mol 1992). According to this view, positive environmental outcomes can be compatible with economic growth, and technology—such as hybrid cars or scrubbers that reduce industrial contaminants emitted from factory smokestacks—has the potential to mitigate environmental ills. Spaargaren and Mol (1992, 339–40) argue that ecological modernization will lead to fewer leakages from systems of production and recycling, more efficient use of renewable energy, and improved quality of production processes and products. Social and institutional transformations envisioned under ecological modernization include a change in the role of science and technology from a source of environmental problems to a source of solutions; the increased involvement and importance of social movements in the core of environmental decision making; and a change in our thinking so that economic and environmental interests are no longer pitted against one another (Mol and Sonnenfeld 2000, 6–7).

Despite their laudable goals, ecological modernization and sustainable development remain difficult to clearly define. Many have pointed to a deeply problematic contradiction between the concept of ecological sustainability on the one hand and development based on continuous economic growth on the other (Sinclair 1996). In an effort to find out if real environmental benefits were gained in a specific case, Davidson and MacKendrick (2004) compared the way in which the government of Alberta argued that the tar sands could be developed sustainably, with the actual impact of the province's environmental policies. With the rise of environmental consciousness and the popularization of the idea of sustainable development in the 1970s and '80s, the government of Alberta's reliance upon oil and gas revenues became potentially problematic. By analyzing relevant documents such as government policy papers and conducting interviews with key informants, Davidson and MacKendrick (2004) show how the government mitigated the potential conflict between citizen concern for ecological preservation and pressure to extract resources by claiming that resources would be developed in an environmentally friendly way. Importantly, the authors found that the increased discussion of environmental sustainability over time did not correspond to substantial actions to make practices more environmentally sustainable. They conclude that the concept of sustainable development can be used to hide the reality of negative environmental impacts.

Conclusion

As we have seen, the cultural concept of wilderness has a particular salience for Canadians. But the ways that local communities understand and interact with nature and the environment can change from one time and place to another. In addition, approaches to saving the natural environment vary considerably. Political ecologists argue that capitalism is the root cause of the environmental crisis, while those who favour the positive role of science, technology, and market forces argue that ecological modernization and sustainable development can strike a balance between ecological and economic goals. Issues of environmental justice remind us that social problems are often not separable from environmental problems, an idea that is also central to deep ecology and ecofeminism. Environmental activism can play an important role, as can the involvement of local communities in decision making.

Our planet is currently facing a number of serious ecological and environmental crises, some catastrophic and sudden, such as massive offshore oil spills, and others slower but no less devastating, such as species extinction and climate change. The impact of environmental degradation on entire ecosystems and on human society is significant. In both sociology and in everyday life, it is crucial that we pay attention to the many complex ways in which the natural and human worlds are intimately interwoven. Given the complexity of the natural and social worlds, sociology has an important role to play in analyzing how, and to what effect, lines of demarcation are drawn between what is called natural and what is called social or cultural, as well as the causes, consequences, and solutions to environmental damage.

Questions to Consider

1. How do the concepts of the treadmill of production and ecological modernization differ on the question of whether modern capitalism is environmentally sustainable?
2. What does 'human exceptionalism' mean, and what are some of ways you see it manifested in everyday life?
3. Give an example of how domination of certain groups of people is linked with domination of the environment. How might this relate to the nature/culture dualism?
4. Why might the concept of wilderness actually be a hindrance to environmental sustainability?

23 | What Questions Has Sociology Deserted?

Lorne Tepperman

Introduction

Recently, I have been reading a lot of material outside my field of immediate research interest—problem gambling—to prepare a new textbook that introduces students to sociology. In doing this, I have learned a lot about many different fields of sociology and learned about them from somewhat less familiar perspectives: postmodernism, critical race theory, cultural studies, intersectionality theory, and so on. My reactions to this have been, first, puzzlement, then excitement, then puzzlement again. The excitement comes from confronting new ways of thinking about the world. The puzzlement comes from discovering that a lot of the new work doesn't try to answer questions I have always been interested in answering. This brief paper is about that problem.

Some Background

What has happened to the questions sociology was expected to answer when I entered the field as a student around 50 years ago? Before looking specifically at a few of the questions sociology has deserted—that is, stopped asking without having answered them—let me say a bit about how sociology looked half a century ago.

The first research project I worked on was typical. I served as a research assistant to sociologist P.J. Giffen, a specialist in deviance and addictions. In the summer after my third undergraduate year, I was hired at the former Addiction Research Foundation of Ontario (now, Centre for Addition and Mental Health) to write a report on first drunkenness offenders. Several years earlier, these offenders had been arrested for drunkenness, for the first time ever. I was to find out which of them went on to become repeated or chronic drunkenness offenders who, in turn, stood a good chance of ending up as alcoholics on 'skid row'. My little study was to fit into a larger study of skid-row alcoholics that Professor Giffen and his collaborators had been working on for years.

I analyzed the interview data that had already been collected, gathered new information about the later arrest records of these 50 first offenders, and carried out an elementary statistical analysis of the results. The data showed that first offenders with the least education, least occupational status, and (most important of all) fewest social and family contacts were most likely to become chronic offenders. These were people—all men—without much **social capital** (as we would call it now), cultural capital, human capital, and just plain money. In time, they would be arrested repeatedly, beginning a long downward spiral—a deviant career—that would pass them repeatedly through jails, hostels, and occasionally hospitals. Some would finally die on the streets, in hostels or shabby rooming houses. Their problem was not an above-average level of alcohol addiction; it was a below-average level of social attachment.

This finding about first offenders—so simple yet so powerful—hooked me on sociology. It showed me that sociology could play a role in studying social problems, making social policy, and understanding the plight of poor and isolated people—society's victims. Later, in social theory classes, I learned that this had always been sociology's goal. Sociologists had always tried to study the facts of social life; develop hypotheses, principles, and even 'laws'; and apply these to improving people's lives. The goal of sociology was always to build a better society.

Auguste Comte, who first conceived the idea of 'sociology' in the nineteenth century, imagined a science of human societies that would help humanity make social as well as technological progress. Karl Marx, in turn, imagined that a systematic, sociological study of history would help end inhuman exploitation. The Fabian sociologists of turn-of-the-twentieth-century England and the social-gospel-inspired sociologists of Canada and the United States believed that sociological research could help improve the lives of the poor, weak, and oppressed. Moreover, when I came into sociology in the early 1960s, a youthful wave of idealism once again supported the idea that sociology could fix society by studying and criticizing it. The sociology classrooms were filled with idealistic young people who opposed the Vietnam War, racial oppression, nuclear adventurism, and the historic mistreatment of women; and the discipline responded accordingly.

Of course, that was a long time ago. We are more skeptical today about the possibility of progress or even social improvement. It has become obvious that a century and a half of positivistic sociology—informed by the goals of natural science—has not been enough to erase capitalism, racism, sexism, or many of the other social ills that concerned earlier generations. However, there has been social progress in the last two centuries, and some of it may have resulted from the efforts of sociologists and their students. So, let's not ask whether the goals of early sociology are relevant any more. Put another way, let's ask whether sociology should have 'deserted' questions that were so dear to many sociologists in the nineteenth and twentieth centuries; or whether we should reopen a discussion of these topics.

Some Deserted Questions

Briefly, I will make the case for a few of these 'deserted questions' and, more generally, for using empirical data to answer questions that have important social consequences. Despite all, it may be too early for sociologists to give up on scientific skepticism, empirical rigour, and statistical testing. There are still empirical questions we need to answer. Therefore, here are a few important questions that sociologists have seemingly deserted without having found out the answers.

First, consider the causes and effects of **alienation**. The concept of alienation was popularized, though not invented, by Karl Marx in his 'early manuscripts' of 1848. By 'alienation', Marx meant to suggest a dehumanization that resulted when people were treated as objects or mere cogs in the wheels of capitalism. Subject to exploitation and humiliation, people became estranged from their work, from the things they produced at work, from other workers, and even from themselves. In effect, they became machines, Marx asserted.

In the late 1950s, Melvin Seeman (1959) rebooted the concept of alienation. He did so by combining it with several other sociological and psychological ideas—anomie, estrangement, isolation, and meaninglessness—and, most important, by developing empirical measures of these concepts. His work launched a surge of new research on alienation throughout the late 1950s and 1960s.

Since the 1970s, however, there has been almost no research on alienation in North American sociology. That is not because ordinary people feel less alienated today than they did 50 years ago. Perhaps we are even more alienated today and have grown so used to alienation we do not notice it any more. There is plenty of evidence that people are still estranged from one another—'bowling alone', as Robert Putnam (2000) put it.

Many other people are desperately searching for meaning and social connection in their lives. Perhaps it is their emptiness and demoralization that leads so many people to modern 'addictions'. The new addicts consume food to obesity and mass media to idiocy, use drugs and sex to find meaning, and surf the Net endlessly in hopes of contacting someone about something—perhaps to confirm they are alive. (No longer is religion alone the 'opiate of the masses', as Karl Marx called it; now television and social media play this role.)

So what happened to the study of alienation? Why did sociologists desert the topic? Perhaps if we reopen the discussion, we will find ways to measure and improve the quality of work life (or school life), for a start; and perhaps deal with some of the rampant addiction and mental illness our society is facing.

Consider another social-psychological example of a deserted topic: labelling theory. So-called labelling theory is taught in every introductory textbook and introductory course; however, no one does research on the topic any more. In short, the theory says, people judge people and put values (or labels) on them: good/bad, beautiful/ugly, smart/dumb, and so on. In turn, we tend to live up or live down to the labels other people put on us. A refinement of this is Cooley's theory of the looking-glass self, which says people evaluate themselves according to what they read in other people's eyes. They respond to how others view them, and view themselves similarly. Thus, a person viewed and treated as ugly will feel ugly, and even behave as an ugly person might behave, excluding himself from social life, creating a self-fulfilling prophecy (that is, becoming an 'ugly person' with no friends). Similarly, a person viewed as stupid will lower her academic ambitions, try less hard, and do poorly on tests: again a self-fulfilling prophecy (that is, a stupid person will get bad grades).

Psychologists Robert Rosenthal and Lenore Jacobson (1968), in a classic set of experiments published as *Pygmalion in the Classroom*, showed that when teachers believe a student is dumb, they will give her less help and her grades indeed will drop. That is, she will test as dumb and, in this sense, become dumb. If the same teachers think the student is smart, she will get more attention and higher grades. Thus, labelling can work internally, by attacking people's ambition and self-esteem, and it can work externally, by stigmatizing and excluding people. It works because people come to expect less of themselves if they believe other people expect little of them. It also works because of bias and limited opportunities that follow from labelling.

It is easy to see the merit in this general principle, but obviously, it is not always true (or always false.) Labelling sometimes has these limiting effects and sometimes it does not. This fact might lead us to feel that the theory is trivial or cannot be proven systematically. However, as sociologists, our job is to discover the conditions under which labelling has a harmful effect, versus the conditions under which it does not. After all, people do not respond to everyone's evaluation in the same way; they give much more credence or importance to some people's evaluations than others do. In addition, not everyone has the same power to stigmatize or exclude us. So, instead of deserting the topic of labelling, we should be asking about the conditions under which labelling has harmful effects, and then asking about the ways we can reduce or prevent these harmful outcomes. Doing so might have an important value in various realms—for example, in dealing with the victims of bullying, racial stereotyping, criminalization, or parental abuse.

Consider a third deserted topic: **social distance**. The psychologist Emory Bogardus developed this idea in the 1920s and social researchers used it for decades after, but it has been relatively unused in the last 30 to 40 years. Bogardus's purpose was to develop a way of measuring the distance or closeness between different ethnic or racial groups. In part, his goal was purely scientific: to find which groups feel drawn to, or repelled by, which other groups. Bogardus also saw this measure as a way of assessing social improvement. He wanted to find out whether, increasingly, groups were mixing and assimilating with one another, despite traditional ethnic or racial dislikes (Bogardus 1926, 1947).

In addition, groups have been mixing more. Some groups are still more excluded than other groups—for example, racialized minorities more than non-racialized minorities; and some groups are still more exclusionary than other groups. However, in general, social distance among ethnic and racial groups has been declining in North America over the past 50 years. Ever-fewer signs of overt racism and ever-increasing rates of racial, ethnic, and religious mixing at school, at work, and in marriage, confirm this observation. So, social distance would seem to be a useful measure of social change, yet today it is largely unused, largely deserted.

Similarly, social mobility, a central topic of sociology in the 1950s, 1960s, and 1970s, is virtually unstudied today. The original goal of social mobility research—especially, research on intergenerational social mobility—was to find out whether society was open or closed to talented, educated people from poor families, and whether it was becoming more open over time. Such mobility research led Canada's great sociologist, John Porter (1987), to argue for the expansion of post-secondary education in Canada (and against multiculturalism, which he saw as condoning ethnic enclaves, self-exclusion, and even discrimination.) People who studied social mobility were convinced that, even if perfect equality of condition was unattainable, we might at least aspire to achieving equal opportunity; and we could only assess our progress by measuring intergenerational mobility. Yet again, today very few sociologists or policy-makers pay attention to the issue of social mobility—whether in respect to education or jobs.

Fifty years ago, the dominant sociological belief in North America was 'positivism'—a conviction that you could make sociological laws through empirical analysis. One of the books that impressed young students then with its sheer boldness was by Bernard Berelson and Gary Steiner. Titled *Human Behavior: An Inventory of Scientific Findings* (1964), the book tried to codify everything sociologists knew about various topics close to Berelson's heart. These included public opinion, political behaviour, the effects of reading on people's attitudes, mass communication, and so on. The book may have been misguided even then: likely, it was *never* possible to codify all of social science knowledge, and it never will be. That is because too many social principles are conditional or contextual: how they work depends mainly on the particular setting, situation, or demographic mix.

Yet early sociology, before (say) 1970, mostly believed that the codification of scientific laws of society was possible. Take another example—a book by my former teacher and mentor, George Homans. The book was titled, simply, *The Human Group* (1958). Based on an interesting variety of group studies, the book aimed to discover universal principles that would apply to all groups at all times and places. In this way, it assumed that we could understand the practices of a present-day juvenile gang by studying nineteenth-century Irish peasants, or understand the operation of a winning basketball team by studying a small, preliterate Australian tribe. Homans was right, to a degree: there *are* universal principles of group dynamics, and sociology has come a long way toward understanding them. (For example, they have to do with leadership, group ritual, cohesive norms, setting goals, and the like.) Currently, psychologists, social workers, and management experts are doing the new work on this topic. Sociologists have deserted this eminently sociological topic without discovering the answers to questions such as 'How can we build a winning team?,' 'a happy family?,' 'a contented classroom?,' 'a productive workplace?,' and so on.

Let us return briefly to a general problem in the 'sociology of deserted questions': the failure to look for conditions under which events turn out one way rather than another. Consider the most famous typology, or so-called theory, in sociology: Robert K. Merton's 'anomie theory', also often called 'strain theory'. The theory argues that seemingly bizarre and unrelated types of deviant behaviour are sensible and related to one another. According to Merton (1938), we can best understand them as meaningful, 'functional' adaptations to **anomie**. That is, they are solutions to the fundamental problem caused by modern consumerist capitalism: universal desires but narrowly limited opportunities to satisfy those desires. Thus, these so-called adaptations—crime, mental illness, addiction, and other seemingly alienated approaches to living—make it possible for capitalism to survive. In this way, they are functional to the social and economic system, which is committed to capitalism, and functional to the survival of alienated individuals, who devise a new way of living.

Merton's anomie theory most decidedly does not predict what kinds of people are going to devise what kinds of adaptation, how long they will remain with these adaptations, or why certain adaptations are more common in certain neighbourhoods, communities, or societies than in others. Once again, one might have expected sociology to address this question—that is, to specify the conditions under which crime rates or addiction rates or rates of mental illness will rise in response to this problem of anomie. Yet, instead of addressing this question, sociologists have deserted the topic. We continue, ritualistically, to teach students the anomie typology, but anomie theory is dead: it produces no new research.

There is a danger that we will do the same with another interesting typology or theory, credited to Baumrind (1967). This theory asserts that certain types of parenting are superior to other types. Specifically, authoritative parenting (which combines firm rules with loving support) is found to be superior to three alternative forms of parenting: authoritarian (rules/no love), permissive (love/no rules), and neglectful (no rules/no love). Studies over the past two decades have shown that authoritative parenting is more likely than the other three kinds to produce happy, healthy children. These children tend to do well in school, stay out of trouble with the law, get along well with other people, and respect themselves.

Postmodern sociologists are likely to doubt—even reject—such findings, since they are inclined to oppose the search for universal principles of social life. They correctly point out that, in various parts of the world, people expect different kinds of parenting and, therefore, may adapt to authoritarian parenting (for example) differently than we might do. What is needed now is a series of cross-national studies to discover the universality, or particularity, of Baumrind's findings. Sociologists must avoid the urge to desert this topic before we have clarified the conditions under which Baumrind's theory holds or does not hold. For example, we may want to find out if the theory is valid in urban regions of the world but not in rural regions; in secular parts of the world but not theocratic parts; and in societies that promote gender equality but not in societies where men routinely subordinate women (and children).

Speaking of 'postmodernism', another deserted topic in present-day sociology is 'modernization', a topic that not only dominated sociology 50 years ago but also, in certain senses, is the founding problem of sociology. Remember that the founding thinkers of sociology—Marx, Weber, and Durkheim—were all concerned with the likely effects of urbanization, industrialization, political revolution, new technology, new forms of social organization (e.g., bureaucracy, rule of law) and above all, capitalism. Nineteenth-century sociologists tended to be optimistic about the possibility of 'progress', though they may have disagreed about the shape this progress would, or should, take. They all agreed that a modern, literate, urban industrial society carried more potential for freedom and human fulfillment than traditional rural societies. In particular, they heralded the escape from the traditional constraints of religion, caste, class, and provincialism.

Of course, modernity did not give us everything humanity had expected. We can probably all agree that the twentieth century—however technically and educationally advanced—was a nightmare of war, cruelty, and disappointed hopes. It is hard to believe in progress or modernity today, any more than we can believe in capitalism, communism, nationalism, or organized religion as sources of human empowerment. Once again, we have to ask: under what conditions has modernity worked reasonably well, and under what conditions has it failed dismally? Can we, as sociologists, explain the successes and failures and, as citizens, work to create more successes and fewer failures? Surely, this question is just as relevant today, in the clash between (for example), traditional Islam and modern Western secularism as it was a century or even two centuries ago.

Related to this, and similar in form, is the inequality problem. Early sociologists had hoped to erase social inequality or, at least, avoid and remove its worst harms. Today, we can be certain, based on evidence from the past century or so, that we will never wipe out inequality. We can only reduce it and mitigate it; so once again, sociologists should be asking how successes have been achieved in this domain, and how we can make better social policies, in specific circumstances, to achieve added successes. If we can give up the idea of a fully egalitarian society, we may be able to make better headway solving the problems that, in many parts of the world, are still commonly associated with racism, sexism, and unequal wealth.

It is probably because they understood inequality could never be removed that some of sociology's key figures—including Émile Durkheim and Pitrim Sorokin—developed an interest in the 'social sentiments', especially altruism. (In fact, the great classical economist Adam Smith (1759) began this conversation a century earlier, in discussing the 'moral sentiments' of society.) Clearly, human societies are held together by something more than self-interest; and, despite what economists say, people are more than profit-maximizers. Throughout history, people have risked their lives and belongings for grand ideas and for other people. They have often acted in the interest of things larger than themselves; and it is this almost incomprehensible everyday saintliness that often holds societies together. We see this altruism every day in friendships, families, communities, schools, and workplaces. In fact, the only place we do not see altruism is in the marketplace.

The question that most intrigued Sorokin toward the end of his life was how we might capitalize on altruism to increase social cohesion and improve general well-being (see Sorokin 1950, 1954). What a grand problem that is; and, conceivably, an altruistic society is more attainable than the classless society to which Marx had pledged himself. However, leaving aside the practical attainability of this altruistic society—perhaps the goal of sociologist Amitai Etzioni (1996) and others through present-day 'communitarianism'—at the very least, altruism remains an unanswered question. We know little more about the conditions that promote altruism than Durkheim or Sorokin did a century ago. It too has been deserted.

So, finally, consider the problem of present-day homelessness. Today, many Canadians, sociologists and non-sociologists alike, are concerned about homeless people. Though they are hard to count and often nearly invisible, the homeless lead lives of quiet desperation, ill health, and often, great danger. For various reasons, we are starting to take initiatives to improve their condition, starting with their housing and healthcare. What is interesting is that, as we begin to study and understand the plight of the homeless, we are reminded that they are on the streets not because they are sicker, weaker, or more blame-worthy than the rest of us. Usually, they are on the streets because they have less social capital, cultural capital, human capital, and just plain money. So, 50 years later, it seems that we are returning to a basic concern that we have deserted and ignored: people's lives are often beyond their control. That is why we create social safety nets and why we devise policies of harm reduction.

In short, though many of the questions of 50 years ago have been unjustly deserted, other questions keep resurfacing—often in slightly changed guises. The 'skid-row alcoholic' of yesteryear is the homeless man, woman, or child of today. This may serve as a reminder that important sociological problems do not disappear simply because we choose to ignore them.

Conclusion

In closing, every sociology student needs to learn the history of the discipline. There are reasons for doing so. Many theories and concepts in use today came from earlier thinkers, so we do well to understand what they had origin-ally meant. Many questions debated today were debated, in other terms, by sociologists in earlier generations. Also, the earlier sociologists were just as smart, serious, and dedicated as anyone doing sociology today. Though they may have written in antiquated, even complicated language, they were talking about things that still matter; and often they did so in brilliant, exciting ways.

Therefore, one reason to study the history of sociology is to enter a dialogue with the smartest people who ever thought about societies and social prob-lems. Another reason, as I have argued here, is to revisit and perhaps reopen some of the great sociological questions that later sociologists deserted. Even if most of these earlier sociologists are dead white men; even if they plainly had nothing to say about racism, sexism, ageism, or sexual orientation; even if they talked about communities that no longer exist and people who seem unlike ourselves; even if their predictions were often wrong and their methods were primitive; even if they died long before your sociology professor was born, perhaps even before your grandparents were born—you should still visit and consider their work.

If you do, more likely than not, you will find deserted questions worth pondering.

Questions to Consider

1. Try to think of some other questions in sociology that may have been deserted.
2. Think of some questions in sociology that, in your opinion, should be deserted.
3. What if anything do the deserted topics discussed in this paper have in common?
4. What is the value of modernity as a concept in sociology, and what are its pitfalls?
5. In your view, is sociology particularly likely to desert unanswered questions, or do you think this happens in other fields too (e.g., physics, English literature, criminology, and so on)?

Glossary

Adolescent femininity Socially accepted ways to be a teenage 'girl'.

Alienation The estrangement of people from one another, their work, or the products of their work; more generally, a sense of distance from social relations.

Altruism Behaviour that takes account of the interests of others, in opposition to egoism, selfishness, and self-interested individualism.

Anomie In Merton's use, a gap between cultural goals and social opportunities, created by a strain in the social system of modern capitalism.

Anthropocentrism Ideas, theories, or behaviours centred around the belief that humans are the most important factor or actor in the natural world.

Anthropogenic climate change Change in the overall temperature and climatic patterns of the earth due to elevated greenhouse gas levels (e.g., carbon dioxide and methane) caused by human activities such as the burning of fossil fuels.

Anti-psychiatry movement The predecessor to the mad movement, the anti-psychiatry movement flourished in the 1960s when a group of psychiatrists began critiquing their discipline for failing to recognize the moral judgments embedded within psychiatric diagnoses. The movement continues today.

Call centre A specialized workplace that provides service and/or information over the telephone. Increasingly, call centres also provide Web support, including email handling, fax support, and online chat.

Citizenship A type of identity within a defined territory that is usually deemed 'good' and is typically distinguished from outsider identities that are typically considered to be lacking in some way.

Class Marx claimed that classes are the product of, and defined through, relations to the mode of production. That is, either one owns machines or, conversely, works on these machines. Capitalists control the production of commodities and benefit from their sale. By contrast, workers have access only to their labour power and sell it to owners in exchange for a wage. Contemporary class theorists have expanded this understanding to encompass, among other divisions, the middle classes.

Codification A process by which the experiential, shared cultural voice of an emerging group is transformed into an official, dominant discourse, such that the original demands are reframed and now make sense differently.

Collective conscience A society's shared morality.

Colonialism Historical and enduring processes (i.e., industrial schools, the reserve system, and outlawing of traditions) of subordinating indigenous cultural norms to Euro-Canadian ways of being.

Constitutional orthodoxy The strict adherence to the rule of law and doctrines as set out in a country's constitution.

Cultural studies The evolving study of culture in creative, social, and political contexts. Today it has come to mean a multi-disciplinary and usually critical approach to social formations. Often its study engages with popular cultural forms.

Culture Once reserved for so-called high-brow culture such as classic literature and music, the term now reflects a much broader spectrum of the social exchange and mediation of meaning and embraces popular culture and its technological media.

Deinstitutionalization The movement of people out of psychiatric hospitals and into the community to receive treatment and services.

Discipline A subtle but pervasive form of governance that guides behaviour without the use of law.

Division of labour In his earlier work, Durkheim emphasized this concept to suggest that groups are significantly influenced by the way that they organized their labour and divided the tasks required to accomplish functions required for the survival of a given social formation. He noted that changes from 'primitive' to 'modern' forms of the division of labour were to have important implications for the ways that those societies developed, and for the kinds of subjects (e.g., individuals) they shaped.

Environmental justice A legal process that seeks to redress situations in which environmental problems are felt most by those who benefit from them least.

Emotional labour The management, evocation, and potential commodification of particular forms of emotional expression or suppression of other forms of emotional expression in order to satisfy the feeling rules of a particular social role, job, or relationship.

Ethnomethodology An alternative sociological theory/methodology that examines the tacit, taken for granted practices that constitute everyday social life.

Eugenics A term meaning 'well-born' or 'good genes'. Early eugenicists drew inspiration from the biological sciences and assumed that, like livestock, some humans possess 'better' genes than others. This mentality was the impetus for campaigns promoting forms of social control aimed at improving the racial qualities of future generations.

Existentialism A school of philosophical thought that considered human beings, by their unique nature, as partly undetermined. As such, individuals are required to make free choices among possible courses of action. Such freedom was seen as closely tied to moral responsibility, but with the recognition that there are no moral certainties. In this context, human beings must freely choose actions (without any necessary moral guidelines), but then they are also held responsible for the outcome of the choices they make—the source of considerable 'anxiety'. Under the famous idea of 'existence precedes essence', existential thinking emphasized that by freely choosing particular kinds of existence, human beings could, in essence, become authentic and responsible beings.

Feeling rules Affective rules that define and govern appropriate and inappropriate feeling in various circumstances, which may be at odds with other socially created or personal internalized feelings.

Fictive kin relationships People chosen to be family members that are not legally or biologically related.

Free will The idea that human beings are able to choose ways to act from various courses that might be available to them. Free will and being responsible morally for chosen courses of action often go hand in glove.

Gender policing Practices that pressure, discipline, or penalize people to make them conform to specific standards of masculinity or femininity.

Gender-responsive policy Policy that recognizes quantitative and qualitative differences between men and women's lives and is responsive to their unique needs and experiences. Such policies are intended to eliminate systemic barriers, cultural bias, and gender bias. (Also referred to as *gender-specific* or *women-centred policy*.)

Governance The guiding of behaviour through law, norms, morality, power structures, surveillance, etc. The process and practices that apply to policing vary significantly given the environment in which policing is applied. Governance in the realm of public policing must take into account legal and constitutional accountability and responsibilities.

Homophobia Attitudes and practices that disadvantage, discriminate against, or persecute homosexual people and practices. Homophobia can reside in individuals, but it can also be institutionalized and enforced through law, family, religion, media, employment, and so on. (Alternatively conceptualized as *heterosexism* or *heteronormativity*.)

Identity Our sense of who we are and who others perceive us to be; identities are formed through social interaction.

Ideological domination Ways of thinking and governing that preserve a society's power structure to the disadvantage of those who are ruled.

Ideology Originally associated with the work of Marx and his analysis of how dominant political economies maintain their positions, the term has evolved into a more complex and contested explanation of social power in the face of cultural developments such as mass media and entertainment, and new communication and information technologies.

Indigenous sovereignty The political condition in which indigenous peoples in Canada (including Inuit, First Nations, and Indian people) would govern themselves as a sovereign political community under international law. Sovereignty may include any aspect of economic, political, social, and/or culture.

Individualism   An ideology that gives the individual person rather than the social collective primacy.

Institutional ethnography   A feminist perspective that combines ethnomethodological and Marxist insights to examine how the 'ruling relations' tacitly work to exclude and marginalize women (and others) in Western societies.

Instrumental reason   The applied use of human reason to calculate the most efficient means to a particular goal.

Keynesian welfare state   A system developed after World War II by both federal and provincial governments to provide tax-funded public programs to ensure the basic needs of citizens. These programs rested on a premise of shared citizen entitlement and mutual obligation and were designed as economic instruments to shore up the market in times of economic downturn. In Canada, the programs of the Canadian welfare state were particularly important in articulating a shared sense of national identity.

Knowledge-based economy   An economy in which the knowledge content of existing work has been upgraded, and in which information workers are predominant over other types of workers in the labour force as a whole.

Mad movement   Groups of psychiatric survivors/consumers who fight against the oppressive techniques used by the mental health system. The groups are best known for Mad Pride events that take place around the world.

Male breadwinner model   A view that separates home and work along rigid gender lines, whereby men do paid work and women do care work, which reinforces a nuclear family model (households including only a husband, a wife, and their biological children).

Mass communication   Mass communication describes the process of creating shared meaning between mass media and their audiences. The term refers to the process by which a complex organization, using a variety of technologies (machines) produces a steady stream of public messages aimed at a large, scattered, and diverse audience.

Media effects   The various ways individuals or groups can be influenced by media content.

Research on media effects often addresses dramatic issues such as violence, pornography, or social stereotyping. Debates on media effects often frame discussion on two opposing perspectives: either media messages are powerful stimuli that can persuade or influence peoples' behaviour, or media messages have little influencing power. Communication research since the 1960s tends to support the view that repeated media exposure reinforces values and attitudes that a person already has.

Media literacy   The development and use of a set of skills that enable individuals to critically interpret and evaluate the meanings of messages they encounter in the media. 'Media literacy' also refers to an individual's ability to use the tools of communication to produce as well as understand mediated communication.

Modernity   Modernity represents a particular perspective that Baudelaire captured in three words: the transitory, the fugitive, and the contingent.

Nationalism   Refers to both an ideology seeking to create or defend a specific culture within a given political unit, and to a process: the formation of distinct national states, mostly during a period covering the late nineteenth and twentieth centuries. Some researchers argue that we have now entered a post-national period, but nation states, usually enjoying a fairly high degree of sovereignty, and more rarely cultural homogeneity, remain the most common political structures.

Nation-state   Two separate but often linked concepts.

Nation   A population defined by a common culture, language and/or ethnicity.

State   A sovereign political association located within geographical borders. The combination of 'nation' and 'state' provides strong legitimacy for governments. Note that some nations are without a state (Kurds) and some states are not nations (Hong Kong).

Nature/culture dualism   The binary opposition that divides humans from the rest of existence; it can take a variety of related forms, such as non-human/human, body/mind, and object/subject.

Neo-liberalism   A social, political and economic regulatory system that is characterized by (among other things) the freedom of the market, privatizing government services, and shifting responsibility from government to individuals.

Neo-liberal welfare state A systemic reform in the 1980s, reacting against the perceived weaknesses of the Keynesian welfare state. Some social programs were eliminated, while others saw a drastic reduction in funding and a reorientation in delivery. Neo-liberal social programs emphasize individual, family, and community responsibility; choice in the market place; and freedom from the state.

Normalization A governing practice that makes some ways of being 'normal' and others 'abnormal' and thus in need of interventions.

Olympism According to the Olympic Charter, Olympism is a philosophy of life, exalting and combining in a balanced whole the qualities of body, will, and mind.

Out-migration The departure of people from a region on a temporary or permanent basis.

Pathways to prison Individual or structural factors that may contribute to an individual's involvement in crime and eventual incarceration. Some factors may include homelessness, mental health difficulties, prostitution, victimization, trauma, poor education, unemployment, substance use, economic marginalization, or lack of social support.

Patriarchy This term refers to the structures and practices whereby males explicitly and implicitly exert power over females, and enjoy economic, political, cultural, and material privileges compared to females.

Performativity This term refers to the actions and practices that individuals make in conformance with norms.

Policing A process of regulating and ordering contemporary societies and individuals carried out by police—the civil force of a national, provincial, or local government, responsible for the prevention and detection of crime and the maintenance of public safety and order.

Political ecology A perspective, based on the classical sociology of Marx, on how capitalist economic and political structures transform ecological material into private profit.

Power relations Foucault used this phrase to emphasize his 'relational theory of power'. In short, against a dominant view of power as a top-down phenomenon in which subjects are constrained by a visible and central authority (e.g. a sovereign, a king or queen, etc.), Foucault understood power as 'bottom up' affair. Here, the outcome of local clashes of will effectively shapes subjects, their actions and ultimately the social and political contexts that envelop them. In effect, this means that in his approach to power, Foucault focused on the 'political technologies' developed by local relations, and the ways that people's actions helped to structure the actions of others. In this context, freedom and power are not opposed, since power relations shape the freedoms of a given historical moment.

Private security The broad term used to describe a wide range of private (non-governmental) security-related activities associated with the protection of private property.

Queer theory A theoretical approach based on analyzing societies and cultures from the viewpoints of lesbian, gay, bisexual, and transgendered people. Queer theory focuses, in particular, on showing how concepts of heterosexuality and masculinity depend on the simultaneous covert desire for, and overt denial of, homosexual attraction.

Racial overrepresentation A phenomenon that occurs when a racial group has more of its members in some condition (i.e., unemployed, living in poverty, imprisoned) in greater numbers than the group's population would suggest. For example, as Aboriginals make up 4 per cent of the population, you might predict, other things being equal, that they would represent 4 per cent of the prison population. However, in actuality, Aboriginals make up approximately 18 per cent of the incarcerated adult population. Thus, as a racial group they are overrepresented in the prison population.

Refugee A person outside his or her country of origin who cannot return due to fear of persecution.

Reintegration The process an individual goes through upon returning to the community after a period of incarceration and attempting to overcome a range of social, economic, and personal challenges that can be obstacles to a crime-free lifestyle. (Also referred to as *resettlement* or *re-entry*.)

Sex/gender distinction   This term refers to the discursive separation of sex and gender within modern society whereby sex is associated with biology/nature and gender is associated with culture/society.

'Sixties Scoop'   A government initiative that involved child welfare authorities taking Aboriginal children from their homes, communities, and cultures and adopting or fostering them out to primarily non-Aboriginal families.

Social capital   The types of social relationships—often located in families or communities—that help people achieve high educational and occupational goals.

Social distance   In Bogardus's use, a willingness to admit different (specified) ethnic or racial groups to intimacy with you, your family, friends, or neighbours.

Social investment state   A modification of the neo-liberal welfare state. The child receives primary emphasis in social investment policies, and the objective of social programs is to ensure support for the development of future workers and economic innovators.

Social media   Internet or web-based sites that provide information and content to users and allow, encourage, or even require that those users interact with that content. In contrast to mass communication, which involves the transmission of standardized messages from an organization to a wide audience, social media allows users to respond to content—to express their own views with communicators and with other users.

Society   A group of people unified by a distinct set of normative relations, common interests, and common goals.

Sociology of emotions   Sub-field of sociology that explains the emotions with reference to relationships between social contexts and interactions, power and difference, private and public realms, and body and society.

Sovereignty   The term can have many different meanings, but its most common definition applies to states able to exert independent rule within a given geographic territory. Historically, full sovereignty has only applied to a relatively small number of societies. There are debates currently about the erosion of state sovereignty, although in practice it remains the most common form of political power.

State   A set of institutions that rule over a particular society. While states vary in size, power, and complexity, they share common attributes, including the monopoly of certain forms of power (notably police, justice, and armed forces), the recognition of other states and international institutions, and the centralization of power within a relatively well-defined territory. While many states claim to be nation-states, or states that govern a single national group, many, including Canada, are multinational states.

Statehood   The status of being a state rather than a dependent region or territory.

Theory   A conceptual framework that describes, explains, analyzes, and interprets the social world.

Two-sex model   This term refers to a model of sexual difference in which females and males are understood to have entirely separate (and complementary) bodies (including hormones, chromosomes, gonads, genitalia, and secondary sex characteristics). The two-sex model overturned the one-sex model prevalent within Western discourses before and during the Enlightenment. The one-sex model understood humans to have one body type, with males and females tending toward different external and internal displays of this one body type.

Transnational families   Families whose members, living in other countries, are separated by borders.

References

Abercrombie, Nicholas, Stephen Hill, and Bryan S. Turner. 1984. *Dictionary of sociology.* London: Penguin.

Acoose, Janice. 1995. *Iskewewak kah'ki yaw ni wahkoma kaak: Neither Indian princesses nor easy squaws.* Toronto: Women's Press.

Adam, Barry D. 1978. *The survival of domination.* New York: Elsevier/Greenwood.

———. 1985. 'Age, structure and sexuality'. *Journal of Homosexuality* 11 (3/4): 19–33.

———. 1995. *The rise of a gay and lesbian movement.* New York: Twayne.

———. 1996. 'Structural foundations of the gay world'. In S. Seidman (Ed.), *Queer theory/ sociology.* Cambridge, MA: Blackwell.

———. 1998. 'Theorizing homophobia'. *Sexualities* 1 (4): 387–404.

———. 2004. 'Care, intimacy, and same-sex partnership in the 21st century'. *Current Sociology* 52 (2): 265–79.

———. 2006. 'Relationship innovation in male relationships'. *Sexualities* 9 (1): 5–26.

Adelberg, E., and C. Currie. 1987. *Too few to count: Canadian women in conflict with the law.* Vancouver: Press Gang.

Adkins, Lisa. 2002. *Revisions: Gender and sexuality in late modernity.* Buckingham, UK: Open University Press.

Adorno, Theodor, and Max Horkheimer. 1979 [1944]. 'The culture industry: Enlightenment as mass deception'. In *Dialectic of enlightenment.* London: Verso.

Agger, Ben. 1991. *A critical theory of public life.* London: Falmer Press.

Agocs, Carol. 2000. 'Race and ethnic relations'. In J. Teevan and W.E. Hewitt (Eds.), *Introduction to sociology: A Canadian focus.* Scarborough: Prentice Hall.

Aitken, R. 2008. 'Notes on the Canadian exception: Security certificates in critical context'. *Citizenship Studies* 12 (4): 381–96.

Akyeampong, E.B. 2005. 'Business support services'. *Perspectives on Labour and Income* 6 (5): 5–9.

Albanese, Patrizia. 2010. 'Introduction to Canada's families: Historical and recent variations, definitions, and theories'. In D. Cheal (Ed.), *Canadian Families*, 2–26. Toronto: Oxford University Press.

———. 2005. *Government MLA review of the Private Investigators and Security Guards Act.* Edmonton: Alberta Solicitor General and Public Security.

———. 2010. *Private Investigators and Security Guards Act.* Edmonton: Alberta Queens' Press.

Alfred, Taiaiake. 1999. *Peace, power and right-eousness: An indigenous manifesto.* Toronto: Oxford University Press.

Althusser, Louis. 1971. *Lenin and Philosophy and Other Essays.* Trans. Ben Brewster. New York: Monthly Review Press.

Amadiume, Ifi. 1980. *Male daughters, female husbands.* Toronto: DEC.

Ambert, Anne-Marie. 2006. *One-parent families: Characteristics, causes, consequences, and issues.* Toronto: Vanier Institute of the Family.

Amnesty International. 2004. *Stolen sisters—A human rights response to discrimination and violence against indigenous women in Canada.* http://www.amnesty.ca/ resource_centre/reports.

Anderson, Benedict. 1991. *Imagined communities: Reflections on the origin and spread of nationalism.* New York: Verso.

———. 1998. *The spectre of comparisons: Nationalism, Southeast Asia and the world.* London: Verso.

Anderson, C. 1999. 'Governing Aboriginal justice in Canada: Constructing responsible individuals and communities through tradition'. *Crime, Law and Social Change* 31 (2): 303–26.

Aporta, Claudio. 2009. 'The trail as home: Inuit and their pan-Arctic network of routes'. *Human Ecology* 37 (2): 131–46.

Arditti, J., and A. Few. 2006. 'Mothers' reentry into family life following incarceration'. *Criminal Justice Policy Review* 17 (1): 103–23.

Arnold, Mathew. 1990 [1875]. *Culture and anarchy.* Cambridge, UK: Cambridge University Press.

Assembly of First Nations. 2005. *Our Nations Our Governments: Choosing Our Own Paths.* Report of the Joint Committee of Chiefs and Advisors on the Recognition and Implementation of First Nation Governments. Ottawa: Assembly of First Nations.

Atkinson, J.M. 1971. 'Societal reactions to suicide: The role of coroners' definitions'. In S. Cohen (Ed.), *Images of deviance*. Harmondsworth, UK: Penguin.

———. 1982. *Discovering suicide: Studies in the social organization of sudden death*. London: Macmillan.

Ayling, J., and C. Shearing. 2008. 'Taking care of business: Public police as commercial security vendors'. *Criminology and Criminal Justice* 8 (1): 27–50.

Babooram, A. 2008. 'The changing profile of adults in custody, 2006/2007'. Ottawa: Statistics Canada. Catalogue no. 85-002-X. http://www.statcan.gc.ca/pub/85-002-x/2008010/article/10732-eng.htm#a6.

Bagdikian, Ben. 2000. *The media monopoly*, 6th edn. Boston: Beacon Press.

Bagemihl, B. 1999. *Biological exuberance: Animal homosexuality and natural diversity*. New York: Stonewall Inn Editions.

Baines, Donna. 2004a. 'Caring for nothing: Work organization and unwaged labour in social services'. *Work, Employment and Society* 18 (2): 267–95.

———, and Bonnie Freeman. 2011. 'Intergenerational care work: Mothering, grandmothering, and eldercare'. In C. Krull and J. Sempruch (Eds.), *Demystifying the family/work contradiction*, 67–80. Vancouver: University of British Columbia Press.

Bakan, Abigail, and Audrey Kobayashi. 2000. *Employment equity policy in Canada: An interprovincial comparison*. Ottawa: Status of Women Canada.

Baker, Maureen. 2001. *Families, labour and love: Family diversity in a changing world*. Sydney: Allen and Unwin.

———. 2010. *Choices and Constraints in Family Life*, 2nd edn. Toronto: Oxford University Press.

Balfour, G., and E. Comack. 2006. *Criminalizing women*. Halifax: Fernwood.

Banner, David. 2005. 'Ain't got nothing'. *Certified* (music CD). Big Face/Universal.

Barker, J. 2009. *Women in the criminal justice system: A Canadian perspective*. Toronto: Emond Montgomery Publications Ltd.

Barney, Darin. 2000. *Prometheus wired: The hope for democracy in the age of networked technology*. Vancouver: University of British Columbia Press.

Barris, Stephen. 2005. 'How long will lesbian, gay, bisexual and transgender rights be ignored at the UN?' *Bulletin of the International Gay and Lesbian Rights Association* 117: 22–5.

Barthes, Roland. 1972 [1957]. *Mythologies*. London: Jonathon Cape.

Bartholet, Elizabeth. 2005. 'Abuse and neglect, foster drift, and the adoption alternative'. In S. Haslanger and C. Witt (Eds.), *Adoption matters: Philosophical and feminist essays*, 223–33. Ithaca, NY: Cornell University Press.

Bartky, Sandra Lee. 1997. 'On psychological oppression'. In Mary F. Rogers (Ed.), *Contemporary feminist theory: A text/reader*. Boston: McGraw-Hill.

Basting, Anne Davis. 2001. "God Is a Talking Horse': Dementia and the performance of self'. *The Drama Review* 45: 78–94.

———. 2009. *Forget memory*. Baltimore: Johns Hopkins University Press.

Battle, Ken. 2008. *A $5000 Canada Child Tax Benefit: Questions and answers*. Ottawa: Caledon Institute for Social Policy.

Bauder, David. 2009. 'Study: More Americans think media is biased, inaccurate'. *The Huffington Post*, 14 September.

Baudrillard, Jean. 1983. *Simulations*. New York: Semiotext(e)

Bauman, Zygmunt. 1987. *Legislators and interpreters*. Cambridge, UK: Polity Press.

———. 1988. *Freedom*. Minneapolis: University of Minnesota Press.

———. 1990. *Thinking sociologically*. Oxford, UK: Basil Blackwell.

———. 1992. *Intimations of postmodernity*. London: Routledge.

———. 2000. 'Sociological enlightenment—For whom, about what?' *Theory, Culture and Society* 17 (2): 71–81.

———. 2001a. *Community: Seeking safety in an insecure world*. Cambridge, UK: Polity Press.

———. 2011. *Collateral damage: Social inequalities in a global age*. Cambridge, UK: Polity Press.

Baumrind, Diana. (1967). Child-care practices anteceding three patterns of preschool behavior. *Genetic Psychology Monographs* 75: 43–88.

Bavington, Dean. 2002. 'Managerial ecology and its discontents: Exploring the complexities of control, careful use and coping in resource and environmental management'. *Environments* 30 (3): 3–21.

Bayatrizi, Z. 2008a. 'From fate to risk: The quantification of mortality in early modern statistics'. *Theory, Culture and Society* 25 (1): 121–43.

——. 2008b. *Life sentences*. Toronto: University of Toronto Press.

——. 2009. 'Counting the dead and regulating the living: Early modern statistics and the formation of the sociological imagination (1662–1897)'. *British Journal of Sociology* 60 (3): 603–21.

Beale, Elizabeth. 2008. 'As labour markets tighten, will outmigration trends reverse in Atlantic Canada'. Commentary. May. Halifax: Atlantic Provinces Economic Council.

Beamish, R. 1993. 'Labor relations in sport: Central issues in their emergence and structure in high performance sport'. In A. Ingham and J. Loy (Eds.), *Sport in social development: Traditions, transitions, and transformations*. Champaign, IL: Human Kinetics.

——. 2011. *Steroids: A new look at performance enhancing substances*. Santa Barbara, CA: Praeger.

——, and I. Ritchie. 2004. 'From chivalrous brothers-in-arms to the eligible athlete: Changed principles and the IOC's banned substance list'. *International Review for the Sociology of Sport*. 39: 355–71.

——, and J. Borowy. 1989. *Q: What do you do for a living? A: I'm an athlete*. Kingston, ON: Sport Research Group.

Bean, P. 2008. *Madness and crime*. Portland: Willan Publishing.

Beauchemin, Jacques. 2008. ' Le nationalisme québécois entre culture et identité'. *Ethique publique* 10 (1), 103–15.

Beaudin, M., and S. Breau. 2001. 'Employment, skills and the knowledge economy in Atlantic Canada'. *Maritime Series Monographs*. Moncton: Institut canadien de recherche sur le développement regional/ The Canadian Institute for Research on Regional Development.

Becker, D. 2004. 'Post-traumatic stress disorder'. In P. Caplan and L. Cosgrove (Eds.), *Bias in psychiatric diagnosis*, 207–12. Lanham: Jason Aronson.

Bell, Daniel. 1973. *The coming of post-industrial society*. Basic Books.

Bendelow, Gillian. 2009. *Health, emotion and the body*. Cambridge: Polity Press.

Benford, Robert D., and David A. Snow. 2000. 'Framing processes and social movements: An overview and assessment'. *Annual Review of Sociology* 26: 611–39.

Bengtson, Vern L. 2001. 'The burgess award lecture—beyond the nuclear family: The increasing importance of multigenerational bonds'. *Journal of Marriage and Family* 63 (1): 1–16.

Benjamin, Walter. 1968 [1936]. 'The work of art in the age of mechanical reproduction'. In *Illuminations* (Harry Zohn, trans.). New York: New Left.

Benton Banai, Edward. 1979. *The Mishomis book: The voice of the Ojibway*. St. Paul, MN: Indian Country Press.

Berelson, B. 1959. 'The state of communication research'. *Public Opinion Quarterly* 23 (1): 16.

Berelson, Bernard and Gary A. Steiner. 1964. *Human behavior: An inventory of scientific findings*. New York: Harcourt, Brace & World.

Beresford, P. 2005. 'Social approaches to madness and distress: User perspectives and user knowledges' In J. Tew (Ed.), *Social perspectives in mental health: Developing social models to understand and work with mental distress*, 32–52. London: Jessica Kingsley Publishers.

Bernard, J. (Ed.). 1961. *Teen-age culture*. Special edition of *Annals of the American Academy of Political Social Sciences* v. 338.

Bezanson, Kate. 2010. 'The 'great recession', families and social reproduction'. *Transition* 40 (1): 1–6.

Bibby, Reginald W. 2004. *The future families project: A survey of Canadian hopes and dreams*. Toronto: Vanier Institute of the Family.

Bierly, Margaret. 1985. 'Prejudice toward contemporary outgroups as a generalized attitude'. *Journal of Applied Social Psychology* 15 (2): 189–99.

Bigo, D. 2002. 'Security and immigration: Toward a critique of the governmentality of unease'. *Alternatives* 27: 63–92.

Billings, D., and T. Urban. 1982. 'The socio-medical construction of transsexualism: An interpretation and critique'. *Social Problems* 29: 266–82.

Bindel, Julie. 2004. 'Gender benders, beware'. *Guardian Unlimited* 31 January. http://www.guardian.co.uk/weekend/story/0,3605,1134099,00.html.

Binkley, M. 1994. *Voices from offshore: Narratives of risk and danger in the Nova Scotia deep sea fishery*. St John's, NF: Iser Books.

Bittner, Egon. 1990. *Aspects of police work*. Boston: Northeastern University Press.

Blackstock, C. 2003. 'Same country, same land, 78 countries apart'. Unpublished paper.

Blanchette, K. and S.L. Brown. 2006. *The assessment and treatment of women offenders: An integrative perspective*. New York: John Wiley and Sons.

Bloom, B., B. Owen, and S. Covington. 2004. 'Women offenders and the gendered effects of public policy'. *Review of Policy Research* 21 (1): 31–48.

———. 2006. *A summary of research, practice, and guiding principles for women offenders. The gender-responsive strategies project: Approach and findings*. Washington DC: National Institute of Corrections. http://nicic.org/Library/020418.

Blumer, Herbert, and P.M. Hauser. 1939. *Movies, delinquency and crime*. New York: MacMillan.

Bogardus, Emory S. 1926. 'Social distance in the city'. *Proceedings and Publications of the American Sociological Society* 20: 40–46.

———. 1947. 'Measurement of personal-group relations'. *Sociometry* 10 (4): 306–11.

Boily, Frédéric. 2004. 'Lionel Groulx et l'esprit du libéralisme'. *Recherches sociographiques* 45: 239–57.

Bolin, A. 1994. 'Transcending and transgendering: Male-to-female transsexuals, dichotomy and diversity'. In G. Herdt (Ed.), *Third sex, third gender*. New York: Zone Books.

Booker Loper, A., and L. Levitt. 2011. 'Mental health needs of female offenders'. In T. Fagan and R. Lax (Eds.), *Correctional mental health: From theory to practice*. California: Sage.

Boritch, H. 1992. 'Gender and criminal court outcomes: An historical analysis'. *Criminology* 30: 293–325.

Bouchard, Gérard, and Charles Taylor. 2008. *Building the future. A time for reconciliation*. Report of the Commission de consultation sur les pratiques d'accommodement reliées aux différences culturelles, Gouvernement du Québec.

Bourdieu, P. 1977. *Outline of a theory of practice*. Cambridge, UK: Cambridge University Press.

Bourque, Gilles. 2001. 'Between nations and society'. In Michel Venne (Ed.), *Vive Quebec! New thinking and new approaches to the Quebec nation*. Toronto: Lorimer.

Bradbury, Bettina. 2000. 'Single parenthood in the past: Canadian census categories, 1891–1951, and the "normal" family'. *Historical Methods* 33 (4): 211–17.

———. 2005. The social, economic and cultural origins of contemporary families. In M. Baker (Ed.), *Families: Changing trends in Canada*, 5th edn. Toronto: McGraw-Hill Ryerson.

Brake, Mike. 1980. *The sociology of youth cultures and youth subcultures*. New York: Routledge and Kegan Paul.

Brandon, William. 1986. *New worlds for old: Reports from the New World and their effect on the development of social thought in Europe*. Athens, OH: Ohio University Press.

Bray, Alan. 1982. 'Homosexuality and the signs of male friendship in Elizabethan England'. *History Workshop* 29: 1–19.

Bresson, M. 2003. 'Le lien entre santé mentale et précarité sociale: Une fausse evidence'. *Cahiers Internationaux de Sociolgie* 115: 311–26.

Brinded, P. M., A.I. Simpson, T.M. Laidlaw, N.A. Fairley, and F. Malcolm. 2001. 'Prevalence of psychiatric disorders in New Zealand prisons: A national study'. *Australian and New Zealand Journal of Psychiatry* 35 (2): 166–73.

Britton, Dana. 1990. 'Developmental origins of antihomosexual prejudice in heterosexual men and women'. *Clinical Social Work Journal* 19: 163–75.

Brodie, Janine. 1997. 'Meso-discourses, state forms and the gendering of liberal-democratic citizenship'. *Citizenship Studies* 1 (2): 223–42.

———. 2002. 'An elusive search for community: Globalization and the Canadian national identities'. *Review of Constitutional Studies* 7 (1/2): 155–78.

Brown, George, and Ron Maguire. 1979. *Indian treaties in historical perspective*. Ottawa: Department of Indian Affairs.

Brown, Lyn Mikel. 1998. *Raising their voices: The politics of girls' anger*. Cambridge, MA: Harvard University Press.

Brown, M. 2006. 'Gender, ethnicity, and offending over the life course: Women's pathways to prison in the Aloha State'. *Critical Criminology* 14: 137–58.

Brumberg, Joan Jacobs. 1997. *The body project: An intimate history of American girls*. New York: Vintage.

Buchanan, R. 2000. '1-800 New Brunswick: Economic development strategies, firm restructuring and the local production of 'global' services'. In. J. Jenson and B.d.S. Santos (Eds.), *Globalizing institutions, Case studies in regulation and innovation*, 53–80. Aldershot, UK: Ashgate.

Bullard, D. 1996. *Unequal protection: Environmental justice and communities of color*. San Francisco: Sierra Club Books.

Burbidge, S. 2005. 'The governance deficit: Reflections on the future of public and private policing in Canada'. *Canadian Journal of Criminology and Criminal Justice* 47 (1): 64–85.

Burch, Sarah. 2010. 'Transforming barriers into enablers of action on climate change: Insights from three municipal case studies in British Columbia, Canada'. *Global Environmental Change* 20 (2): 287–97

Burchell, G., C. Gordon, and P. Miller (Eds.). 1991. *The Foucault effect*. Chicago: University of Chicago Press.

Burke, P. 1996. *Gender shock: Exploding the myths of male and female*. New York: Anchor.

Burrell, Gordon, Robert Young, and Richard Price. 1975. *Indian treaties and the law: An interpretation for laymen*. Edmonton: Indian Association of Alberta.

Butler, Judith. 1990. *Gender trouble: Feminism and the subversion of identity*. London: Routledge.

Burstow, B. 2004. 'Progressive psychotherapists and the psychiatric survivor movement'. *Journal of Humanistic Psychology* 44 (2): 141–54.

———, and D. Weitz (Eds.). 1988. *Shrink resistant: The struggle against psychiatry in Canada*. Vancouver: New Star Books, 1988.

Butler, Judith. 1990. *Gender Trouble: Feminism and the subversion of identity*. New York: Routledge.

———. 1993b. 'Critically queer'. *GLQ* 1 (1): 17–32.

———. 2004. *Undoing gender*. New York and London: Routledge.

Butler, P.M., and R. Smith. 2003. 'Environmental sociology and the explanation of environmental reform'. *Organization and Environment* 16 (3): 306–44.

Byrne, Bridget. 2003. 'Reciting the self: Narrative representations of the self in qualitative interviews'. *Feminist Theory* 4 (1): 29–49.

Cairns, Alan C. 2000. *Citizens plus: Aboriginal peoples and the Canadian state*. Vancouver: University of British Columbia Press.

Cajete, Gregory. 1999. *Native science: Natural laws of interdependence*. Santa Fe, NM: Clear Light Publishers.

Calverley, D. 2010. 'Adult correctional services in Canada 2008/2009'. 2010 component of Statistics Canada catalogue no. 85-002-X. *Juristat* 30 (3) Fall. Ottawa: Statistics Canada.

Campbell, Colin, Charlie Gillis, and Kate Lunau. 2008. 'Shouldn't we be fighting back? What parents, regulators and internet service providers are doing to manage online porn'. *Maclean's,* June 18. http://www.macleans.ca/culture/lifestyle/article.jsp?content=20080618_18381_18381

Camus, Albert. 1991 [1947]. *The plague*. New York: Vintage.

Canada. 1982. *Canadian Charter of Rights and Freedoms*. Ottawa: Government Printer.

Canada, Citizenship and Immigration Canada. 2008a. 'Applying for permanent residence—Business class applicants: Investors, entrepreneurs, self-employed persons (IMM 4000)'. http://www.cic.gc.ca/english/information/applications/guides/4000E5.asp.

———. 2008b. 'Applying for permanent residence—Business class applicants: Investors, entrepreneurs, self-employed persons (IMM 4000): Selection criteria'. http://www.cic.gc.ca/english/information/applications/guides/4000E4.asp.

———. 2009a. 'Facts and figures: Immigration overview: Permanent and temporary residents'. http://www.cic.gc.ca/english/pdf/research-stats/facts2008.pdf.

———. 2009b. 'Facts and figures: Immigration overview: Permanent and temporary Residents— Permanent residents by category, 2005–2009'. http://www.cic.gc.ca/english/resources/statistics/facts2009/permanent/01.asp.

———. 2009c. 'Application for permanent residence: Federal skilled worker class

(IMM 7000)'. http://www.cic.gc.ca/english//
information/applications/guides/EG72.
asp#factors.

———. 2010a. 'Canada—Permanent residents
by category, 2006–2010'. http://www.cic.
gc.ca/english/resources/statistics/facts2010-
summary/01.asp.

———. 2010b. 'The citizenship test'. http: //
www.cic.gc.ca/english/citizenship/cit-test.
asp.

———. 2010c. 'Update: priority processing
measures in Haiti (May 25, 2010)'. http: //
www.cic.gc.ca/english/department/media/
notices/notice-haiti42.asp

Canadian Broadcasting Corporation (CBC).
2005. *Running off track: The Ben Johnson
story.* Video clip. http: //archives.cbc.ca/
IDD-1-41-1392/sports/ben_johnson.

———. 2009. 'Top gun—Dr. David Walsh,
media in the family'. CBC News: *the fifth
estate.* Originally aired 6 March 2009. http: //
www.youtube.com/watch?v=29Ki2IrG0b0.

Canadian Centre for Policy Alternatives. 2011.
'Canada's income gap, the richest 20%
vs. the poorest 20%'. 18 July. http://www.
policyalternatives.ca/newsroom/updates/
you-oughta-know-canadas-income-gap-
richest-20-vs-poorest-20.

Canadian Centre on Substance Abuse. 2006.
Fact sheet: Self-harm among Criminalized
women. http://www.ccsa.ca/2006%20
CCSA%20Documents/ccsa-011338-2006-e.
pdf.

Canadian Council on Social Development.
2003a. *Campaign 2000: Report card on
child poverty in Canada.* Ottawa: Canadian
Council on Social Development.

———. 2003b. *Aboriginal children in poverty
in urban communities.* http://www.ccsd.ca/
pr/2003/aboriginal.htm.

———. 2004. *Percentage change in welfare
benefits in Canada.* http://www.ccsd.ca/
factsheets/fs_96wel.htm

———. 2008. *Family security in insecure times:
The case for a poverty reduction strategy
for Canada: 2008 report card on child and
family poverty in Canada.* Ottawa: Canadian
Council on Social Development.

———. 2010. *Campaign 2000: Report card on
child poverty in Canada.* Ottawa: Canadian
Council on Social Development.

Canadian Human Rights Commission (CHRC).
2003. *Protecting their rights: A systematic
review of human rights in correctional
services for federally sentenced women.* http://
www.chrc-ccdp.ca/legislation_policies/con-
sultation_report-eng.aspx.

Canadian Press. 2007. Nuclear family still
thrives in some parts of Canada. 12
September. http://www.ctv.ca/CTVNews/
Canada/20070912/nuclear_family_070912/.

———. 2008. Auditor: Foster care failing Native
children. 6 May. http://www.thestar.com/
News/Canada/article/422012.

———. 2010. 'Bill targets 'ghost' immigration
consultants'. *Toronto Star* (online edition) 8
June: http://www.thestar.com/news/canada/
article/820462--bill-targets-ghost-immigra-
tion-consultants.

Cancian, Francesca M. 1986. 'The feminization
of love'. *Signs* 11: 692–709.

Caplan, P.J. 1995. *They say you're crazy: How
the world's most powerful psychiatrists
decide who's normal.* Reading, MA.:
Addison-Wesley.

Carbone-Lopez, Kristin, and Candace
Kruttschnitt. 2010. 'Risky relationships?
Assortative mating and women's experiences
of intimate partner violence'. *Crime and
Delinquency* 56 (3): 358–84.

Cardinal, Harold, and Walter Hildebrandt. 2000.
*Treaty elders of Saskatchewan: Our dream
is that our peoples will one day be clearly
recognized as nations.* Calgary: University of
Calgary Press.

Carlen, P. 2002. 'New discourses of justification
and reform for women's imprisonment
in England'. In P. Carlen (Ed.), *Women
and punishment: A struggle for justice.*
Cullompton, UK: Willan.

Carr, Nicholas. 2008. 'Is Google making us
stupid?' *The Atlantic.* http://www.theatlantic.
com/doc/200807/google

Carrington, P., and J. Schulenberg. 2004.
'Introduction: The Youth Criminal Justice
Act: A new era in Canadian juvenile justice?'
*Canadian Journal of Criminology and
Criminal Justice* 46 (2): 219–23.

Carter, Sarah. 1990. *Lost harvests: Prairie Indian
reserve farmers and government policy.*
Montreal and Kingston: McGill-Queen's
University Press.

Castles, S., and M. Miller. 1998. *The age of migration.* 2nd edn. New York: Guilford.

Catton, William R., Jr., and Riley E. Dunlap.
1980. 'A new ecological paradigm for

post-exuberant sociology'. *American Behavioral Scientist* 24 (1): 15–47.

Celinska, K., and J. Siegel. 2010. 'Mothers in trouble: Coping with actual or pending separation from children due to incarceration'. *The Prison Journal* 1 (90): 447–74.

Chamberlin, J. 1990. 'The ex-patients movement: Where we've been and where we're going'. *The Journal of Mind and Behavior* 11 (3–4): 323–36.

Charland, Maurice.1986. 'Technological nationalism.' *Canadian Journal of Political and Social Theory* 10 (1): 196–220.

Chase, C. 1998. 'Affronting reason'. In D. Atkins (Ed.), *Looking queer*, 205–20. New York: Harrington Park Press.

Chomsky, Noam. 2006. *Language and mind*. New York: Cambridge University Press.

Chui, T., K. Tran, and H. Maheux. 2007. 'Immigration in Canada: A portrait of the foreign-born population, 2006 census'. Statistics Canada, catalogue no. 97-557-XIE.

Ciara and Missy Elliot. 2004. '1, 2 Step'. *Goodies* (music CD). LaFace and Sho'nuff Records.

Cicourel, A.V. 1967. 'Fertility, family planning and the social organization of family life: Some methodological issues'. *Journal of Social Issues* 23 (4): 57–81.

———. 1968. *The social organization of juvenile justice*. New York: John Wiley and Sons.

———. 1973. *Theory and method in a study of Argentine fertility*. New York: John Wiley and Sons.

———, and J.I. Kitsuse. 1963. *The educational decision-makers*. Indianapolis, IN: Bobbs-Merrill.

Clanton, Gordon. 1989. 'Jealousy in American culture, 1945–1985'. In David D. Franks and E. Doyle McCarthy (Eds.), *The sociology of the emotions: Original essays and research papers*, 157–66. Greenwich, CT: : Press.

Clark, C. 1999. 'Failed business immigrants free to stay in Canada: 40% don't meet their obligations'. *National Post*, October 11: A1.

Clark, T. 1997. *Art and propaganda in the twentieth century*. New York: Calmann and King.

Clark, Warren. 2007. 'Delayed transitions of young adults'. *Canadian Social Trends* 84 (Winter): 14–22.

Clio Collective. 1987. *Quebec women: A history*. Toronto: Women's Press.

Coates, Ken. 1999. 'The 'gentle' occupation: The settlement of Canada and the dispossession of the First Nations'. In Paul Havemann (Ed.), *Indigenous peoples rights in Australia, Canada and New Zealand*, 141–61. Auckland, NZ: Oxford University Press.

Cockerham, W.C. 2003. *Sociology of mental disorder*. New Jersey: Prentice Hall.

Cohen, O. 2005. 'How do we recover? An analysis of psychiatric survivor oral histories'. *Journal of Humanistic Psychology* 45 (3): 333–54.

Cohen, Robin. 1996. 'Diasporas and the nation-state: From victims to challengers'. *International Affairs* 72 (3): 507–20.

Cohen, S. 1985. *Visions of social control: Crime, punishment and classification*. Cambridge, UK: Polity Press.

Colapinto, J. 2000. *As nature made him: The boy who was raised as a girl*. Toronto: HarperCollins.

Coleman, James S. 1961. *Adolescent society: The social life of the teenager and its impact on education*. New York: Free Press of Glencoe.

Collins, Patricia Hill. 1990. *Black feminist thought: Knowledge, consciousness, and the politics of empowerment*. New York: Routledge.

———. 2000. *Black feminist thought: Knowledge, consciousness, and the politics of empowerment*, revised 10th anniversary edn. New York: Routledge.

———. 2005. *Black sexual politics. African Americans, gender and the new racism*. New York: Routledge.

Comack, E. 1996. *Women in trouble*. Halifax: Fernwood.

Comte, Auguste. 1975. *Auguste Comte and positivism: The essential writings*. Gertrude Lenzer, Ed. Chicago: University of Chicago Press.

Connell, R.W. 1987. *Gender and power*. Stanford, CA: Stanford University Press.

———. 2004. 'Encounters with structure'. *International Journal of Qualitative Studies in Education* 17 (1): 11–28.

Connolly, P. 1989. 'Hearings on steroids in amateur and professional sports: The medical and social costs of steroid abuse'. Testimony before the United States Senate Committee on the Judiciary. 101st Congress, 1st session, 3 April, 9 May.

Conrad, P. 2007. *The medicalization of society: On the transformation of human conditions into treatable disorders*. Baltimore: Johns Hopkins University Press.

Constatine, M.G. 2006. 'Institutional racism against African Americans: Physical and mental health implications'. In M.G. Constatine and D.W. Sue (Eds.), *Addressing racism: Facilitating cultural competence in mental health and educational* settings, 33–41. Hoboken, NJ: John Wiley and Sons.

Cook, J.A., and J.A. Jonikas. 2002. 'Self-determination among mental health consumers/survivors: Using lessons from the past to guide the future'. *Journal of Disability Policy Studies* 13 (2): 88–96.

Coontz, Stephanie. 2010. 'The evolution of American families'. In Barbara J. Risman (Ed.) *Families as they really are*. New York: W.W. Norton and Company: 30–48.

Cormier, Jeffrey, and Philippe Couton. 2004. 'Civil society, mobilization and communal violence: Quebec and Ireland, 1890–1920'. *Sociological Quarterly* 45 (3): 487–508.

Cornell, Drucilla. 2005. 'Adoption and its progeny'. In S. Haslanger and C. Witt (Eds.), *Adoption matters: Philosophical and feminist essays*. Ithaca, NY: Cornell University Press.

Cornell, Stephen E. 1998. *The return of the Native: American Indian political resurgence*. New York: Oxford University Press.

———, and Douglas Hartmann. 1998. *Ethnicity and race*. Thousand Oaks, CA: Pine Forge Press.

Correctional Service of Canada. 1990. *Creating choices: The report of the Task Force on Federally Sentenced Women*. Ottawa: Correctional Service of Canada.

———. 1998. *Women convicted of homicide serving a federal sentence*. Ottawa: Correctional Service of Canada. http://www.csc_scc.gc.ca/text/prgrm/fsw/homicide/toc_e.shtml.

———. 2007. Statistical Overview 2007 CSC—Women Offender Sector. Ottawa: Correctional Service of Canada. http://www.csc-scc.gc.ca/text/prgrm/fsw/wos33/docs/wos33_stat-ovrvw_2007-eng.pdf.

———. 2010 *Woman offenders: Statistical overview, 2009–2010*. Ottawa: Correctional Service of Canada, Women Offender Sector. http://www.csc-scc.gc.ca/text/prgrm/fsw/wos_Stat_09_10/wos_stat_09_10-eng.pdf.

Corrigan, Philip, and Derek Sayer. 1985. *The great arch: English state formation as cultural revolution*. Oxford, UK: Basil Blackwell.

Cossman, Brenda, Shannon Bell, Lise Gotell, and Becki Ross. 1997. *Bad attitudes on trial*.

Toronto: University of Toronto Press.

Coubertin, Pierre de. 2000. *Olympism: Selected writings*. Norbert Muller, Ed.. Lausanne, Switzerland: International Olympic Committee.

Couldry, Nick. 2009. 'Teaching us to fake it. The ritualized norms of television's "reality" games'. In Susan Murray and Laurie Oullette (Eds.), *Reality TV: Remaking television culture*, 2nd edn, 82–99. New York: New York University Press.

Covell, K., and B. Howe. 2001. *The challenge of children's rights for Canada*. Waterloo, ON: Wilfred Laurier University Press.

Covington, S., and B. Bloom. 2006. 'Gender responsive treatment and services in correctional settings'. *Women and Therapy* 29 (3–4): 9.

Creese, G., and R. Dowling. 2001. 'Gendering immigration: The experience of women in Sydney and Vancouver'. *Progress in Planning* 55 (3): 153–62.

Cronon, William. 1998. 'The trouble with wilderness, or getting back to the wrong nature'. In Michael P. Nelson and J. Baird Callicott (Eds.), *The Great New Wilderness Debate*. Athens, Georgia: University of Georgia Press.

Crossley, M. L., and N. Crossley. 2001. 'Patient voices, social movements and the habitus: How psychiatric survivors "speak out"'. *Social Science and Medicine* 52 (10): 1477–89.

CUPE Ontario. 2008. 'Creator of Quebec child care system to be honoured on Child Care Worker Appreciation Day'. 20 October. http://www.cupe.on.ca/doc.php?document_id=572&lang=en

Currie, Dawn H., Deirdre Kelly, and Shauna Pomerantz. 2009. '*Girl power': Girls reinventing girlhood*. New York: Peter Lang.

Curry, Bill, and Gloria Galloway. 2008. 'We are sorry'. *Globe and Mail,* 12 June. http://www.theglobeandmail.com/news/national/article690958.ece.

Curtis, B. 2001. *The politics of population*. Toronto: University of Toronto Press.

Dahrendorf, Ralph. 1973. *Homo sociologicus*. London: Routledge and Kegan Paul.

Dain, N. 1989. 'Critics and dissenters: Reflections on "anti-psychiatry" in the United States'. *Journal of the History of the Behavioral Sciences* 25 (1): 3–25.

Dalby, Simon. 2003. 'Green Geopolitics.' In John Agnew, Katharyne Mitchell, and Gearóid Ó Tuathail (Eds.), *A companion guide to political geography*. Oxford: Blackwell: 440–54.

Daly, Kathleen. 1992. Women's pathways to felony court: Feminist theories of law breaking and problems of representation. *Review of Law and Women's Studies* 2: 11–52.

Dant, Tim. 2003. *Critical social theory*. London: Sage.

Das Gupta, Tania. 2000. 'Families of native people, immigrants, and people of colour.' In Nancy Mandell and Ann Duffy (Eds.), *Canadian families: diversity, conflict and change*, 146–87. Toronto: Harcourt Brace.

Daston, L., and K. Park. 1998. *Wonders and the order of nature*. New York: Zone Books.

Davidson, Debra J. and Norah MacKendrick. 2004. 'All dressed up with nowhere to go: The discourse of ecological modernization in Alberta'. *Canadian Review of Sociology and Anthropology* 41 (1): 47–65.

Davis, Angela. 2001. 'Racism, birth control and reproductive rights'. In A. Davis (Ed.), *Women, race and class*, 202–21. London: Women's Press.

Davis, S. 2006. *Community mental health in Canada: Theory, policy, and practice*. Vancouver: University of British Columbia Press.

Debbané, Anne-Marie, and Roger Keil. 2004. 'Multiple disconnections: Environmental justice and urban water in Canada and South Africa'. *Space and Polity* 8 (2): 209–25.

DeHart, D. 2008. 'Pathways to prison: Impact of victimization in the lives of incarcerated women'. *Violence Against Women* 14 (12): 1362–81.

Deleuze, Gilles. 1988. *Michel Foucault*. (Paul Bové, trans.). Minneapolis, MN: University of Minnesota Press.

———. 1993. *The fold: Leibniz and the baroque*. (Tom Conley, trans.). Minneapolis, MN: University of Minnesota Press.

Dell, Colleen Anne, C. Fillmore, and J. Kilty. 2009. 'Looking back 10 years after the Arbour inquiry: Ideology, policy, Practice and the federal female prisoner'. *Prison Journal* 89: 286–308.

Della-Mattia, E. 2004. 'Martin fingers Liberals for child benefit clawback'. *Sault Star* 22 November: A4.

Demerson, V. 2004. *Incorrigible*. Waterloo: Wilfred Laurier University Press.

Denov, M. 2004. 'Children's rights, juvenile justice, and the UN Convention on the Child: Implications for Canada'. In K. Campbell (Ed.), *Understanding youth justice in Canada*. Toronto: Pearson.

Derrida, Jacques. 1976. *Of grammatology*. Baltimore, MD: Johns Hopkins University Press.

de Vries, Brian. 2010. '*Friendship and family: The company we keep*'. *Transition: Creating Families* 40 (4). http://www.vifamily.ca/media/node/765/attachments/VIF_trans_winter2010E_121010-3.pdf.

Dewing, Michael. 2010. *Social media 2. Who uses them?* Library of Parliament background paper. Ottawa: Library of Parliament.

Dickinson, John A., and Brian Young. 2000. *A short history of Quebec*. Montreal and Kingston: McGill-Queen's University Press.

Diners, Gail. 2011. *Gender, race and class in media: A critical reader*. Thousand Oaks, CA: Sage.

Doane, Mary Anne. 1982. 'Film and the masquerade: Theorizing the female spectator'. *Screen* 23 (3/4): 81.

Donzelot, J. 1984. *L'invention du social*. Paris: Fayard.

Doob, A., and C. Cesaroni. 2004. *Responding to youth crime in Canada*. Toronto: University of Toronto Press.

Doran, N.. 1994. 'Risky business: Codifying embodied experience in the Manchester Unity of Oddfellows'. *Journal of Historical Sociology* 7 (2), 131–54.

———. 1996. 'From embodied 'health' to official 'accidents': Class, codification and the early British factory legislation, 1831–1844'. *Social and Legal Studies* 5 (4): 523–46.

———. 2001. 'Governmentality and class: Some preliminary remarks on cultural incorporation'. Paper presented at the 'Governmentality and Freedom for Whom and for What?' session of the Canadian Sociological Association annual conference, Quebec City, 30 May.

———. 2003. 'Resisting Insurance technology: Some lessons from mid-nineteenth-century England'. Paper presented at the 'Vital Politics: Health, Politics and Bioeconomics into the 21st century' conference, London School of Economics, London, UK, September 5–7.

———. 2004. 'Re-writing the social, re-writing sociology: Donzelot, genealogy and working class bodies'. *Canadian Journal of Sociology* 29 (3): 333–57.

———. 2008. 'Decoding "encoding" in a cultural studies' classic: Moral panics, media portrayals and Marxist presuppositions'. *Theoretical Criminology* 12 (2): 191–221.

Doucet, Andrea. 2004. 'Fathers and the responsibility for children: A puzzle and a tension'. *Atlantis: A Women's Studies Journal: Special Issue on the Politics of Unpaid Work* 28 (2): 103–14.

———. 2006a. *Do men mother?* Toronto: University of Toronto Press.

———. 2006b. '"Estrogen-filled worlds": Fathers as primary caregivers and embodiment'. *Sociological Review* 23 (4): 695–715.

———. 2011. 'What impedes fathers' participation in care work? Theorizing the community as an institutional arena'. In C. Krull and J. Sempruch (Eds.), *A life in balance? Reopening the family–work debate*, 115–29. Vancouver: University of British Columbia Press.

Douglas, Jack. 1967. *The social meaning of suicide*. Princeton, NJ: Princeton University Press.

———. 1970a. *Freedom & tyranny: Social problems in a technological society*. New York: Knopf.

———. 1970b. 'Understanding everyday life'. In J. Douglas (Ed.), *Understanding everyday life: Toward the reconstruction of sociological knowledge*, 3–44. Chicago: Aldine.

———, and John Johnson. 1977. *Existential sociology*. New York: Cambridge University Press.

Douglas, M. 2002. 'Neediest children feel sting'. *Kamloops Daily News* 22 April: A1.

Dover, K.J. 1978. *Greek homosexuality*. New York: Vintage.

Downes, Daniel. 2011. 'No contest: *American Idol* and the culture of competition'. In Carlen Lavigne and Heather Marcovitch (Eds.), *American remakes of British television. Transformations and mistranslations*. Lanham, MD: Lexington Books: 17–34.

Downes, David., P. Rock, and C. McCormick. 2009. *Understanding deviance: Canadian edition*. Toronto: Oxford University Press.

Dreby, Joanna. 2006. 'Honor and virtue: Mexican parenting in the transnational context'. *Gender and Society* 20 (1): 32–59.

Dubin, C. 1990. *Commission of inquiry into the use of drugs and banned practices intended to increase athletic performance*. Ottawa: Canadian Government Publishing Centre.

Duffy, Ann, and Norene Pupo. 2011. 'Employment in the new economy and the impact on Canadian families'. In C. Krull and J. Sempruch (Eds.), *Demystifying the family/work contradiction*, 98–114. Vancouver: University of British Columbia Press.

Durkheim, Émile. 1964 [1895]. *The rules of sociological method*. George G. Catlin, Ed. (Sarah A. Solovay and John H. Mueller, trans.). New York: Free Press.

———. 1952 [1897]. *Suicide: A study in sociology*. London: Routledge and Kegan Paul.

———. 1989 [1893]. *The division of labour in society*. (W.D. Halls, trans.). London: Macmillan.

Ehrenreich, Barbara. 2001. *Nickel and dimed: On (not) getting by in America*. New York: Henry Holt and Company.

Eichler, Margrit. 2000. 'In/equity and un/sustainability: Exploring intersections'. *Environments* 28 (2): 1–9.

Engels, Friedrich. 1972. 'The origin of the family, private property, and the state'. In Robert C. Tucker (Ed.), *The Marx-Engels reader*, 2nd edn. New York: Norton: 734–59.

Erikson, E.H. 1968. *Identity: Youth and crisis*. New York: Norton.

Etzioni, Amitai. 1996. 'The responsive community: A communitarian perspective'. Presidential address, American Sociological Association, 20 August 1995. *American Sociological Review*, February 1996: 1–11.

Everett, B. 1994. 'Something is happening: The contemporary consumer and psychiatric survivor movement in historical context'. *The Journal of Mind and Behavior* 15 (1/2): 55–70.

Everndon, Neil. 1992. *The social creation of nature*. Baltimore: Johns Hopkins University Press.

Faludi, Susan. 1999. *Stiffed*. New York: Morrow.

Fausto-Sterling, A. 2000. *Sexing the body: Gender politics and the construction of sexuality*. New York: Basic Books.

Featherstone, Mike. 1988. 'In pursuit of the postmodern: An introduction'. *Theory, Culture and Society* 5 (2/3): 195–216.

Feld, B. 2000. 'Juveniles' waiver of legal rights: Confessions, Miranda, and the right to counsel'. In T. Grisso and R.G. Schwartz (Eds.), *Youth on trial: A developmental perspective on juvenile justice*. Chicago: University of Chicago Press.

Fillmore, C., C.A. Dell, and The Elizabeth Fry Society of Manitoba. 2000. *Prairie women, violence and self-harm*. http://www.pwhce.ca/pdf/self-harm.pdf.

Finnie, R. 2000. *Who moves? A panel logit model analysis of inter-provincial migration in Canada*. Ottawa: Business and Labour Market Analytical Division, Statistics Canada.

Fiske, John. 2010. *Understanding popular culture*, 2nd edn. New York: Routledge.

Fogg-Davis, Hawley. 2005. 'Racial randomization: Imagining non-discrimination in adoption'. In Sally Haslanger and Charlotte Witt (Eds.), *Adoption matters: philosophical and feminist essays*, 247–64. Ithaca, NY: Cornell University Press.

Fontaine, Louise. 1993. *Un labyrinthe carré comme un cercle; Enquête sur le ministère des communautés culturelles et de l'immigration et sur ses acteurs réels et imaginés*. Montréal: L'Étincelle.

Food Banks Canada. 2010. *Hunger Count 2010: A comprehensive report on hunger and food bank use in Canada, and recommendations for change*. http://www.foodbankscanada.ca/documents/HungerCount2010_web.pdf.

Ford, James D., Tristan Pearce, Justin Gilligan, Barry Smit, and Jill Oakes. 2008. 'Climate change and hazards associated with ice use in Northern Canada'. *Arctic, Antarctic, and Alpine Research* 40 (4): 647–59.

Foster, Jennifer, and L. Anders Sandberg. 2005. 'Friends or foe? Invasive species and public green space in Toronto'. *The Geographical Review* 94 (2): 178–98.

Foster, John Bellamy. 1994. *The vulnerable planet: A short economic history of the environment*. New York: Monthly Review Press.

Foucault, Michel. 1977. *Discipline and punish: The birth of the prison*. (A. Sheridan, trans.) New York: Pantheon.

———. 1978. *The History of Sexuality, Vol. 1: An Introduction*. New York: Random House.

———. 1980a. *Power/knowledge: Selected interviews and other writings, 1972–1977*. New York: Pantheon.

———. 1982. 'The subject and power'. In Hubert Dreyfus and Paul Rabinow, *Michel Foucault: Beyond structuralism and hermeneutics*. Chicago: University of Chicago Press.

———. 1988 [1964]. *Madness and civilization: A history of insanity in the Age of Reason*. R. Howard, Trans. New York: Vintage Books.

Francis, C. 1990. *Speed trap: Inside the biggest scandal in Olympic history*. Toronto: Lester and Orpen Dennys.

Francis, D., and S. Hester. 2004. *An invitation to ethnomethodology*. London: Sage.

Franke, W.F., and B. Berendonk. 1997. 'Hormonal doping and androgenization of athletes: A secret program of the German Democratic Republic government'. *Clinical Chemistry* 43 (7): 1262–79.

Frese, F. 1997. 'The mental health service consumer's perspective on mandatory treatment'. *New Directions for Mental Health Services* 75: 17–26.

Freud, Sigmund. 1966 [1913]. 'The dream work'. In *Introductory lectures on psychoanalysis* (James Strachey, trans.). New York: Norton.

Frideres, James S. 1974. *Canada's Indians: Contemporary conflicts*. Scarborough, ON: Prentice Hall.

———. 1998. *Aboriginal peoples in Canada: Contemporary conflicts*. Scarborough, ON: Prentice Hall Allyn and Bacon Canada.

Friedan, Betty. 1963. *The feminine mystique*. New York: Dell.

Frisby, David. 1992. *Simmel and since: Essays on Georg Simmel's social theory*. London: Routledge.

Fudge, Judy. 2002. 'From segregation to privatization: Equality, the law and women public servants 1908–2001'. In Brenda Cossman and Judy Fudge (Eds.), *Privatization, law and the challenge to feminism*, 86–127. Toronto: University of Toronto Press.

Gaetz, Stephen, and Bill O'Grady. 2006. *The missing link: Discharge planning, incarceration and homelessness*. Ontario: JHS.

Galloway, D. 2000. 'The dilemmas of Canadian citizenship law'. In T.A. Aleinikoff and D. Klusmeyer (Eds.), *From migrants to citizens: Membership in a changing world*. Washington: Carnegie Endowment for International Peace.

Garfinkel, Harold, in collaboration with R. Stoller. 1967. *Studies in ethnomethodology*. Cambridge, UK: Polity Press.

————. 1974. 'The origins of the term 'ethnomethodology''. In R. Turner (Ed.), *Ethnomethodology*, 15–18. Harmondsworth, UK: Penguin.

————. 1986. *Ethnomethodological studies of work*. New York: Routledge and Kegan Paul.

Gartner, R., C. Webster, and A. Doob. 2009. 'Trends in women's imprisonment in Canada'. *Canadian Journal of Criminology and Criminal Justice* (April): 170–198.

Gee, James Paul. 2000–1. 'Identity as an analytic lens for research in education'. *Review of Research in Education* 25: 99–125.

————. 2002. *An introduction to discourse analysis: Theory and methods*. London: Routledge.

Gellner, Ernest. 1997. *Nationalism*. New York: New York University Press.

Gelsthorpe, L., and Morris, A. 2002. 'Women's imprisonment in England and Wales: A penal paradox'. *Criminology and Criminal Justice* 2 (3): 277–30.

George, Nelson. 1998. *Hip hop America*. New York: Penguin.

Giddens, Anthony. 1984. *The constitution of society*. Berkeley: University of California Press.

Gilbert, D. 1980. *The miracle machine*. New York: Coward, McCann and Geoghegan.

Gillis, John R. 1988. 'From ritual to romance: Toward an alternative history of love'. In Peter N. Stearns, and Carol Zisowitz Stearns (Eds.), *Emotion and social change: Toward a new psychohistory*, 87–121. New York: Holmes and Meier.

Gitlin, Todd. 2002. *Media unlimited*. New York: Owl.

Gleeson, Kate, and Hannah Frith. 2004. 'Pretty in pink: Young women presenting mature sexual identities'. In Anita Harris (Ed.), *All about the girl: Culture, power and identity*. New York: Routledge.

Global Forest Watch. 2006. *Canada's large intact forest landscapes, updated analysis: Executive summary*. http://www.globalforestwatch.org/english/canada/pdf/Canada_LIFL_2006_Exec_Summary.pdf.

Goffman, Erving. 1961. *Asylums*. London: Penguin.

————. 1971. *The presentation of self in everyday life*. Harmondsworth, UK: Penguin.

————. 1976. *Gender advertisements*. London: Macmillan.

Goldman, B. 1984. *Death in the locker room: Steroids and sports*. South Bend, IN: Icarus.

Goldthorpe, J. 1968. *The affluent worker: Political attitudes and behaviour*. Cambridge, UK: Cambridge University Press.

————. 1969. *The affluent worker in the class structure*. Cambridge, UK: Cambridge University Press.

————, D. Lockwood, F. Bechhofer, and J. Platt. 1968. *The affluent worker: Industrial attitudes and behaviour*. Cambridge, UK: Cambridge University Press.

Gouldner, A. 1970. *The coming crisis of Western sociology*. New York: Basic Books.

Gramsci, Antonio. 1992. *Prison notebooks*. Joseph A. Buttigieg, Ed. New York: Columbia University Press.

Grandin, Temple. 1995. *Thinking in pictures: And other reports from my life with autism*. New York: Doubleday.

————, and Catherine Johnson. 2004. *Animals in translation: Using the mysteries of autism to decode animal behavior*. Riverside, NJ: Scribner.

————, and Margaret M. Scariano. 1986. *Emergence, labeled autistic*. Novato, CA: Arena Press.

Green, M., and B. Oakley. 2001. 'Elite sport development systems and playing to win: Uniformity and diversity in international approaches'. *Leisure Studies* 20: 247–67.

Greenberg, David. 1988. *The construction of homosexuality*. Chicago: University of Chicago Press.

Gubrium, Jaber F., and James A. Holstein. 1998. 'Narrative practice and the coherence of personal stories'. *Sociological Quarterly* 39: 163–87.

Guttmann, A. 2002. *The Olympics: A history of the modern Games*. Urbana and Chicago: University of Illinois Press.

Habermas, Jürgen. 1971. *Towards a rational society: Student protest, science and politics*. Boston: Beacon.

————. 1975. *Legitimation crisis*. (T. McCarthy, trans.). Boston: Beacon.

Hacking, I. 1982. 'Biopower and the avalanche of printed numbers'. *Humanities in Society* 5 (1): 279–95.

Haggerty, K. 2001. *Making crime count*. Toronto: University of Toronto Press.

Hall, Stuart. 1959. 'Deviance, politics and the media'. In P. Rock and M. McIntosh (Eds.), *Deviance and social control*. London: Tavistock.

———, and Paddy Whannel. 1998. 'The young audience'. In John Storey (Ed.), *Cultural theory and popular culture*, 2nd edn. Hemel Hampstead, UK: Prentice Hall.

Halperin, David. 1990. *One hundred years of homosexuality*. New York: Routledge.

———. 1995. *Saint Foucault*. New York: Oxford University Press.

———. 2002. *How to do the history of homosexuality*. Chicago: University of Chicago Press.

Haluza-Delay, Randolph. 2007. 'Environmental justice in Canada'. *Local Environment* 12 (6): 557–63.

Hamilton, Lawrence C., and Melissa J. Butler. 2001. 'Outport adaptations: Social indicators through Newfoundland's cod crisis'. *Human Ecology Review* 8 (2): 1–11.

Hamilton, R. 2004. *Gendering the vertical mosaic: Feminist perspectives on Canadian society*. 2nd edn. Toronto: Pearson.

Hannah-Moffat, K. 2009. 'Gridlock or mutability: Reconsidering "gender" and risk assessment'. *Criminology and Public Policy* 8 (1): 221–29.

———, and M. Shaw. 2001. *Taking risks: Incorporating gender and culture into the assessment and classification of federally sentenced women in Canada*. Ottawa: Status of Women Canada.

Hannigan, John. 2006. *Environmental Sociology: A Social Constructionist Perspective*, 2nd edn. London: Taylor & Francis.

Hansen, Karen V. 2005. *Not-so-nuclear families: Class, gender and networks of care*. New Brunswick, NJ: Rutgers University Press.

Haraway, Donna. 1988. 'Situated knowledges: The science question in feminism and the privilege of partial perspective'. *Feminist Studies* 14 (3): 575–99.

Hardin, Herschel. 1985. *Closed circuits. The sell-out of Canadian television*. Toronto: Douglas & McIntyre.

Harding, S. 1986. *The science question in feminism*. Ithaca, NY: Cornell University Press.

Harré, Rom, and Robert Finlay-Jones. 1986. 'Emotion talk across times'. In Rom Harré (Ed.), *The social construction of emotions*, 220–33. Oxford, UK: Basil Blackwell.

Harrison, D., and L. Laliberté. 1994. *No life like it*. Toronto: Lorimer.

Hartsock, N. 1987. 'Rethinking modernism: Minority vs. majority theories'. *Cultural Critique* 7: 187–206.

Haslanger, Sally. 2005. 'You mixed? Racial identity without racial biology'. In Haslanger and Witt (Eds.), *Adoption matters: Philosophical and feminist essays*, 265–89. Ithaca, NY: Cornell University Press.

———, and Charlotte Witt (Eds.). 2005. *Adoption matters: Philosophical and feminist essays*. Ithaca, NY: Cornell University Press.

Hausman, B. 1995. *Changing sex: Transsexualism technology and the idea of gender*. Durham, NC: Duke University Press.

Hayman, S. 2006. *Imprisoning our sisters: The new federal women's prisons in Canada*. Kingston, ON: McGill-Queens University Press.

Hearn, Alison. 2009. 'Hoaxing the "real". On the metanarrative of reality television'. Susan Murray and Laurie Oullette (Eds.), *Reality TV. Remaking television culture*, 2nd edn., 165–78. New York: New York University Press.

Hebdige, Dick. 1979. *Subculture: The meaning of style*. London: Methuen.

Hedges, Chris. 2009. *Empire of illusion: The end of literacy and the triumph of spectacle*. Toronto: Knopf.

Heimer, Karen, and Candace Kruttschnitt. 2006. *Gender and crime: Patterns in victimization and offending*. New York: New York University Press.

Henderson, James (Sakej). 1994a. 'Empowering treaty federalism'. *Saskatchewan Law Review* 58: 269.

———. 1994b. 'Implementing the treaty order'. In Richard Gosse, James Youngblood Henderson, and Roger Carter (Eds.), *Continuing Poundmaker's and Riel's quest: Presentations made at a conference on Aboriginal peoples and justice*. Saskatoon: Purich.

Henley, Nancy, and Fred Pincus. 1978. 'Interrelationship of sexist, racist and antihomosexual attitudes'. *Psychological Reports* 42 (1): 83–90.

Hennessy, Rosemary. 1995. 'Queer visibility in commodity culture'. In L. Nicholson and S. Seidman (Eds.), *Social postmodernism: Beyond identity politics*. Cambridge, UK: Cambridge University Press.

Herdt, Gilbert. 1984. *Ritualized homosexuality in Melanesia*. Berkeley: University of California Press.

Herek, Gregory. 1988. 'Heterosexuals' attitudes

toward lesbians and gay men'. *Journal of Sex Research* 25 (4): 451–77.

Herman, Edward, and Noam Chomsky. 1988. *Manufacturing consent: The political economy of the mass media.* New York: Pantheon.

Hermer, Joe, and Janet Mosher. 2002. *Disorderly people: Law and the politics of exclusion in Ontario.* Halifax: Fernwood.

Hewitt, John P. 1998. *The myth of self-esteem: Finding happiness and solving problems in America.* New York: St. Martin's.

Hilbert, Richard. 1992. *The classical roots of ethnomethodology: Durkheim, Weber and Garfinkel.* Chapel Hill: University of North Carolina Press.

Hill, Richard. 1992. 'Continuity of Haudenosaunee government'. In Jose Barreiro (Ed.), *Indian roots of American democracy.* Ithaca, NY: Akwe: don Press, Cornell University.

Hird, M.J. 2000. 'Gender's nature: Intersexuals, transsexualism and the 'sex'/'gender' binary'. *Feminist Theory* 1 (3): 347–64.

Hird, M.J. (2003a). 'Considerations for a psycho-analytic theory of gender identity and sexual desire: The case of intersex'. *Signs: Journal of Women in Culture and Society* 28 (4): 1067–92.

———. (2003b). 'A typical gender identity conference? Some disturbing reports from the therapeutic front lines'. *Feminism and Psychology* 13(2): 181–99.

———. 2004. *Sex, gender and science.* Basingstoke, UK: Palgrave Macmillan.

———, and J. Germon. 2001. 'The intersexual body and the medical regulation of gender'. In K. Backett-Milburn and L. McKie (Eds.), *Constructing Gendered Bodies,*162–78. London: Palgrave.

Hobbes, Thomas. 1989 [1651]. *The leviathan.* Belmont, CA: Wadsworth.

Hoberman, J. 1984. *Sport and political ideology.* Austin: University of Texas Press.

Hobsbawm, Eric J. 1992. *Nations and nationalism since 1780: Programme, myth, reality.* Cambridge, UK: Cambridge University Press.

Hochschild, Arlie Russell. 1983. *The managed heart: The commercialization of human feeling.* Berkeley: University of California Press.

———. 1990. *The second shift: Working parents and the revolution at home.* New York: Viking.

———. 1998. 'The sociology of emotion as a way of seeing'. In Gillian Bendelow and Simon J. Williams (Eds.), *Emotions in social life: Critical themes and contemporary issues,* 5–15. London and New York: Routledge.

———. 2003. *The commercialization of intimate life: Notes from home and work.* Berkeley: University of California Press.

Hogeveen, B. 1999. 'An intrusive and corrective government: Political rationalities and the governance of Plains Aboriginals 1870–1890'. In R. Smandych (Ed.), *Governable places: Readings on governmentality and crime control.* Aldershot, UK: Dartmouth.

———. 2005. '"If we are tough on crime, if we punish crime, then people get the message": Constructing and governing the punishable young offender in Canada during the late 1990s'. *Punishment and Society* 7 (1): 73–89.

Hollingshead, A.B. 1949. *Elmtown's youth: The impact of social classes on adolescents.* New York: John Wiley and Sons.

Holmshaw, J., and S. Hillier. 2000. 'Gender and culture: A sociological perspective to mental health problems in women'. In D. Kohen (Ed.), *Women and mental health.* London: Routledge.

Homans, George. *The human group.* 1950. New York: Harcourt, Brace and Company.

Hondagneu-Sotelo, P. 2007. *Domestica: Immigrant workers cleaning and caring in the shadows of affluence,* 2nd edn. Berkeley, CA: University of California Press.

Hood-Williams, John. 1996. 'Goodbye to sex and gender'. *Sociological Review* 49 (1): 1–16.

Huddart-Kennedy, Emily, Thomas M. Beckley, Bonita L. McFarlane, and Solange Nadeau. 2009. 'Why we don't "walk the talk": Understanding the environmental values/behaviour gap in Canada'. *Research in Human Ecology* (16) 2:151–60.

Hunt, Alan. 1999. *Governing morals: A social history of moral regulation.* Cambridge, UK: Cambridge University Press.

———, and Gary Wickham. 1994. *Foucault and the law: Towards a sociology of law as governance.* London: Pluto.

Iacovetta, Franca. 1999. 'Gossip, contest and power in the making of suburban bad girls: Toronto, 1945–60'. *Canadian Historical Review* 80 (4): 585–623.

———. 2006. 'Recipes for democracy? Gender, family, and making female citizens in Cold War Canada'. In A. Glasbeek (Ed.), *Moral* regulation and governance in Canada, 169–87. Toronto: Canadian Scholars' Press.

Illouz, Eva. 2008. Saving the modern soul: Therapy, emotions, and the culture of self-help. Berkeley: University of California Press.

Institut de la Statistique du Québec. 2010. 'Immigrants selon la connaissance du français et de l'anglais, Québec, 1980–2009'. Québec: Gouvernement du Québec. http://www.stat.gouv.qc.ca/donstat/societe/demographie/migrt_poplt_imigr/607.htm.

Isin, E. 2002. Being political: Genealogies of citizenship. Minneapolis: University of Minnesota Press.

———, and B. Turner. 2007. 'Investigating citizenship: An agenda for citizenship studies'. Citizenship Studies 11: 5–17.

Ivison, Duncan. 1997. The self at liberty: Political liberty and the arts of government. Ithaca, NY: Cornell University Press.

Jackson, C. 2000. 'Waste and whiteness: Zora Neale Hurston and the politics of eugenics'. African American Review 34 (Winter): 639–60.

Jackson, M. 1989. 'Locking up Natives in Canada'. University of British Columbia Law Review 23 (special issue): 213–40.

Jaggar, Alison M. 1989. 'Love and knowledge: Emotion in feminist epistemology'. In Alison M. Jaggar and Susan R. Bordo (Eds.), Gender/body/knowledge: Feminist reconstructions of being and knowing, 145–71. New Brunswick, NJ: Rutgers University Press.

Jaimes, M. Annette (Ed.). 1992. The state of Native America: Genocide, colonization and resistance. Boston: South End Press.

Jarman, Jennifer, Peter Butler, and Donald Clairmont. 1997. 'Sweatshops and teleprofessionalism: An investigation of life and work in the teleservice industry'. Paper presented at the Second International Telework Conference, Building Actions on Ideas, Amsterdam.

Jeffreys, S. 1990. Anticlimax. London: Women's Press.

———. 2003. Unpacking queer politics: A lesbian feminist perspective. Oxford, UK: Polity Press.

Jenson, J., and D. Saint-Martin. 2003. 'New routes to social cohesion? Citizenship and the social investment state'. Canadian Journal of Sociology 28 (1): 77–99.

———, and M. Sineau. 2001. Who cares? Women's work, childcare and welfare state redesign. Toronto: University of Toronto Press.

Johansen, Bruce E. 1982. Forgotten founders: How the American Indian helped shape democracy. Boston: Harvard Common Press.

Johnson, H. 2006. 'Concurrent drug and alcohol dependency and mental health problems among incarcerated women'. The Australian and New Zealand Journal of Criminology 39 (2): 190–217.

Johnson, Steven. 2005. Everything bad is good for you. New York: Riverhead.

Johnsrude, L. 1999. 'Budget restraints hurt children'. Edmonton Journal, 7 August: A3.

Johnston, Les, and Clifford Shearing. 2003. Governing security: Explorations in policing and justice. London: Routledge.

Jones, Alison. 1993. 'Becoming a "girl": Poststructuralist suggestions for educational research'. Gender and Education 5 (2): 157–67.

Jones, T. 2003. 'The governance and accountability of policing'. In Tim Newburn (Ed.), Handbook of policing. Collompton, UK: Willan.

———, and T. Newburn. 1998. Private security and public policing. Oxford, UK: Police Studies Institute, Clarendon.

Jordan, Mark. 1997. The invention of sodomy in Christian theology. Chicago: University of Chicago Press.

Jordison, S., and D. Kieran (Eds.). 2004. Crap towns II. London: Boxtree.

Kashima, Yoshihisa, and Margaret Foddy. 2002. 'Time and self: The historical construction of the self'. In Yoshihisa Kashima, Margaret Foddy, and Michael Platon (Eds.), Self and identity: Personal, social, and symbolic, 180–206. Mahwah, NJ: Lawrence Erlbaum Associates.

Kayser, B., and A. Smith. 2008. 'Globalisation of anti-doping: The reverse side of the medal'. British Medical Journal 337 (July): 85–87.

Keane, T.M., A.K. Silberbogen, and M.R. Weirerich. 2008. 'Post-traumatic stress disorder'. In J. Hunsley and E.J. Mash (Eds.), Assessments that Work, 293–316. Oxford: Oxford University Press.

Keating, Michael. 2004. 'European integration and the nationalities question'. Politics and Society 32: 367–88.

Keen, Andrew. 2007. The cult of the amateur:

How today's internet is killing our culture. New York: Doubleday.

Kelley, N., and M. Trebilcock. 1998. *The making of the mosaic: A history of Canadian immigration policy.* Toronto: University of Toronto Press.

Kellough, Gail, and Scot Wortley. 2002. 'Remand for plea: Bail decisions and plea bargaining as commensurate decisions'. *British Journal of Criminology* 42: 186–210.

Kelly, Deirdre M., Shauna Pomerantz, and Dawn H. Currie. 2005. 'Skater girlhood and emphasized femininity: "You can't land an ollie properly in heels"'. *Gender and Education* 17 (3): 129–48.

Kessler, S. 1990. 'The medical construction of gender: Case management of intersexed infants'. *Signs: Journal of Women in Culture and Society* 16: 3–26.

Killanin, L. 1976. 'Eligibility and amateurism'. In L. Killanin and J. Rodda (Eds.), *The Olympic Games: 80 years of people, events and records.* Don Mills, ON: Collier Macmillan.

Kimball, J.N. 2007. 'Electroconvulsive therapy—an outdated treatment, or one whose time has come?' *Southern Medical Journal* 100 (5): 462–63.

Kinsman, Gary. 1996. *The regulation of desire.* Montreal: Black Rose.

———, and Patrizia Gentile. 2010. *The Canadian war on queers.* University of British Columbia Press.

Kitwood, Tom. 1997. *Dementia reconsidered: The person comes first.* Buckingham, UK: Open University Press.

Klein, Naomi. 2000. *No logo.* Toronto: Knopf.

Kleinman, Zoe. 2009. 'Children who use technology are "better writers"'. BBC News, 3 December. http://news.bbc.co.uk/go/pr/fr/-/2/hi/technology/8392653.stm.

Kong, R., and K. AuCoin. 2008. 'Female offenders in Canada'. Statistics Canada catalogue no. 85-002-XIE, *Juristat* 28 (1). Ottawa: Statistics Canada.

Kontos, Pia. 2004. 'Ethnographic reflections on selfhood, embodiment and Alzheimer's Disease'. *Ageing and Society* 24: 829–49.

Kovach, Margaret. 2005. 'Emerging from the margins: Indigenous methodologies'. In Leslie Brown and Susan Strega (Eds.), *Research as resistance: Critical, indigenous and anti-oppressive approaches.* Toronto: Canadian Scholars Press.

Krull, Catherine. 2006. 'Historical and cross-cultural perspectives on family life'. In Anne-Marie Ambert (Ed.), *One-parent families: Characteristics, causes, consequences,* and issues, 31–57. Toronto: Vanier Institute of the Family.

———. 2010. 'Investing in families and children: Family policies in Canada'. In D. Cheal (Ed.), *Canadian families,* 254–73. Toronto: Oxford University Press.

———. 2011. 'Destabilizing the nuclear family ideal: Thinking beyond essentialisms, universalisms and binaries'. In C. Krull and J. Sempruch (Eds.), *Demystifying the family/work* contradiction, 1–29. Vancouver: University of British Columbia Press.

———, and J. Sempruch (Eds.). 2011. *A life in balance? Reopening the family–work debate.* Vancouver: University of British Columbia Press.

Krupnik, Igor and Dyanna Jolly. 2002. *The earth is faster now: Indigenous observations of Arctic environmental change.* Fairbanks, Alaska: Arcus.

Kuhn, T.S. 1970. *The structure of scientific revolutions,* 2nd edn. Chicago: University of Chicago Press.

Kumar, K. 1995. *From post-industrial to postmodern society: New theories of the contemporary world.* Oxford: Blackwell.

Kunz, W. A. 2006. *Culture conglomerates: Consolidation in the motion picture and television Industries.* Lanham, MD: Rowan and Littlefield.

Kutchins, H., and S.A. Kirk. 1997. *Making us crazy—DSM: The psychiatric bible and the creation of mental disorders.* New York: The Free Press.

Kymlicka, Will. 1998. *Finding our way: Rethinking ethnocultural relations in Canada.* Toronto: Oxford University Press.

———. 2000. 'Nation-building and minority rights: Comparing west and east'. *Journal of Ethnic and Migration Studies* 26: 183–212.

Laczko, Leslie S. 2000. 'Canada's linguistic and ethnic dynamics in an evolving world-system'. In Thomas D. Hall (Ed.), *A world-systems reader: New perspectives on gender, urbanism, cultures, indigenous peoples, and ecology,* 131–42. Lanham, MD: Rowman and Littlefield.

Ladner, Kiera. 2000. 'Women and Blackfoot nationalism'. *Journal of Canadian Studies* 35 (2): 35–62.

————. 2003. 'Treaty federalism: An indigenous view of Canadian federalisms'. In François Rocher and Miriam Smith (Eds.), *New trends in Canadian federalism*, 2nd edn, 167–94. Peterborough, ON: Broadview.

Laforest, Guy. 2001. 'The true nature of sovereignty: Reply to my critics concerning Trudeau and the end of a Canadian dream'. In Ronald Beiner and Wayne Norman (Eds.), *Canadian political philosophy*. Don Mills, ON: Oxford University Press.

Laing, R.D. 1971. *The politics of the family and other essays*. New York: Pantheon Books.

Laishes, J. 2002. *The 2002 mental health strategy for women offenders*. Correctional Services Canada. http://www.csc-scc.gc.ca/text/prgrm/fsw/mhealth/toc-eng.shtml.

Laitin, David D. 1998. *Identity in formation: The Russian-speaking populations in the near abroad*. Ithaca, NY: Cornell University Press.

Lan, Pei-Chia. 2003. Maid or madam? Filipina migrant workers and the continuity of domestic labor. *Gender and Society* 17 (2): 187–208.

Lang, Sabine. 1998. *Men as women, women as men*. Austin: University of Texas Press.

Laqueur, T. 1990. *Making sex*. Cambridge, MA: Harvard University Press.

Larsen, Knud, Rodney Cate, and Michael Reed. 1983. 'Antiblack attitudes, religious orthodoxy, permissiveness and sexual information'. *Journal of Sex Research* 19: 105–18.

Latour, Bruno. 1993. *We have never been modern*. New York: Harvester Wheatsheaf.

Lazarsfeld, P., B. Berelson, and H. Gaudet. 1944. *The peoples' choice*. New York: Duell, Sloan and Pearce.

Le Bourdais, Céline, and Évelyne Lapierre-Adamcyk. 2004. 'Changes in conjugal life in Canada: Is cohabitation progressively replacing marriage?' *Journal of Marriage and Family* 66: 929–42.

Leavis, F.R. 1999 [1930]. *Mass civilisation and minority culture*. Cambridge, UK: Minority Press.

LeBaron, Michelle. 2004. 'Learning new dances: Finding effective ways to address intercultural disputes'. In Catherine Bell and David Kahane (Eds.), *Intercultural dispute resolution*. Vancouver: University of British Columbia Press.

Lee, Jennifer. 2005. 'The man date'. *New York Times* 10 April: 1.

Lehnertz, K. 1979. *Berufliche Entwicklung der Amateurspitzensportler in der Bundesrepublik Deutschland* [Occupational development of amateur elite athletes in the Federal Republic of Germany]. Schorndorf, Germany: Karl Hofmann Verlag.

Lewis, J. 2001. 'Legitimizing care work and the issue of gender equality'. In M. Daly (Ed.), *Care work: The quest for security*. Geneva: International Labour Office.

Ley, C. 2003. 'Seeking homo economicus: The Canadian state and the strange story of the Business Immigration Program'. *Annals of the Association of American Geographers* 93 (2): 426–41.

Li, Geoffrey. 2008. 'Private security and public policing'. *Juristat* 28 (10). http://www.statcan.gc.ca/pub/85-002-x/2008010/article/10730-eng.pdf.

Lippert, R. 1998. 'Canadian refugee determination and advanced liberal government'. *Canadian Journal of Law and Society* 13: 177–207.

————R. 1999. 'Governing refugees: The relevance of governmentality to understanding the international refugee regime'. *Alternatives* 24 (3): 295–328.

————. 2010. 'Wither sanctuary?' *Refuge* 26 (1) (In Press).

Little Bear, Leroy. 2004. 'Aborginal paradigms: Implications for relations to land and treaty making'. In Kerry Wilkins (Ed.), *Advancing Aboriginal claims: Visions, strategies, directions*, 26–8. Saskatoon: Purich.

Little, Margaret Hillyard. 2011. 'The increasing invisibility of mothering'. In C. Krull and J. Sempruch (Eds.), *A life in balance? Reopening the family–work* debate, 194–205. Vancouver: University of British Columbia Press.

Loader, I. 2000. 'Plural policing and democratic governance'. *Social and Legal Studies* 9 (3): 323–45.

————, and N. Walker. 2001. 'Policing as a public good: Reconstituting the connection between policing and the state'. *Theoretical Criminology* 5 (1): 9–35.

Lowe, Elaine. 2006. 'What a difference 50 years makes: Coming of age, then and now' (issue title). *Transition Magazine* 36 (1).

Lupton, Deborah. 1998. *The emotional self*. London: Sage.

Luxton, Meg. 1997. 'Feminism and families:

The challenge of neo-conservatism'. In Meg Luxton (Ed.), *Feminism and families: Critical policies and changing* practices, 10–26. Halifax: Fernwood.

———, and June Corman. 2001. *Getting by in hard times: Gendered labour at home and on the job.* Toronto: University of Toronto Press.

Lyotard, J.F. 1984. *The postmodern condition: A report on knowledge.* Manchester, UK: Manchester University Press.

MacDonald, A.P., Jr, J. Huggins, S. Young, and R.A. Swanson. 1973. 'Attitudes toward homosexuality'. *Journal of Consulting and Clinical Psychology* 40 (1): 161.

MacDonald, H. 2010. 'Who counts? Nuns, work, and the census of Canada'. *Histoire sociale/ Social History* 86 (November): 369–91.

Machlup, F. 1962. *The production and distribution of knowledge in the United States.* Princeton, NJ: Princeton University Press.

Macionis, John J., and Linda M. Gerber. 2005. *Sociology.* 5th edn. Toronto: Prentice Hall.

MacKay, R. 1974. 'Standardised tests: Objective/ objectified measures of 'competence''. In A.V. Cicourel, K.H. Jennings, S.H. Jennings, K.C. Leiter, R. MacKay, H. Mehan, and D.R. Roth (Eds.), *Language use and school performance*, 218–47. New York: Academic Press.

Macklin, A. 2003. 'Dancing across borders: 'Exotic dancers', trafficking, and Canadian immigration policy'. *International Migration Review* 37 (1): 464–500.

Maclure, Jocelyn. 2003. *Quebec identity: The challenge of pluralism.* Montreal and Kingston: McGill-Queen's University Press.

Magder, Ted. 2009. 'Television 2.0. The business of American television in transition'. In Susan Murray and Laurie Oullette (Eds.), *Reality TV. Remaking television culture*, 2nd edn, 141–64. New York: New York University Press.

Mandell, Nancy, and Sue Wilson. 2011. 'Intergenerational Care Work: Mothering, Grandmothering, and Eldercare'. In C. Krull and J. Sempruch (Eds.), *A life in balance? Reopening the family–work debate*, 30–46. Vancouver: University of British Columbia Press.

Mannheim, Karl. 1952. 'The problem of generations'. In P. Kecskemeti (Ed.), *Essays on the sociology of knowledge.* New York: Routledge and Kegan Paul.

Markusoff, J. 2007. 'Albertans losing at track,

Grits say: Wagers up only slightly despite $190M in aid'. *Edmonton Journal*, 18 January: A1.

Marshall, T. 1996. 'The evolution of restorative justice in Britain'. *European Journal on Criminal Policy and Research* 4 (4): 21–43.

Martineau, Harriet. 1983 [1869]. *Autobiography.* London: Virago.

Marx, Karl. 1970 [1859]. *A contribution to the critique of political economy.* M. Dobb, Ed. (S.W. Ryazanskaya, trans.). Moscow: Progress Publishers.

———. 1973 [1939]. *Grundrisse.* (M. Nicolaus, trans.). Harmondsworth, UK: Penguin.

———. 1975 [1852]. 'The 18th Brumaire of Louis Bonaparte'. In *Karl Marx, Friedrich Engels: Collected works*, 11: 99–197. London: Lawrence and Wishart.

———. 1976 [1867]. *Capital.* v. 1. Harmondsworth, UK: Penguin.

———, and Friedrich Engels. 1947 [1846]. *The German ideology.* New York: International Publishers.

———, and ———. 1948 [1848]. *Manifesto of the Communist Party.* New York: International Publishers.

———, and ———. 1976. *Collected works, vol 5.* London: Lawrence and Wishart.

Matas, R. 2005. 'Vancouver man charged with human trafficking'. *Globe and Mail* 14 April: S3.

Mathews, H. 2001. 'Citizenship, youth councils and young people's participation'. *Journal of Youth Studies* 4 (3): 299–318.

Maupin, A. 2007. *Michael Tolliver lives.* San Francisco, CA: HarperCollins.

McDaniel, Susan A. 1997. 'Intergenerational transfers, social solidarity, and social policy: Unanswered questions and policy challenges'. *Canadian Public Policy/ Canadian Journal on Aging* (joint issue) 23 (Supplement 1): 1–21.

———. 2001. '"Born at the right time?" gendered generation and webs of entitlement and responsibility'. *Canadian Journal of Sociology* 26 (2): 193–214.

———. 2002. 'Women's changing relations to the state and citizenship'. *Canadian Review of Sociology and Anthropology* 9 (2): 125–49.

———. 2003. 'Pensions, privilege and poverty: another "take" on intergenerational equity'. In Jacques Veron, Sophie Pennec, and Jacques Legare (Eds.), *Ages, générations* et contrat social: L'état providence face aux changements démographiques, 259–78. Paris: Institut national de la recherche scientifiques.

———. 2008. 'The "growing legs" of generation as a policy construct: reviving its family meaning'. Journal of Comparative Family Studies 40 (2): 243–53.

McDiarmid. Jessica. 2006. 'The Asper-ization of Canadian news. Media concentration continues despite Senate warning'. King's Journalism Review 12: 1–6.

McKenzie, K., and K. Bhui. 2007. 'Institutional racism in mental health care: Services have some way to go before they meet the challenges of a multicultural society'. British Medical Journal 334: 649–50.

McLean, A. 1995. 'Empowerment and the psychiatric consumer/ex-patient movement in the united states: contradictions, crisis and change'. Social Science & Medicine 40 (8): 1053–71.

McLean, Archie. 2006. 'Morton stakes out far right in leadership race: Clarity on issues hallmark of professor turned politician'. Edmonton Journal, 14 October. http://www2.canada.com/edmontonjournal/features/passingthetorch/story.html?id=188c1580-a6cd-4ff1-8cc6-a227603f3b9f.

———. 2010. 'Who is Ted Morton, Alberta's new finance minister?' Edmonton Journal, 17 January. http://communities.canada.com/edmontonjournal/blogs/electionnotebook/archive/2010/01/17/who-is-ted-morton-alberta-s-new-finance-minister.aspx.

McLuhan, Marshall. 1994 [1964]. Understanding media: The extensions of man. Cambridge, MA: MIT Press.

McNay, Lois.. 1993. Foucault and feminism: Power, gender and the self. Boston: Northeastern University Press.

———. 1994. Foucault: A critical introduction. New York: Continuum Publishers.

McRobbie, A. 1980. 'Settling accounts with subcultures: A feminist critique'. Screen Education 34: 37–49.

Mead, George Herbert. 1934. Mind, self, and society. Chicago: University of Chicago Press.

Mears, Ashley, and Finlay, William. 2005. 'Not just a paper doll: How models manage bodily capital and why they perform emotional labor'. Journal of Contemporary Ethnography 34: 317–43.

Mental Health Commission of Canada. 2009. Towards recovery and well being: A framework for a mental health strategy for Canada. Ottawa: Mental Health Commission of Canada http://www.mentalhealthcommission.ca/SiteCollectionDocuments/board-docs/15507_MHCC_EN_final.pdf.

Merchant, Carolyn. 1980. The death of nature: Women, ecology, and the scientific revolution. San Francisco: Harper and Row.

———. 2008. 'Introduction'. In Carolyn Merchant (Ed.), Ecology, 2nd edn. 1–27. New York: Humanity Books.

Mercredi, Ovide, and Mary Ellen Tupel. 1993. In the rapids: Navigating the future of First Nations. Toronto: Viking.

Merton, Robert K. 1938. 'Social structure and anomie'. American Sociological Review 3 (5): 672–82

Metzner, Jeffrey L., and Jamie Fellner. 2010. 'Solitary confinement and mental illness in US prisons: A challenge for medical ethics.' The Journal of the American Academy of Psychiatry and the Law 38 (1): 104–8.

Meyer, Manu Aluli. 2001. 'Acultural assumptions of empiricism: A Native Hawaiian critique'. Canadian Journal of Native Education 24 (2): 188–98.

Milan, Anne. 2000. 'One hundred years of families'. Canadian Social Trends, Statistics Canada catalogue no. 11-008 (Spring): 2–13.

Miller, David. 1991. Liberty. Oxford, UK: Oxford University Press.

Mills, C. Wright. 1959. The sociological imagination. Oxford, UK: Oxford University Press.

———. 1963. Power, politics and people: The collected essays of C. Wright Mills. Introduction by Irving Louis Horowitz (Ed.). New York: Oxford University Press.

———. 2004. 'The promise of sociology'. In John J. Macionis, Nijole V. Benokraitis, and Bruce Ravelli (Eds.), Seeing ourselves: Classic, contemporary, and cross-cultural readings in sociology, Canadian edition, 1–4. Toronto: Pearson.

Mills, D. 2002. 'Children will be protected despite cutbacks'. National Post 3 October.

Milner, Murray, Jr. 2004. Freaks, geeks, and cool kids: American teenagers, schools, and the culture of consumption. London: Routledge.

Moi, T. 1991. 'Appropriating Bourdieu: Feminist theory and Pierre Bourdieu's sociology of culture'. *New Literary History* 22 (4): 1017–49.

Mol, Arthur P. J., and David A. Sonnenfeld. 2000. 'Ecological modernisation around the world: An introduction'. *Environmental Politics* 9 (1): 1–14.

Money, J. 1985. 'The conceptual neutering of gender and the criminalisation of sex'. *Archives of Sexual Behaviour* 14: 279–91.

Monture-Angus, Patricia. 1995. *Thunder in my soul: A Mohawk woman speaks*. Halifax: Fernwood.

———. 1999. *Journeying forward: Dreaming First Nations independence*. Halifax: Fernwood.

Moretti, Marlene M., Candice L. Odgers, and Margaret A. Jackson. 2004. *Girls and aggression: Contributing factors and intervention principles*, vol. 19. New York: Kluwer Academic/Plenum.

Morgan, Lewis Henry. 1851. *The League of the Ho-dé-no-sau-nee*. Rochester, NY: Sage.

———. 1985 [1877]. *Ancient society*. Foreword by Elisabeth Tooker. Tucson: University of Arizona Press.

Morin, Stephen, and Ellen Garfinkle. 1978. 'Male homophobia'. *Journal of Social Issues* 34 (1): 29–47.

Morrison, T. 1992. *Playing in the dark: Whiteness and the literary imagination*. New York: Vintage.

Morton, Ted. 1998. 'Why family matters'. *Calgary Sun*, 1 November. http://fathersforlife.org/families/morton.htm.

Mosco, Vincent. 2009. *The political economy of communication*, 2nd edn. Seven Oaks, CA: Sage.

Moyers, Bill. 2007. 'Society on steroids: A Bill Moyers essay'. http://www.pbs.org/moyers/journal/blog/2007/12/society_on_steroids_a_bill_moy.html.

MRSB Consulting Services. 2003. 'PEI urban call centre labour market profile'. Charlottetown, PE: PEI Labour Market Development Agreement, Human Resources Development Canada and PEI Department of Development and Technology.

Mulvey, Laura. 1975. 'Visual pleasure and narrative cinema'. *Screen* 16 (3): 6–18.

Murphy, C. 1998. 'Policing postmodern Canada'. *Canadian Journal of Law and Society* 13 (2): 1–28.

———, and C. Clarke. 2005. 'Policing communities and communities of policing: A comparative study of policing and security in two Canadian communities'. In Dennis Cooley (Ed.), *Re-imagining policing in Canada*. Toronto: University of Toronto Press.

Murphy, Raymond. 2009. *Leadership in disaster: Learning for a future with global climate change*. Montreal and Kingston: McGill-Queen's University Press.

Murray, Janet H. 1998. *Hamlet on the holodeck. The future of narrative in cyberspace*. Cambridge, MA.: MIT Press.

Murray, Susan and Laurie Oullette (Eds.). 2009. *Reality TV. Remaking television culture*, 2nd edn. New York: New York University Press.

Murray, Stephen. 2000. *Homosexualities*. Chicago: University of Chicago Press.

Naess, Arne. 2008. 'Deep ecology'. In Carolyn Merchant (Ed.), *Ecology*, 2nd edn. 143–47. New York: Humanity Books.

Namaste, V. 2005. *Sex change, social change: Reflections on identity, institutions and imperialism*. London: Women's Press.

Nataf, Z. 1998. 'Whatever I feel . . .' *New Internationalist* April: 22–25.

National Council of Welfare. 2006. *Welfare incomes 2005*. Ottawa: National Council of Welfare.

Nelson, Lise. 1999. 'Bodies (and spaces) do matter: The limits of performativity'. *Gender, Place and Culture* 6 (4): 331–53.

Nelson, Margaret K. 2006. 'Families in not-so-free fall: A response to comments'. *Journal of Marriage and Family* 68 (4): 817–23.

Neumann, C.M., D.L. Forman, and J.E. Rothlein. 1998. 'Hazard screening of chemical releases and environmental equity analysis of populations proximate to toxic release inventory facilities in Oregon'. *Environmental Health Perspectives* 106 (4): 217–26.

Novek, Joel. 2003. 'Intensive hog farming in Manitoba: Transnational treadmills and local conflicts'. *Canadian Review of Sociology and Anthropology* 40 (1): 1–2.

O'Connor, James. 1998. *Natural causes: Essays in ecological Marxism*. New York: Guilford Press.

O'Connor, Julia, Ann Shola Orloff, and Sheila Shaver. 1999. *States, markets, families: gender, liberalism and social policy in Australia, Canada, Great Britain and the United States*. Cambridge, UK: Cambridge University Press.

Office of the Correctional Investigator (OCI). 2008. *Annual report of the correction investigator, 2008–2009*. Ottawa: Minister of Public Works and Government Services.

O'Hara, K. 1998. *Comparative family policy: Eight countries' stories*. Ottawa: Canadian Policy Research Network.

Organisation for Economic Co-operation and Development (OECD). 2008. *Growing up unequal? Income distribution and poverty in* OECD *countries*. http://www.oecd.org/document/53/0,3746, en_2649_33933_41460917_1_1_1_1,00.html.

Ontario. 2003. *Private Investigators and Security Guards Act: Discussion paper*. Toronto: Ontario Ministry of Public Safety and Security. June.

———. 2004. Bill 88: An Act to Amend the Private Investigators and Public Security Guards Act. Toronto: Legislative Assembly of Ontario. June.

Oudshoorn, N. 1994. *Beyond the natural body: An archaeology of sex hormones*. London and New York: Routledge.

Owram, Douglas. 1999. 'The family at mid-century' (issue title). *Transition Magazine* 29 (4).

Parkes D., and Pate K. 2006. 'Time for accountability: Effective oversight of women's prisons'. *Canadian Journal of Criminology and Criminal Justice* (April): 251–85.

Parkins, John R. 2008. 'The metagovernance of climate change: Institutional adaptation to the mountain pine beetle epidemic in British Columbia'. *Journal of Rural and Community Development* 3 (2): 7–29.

———, and Debera J. Davidson. 2008. 'Constructing the public sphere in compromised settings: Environmental governance in the Alberta forest sector'. *Canadian Review of Sociology* 45 (2): 177–96.

Parsons, Talcott, and Robert Bales (Eds.). 1955. *Family, socialization and interaction process*. Glencoe, IL: Free Press.

Patten, Christopher. 1999. *The Report of the Independent Commission on Policing in Northern Ireland*. London: HMSO.

Pavlich, George C. 2000. *Critique and radical discourses on crime*. Aldershot, UK: Ashgate.

———. 2005. 'Experiencing critique'. *Law and critique* 16: 95–112.

Pearce, Tristan, Barry Smit, Frank Duerden,

James D. Ford, Annie Goose, and Fred Kataoyak. 2010. 'Inuit vulnerability and adaptive capacity to climate change in Ulukhaktok, Northwest Territories, Canada'. *The Polar Record* 46 (237): 157–77.

Peck, Jamie. 2001. *Workfare states*. New York: Guilford.

———, Nik Theodore, and Neil Brenner. 2009. 'Postneoliberalism and its malcontents'. *Antipode* 41 (S1): 94–116.

Peers, Laura. 1996. 'Subsistence, secondary literature and gender bias: The Saulteaux'. In Christine Miller, Patricia Chuchryk, Maria Smallface Marule, Brenda Manyfingers, and Cheryl Deering (Eds.), *Women of the First Nations: Power, wisdom and strength*. Winnipeg: University of Manitoba Press.

Penley, Constance, and Andrew Ross. 1991. *Technoculture*. Minnesota: University of Minnesota Press.

Perrault, S., and S. Brennan. 2010. *Criminal victimization in Canada, 2009*. Ottawa: Statistics Canada. http://www.statcan.gc.ca/pub/85-002-x/2010002/article/11340-eng.htm.

Peterson-Badali, M., and R. Abramovich. 1992. 'Children's knowledge of the legal system: Are they competent to instruct legal counsel?' *Canadian Journal of Criminology* 34 (2): 139–60.

Pew Research Center for the People and the Press. 2010. *Ideological news sources: Who watches and why*. Washington DC: Pew Research Center for the People and the Press, 2010.

Pfohl, S. 1994. *Images of deviance and social Control: A sociological history*, 2nd edn. New York: McGraw-Hill.

Phoenix, Ann, Stephen Frosh, and Rob Pattman. 2003. 'Producing contradictory masculine subject positions'. *Journal of Social Issues* 59 (1): 179–95.

Pipher, Mary. 1994. *Reviving Ophelia: Saving the selves of adolescent girls*. New York: Ballantine.

Platt, B. 2010. 'A sanctuary of conscience'. *United Church Observer*. http://www.ucobserver.org/justice/2010/01/war_resister_rodney_watson.

Police Futures Group. 2005. 'Private policing'. www.policefutures.org/docs/PFG_Private_Policing.

Pollack, S. 2005. 'Taming the shrew: Regulating

prisoners through women-centered mental health programming'. *Critical Criminology* 13 (1): 71–87.

———. 2009. '"You can't have it both ways": Punishment and treatment of imprisoned women'. *Journal of Progressive Human Services* 20 (2), 112–28.

Pomerantz, Shauna, Dawn H. Currie, and Deirdre M. Kelly. 2004. 'Sk8er girls: Skateboarders, girlhood and feminism in motion'. *Women's Studies International Forum* 27 (5/6): 547–57.

Ponting, J. Rick, and Roger Gibbins. 1980. *Out of irrelevance: A socio-political introduction to Indian affairs in Canada.* Scarborough, ON: Butterworth.

Poster, Mark. 1995. *The second media age.* Chicago: Polity Press.

Porter, John. 1987. *The measure of Canadian society: Education equality and opportunity.* Ottawa: Carleton University Press

Postman, Neil. 1985. *Amusing ourselves to death. Public discourse in the age of show business.* New York: Penguin

———. 1992. *Technopoly: The surrender of culture to technology.* New York: Vintage.

Potter, Russell A. 1995. *Spectacular vernaculars: Hip hop and the politics of postmodernism.* New York: SUNY Press.

Prasad, A. 2005. 'Reconsidering the socio-scientific construction of sexual difference: The case of Kimberly Nixon'. *Canadian Woman Studies* 24 (2/3).

Pratt, Anna. 2005. *Securing borders: Deportation and detention in Canada.* Vancouver: University of British Columbia Press.

Pratte, André (Ed.). 2008. *Reconquering Canada: Quebec federalists speak up for change.* Toronto: Douglas & McIntyre.

Prentice, A., P. Bourne, G. Cuthbert Brandt, B. Light, W. Mitchinson, and N. Black. 1988. *Canadian women: A history.* Toronto: Harcourt, Brace and Jovanovich.

Presse, L.D., and R.D. Hart. 1999. Variables associated with parasuicidal behaviours by female offenders during a cognitive-behavioural treatment program. *Canadian Psychology* 40 (2a): 108.

Prestholdt, Jeremy. 2009. 'The afterlives of 2pac: Imagery and alienation in Sierra Leone and beyond'. *Journal of African Cultural Studies* 21 (2): 197–218.

Price, John A. 1981. 'Native studies in Canadian universities and colleges'. *Canadian Journal of Native Studies* 2 (1): 349–61.

Putnam, R. 2000. *Bowling alone: The collapse and revival of American community.* New York: Simon and Schuster.

Raboy, Marc. 1990. *Missed opportunities. The story of Canadian broadcast policy.* Montreal and Kingston: McGill-Queen's Press.

Rae, Heather. 2002. *State identities and the homogenisation of peoples.* Cambridge, UK: Cambridge University Press.

Ramsay, Richard, and Pierre Tremblay. 2005. 'Bisexual, gay, queer male suicidality'. University of Calgary. http://www.fsw.ucalgary.ca/ramsay/homosexualitysuicide.

Ray, Regan. 2008. 'CBC-commissioned report says public broadcaster's election coverage "fair and balanced"'. 23 October. http://j-source.ca/article/cbc-commisioned-report-says-public-broadcasters-election-coverage-fair-and-balanced

Raymond, J. 1994. *The transsexual empire.* New York: Teachers College Press.

Reay, Diane. 2005. 'Beyond consciousness? The psychic landscape of social class'. *Sociology* 39: 911–28.

Reiman, J. 1979. *The rich get richer and the poor get prison: Ideology, class and criminal justice.* New York: John Wiley and Sons.

Reiner, Robert .1993. *The politics of the police.* Oxford: Oxford University Press.

Reitsma-Street, M. 1999. 'Justice for Canadian girls: A 1990s update'. *Canadian Journal of Criminology* 41 (3): 335–58.

Reitz, J. (Ed.). 2003. *Host societies and the reception of immigrants.* San Diego: Center for Comparative Immigration Research, University of California.

Rich, Adrienne. 1989. 'Compulsory heterosexuality and lesbian existence'. In L. Richardson and V. Taylor (Eds.), *Feminist frontiers II.* New York: Random House.

———. 2001. 'Challenges incarcerated women face as they return to their communities: Findings from life history interviews'. *Crime and Delinquency,* 47, 368–89.

Richie, B. 2001. 'Challenges incarcerated women face as they return to their communities: Findings from life history interviews'. *Crime and Delinquency* 47: 368–89.

Ridout, Vanda. 2003. *The continentalization of Canadian telecommunications: The politics of regulatory reform.* Montreal and Kingston:

McGill-Queen's University Press.

Ringrose, Jessica. 2008. ' "Every time she bends over, she pulls up her thong": Teen girls negotiating discourses of competitive, heterosexualized aggression'. *Girlhood Studies: An Interdisciplinary Journal* 1 (1): 33–59.

Riordan, J. 1977. *Sport in Soviet society*. Cambridge, UK: Cambridge University Press.

Rissmiller, D J., and J.H. Rissmiller. 2006. 'Evolution of the anti-psychiatry movement into mental health consumerism'. *Psychiatric Services* 57: 863–66.

Roberts, Dorothy. 2005. 'Feminism, race and adoption policy'. In S. Haslanger and Charlotte Witt (Eds.), *Adoption matters: Philosophical and feminist essays*, 234–56. Ithaca, NY: Cornell University Press.

Roberts, J., and R. Melchers. 2003. 'The incarceration of Aboriginal offenders'. *Canadian Journal of Criminology* 45 (2): 170–89.

Robertson, Roland. 1990. 'After nostalgia? Willful nostalgia and the phases of globalization'. In Bryan S. Turner (Ed.), *Theories of modernity and postmodernity*. London: Sage.

Röder, H. 2002. *Von der 1. zur 3. Förderstufe* [From the first to the third level for advancement]. http://www.sport-ddr-roeder.de/kapitel_10_0.htm.

Roediger, D. 1991. *Wages of whiteness: Race and the making of the American working-class*. New York: Verso.

Rogers, A., and D. Pilgrim. 2010. *A sociology of mental health and illness*, 4th edn. Buckingham, UK: Open University Press.

Rosaldo, Renato. 1989. *Culture and truth: The remaking of social analysis*. Boston: Beacon Press.

———. 1991. 'Governing by numbers: Figuring out democracy'. *Accounting, Organizations and Society* 16 (7): 673–92.

———. 1999. *Powers of freedom*. Cambridge, UK: Cambridge University Press.

Rose, Tricia. 1994. *Black noise: Rap music and black culture in contemporary America*. Middletown, CT: Wesleyan University Press.

Roseneil, Sasha, and Shelley Budgeon. 2004. 'Cultures of intimacy and care beyond "the family": Personal life and social change in the early 21st century'. *Current Sociology* 52 (2): 135–59.

Rosenhan, D. L. 1973. 'On being sane in insane places'. *Science* 179 (4070): 250–58.

Rosenthal, Robert and Lenore Jacobson. 1968. *Pygmalion in the classroom*. New York: Holt, Rinehart and Winston.

Rothblatt, M. 1995. *The apartheid of sex*. New York: Crown.

Rothman, Sheila M. 1978. *Women's proper sphere*, New York: Basic Books.

Rousseau, Jean-Jacques. 1983 [1762]. *The social contract and discourses*. London: J.M. Dent and Sons.

Royal Commission on Aboriginal Peoples. 1993. *Aboriginal peoples and the justice system*. Ottawa: Minister of Supply and Services.

———. 1996. *Bridging the cultural divide: A report on Aboriginal peoples and criminal justice in Canada*. Ottawa: Minister of Supply and Services.

Rozanova, Julia, Herbert C. Northcott, and Susan A. McDaniel. 2006. 'Seniors and portrayals of intra-generational and inter-generational inequality in the *Globe and Mail*'. *Canadian Journal on Aging* 25 (4): 373–86.

Rubin, Beth A., and Charles J. Brody. 2005. 'Contradictions of commitment in the new economy: Insecurity, time, and technology'. *Social Science Research* 34: 843–61.

Rubin, Gayle. 1975. 'The traffic in women'. In R. Reiter (Ed.), *Toward an anthropology of women*. New York: Monthly Review.

Rusnock, A. 2002. *Vital accounts*. Cambridge, UK: Cambridge University Press

Russell, D. 1995. *Women, madness & medicine*. Cambridge, UK: Polity Press.

Ryan, A.J. 1976. 'Athletics'. In C. Kochakian (Ed.) *Anabolic-androgenic steroids. Handbook of experimental pharmacology*, v. 43. New York: Springer-Verlag.

Saccoccio, Sabrina. 2007. 'Revenge of the only children'. CBC News in Depth, 3 July. http://www.cbc.ca/news/background/family/only-children.html.

Saetnan, A. R., H. M. Lomell, and S. Hammer. 2011. *The mutual construction of statistics and society*. New York: Routledge.

Sagan, D. 1992. 'Metametazoa: Biology and multiplicity'. In J. Crary and S. Kwinter (Eds.), *Incorporations*, 362–85. New York: Urzone.

Saint-Martin, Denis. 2007. 'From the welfare state to the social investment state: A new paradigm for Canadian social policy?' In Michael Orsini and Miriam Smith (Eds.),

Critical Policy Studies, 279–98. Vancouver: University of British Columbia Press.

Saint-Simon, Henri de. 1814. 'The reorganization of Europe'. In F.M.H. Markham (Ed.), *Henri Comte de Saint-Simon: Selected writings*. Oxford: Basil Blackwell.

Salazar Parreñas, Rhacel. 2005. *Children of global migration: Transnational families and gendered woes*. Palo Alto, CA: Stanford University Press.

———. 2008. *The force of domesticity: Filipina migrants and globalization*. New York: New York University Press.

Salisbury, E.J., P. van Voorhis, and G.V. Spiropoulos, 2009. 'The predictive validity of a gender-responsive needs assessment: An exploratory study'. *Crime & Delinquency* 55 (4): 550–85.

Sandilands, Catriona. 2005. 'Where mountain men meet the lesbian rangers: Gender, nation, and nature in the rocky mountain national parks'. In Melody Hessing, Rebecca Raglon, and Catriona Sandilands (Eds.), *This elusive land: Women and the Canadian environment*, 142–62. Vancouver: University of British Columbia Press.

Sapir, Edward. 1929. 'The status of linguistics as a science'. *Language* 5: 207–14.

Sartre, Jean-Paul. 1964 [1938]. *Nausea*. (L. Alexander, trans.). New York: Penguin.

———. 1970. 'An existentialist's view of freedom'. In R. Dewey and J. Gould (Eds.), *Freedom, its history, nature and varieties*. London: Macmillan.

Satsan (Herb George). 2005. National Centre for First Nations Governance website, www.fngovernance.org.

Satz, Debra. 2007. 'Remaking families: A review essay'. *Signs* 32 (2): 523–38.

Satzewich, Vic. 1990. 'The political economy of race and ethnicity'. In P. Li (Ed.), *Race and ethnic relations in Canada*, 251–68. Toronto: Oxford University Press.

———, and Terry Wotherspoon. 1993. *First Nations: Race, class and gender relations*. Toronto: Nelson.

Saussure, Ferdinand. 1983 [1916]. *Course in general linguistics*. London: Duckworth.

Sauvé, Roger. 2011. *The current state of Canadian family finances: 2010 report*. Vanier Institute of the Family. http://www.vifamily.ca/media/node/783/attachments/family-finance2010.pdf.

Savage, S., and S. Charman. 1996. 'Managing change'. In F. Leishman, B. Loveday, and S. Savage (Eds.), *Core issues in policing*. London: Longman.

Schiebinger, L. 1993. *Nature's body*. London: Pandora.

Schnaiberg, Allen, and Kenneth Alan Gould. 1994. 'Treadmill predispositions and social responses: Population, consumption and technological change'. In Allan Schnaiberg and Kenneth Alan Gould (Eds.), *Environment and society: The enduring conflict*, 68–91. New York: St. Martin's Press.

Schudson, Michael. 1991. 'The sociology of news production revisited'. In James Curran and Michael Gurevitch (Eds.), *Mass Media and Society*, 141–59. London: Arnold.

Schutz, Alfred. 1962. *Collected papers, volume 1*. The Hague: Martinus Nijhoff.

Scott, Susie. 2006. 'The medicalisation of shyness: From social misfits to social fitness'. *Sociology of Health and Illness* 28: 133–55.

Scott, Wilbur, and Sandra Stanley. 1994. *Gays and lesbians in the military*. Hawthorne, NY: Aldine de Gruyter.

Sealy, P., and P.C. Whitehead. 2004. 'Forty years of deinstitutionalization of psychiatric services in Canada: An empirical assessment'. *Canadian Journal of Psychiatry* 49 (4): 249–57.

Sedgwick, Eve. 1990. *Epistemology of the closet*. Berkeley: University of California.

Seeman, Melvin. 1959. 'On the meaning of alienation'. *American Sociological Review* 24 (6): 783–91.

Seidman, Steven. 1991. 'Postmodern anxiety: The politics of epistemology'. *Sociological Theory* 9 (2): 180–90.

Seltzer, Richard. 1992. 'The social location of those holding antihomosexual attitudes'. *Sex Roles* 26 (9/10): 391–8.

Senn, A. 1999. *Power, politics and the Olympic Games*. Champaign, IL: Human Kinetics.

Sennett, Richard. 1992. *The fall of public man*. New York: Norton.

Shanahan, Suzanne. 2007. 'Lost and found: The sociological ambivalence toward childhood'. *Annual Review of Sociology* 33: 407–28.

Sharrock, W., and B. Anderson. 1986. *The ethnomethodologists*. London: Tavistock.

Shaw, Karena. 2004. 'The global/local politics of the great bear rainforest'. *Environmental Politics* 13 (2): 373–92.

Shaw, M. and S. Hargreaves 1994. 'Ontario women in conflict with the law: A survey of women in institutions and under community supervision in Ontario'. Toronto: Ministry of the Solicitor General and Correctional Services.

Shearing, C., and Jennifer Wood. 2003. 'Nodal governance, democracy and new denizens'. *Journal of Law and Society* 30 (3): 400–19.

Shearing, C., and P. Stenning. 1982. *Private security and private justice: The challenge of the eighties*. Montreal: Institute for Research on Public Policy.

Shields, Stephanie A. 2002. *Speaking from the heart: Gender and the social meaning of emotion*. Cambridge, UK: Cambridge University Press.

———. 2002. 'The two traditions in the sociology of emotions'. In Jack Barbalet (Ed.), *Emotions and Sociology*, 10–32. Oxford: Blackwell Publishing/The Sociological Review.

Siemiatycki, M., and E. Isin. 1998. 'Immigration, diversity and urban citizenship in Toronto'. *Canadian Journal of Regional Science* 20: 73–102.

Siltanen, Janet, and Andrea Doucet. 2008. *Gender relations in Canada: Intersectionality and beyond*. Toronto: Oxford University Press.

Simmel, Georg. 1990 [1900]. *The philosophy of money*. David Frisby (Ed.). (Tom Bottomore and David Frisby, trans.). London and New York: Routledge.

Simpson, Mark. 1994. *Male impersonators*. London: Cassell.

Simpson, S., J.L. Yahner, and L. Dugan. 2008. 'Understanding women's pathways to jail: Analysing the lives of incarcerated women'. *The Australian and New Zealand Journal of Criminology* 41 (1), 84–108.

Sinclair, Peter R. 1996. 'Sustainable development in fisheries dependent regions? Reflections on Newfoundland cod fisheries'. *Sociologia Ruralis* 36 (2): 224–35.

Sisters in Spirit. 2005. http://www.sistersinspirit.ca/enghome.htm.

Smart, B. 1985. *Michel Foucault*. London: Tavistock.

Smart, Carol. 1976. *Women, crime and criminology*. London: Routledge and Kegan Paul.

———. 1989. *Feminism and the power of law*. London: Routledge.

———, and Bren Neale. 1999. *Family fragments*. Cambridge, UK: Polity Press.

Smith, Adam. 1759. *The theory of moral sentiments*. London: A. Millar.

Smith, D. 1974a. 'The ideological practice of sociology'. *Catalyst* 2: 39–54.

———. 1974b. 'The social construction of documentary reality'. *Sociological Inquiry* 44 (4): 257–68.

———. 1975. 'The statistics on mental illness: What they will not tell us about women and why'. In D. Smith and S. David (Eds.), *Women look at psychiatry*, 73–119. Vancouver: Press Gang Publishers.

———. 1978. '"K is mentally ill": The anatomy of a factual account'. *Sociology* 12 (1): 25–53.

———. 1987. *The everyday world as problematic: A feminist sociology*. Toronto: University of Toronto Press.

———. 1990a. 'The statistics on women and mental illness: The relations of ruling they conceal'. In *The conceptual practices of power*, 107–38. Toronto: University of Toronto Press.

———. 1990b. 'No one commits suicide: Textual analyses of ideological practices'. In *The Conceptual Practices of Power*, 140–73. Toronto: University of Toronto Press.

———. 1999. *Writing the social: Critique, theory and investigations*. Toronto: University of Toronto Press.

Snider, L. 2003. 'Constituting the punishable woman: Atavistic man incarcerates postmodern woman'. *British Journal of Sociology* 43 (2): 354–78.

Snider, L. 2004. 'Female punishment: From punishment to backlash'. In C. Sumner (Ed.), *The Blackwell companion to criminology*. Malden, MA: Blackwell.

Snow, D.A., S.G. Baker, A. Leon, and M. Martin. 1986. 'The myth of pervasive mental illness among the homeless'. *Social Problems* 33 (5): 407–23.

Sokoloff, Natalie. 2005. 'Women prisoners at the dawn of the 21st century'. *Women and Criminal Justice* 16 (1–2): 127–37.

Solomon, Arthur, with Michael Posluns. 1990. *Songs for the people: Teachings on the natural way*. Toronto: NC Press.

Sontag, S. 1980. 'Fascinating fascism'. In *Under the sign of Saturn*, 73–105. New York: Farrar, Straus and Girous.

Soroka, Stuart. 2007. *Canadian perceptions of*

the health care system: A report to the health council of Canada. Toronto: Health Council of Canada.

Sorokin, Pitirim A. 1950. *Altruistic love: A study of American 'good neighbors' and Christian saints* . Boston: Beacon Press.

———. 1954. *The ways and power of love: Types, factors, and techniques of moral transformation.* Boston: Beacon Press.

Spaargaren, Gert, and Arthur P.J. Mol. 1992. 'Sociology, environment, and modernity: Ecological modernization as a theory of social change'. *Society and Natural Resources* 5: 323–44.

Speer, A. 1969. *Erinnerungen* [Memoirs]. Berlin: Verlag Ullstein.

Spencer, Emily. 2006. 'Lipstick and high heels: War and the feminization of women in *Chatelaine* magazine, 1928–1956'. Ph.D. dissertation, Royal Military College of Canada, Kingston, Ontario.

Spitzer, G., H.-J. Teichler, and K. Reinartz (Eds.). 1998 [1952]. 'Das Staatliche Komitee für Körperkultur und Sport übernimmt die wesentlichen Funktionen des Sportausschusses [The State Committee for Physical Culture and Sport takes over the essential functions of the Sport Committee]'. In *Schlüsseldokumente zum DDR-Sport. Ein sporthistorischer Überblick in Originalquellen. Schriftenreihe: Sportentwicklungen in Deutschland* [*Key documents in GDR Sport. A historical overview of sport through original sources: Sport development in Germany*], v. 4. Aachen, Germany: Meyer & Meyer Verlag.

Stacey, Judith. 1996. *In the name of the family: Rethinking family values in the postmodern age.* Boston: Beacon Press.

———. 2004. 'Cruising to familyland: Gay hypergamy and rainbow kinship'. *Current Sociology* 52: 181–97.

Starr, Paul. 2004. *The creation of the media. Political origins of modern communication.* New York: Basic Books.

Statistics Canada. 2000. *Youth in custody and community services in Canada, 1998–9.* Ottawa: Centre for Justice Statistics.

———. 2004a. *Labour force estimates by detailed occupation, sex, Canada, province, annual average, 1987–2004.* Ottawa: Statistics Canada.

———. 2005. Divorces. *The Daily,* 9 March.

http://www.statcan.gc.ca/daily-quotidien/050309/dq050309b-eng.htm.

———. 2006a. 'Average hourly wages of employees by selected characteristics and profession, unadjusted data, by province'. *Labour force survey, April 2005.* http://www40.statcan.ca/101/cst01/labour69a.htm.

———. 2006b. Violence against Aboriginal women: Statistical trends. Ottawa: Statistics Canada.

———. 2007. *Quarterly demographic estimates: January to March 2007, preliminary.* Ottawa: Statistics Canada.

———. 2008. Census snapshot—Immigration in Canada: A portrait of the foreign-born population, 2006 census. *Canadian Social Trends* (April).

Steckley, John. 2003. *Aboriginal voices and the politics of representation in Canadian introductory sociology books.* Toronto: Canadian Scholars Press.

Steffensmeier, D., and E. Allan. 1998. 'The nature of female offending: Patterns and explanations'. In R.T. Zaplin (Ed.), *The female offender: Critical perspectives and effective treatment intervention* 5–29. Gaithersburg: Aspen.

Stenfert Kroese, B., and G. Holmes. 2001. '"I've never said 'no' to anything in my life": Helping people with learning disabilities who experience psychological problems'. In C. Newnes, G. Holmes, and C. Dunn (Eds.), *This is madness too: Critical perspectives on mental health services,* 71–80. Ross-on-Wye: PCCS Books.

Stenning, Philip. 2009. 'Governance and accountability in a plural policing environment – the story so far'. *Policing* February 8.

Stoddart, Mark, C.J. (2011). '"If we wanted to be environmentally sustainable, we'd take the bus": Skiing, mobility and the irony of climate change' *Human Ecology Review.*

———, and D.B. Tindall. 2010. '"We've also become quite good friends": Environmentalists, social networks and social comparison in British Columbia, Canada'. *Social Movement Studies* 9 (3): 253–71.

Straubhaar, J. and R. LaRose. 2000. *Media now: Communications media in the information age.* Belmont, CA: Wadsworth.

Stroeve, J., M. Serreze, S. Drobot, S. Gearheard, 'M. Holland, J. Maslanik, W. Meier, and T.

Scambos. 2008. 'Arctic sea ice extent plummets in 2007'. *EOS, Transactions, American Geophysical Union* 89 (2): 13–20.

Strohschein, Lisa. 2007. 'Challenging the presumption of diminished capacity to parent: Does divorce really change parenting practices?' *Family Relations* 56: 358–68.

Stroman, D.F. 2003. *The disability rights movement: From deinstitutionalization to self-determination*. Lanham: University Press of America.

Sturken, Marita, and Lisa Cartwright. 2009. *Practices of looking: An introduction to visual culture*. New York: Oxford University Press.

Stychin, Carl. 1998. *A nation by rights*. Philadelphia: Temple University Press.

Sudnow, D. 1967. *Passing on: The social organization of dying*. Englewood Cliffs, NJ: Prentice Hall.

Szasz, T. 1989. *Law, liberty, and psychiatry: An inquiry into the social uses of mental health practices*. Syracuse, NY: Syracuse University Press.

———. 1990. *Sex by prescription*. Syracuse, NY: Syracuse University Press.

Tanner, J. 1996. *Teenage troubles: Youth and deviance in Canada*. Scarborough, ON: Nelson.

Taras, David. 2001. *Power and betrayal in the Canadian media*. Peterborough: Broadview Press.

Taylor, Catherine, and Tracey Peter. 2011. 'We are not aliens, we're people, and we have rights'. *Canadian Review of Sociology* 48 (2): in press.

Taylor, J. 1995. 'The third sex'. *Esquire* 123 (4): 102–12.

Teeter, Brad. 2005. 'Court slams BC bullying'. *Xtra!* 534: 22.

Teichler, H.-J. 1975. 'Berlin 1936—ein sieg der NS-propaganda? [Berlin 1936—A victory for Nazi propaganda?]'. *Stadion* 2: 265–306.

Tew, J. 2005. 'Core themes of social perspectives'. In J. Tew (Ed.), *Social perspectives in mental health: Developing social models to understand and work with mental distress*, 13–31. London: Jessica Kingsley Publishers.

Theriault, Joseph-Yvon. 2002. *Critique de l'américanité*. Montréal: Éditions Québec-Amérique.

Thiessen, V., and J. Blasius. 2002. 'The social distribution of youth's images to work'. *Canadian Review of Sociology and Anthropology* 39 (1): 49–78.

Thobani, S. 2000. 'Closing ranks: Racisms and sexism in Canada's immigration policy'. *Race and Class* 42: 35–55.

Thomas, Robina. 2005. 'Honouring the oral traditions of my ancestors through storytelling'. In Leslie Brown and Susan Strega (Eds.), *Research as resistance: Critical, indigenous and anti-oppressive approaches*. Toronto: Canadian Scholars Press.

Thornton, Russell. 1998. 'Institutional and intellectual histories of Native American studies'. In Russell Thornton (Ed.), *Studying Native America: Problems and prospects*. Madison: University of Wisconsin Press.

Throsby, Karen, and Rosalind Gill. 2004. '"It's Different for Men": Masculinity and In Vitro Fertilization (IVF)'. *Men and Masculinities* 6 (4): 330–48.

Tipper, Jenni, and Roger Sauvé. 2010. 'The risks and realities of recovery'. *Transition* 40 (1): 1–6.

Tobias, John L. 1998. 'Canada's subjugation of the Plains Cree, 1879–1885'. In Ken Coates and Robin Fisher (Eds.), *Out of the background: Readings on Canadian Native history*. 2nd edn, 150–76. Toronto: Irwin.

Todd, J., and T. Todd. 2001. 'Significant events in the history of drug testing and the Olympic movement: 1960–1999'. In W. Wilson and E. Derse (Eds.), *Doping in elite sport: The politics of drugs in the Olympic movement*. Champaign, IL: Human Kinetics.

Todd, T. 1987. 'Anabolic steroids: The gremlins of sport'. *Journal of Sport History* 14 (1): 87–107.

Torpey, J. 2000. *The invention of the passport: Surveillance, citizenship and the state*. Cambridge, UK: Cambridge University Press.

Tran, K., S. Kustec, and T. Chui. 2005. 'Becoming Canadian: Intent, process, and outcome'. *Canadian Social Trends*. Statistics Canada catalogue no. 11-008.

Trend, David. 2007. *The myth of media violence. A critical introduction*. Oxford: Blackwell.

Tuchman, Gay. 1980. *Making news: A study in the construction of reality*. New York: Free Press.

Turcotte, Martin. 2006. 'Parents with adult children living at home'. *Canadian Social Trends* 80 (Spring): 2–10.

Turner, Bryan S. 1990. 'Periodization and politics in the postmodern'. In Bryan S. Turner (Ed.), *Theories of modernity and postmodernity*. London: Sage.

Turner, R. 1974. 'Words, utterances and activities'. In R. Turner (Ed.), *Ethnomethodology*, 197–215. Harmondsworth, UK: Penguin.

United Nations (UN). 2008. *Draft United Nations rules for the treatment of women prisoners and non-custodial measures for women offenders*. Commission on Crime Prevention and Criminal Justice, 18th session, Vienna. http://zh.unrol.org/files/ECN152009_CRP8.pdf.

Urry, John. 2004. 'The "system" of automobility'. *Theory, Culture & Society* 21: 25–39.

Ussher, J.M. 1991. *Women's madness: Misogyny or mental illness?* New York: Harvester Wheatsheaf.

Valverde, M. 1991. *The age of light, soap, and water: Moral reform in English Canada, 1885–1925*. Toronto: McClelland & Stewart.

———. 1999. 'Democracy in governance: Socio-legal framework'. Report for the Law Commission of Canada, University of Toronto.

Vanier Institute of the Family. 2008. 'Grandmother, Grand-père, Anaanatsiaq, Popo . . .'. *Fascinating Families* 11 (October 15). http://www.vifamily.ca/media/node/264/attachments/FF11.pdf.

———. 2010a. 'Two incomes the norm . . . and the necessity'. *Fascinating Families* 25 (February). http://www.vifamily.ca/sites/default/files/ff25.pdf.

———. 2010b. 'Children growing up in stepfamilies'. *Fascinating Families* 31 (October). http://www.vifamily.ca/media/node/513/attachments/stepfamilies.pdf.

———. 2010c. 'Families count IV: Family diversity'. *Transition* 40 (2): 5–14.

———. 2010d. 'Families count IV: Family economic security and caring'. *Transition* 40 (3): 4–11.

———. 2010e. 'Families working shift'. *Fascinating Families* 26 (March). http://www.vifamily.ca/media/node/79/attachments/ff26.pdf.

Venables, Robert W. 1992. 'American Indian influences on the America of the founding fathers'. In Oren Lyons (Ed.), *Exiled in the land of the free: Democracy, Indian nations, and the U.S. Constitution*, 74–124. Sante Fe, NM: Clear Light Publishers.

Venne, Michel. 2001. *Vive Quebec! New thinking and new approaches to the Quebec nation*. Toronto: James Lorimer & Company.

Vicinus, Martha. 1992. 'They wonder to which sex I belong'. *Feminist Studies* 18 (3): 467–97.

Vipond, Mary. 1992. *Mass media in Canada*, revised edn. Toronto: James Lorimer & Company.

Wacquant, L. 1999. 'Urban marginality in the coming millennium'. *Urban Studies* 36 (10): 1639–47.

———. 2001. 'Deadly symbiosis: When ghetto and prison mesh'. *Punishment and Society* 3 (1): 95–134.

Walcott, Rinaldo. 2000. *Rude: Contemporary black Canadian cultural criticism*. Toronto: Insomniac Press.

Walker, Janet. 2003. 'Radiating messages: An international perspective'. *Family Relations* 52: 406–17.

Walmsley, R. 2006. *World female imprisonment list*. London: King's College, International Centre for Prison Studies.

Warrior, Robert. 1996. *Like a hurricane: The Indian movement from Alcatraz to Wounded Knee*. New York: New Press.

Waters, Johanna L. 2002. 'Flexible families? Astronaut households and the experiences of mothers in Vancouver, British Columbia'. *Social and Cultural Geography* 3: 117–34.

Watt-Cloutier, Sheila. 2007. Testimony presented at the Inter-American Commission of Human Rights, 1 March 2007. http://earthjustice.org/news/press/2007/nobel-prize-nominee-testifies-about-global-warming.

Weatherford, Jack. 1988. *Indian givers: How the Indians of the Americas transformed the world*. New York: Fawcett Columbine.

Weber, Max. 1904–5. *The Protestant ethic and the spirit of capitalism*. (Talcott Parsons, trans.). New York: Charles Scribner's Sons.

———. 1948. *From Max Weber: Essays in sociology*. H. Gerth and C. Wright Mills (Eds.). London: Routledge and Kegan Paul.

Weber, M. 1980. *Basic concepts in sociology*. New York: Citadel.

Weeks, Jeffrey. 1995. *Invented moralities*. New York: Columbia University Press.

Weissman, Aerlyn. 2002. *Little Sisters vs. Big Brother*. Video.

White, Emily. 2002. *Fast girls: Teenage tribes and the myth of slut*. New York: Scribner.

Whitehouse, Peter J., and Daniel George. 2008. *The myth of Alzheimer's*. New York: St. Martin's Press.

Whorf, Benjamin L. 1956. *Language, thought and reality: Selected writings*. John B. Caroll (Ed.). Cambridge, MA: Technology Press of Massachusetts Institute of Technology.

Wiegers, Wanda. 2007. 'Child-centred advocacy and the invisibility of women in poverty discourse and social policy'. In Dorothy Chunn, Susan Boyd and Hester Lessard (Eds.), *reaction and resistance: Feminism, law, and social change*, 229–61. Vancouver: University of British Columbia Press.

Wilson, S. 1996. 'Consumer empowerment in the mental health field'. *Canadian Journal of Community Mental Health*, 15 (2): 69–85.

Wittgenstein, L. 1953. *Philosophical investigations*. Oxford, UK: Blackwell.

World Commission on Environment and Development. 1987. *Our common future*. Oxford: Oxford University Press.

World Resources Institute. 2006. 'Canada's boreal forests represent 25 percent of planet's remaining intact forests'. http://www.wri.org/stories/2006/09/canadas-boreal-forests-represent-25-percent-planets-remaining-intact-forests.

Wrong, Dennis. 1988. *Power: Its forms, bases and uses*. Oxford, UK: Blackwell.

Yearley, Steven. 1992 'Green ambivalence about science: Legal-rational authority and the scientific legitimation of a social movement'. *The British Journal of Sociology* 43 (4): 511–32.

Yesalis, C., and M. Bahrke. 2002. 'History of doping in sport'. *International Sports Studies* 24 (1): 42–76.

Youdell, Deborah. 2005. 'Sex-gender-sexuality: How sex, gender and sexuality constellations are constituted in secondary schools'. *Gender and Education* 17 (3), 249–70.

Young, Brigitte. 2001. 'The 'mistress' and the 'maid' in the globalized economy'. *Socialist Register* 37: 287–327.

Young, I.M. 1990. *Justice and the politics of difference*. Princeton, NJ: Princeton University Press.

Young, Nathan. 2008. 'Radical neoliberalism in British Columbia: Remaking rural geographies'. *Canadian Journal of Sociology* 33 (1): 1–36.

Zittrain, Jonathan. 2008. *The future of the internet and how to stop it*. New Haven: Yale University Press.

Zucker, K.J., and R.L. Spitzer. 2005. 'Was the gender identity disorder of childhood diagnosis introduced into *DSM-III* as a backdoor maneuver to replace homosexuality? A historical note'. *Journal of Sex and Marital Therapy* 31 (1): 31–42.

Index